THE ART OF ENVIRONMENTAL LAW

Environmental law has aesthetic dimensions. Aesthetic values have shaped the making of environmental law, and in turn such law governs many of our nature-based sensory experiences. Aesthetics is also integral to understanding the very fabric of environmental law, in its institutions, procedures and discourses. The Art of Environmental Law, the first book of its kind, brings new insights into the importance of aesthetic issues in a variety of domains of environmental governance around the world, from climate change to biodiversity conservation. It also argues for aesthetics, and relatedly the arts, to be taken more seriously in the practice of environmental law so as to improve our emotional and ethical capacities to address the upheavals of the Anthropocene.

The Art of Environmental Law

Governing with Aesthetics

Benjamin J Richardson
Professor of Environmental Law
University of Tasmania

·HART·
OXFORD · LONDON · NEW YORK · NEW DELHI · SYDNEY

HART PUBLISHING

Bloomsbury Publishing Plc

Kemp House, Chawley Park, Cumnor Hill, Oxford, OX2 9PH, UK

HART PUBLISHING, the Hart/Stag logo, BLOOMSBURY and the Diana logo are
trademarks of Bloomsbury Publishing Plc

First published in Great Britain 2019

A catalogue record for this book is available from the British Library.

Library of Congress Cataloging-in-Publication data

Names: Richardson, Benjamin J, author.

Title: The art of environmental law : governing with aesthetics / Benjamin J Richardson,
Professor of Environmental Law, University of Tasmania.

Description: Oxford, UK Hart Publishing, an imprint of Bloomsbury Publishing, 2019. |
Includes bibliographical references and index.

Identifiers: LCCN 2019031200 (print) | LCCN 2019031201 (ebook) |
ISBN 9781509924608 (hardback) | ISBN 9781509924615 (Epub)

Subjects: LCSH: Environmental law, International—Philosophy. |
Law and aesthetics. | Environmentalism in art.

Classification: LCC K3585 .R53 2019 (print) | LCC K3585 (ebook) | DDC 344.04/6—dc23

LC record available at https://lccn.loc.gov/2019031200

LC ebook record available at https://lccn.loc.gov/2019031201

ISBN: HB: 978-1-50992-460-8
        ePDF: 978-1-50992-462-2
        ePub: 978-1-50992-461-5

Typeset by Compuscript Ltd, Shannon
Printed and bound in Great Britain by CPI Group (UK) Ltd, Croydon CR0 4YY

To find out more about our authors and books visit www.hartpublishing.co.uk.
Here you will find extracts, author information, details of forthcoming events
and the option to sign up for our newsletters.

For Kura

Acknowledgements

THIS BOOK WAS a long time in coming. It comes from my long-standing interest in environmental art and aesthetics, and desire to investigate how they relate to environmental law, which I have taught and researched throughout my peripatetic academic career. I am grateful to my teachers of art history and theory at the University of Auckland and University of Tasmania who helped me understand the field and build the foundational knowledge from which this book would grow. I have also benefited greatly from being in a family of professional artists; thank you for encouraging me to pursue this project.

My ideas have also benefited from feedback from academic colleagues and audiences at workshops and seminars where I presented some of my research, including at the law faculties at Tilburg University, King's College London, the University of Cape Town and North-West University. In particular, I am grateful for advice from Afshin Akhtar-Khavari, Emily Barritt, Megan Bowman, Heather Forrest, Floor Fleurke, Antje Neumann, Kees Bastmeijer, Sandy Paterson, Willemien du Plessis and Anel du Plessis. Also, I am indebted to some insights from the artists working my own institution, the University of Tasmania, especially Jan Hogan (and her partner Keven Francis), Carolyn Philpott, Martin Walch, Abbey MacDonald and Annalise Rees. Friend Maria Riedl was also fantastic in her endless research tips on environmental art and activism. Thank you also to the various artists, museums and libraries for permission to reuse images of their works in my book.

I also appreciate the advice offered by the anonymous peer reviewers of my initial book proposal, and some papers I previously published where I developed some preliminary ideas on aesthetics and art in environmental law. Some parts of this book are adaptations of my articles in the periodicals *Climate Law* (2018), *Transnational Environmental Law* (2019) and the *Windsor Yearbook of Access to Justice* (2019), as cited where relevant. Finally, many thanks to the editorial staff at Hart Publishing/Bloomsbury, as well as Maria Skrzypiec, for preparing this monograph through its final stages for publication.

Contents

PART III
ASPIRATIONS

'Earth without Art is just Eh'.

Demetri Martin

'No one will protect what they don't care about; and no one will care
about what they have never experienced'.

David Attenborough

'It is only shallow people who do not judge by appearances. The true
mystery of the world is the visible, not the invisible'.

Oscar Wilde

'We can only be ethical in relation to something we can see, feel,
understand, love, or otherwise have faith in'.

Aldo Leopold

'Those who contemplate the beauty of the earth find reserves
of strength that will endure as long as life lasts'.

Rachel Carson

'I think having land and not ruining it is the most beautiful
art anybody could ever want to own'.

Andy Warhol

'Art is not a mirror to reflect reality, but a hammer with which to shape it'.

Bertolt Brecht

'Aesthetics is not a luxury, but a universal human desire'.

Virginia Postrel

List of Acronyms and Abbreviations

ANZ	Australia and New Zealand Bank
ATE	Aboriginal Tent Embassy
AONB	Areas of Outstanding Natural Beauty
CBD	Convention on Biological Diversity
CCAMLR	Commission for the Conservation of Antarctic Marine Living Resources
CO_2	Carbon dioxide
COP	Conference of the Parties
CSR	Corporate social responsibility
DPIPWE	Department of Primary Industries, Parks, Water and Environment (Tasmania)
EIA	Environmental impact assessment
FAO	UN Food and Agriculture Organization
GDP	Gross domestic product
GHG	Greenhouse gas
GIS	Geographic information system
GMO	Genetically modified organism
IP	Intellectual property
IPCC	Intergovernmental Panel on Climate Change
IUCN	International Union for Conservation of Nature
LCA	Landscape character assessment
NEPA	National Environmental Policy Act
NGO	Non-governmental organisation
NSW	New South Wales
ROV	Remotely operated vehicle
SER	Society for Ecological Restoration

TMAG	Tasmanian Museum and Art Gallery
UK	United Kingdom
UN	United Nations
UNESCO	United Nations Educational, Scientific and Cultural Organization
UNFCCC	United Nations Framework Convention on Climate Change
US	United States of America
WWF	World Wide Fund for Nature

List of Figures

Part I

Foundations

1

Environmental Aesthetics and Art

I. TAKING AESTHETICS SERIOUSLY

THE COVER OF my book features John Kane's painting *The Monongahela River Valley, Pennsylvania*, composed in 1931. It's one of several of his depictions of the surging industrialisation he encountered that evokes contrasting imagery of environmental change. An American folk artist, Kane celebrated the march of progress in a landscape teeming with activity that he personally laboured in: railroad trains, a steamboat and, most prominently in this painting, the billowing smokestacks of the behemoth steel mills sprawled along the Pittsburgh river valley. Yet this industrial topography competes with a bucolic landscape in the background, with gentle hills dotted with trees and cottages, which Kane admired equally. When asked of his interest in this subject, Kane replied, 'because I find beauty everywhere in Pittsburgh'.[1] Many environmentalists would disagree however, preferring the aesthetic of less adulterated nature to that bearing the imprint of human activity.

Public campaigns to save forests, rivers and other natural wonders often emphasise their aesthetic virtues, a concept relating to human sensory perceptions that I will later in this chapter define more clearly. Natural beauty has been the touchstone of this aesthetic value. The International Union for Conservation of Nature (IUCN) affirms in its founding 1948 Statute that: 'natural beauty is one of the sources of inspiration of spiritual life, and the necessary framework for the needs of recreation'.[2] In 1962, the United Nations Educational, Scientific and Cultural Organization (UNESCO) echoed similar sentiments in declaring nature's aesthetic values 'a powerful, physical, moral and spiritual regenerating influence'.[3] These sentiments also inhabit legal philosophy. John Finnis, a defender of natural law, enumerated seven basic goods that bring value to human lives that he believed the law should protect, one being aesthetic experiences.[4]

---

[1] Quoted in DB Burke, *American Paintings in the Metropolitan Museum of Art, Volume III: A Catalogue of Works by Artists Born between 1846 and 1864* (Metropolitan Museum of Art) 375.

[2] Statute of the International Union for the Conservation of Nature and Natural Resources, October 1948, preamble.

[3] UNESCO, *Recommendation Concerning the Safeguarding of the Beauty and Character of Landscapes and Sites*, 11 December 1962, preamble.

[4] J Finnis, *Natural Law and Natural Rights* (Oxford University Press, 2011) 87–88.

The appeal to aesthetics permeates the history of environmental politics and governance. The inauguration of the world's first national park,[5] at Yellowstone in the United States (US), was aided by the artists Thomas Moran, Frank Hayes and William Henry Jackson, whose portrayals of its grandeur through their photography and paintings helped convince Congress in 1872 to preserve the deep, glacier-carved valleys and mountains for posterity. The aesthetic disfigurement of nature has also galvanised action, such as the famous 'Keep America Beautiful' anti-littering campaigns.[6] The arts have helped publicise ugly aesthetics, such as the mining and industrial scars revealed graphically by Canadian photographer Edward Burtynsky. The aesthetics of human suffering connected to environmental adversity can also seize attention. In the Brazilian city of São Paulo a severe water crisis intensified in 2015, exacerbated by a drought and the failure of municipal authorities to take preventive measures. The suffering communities collaborated with artists to express their grievances, painting colourful murals around the city, such as images of drought-related themes and ripostes questioning government policy, such as the example in Figure 1.1 on the legs of a bridge spanning São Paulo's principal water source.[7]

Figure 1.1 São Paulo mural by Thiago Mundano, 2015; photograph by Frederick Bernas

---

[5] Although, some believe the world's oldest park is the Bogd Khan Uul nature reserve in Mongolia, designated in 1783 by the Qing Dynasty rulers: National Geographic, 'These are the World's Oldest National Parks', www.nationalgeographic.com/travel/national-parks/worlds-first-protected-lands-conservation-yellowstone.

[6] The sponsoring organisation Keep America Beautiful was established in 1953: www.kab.org.

[7] F Bernas, 'São Paulo Water Crisis is Source of Wave of Brazilian Art Activism' *The Guardian* (Australia edition) 10 March 2015.

Occasionally the law formally and explicitly acknowledges some of these aesthetic issues or concerns. The United Kingdom's (UK) National Parks and Access to the Countryside Act 1949 serves 'the purpose of conserving and enhancing the natural beauty',[8] and British law now provides for designating 'Areas of Outstanding Natural Beauty'.[9] International law has also embraced this agenda to some extent. The World Heritage Convention 1972 serves to safeguard 'areas of outstanding universal value from the point of view of [...] natural beauty', such as China's Danxia geological wonders and Australia's Great Barrier Reef.[10] Much environmental law however, as we will later learn, is insouciant about this realm, despite the influence of aesthetic appreciation on our environmental values and behaviour.

My book is devoted to showing how insights from aesthetics can enrich the study and understanding of environmental law. Aesthetics, be they relating to pictorial, musical or other art forms, can provide insights into environmental law that conventional modes of inquiry have relegated to the periphery. In arguing for aesthetics to be taken seriously, my book also highlights some problems associated with the aesthetic dimensions of environmental law. It is not enough simply to argue for the pertinence of aesthetic inquiry to environmental regulation and policy; we should also consider how aesthetics could improve governance and quell environmental risks.

Of the problems for environmental law that may come with aesthetics, one is that while aesthetic appreciation can gratify human sensory needs, it may lack intrinsic connection to the well-being of other species or the biosphere at large. It is naive to assume that what people find beautiful, they protect. As Kane's painting shows, individuals' aesthetic tastes can deviate from acceptable pollution control or nature conservation. Some may enjoy the look of industrial or urbanised landscapes despite their diminished biodiversity. Aesthetic tastes can also directly drive the destructive refashioning of nature to make it more appealing, for instance via introducing attractive but harmful exotic species. And even where authorities prioritise nature's beauty for protection, it may skew societal attention to the most aesthetically spectacular – the Yellowstones of the world – while neglecting the aesthetically mundane but possibly ecologically significant biomes.

Aesthetic preferences are complex and open to diverse interpretation both within and between cultures. At stake is more than the colloquial refrain that 'beauty is in the eye of the beholder'. Disputes over mining, forestry and other environmentally burdensome activity where aesthetic values are at stake can rarely be divorced from their social context. For working class labourers, a polluting factory provides a source of employment and companionship (as reflected in

---

[8] 1949, c 97, 12–14 Geo 6, s 5(1).
[9] Countryside and Rights of Way Act 2000, c 37, ss 82–89.
[10] (1972) 11 ILM 1358, art 2.

Kane's experience) while for the affluent and educated such places invite disdain. Even among avowed environmentalists, aesthetics can etch sharp divisions: wind turbines are welcomed by many for combatting climate change but can arouse opposition if such 'ugly' facilities inhabit their own locales. These differences can enfeeble the law's efforts to forge consistent and predictable methods of governing environmental activities.

Differences in aesthetic appreciation also shift over time, as Kane's painting of ebullient industrialisation should suggest from our vantage, further challenging the normative strength of so-called 'timeless' aesthetic values. To indulge this point for a moment, consider the shifting sentiments about the koala (*Phascolarctos cinereus*), the arboreal marsupial now beloved as one of Australia's premier tourist ambassadors. Until the early twentieth century it was slaughtered wholesale, especially in Queensland (illustrating also how nature's aesthetic qualities such as animal furs can directly drive destructive practices). Then, in 1919, Norman Lindsay published his picaresque children's tale, *The Magic Pudding: Being the Adventures of Bunyip Bluegum and his Friends Bill Barnacle and Sam Sawnoff.* The principal character in his bestseller was Bunyip Bluegum, a koala, who helped endear the creature to the public and contributed to its improved legal standing. An anthropomorphic koala called Blinky Bill was also the protagonist in the Australian illustrated children's books authored by Dorothy Wall in the 1930s (see Figure 1.2).[11] *The Adventures of Blinky Bill*, depicted in colourful, cartoon-like illustrations, evoked similar endearment. The tide began to turn: Queensland's Fauna Protection Act 1937 gave permanent protection to the koala and later, in 1971, the species became Queensland's official animal emblem 'after a newspaper poll showed strong public support for this endearing marsupial'.[12]

Taking aesthetics seriously also involves determining how to reconcile aesthetic and non-aesthetic considerations in environmental governance. Scientific and economic criteria more commonly substantiate environmental rules and standards. Scientific knowledge injects supposedly objective and consistent criteria for decisions, as evident in procedures for environmental assessments of development proposals, setting pollution standards and managing endangered species, among many applications. Science offers additional rationales for action, such as that the natural environment offers life-supporting services including clean air, water and fertile soil, and it underpins technological innovations to mitigate our impacts, such as through solar and wind power. Economics comes into play too in numerous ways, such as cost-benefit analyses of proposed environmental policies, quantification of the economic benefits of ecosystem services, and financial incentives including carbon taxes to reduce greenhouse gas (GHG) emissions. In these domains, policy-makers assume individuals to

[11] D Wall, *Blinky Bill: The Quaint Little Australian* (Angus and Robertson, 1933).
[12] Queensland Government, 'Animal Faunal Emblem', www.qld.gov.au/about/how-government-works/flags-emblems-icons/animal-emblem.

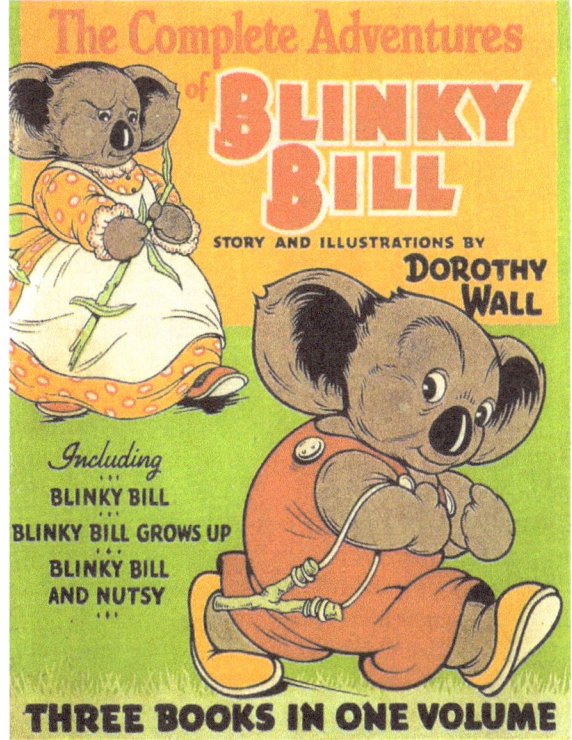

Figure 1.2   Cover of Dorothy Wall's *Blinky Bill* (Angus and Robertson, 1939)

be sufficiently rational and self-interested to understand and respond appropriately to improved information and clearer incentives, while the 'subjective' and 'superficial' emotional values seemingly associated with aesthetics get marginalised from environmental governance.

While the natural sciences and economic incentives have undoubtedly often reshaped modern environmental law for the better, they lack a complete solution. The shortcomings of environmental law generally do not occupy my book, with much already written about them.[13] Less well acknowledged is that our failure to manage the environment wisely stems more often not from lack of knowledge, but from lack of affection and altruism – values that aesthetic appreciation can help nurture. Aesthetic values help to define people's sense of place in nature, and forge the emotional and ethical relationships that can engender stronger environmental law. Whether visual, auditory, tactile or olfactory, sensory stimulation from our environment can generate more visceral feelings

---

[13] See my other work: BJ Richardson, *Time and Environmental Law: Telling Nature's Time* (Cambridge University Press, 2017); BJ Richardson and S Wood (eds), *Environmental Law for Sustainability* (Hart Publishing, 2006).

than are attainable by mere intellectual representation of environmental issues through technical data or expert reasoning.[14] Positive aesthetic experiences can motivate communities to protect nature by finding values in it not captured by scientific accounts, while negative aesthetic experiences can also jolt our perception of nature. The growing space for public participation in environmental decision making, including community consultation rights and access to courts, offers one of the best routes for incorporating aesthetic values into environmental law even if the law does not explicitly affirm them.

The seductive power of aesthetic appreciation, however, may also be manipulated to deceive and harm the public, as exemplified by corporate greenwashing and government propaganda. Seductive beauty is harnessed by the business world in its communications to sway consumers and investors to part with their money. The evocative music and imagery flaunted in corporate marketing can bolster the perception of businesses' supposedly eco-friendly credentials as expressed in terms of being 'carbon neutral' or 'sustainable', for instance. The public can be lulled into complacency by such nonsense, especially in the absence of regulatory oversight to curb misinformation.

We need to take aesthetics seriously, but clearly an aesthetic turn in environmental law should not infer a laissez-faire approach in which regulators merely defend individuals' opportunities to experience natural beauty, as Finnis implies. To counter the foregoing outlined difficulties, the law must support a *critical aesthetics* that contributes to environmentally sound decisions. The *Art of Environmental Law* champions a pedagogic, curatorial style of law. Curating spans a variety of interventions, from active protection of positive aesthetic experiences to curbing the deceptive and harmful practices associated with corporate greenwashing. A critical aesthetics thus takes aesthetic appreciation beyond a purely sensory experience of individuals to one linked to vital collective issues relating to environmental science, civic environmentalism, social accountability and other dimensions that bear on the quality of environmental governance. Thereby, aesthetic appreciation of landscapes and wildlife combines with their historical, cultural and political dimensions as much as their physical properties.[15]

This agenda thus centres on our *relationships* with nature rather demoting it merely to an object of distanced appreciation. Relationships accommodate our sense of place in nature, and the power of aesthetic experiences to deepen people's emotional gratification and moral valuation of the natural world. This bodily engagement could be as beguiling simple as walking (or swimming), as Christopher Tilley advocates. Such journeys through nature collect 'continuous

[14] R Lumber, M Richardson and D Sheffield, 'Beyond Knowing Nature: Contact, Emotion, Compassion, Meaning, and Beauty are Pathways to Nature Connection' (2017) 12(5) *PLOS One*, https://doi.org/10.1371/journal.pone.0177186.
[15] J Vergunst et al, 'Introduction: Landscapes Beyond Land' in A Arnason et al (eds), *Landscapes Beyond Land: Routes, Aesthetics and Narratives* (Berghahn Books, 2012) 1.

visions, smells, tactilities, sounds and tastes', he found.[16] Likewise, aesthetician Arnold Berleant values lived experience within nature, as participants, not observers.[17] These ideas thus try to overcome any ontological separation of humankind and nature that the aesthetic gaze can imply. Activities such as citizen science and community eco-restoration projects are among the means by which the populace can aesthetically appreciate nature in active ways while improving their ecological literacy and making a grassroots impact. As well, opening ourselves to more intimate aesthetic appreciation of other species and their environs requires that we respect the agency of nature in a reciprocal relationship. A critical aesthetics thus must include an aesthetic of vulnerability by which we respect rather than subjugate natural forces, even if they sometimes make our lives less comfortable and convenient. Being vulnerable has formative implications for environmental law, be it from decisions about adapting to climate change sequalae to co-existing with animals that may endanger us.

The arts mediate some of these relationships, especially where one has few opportunities for direct aesthetic appreciation of nature outside human-dominated places. Both for representing the natural world and enabling novel practical engagement with it, the arts can open human imagination across the enlarging temporal and spatial dimensions of the Anthropocene. They can help people to grasp more insightfully environmental shifts such as climate change outside of their own daily lives and localities, and engender attitudinal and behavioural shifts. And the arts can aid strategic interventions by dissident activists challenging destructive corporate or government practices.

In sum, sensory appreciation of the natural world, including as mediated by the arts, matters because of its capacity to shape the ethical and political imagination of the society and thereby the progressive development of environmental law. A richer and more critical sensory awareness of nature's beauty or disfigurement can stimulate deeper ethical and political deliberation about humankind's place in nature, our environmental impacts, the interests of non-human life and other dimensions that underpin environmental laws and policies.

II. OUTLINE OF THE BOOK

My book is not the first scholarship to investigate environmental law and aesthetics, but this field has not enjoyed the attention lavished on many other aspects of environmental law. The few pioneers include John Costonis, who examined aesthetics in US urban development regulation,[18] and Tim Bonyhady's

---

[16] C Tilley, 'Walking: The Past in the Present' in Arnason, *Landscapes Beyond Land* (above n 15) 15, 18.

[17] A Berleant, *Living in the Landscape: Toward an Aesthetics of Environment* (University of Kansas Press, 1997).

[18] J Costonis, *Icons and Aliens: Law, Aesthetics and Environmental Change* (University of Illinois Press, 1999).

account of Australian landscape art and literature in the emergence of its first environmental laws.[19] David Schorr has also tracked correlations between art and the history of environmental law.[20] Cultural heritage law scholarship sometimes forages into this domain, as in Ben Boer's work.[21] In international law, Alice Palmer has evaluated aesthetic criteria in World Heritage Convention decision-making.[22] And several legal philosophers have delved into some of the conceptual bridges between aesthetics and environmental law, notably Andreas Philippopoulos-Mihalopoulos[23] and Afshin Akhtar-Khavari.[24]

My book builds on this founding literature in offering a wider ranging account of the interface between aesthetics and environmental law across a variety of cultures, contexts and histories. This chapter continues by investigating the foundational issues, unpacking the nature of environmental aesthetics and art, and then discerning their influence on human attitudes and practices. Chapter 2 shifts the focus to the law, examining how aesthetics and the arts have influenced environmental law, from inspiring new regulations to the codification of aesthetic values in legal doctrine, as well as the aesthetic qualities of environmental law itself. I canvass the major challenges of governing with aesthetics in Chapter 3, such as the bias for aesthetically 'special' nature and the impact of negative aesthetics. This chapter thus helps us to understand the issues that must be resolved before aesthetics can play a larger role in governing environmental activities. Together, these chapters constitute Part I, devoted to understanding the conceptual, empirical and doctrinal foundations of aesthetics and the arts in environmental law.

Part II, 'Stories', comprises four chapters that delve into specific case studies. Chapter 4 unveils the role of aesthetics in colonising nature, such as the history of reshaping landscapes and their wildlife in order to appease societies' aesthetic preferences. The second story, in Chapter 5, examines aesthetics in business marketing and corporate social responsibility, and the difficulties the law faces in disciplining deceptive corporate communications. In Chapter 6, I tackle the aesthetics of ecological restoration and its legal frameworks; aesthetic considerations have become both a hindrance and help for ecological recovery. Climate change law's encounters with aesthetics and the arts deliver the final story, in Chapter 7. I highlight the challenges of imagining and appreciating the aesthetic values of a changing planet, as well as conflicts over aesthetic values arising in climate change mitigation and adaptation laws, such as with industrial wind farms.

---

[19] T Bonyhady, *The Colonial Earth* (Melbourne University Press, 1999).

[20] D Schorr, 'Art and the History of Environmental Law' (2015) 2 *Critical Analysis of Law* 322.

[21] B Boer and G Wiffin, *Heritage Law in Australia* (Oxford University Press, 2006).

[22] A Palmer, 'Legal Dimensions to Valuing Aesthetics in World Heritage Decisions' (2017) 26(5) *Social and Legal Studies* 581.

[23] A Philippopoulos-Mihalopoulos, *Spatial Justice: Body, Lawscape, Atmosphere* (Routledge, 2015).

[24] A Akhtar-Khavari, 'Fear and Ecological (in)Justice in Edvard Munch's The Scream of Nature' (2015) 6(2) *Nordic Journal of Law and Social Research*, http://jlsr.tors.ku.dk/issues/nnjlsr-06.

My book concludes in Part III, with reflections on developing a critical aesthetics for environmental law. Sort of analogous to how the public's experience of art in galleries and museums is curated, I use 'curating' for conceptualising how environmental law should engage with aesthetic values to facilitate pro-environmental practices. In most cases, aesthetics cannot be codified into prescriptive criteria that lawmakers can mechanically implement or adjudicate, but the legal system can elevate its importance, stimulate opportunities for public engagement and offer interpretive guidance. Reforms to institutionalise curating should extend beyond conventional governance processes of environmental law to address the law's wider role in creating and protecting public spaces for debate and constructive, non-violent dissent including artistic expression.

As is surely already obvious, my study embraces interdisciplinarity. At least half my referenced literature is not even ostensibly in the realm of law. That's a conscious choice, as to rigorously investigate the aesthetic dimensions of environmental law requires engaging closely with the theories and debates in the disciplines of art criticism and aesthetics philosophy. These include the basis for socially defensible aesthetic judgements, the potential of the arts to shape environmental values and behaviours, and how one can curate aesthetic appreciation.

My study is equally unconventional in its multi-jurisdictional scope. I appraise a variety of key trends and precedents worldwide rather than dwell on any specific country. Many examples come from the Western world, notably from Oceania, the European Union and North America, partly because they have played a disproportionately seminal role in environmental law globally, as well as owing to my personal familiarity with them over my peripatetic academic career. I don't, however, wish to trivialise the importance of non-Western precedents and practices, be they associated with Indigenous peoples or the Global South, and I incorporate a variety of examples, especially from South Africa, as far as attainable within the limits a single book allows. Invariably, of course, omissions from some countries or regions exist, but I am aiming not to write an exhaustive account, but rather to build the foundations for a new field of environmental law research.

The affliction of much critical legal scholarship is to write excessively in abstractions, thus obscuring the meaning of some elementary issues. Wishing to avoid the miasma of such writings, this book is grounded in some familiar examples, from wind farms to corporate environmental marketing, that readers will have personally encountered or read about. The case studies in Part II, where the broader theoretical issues are connected to practical examples, were chosen for several reasons. Firstly, they offer deep insights into the interface between aesthetics and environmental law, such as Chapter 5's analysis of ecological restoration, which has a strong aesthetic dimension in that laws in this realm often emphasise the goal of improving the appearance of degraded landscapes. Secondly, Part II engages with some of the most serious environmental problems of the Anthropocene, notably climate change. Thirdly, the case studies capture different phases in the development of environmental law, from the largely historical perspective in Chapter 4, on 'Vanquished Nature', to the emerging and future governance of climate change, in Chapter 7. The fourth rationale is to assess the role of non-state actors in environmental governance, a perspective that comes out most strongly in Chapter 6's account of business aesthetics and corporate social responsibility, as well as in the final chapter's analysis of 'culture jamming' by civil society activists. Together, these examples enable readers to appreciate the variety of key interactions between aesthetics and environmental law.

The heterogeneous research methods and case studies of this book reflect the broader reality that the governance dimensions of environmental aesthetics lack a bespoke research methodology. The same could be said for much scholarship on environmental law. It commonly rests on arguments about doctrinal and philosophical issues rather than addressing empirical questions about the quantified impact or efficacy of governance.[25] Empirical evaluation of environmental law and policy faces several practical barriers, including measuring parameters that we cannot easily compute, and the associated challenge of correlating cause and effect in complex legal phenomena whose relationships we may not decipher except over many years. Environmental law research has a strong axiological character, being concerned with ethics and values, a quality equally applicable to this book. It is predicated on the assumption of the importance of the natural environment to human wellbeing and the importance of social and institutional changes to improve environmental practices. Core concepts that underpin my thesis relating to the value of natural beauty and aesthetic appreciation reflect value-laden and contested choices.

My approach has some affinity with the policy research framework elaborated by Ann Majchrzak and Lynne Markus, and as some scholars of environmental law have recommended.[26] They use an empirical-inductive approach, emphasising discourse and reasoning, in contrast to the scientific hypothesis-testing approach. The dimensions of the social problem and relevant concepts and explanatory theories must first be identified.[27] Thereafter, one can assess the merits of future courses of action that may resolve these social problems. Thirdly, a normative stance is introduced, with recommendations for future action that may resolve these policy or governance problems. Overall, the form of research is partly descriptive, by harnessing scholarly disciplines that seek to understand the causes and effects of environmental activities or governance policies, and

---

[25] C McGrath, *Does Environmental Law Work? How to Evaluate the Effectiveness of Environmental Legal Systems* (Lambert Academic Publishing, 2010).

[26] P Martin and D Craig, 'Accelerating the Evolution of Environmental Law through Continuous Learning from Applied Experience' in P Martin and A Kennedy (eds), *Implementing Environmental Law* (Edward Elgar, 2015) 27.

[27] A Majchrzak and L Markus, *Methods for Policy Research: Taking Socially Responsible Action* (Sage, 2014).

also normative (and thus value-dependent) by recommending better approaches. With a pragmatic orientation, it helpfully illuminates not only what happens, but also why it happens and how we might do better.

On the other hand, this approach won't be satisfying to traditional 'black-letter' lawyers. This is a book for scholars interested in understanding environmental law in its cultural and political context, and interested in normative enquiries as much as in understanding the world as it is. Understanding the role of aesthetics and the arts in environmental law certainly involves issues of formal legal doctrine, such as attempts to codify natural beauty into rules. But the subject matter of this book also demands transcending positivist thinking, and incorporating insights from art theory and the philosophy of aesthetics, as well as environmental history, cultural geography and other disciplines.

Unusual for an environmental law monograph but essential in my case, this book contains many illustrations. I would have liked to include more but the publisher limited me to 50 images. The absence of relevant illustrations in some cases, however, should not diminish the text, as the examples I discuss are generally available on the Internet. So please keep your laptop browser open as a constant companion whilst reading.

Finally, on methodology, I wish to comment briefly on references to 'nature' itself. Some scholars such as Timothy Morton have questioned reliance on this language, raising concerns about creating a nature–humankind divide.[28] When referring to 'natural beauty' or 'environmental aesthetics' we may imply a pristine or untouched realm existing separately from human civilization. That is implausible. Human beings are animals, evolving from primate ancestors, and like all animals we are born, we develop, we eat, we breed and eventually we die. And like many other animals, we also change our environment: the Earth, perhaps with the exception of much of Antarctica, has experienced the effects of human activity directly or indirectly. Another way to conceive of nature is the natural systems that function without the agency of humankind. In this sense, explains philosopher Glenn Parsons, 'an automobile [and] the arrangement of plants in a garden are all non-natural, since each has come about through the voluntary and intentional agency of human beings', in comparison to other natural processes such 'as the fall of rain and the mating behaviours of birds' that function without human agency.[29] As Parsons recognises, this distinction retains some difficulty too, because it overlooks how the natural sciences such as evolutionary biology show that humankind is part of nature as much as any other organism in the tree of life. And our 'scientific' interpretation of natural phenomena can also be value-laden.

Still, I see value in retaining the concept of nature for this book's study. If we treat human environmental behaviours and impacts such as climate change as

---

[28] T Morton, *Ecology Without Nature: Rethinking Environmental Aesthetics* (Harvard University Press, 2007).

[29] G Parsons, *Aesthetics and Nature* (Continuum International Publishing, 2008) 2–3.

just 'natural processes and outcomes' we risk hampering our ability to refer to and take seriously such phenomena. Concurring here, art historian and cultural critic TJ Demos advocates that we speak explicitly about 'nature' because of the powerful value of such language for highlighting the importance of protecting the biosphere's integrity from anthropogenic devastation and degradation.[30] This book's references to 'nature' and its 'aesthetic values' are not intended to imply that they exist outside of the human presence, nor that they exist without human interpretation; but we should emphasise the agency of ecological processes and other creatures, which the language of 'nature' can respect.

III. THE CONCEPT OF THE AESTHETIC

The term 'aesthetic' derives from the ancient Greek *aisthetikos*, relating to human sensory perception. Our sensory apparatus, namely how the brain receives information about the world and the body, is commonly divided into five types – sight, hearing, touch, taste, and smell – although scientists identify a wider panoply including the gustatory, kinaesthetic and vestibular.[31] We don't, however, aesthetically appreciate our world robotically through our senses but via our emotional and psychological states. In modern English usage in its adjectival form, the aesthetic commonly relates to the appreciation of beauty or other sensed qualities, such as how we describe scenery of aesthetic appeal. As a noun, aesthetics denotes the philosophy or principles relating to the practice of art, the aesthetic properties of objects or places, and thirdly, aesthetic experiences and judgements.

These three foci of aesthetics all have relevance to environmental issues.[32] The study of art involves a variety of elements including its perceptible form, as a way of representation of the world, and as a mode of communication, and all matter for how people engage with the natural world. Aesthetic properties are perceptual features of things associated with their beauty, ugliness, grace, harmony, balance and numerous other qualities, again being qualities that people can associate with nature such as its range of amazing symmetries from starfish to snowflakes. The study of aesthetic experiences refers to states of mind including emotions and attitudes, such as disinterestedness, non-instrumentality and contemplation. Aesthetic judgements come from such experiences, expressing the value perceived by the observer.

Lately the aesthetic has garnered a broader meaning beyond its traditional association in Western philosophy with fine art and beauty. With the

---

[30] TJ Demos, *Decolonizing Nature: Contemporary Art and the Politics of Ecology* (Sternberg Press, 2016).

[31] See C Jarrett, *Great Myths of the Brain* (Wiley-Blackwell, 2014) 235–42.

[32] This discussion draws on J Levinson, 'Philosophical Aesthetics: An Overview' in J Levinson (ed), *The Oxford Handbook of Aesthetics* (Oxford University Press, 2005) 3, 5–7.

'aestheticization of the lifeworld', as Gernot Böhme conceptualises cultural trends unfolding in Western societies,[33] scholars increasingly link aesthetics to a variety of expressive activities including business and political communications.[34] A number of aestheticians, notably Yuriko Saito and Andrew Light, advocate an 'everyday aesthetics' that encompasses 'aesthetic practices [that] permeate people's daily lives' through ordinary objects and activities from cooking to tool-making.[35] Through such enquiries, we are reverting to the etymology of aesthetics, *aisthetikos*, meaning that pertaining to sensory perception. My book embraces this broad understanding because it best captures our complex and diverse aesthetic relationships with the natural world.

The concept of the aesthetic has also expanded to encompass both positive and negative experiences. Many traditional and contemporary aestheticians treat it as associated with enjoyable sensory experiences,[36] such as scenic landscapes and sumptuous fine art, but the origins of the term lack such qualifications. Referring to its Greek roots, Paul Duncum reminds us that aesthetics 'allows us to address agreeable experience but also disagreeable experience, the pleasant but also the unpleasant'.[37] Using the concept of the aesthetic in an even-handed way allows us to critically appreciate how aesthetic experiences have diverse effects, such as the problematic use of aesthetic factors for business and political purposes.

With this semantic expansion have come difficulties determining whether or how aesthetic experiences differ from other human feelings and experiences, such as sexual or gastronomic gratification.[38] Glenn Parsons and Allen Carlson caution against the inclusion of purely bodily sensations, like 'the pleasures of exercising, taking a bath, drinking lemonade or engaging in sexual activity', because this would render the aesthetic ridiculously broad.[39] Jacobsen argues that the core of aesthetics processing sits in mediating contemplation, such as an assessment of beauty, rather than a judgement formed by memory-based evaluation.[40] Elisabeth Schellekens and Peter Goldie's study of the 'aesthetic mind' ties aesthetic experiences to emotional and cognitive reactions.[41]

---

[33] G Böhme, *The Aesthetics of Atmospheres* (Routledge, 2016).

[34] G Mazzalovo, *Brand Aesthetics* (Palgrave Macmillan, 2012) 1; A Strati, *Organization and Aesthetics* (Sage, 1999) 184–88.

[35] Y Saito, *Aesthetics of the Familiar: Everyday Life and World-Making* (Oxford University Press, 2017) 1; A Light and JM Smith (eds), *The Aesthetics of Everyday Life* (Columbia University Press, 2005).

[36] J Dewey, *Art as Experience* (Capricorn Press, 1958) 46.

[37] P Duncom, 'Aesthetics, Popular Visual Culture and Designer Capitalism' (2007) 26(3) *Journal of Art and Design Education* 287, quoted in Saito, *Aesthetics of the Familiar* (above n 35) 28.

[38] See eg J Levinson, 'What is Aesthetic Pleasure?' in *The Pleasures of Aesthetics: Philosophical Essays* (Cornell University Press, 1996) 1.

[39] G Parsons and A Carlson, *Functional Beauty* (Oxford University Press, 2008) 178.

[40] T Jacobsen, 'Bridging the Arts and Sciences: A Framework for the Psychology of Aesthetics' (2006) 39 *Leonardo* 155, 158.

[41] E Schellekens and P Goldie (eds), *The Aesthetic Mind: Philosophy and Psychology* (Oxford University Press, 2011).

By contrast, Yuriko Saito challenges distinctions between distal and proximal senses, or mind-body dualism, as unhelpful because physiological responses in their wider context can shape aesthetic experiences (eg the taste of food in a restaurant) and because such a distinction might result in excluding a wide range of 'everyday aesthetics'. Instead, she recommends that we embrace a broad understanding of aesthetic qualities but differentiate them according to their significance and impact.[42] These debates cannot be resolved here, but my book takes the more inclusive view of aesthetics because of the overlapping and intertwined distal and proximal senses involved in nature aesthetics that legal governance must take into account holistically.

Aesthetic expression and appreciation are innate to the human species, as demonstrated by how every society in history has created music and visual art. Even our related hominoid ancestors did so. Archaeologists have found in Neanderthal-occupied caves in southern Europe ochred and perforated marine shells at least 115,000 years old, while evidence from Africa shows that *Homo sapiens* 70,000 years ago were fashioning jewellery from seashells.[43] This capacity for symbolic thought, expressing culture through visual art and music, dance and other artistic media, informs much human behaviour. Sensual experiences are more than a lower-order need to be satiated only after one is fed, clothed and sheltered, as need and desire are intimately bound. In the 1940s, psychologist Abraham Maslow pioneered his model of a 'hierarchy' of needs, a theory of psychological wellbeing predicated on fulfilling core human wants in priority, beginning with basic survival and escalating to other, supposedly less critical needs including physiological necessities of belonging, esteem and happiness.[44] This view is misleading if it demotes aesthetic experiences. People prefer food that smells delicious, while our adrenaline stirs on the sight of an attractive sexual partner. In nature too, colours, shapes and sounds influence the success of many living creatures that 'thrive on being attractive – feathers are colourful, flowers are scented, fruits tastes sweet', and birds 'use pitch, melody, and rhythm to distinguish themselves in the concert hall of the forest'.[45] Nature's aesthetics also benefit our own survival: research suggests that human environmental preferences are consistently focused on access to natural light, views of landscapes with diverse features, diurnal and seasonal cycles, and other natural elements that aid human wellbeing.[46]

A fundamental cleavage in the study of aesthetics is the tension between the ideal of universal principles underpinning aesthetic appreciation and the

---

[42] Saito, *Aesthetics of the Familiar* (above n 35) 40–41.

[43] DL Hoffman et al, 'Symbolic Use of Marine Shells and Mineral Pigments by Iberian Neandertals 115,000 Years Ago' (2018) 4(2) *Science Advances*, doi: 10.1126/sciadv.aar5255; L Hosey, *The Shape of Green* (Island Press, 2012) 20.

[44] A Maslow, 'A Theory of Human Motivation' (1943) 50(4) *Psychological Review* 370.

[45] Hosey, *The Shape of Green* (above n 43) 6, 21.

[46] S Kellert, J Heerwagen and M Madot, *Biophilic Design: The Theory, Science and Practice of Bringing Buildings to Life* (Wiley, 2008).

variable influence of individual psychology and cultural context. The distinction between objective and subjective views has often been framed in terms of whether one maintains that objects possess specific aesthetic properties such as beauty derived from symmetry and complexity, or whether aesthetic judgement depends on what pleases the senses, with beauty merely 'in the eye of the beholder'? An objective aesthetics has also been theorised as attainable from the latter realm if viewers can adopt and share a certain mode of aesthetic appreciation. Understanding these different positions is an important background for legal governance because they have implications for whether environmental aesthetics can be subject to meaningful public discourse and shared legal standards.

In contrast to the Enlightenment's efforts to replace mythology with science, and superstition with rationality, in the realm of sensual experiences the belief has endured that certain aspects of the human experience, the sensual or aesthetic, defy orthodox reasoning. While all able-bodied individuals have the capacity for sensual experiences, we might not ascribe the same meaning to them because aesthetic judgements are cognitively and culturally mediated. The famous Mount Fuji astonishes tourists as a scenic icon but local Shinto believers may be enamoured more by its spiritual significance.[47] A similar dyadic interpretation infuses landscapes occupied by Indigenous peoples: an empty 'wilderness' of scenic purity to a foreigner is a cultural landscape to its Aboriginal custodians.[48] In a 2017 decision of the Supreme Court of Canada, citizens of the Ktunaxa Nation objected to the planning permission for a ski resort, contending that the development would alienate the Grizzly Bear Spirit, a powerful spirit in Ktunaxa cosmology.[49] More frequently encountered aesthetics disagreements for readers relate to artistic taste: admirers of Rembrandt Harmenszoon van Rijn's *The Night Watch* (1642) may be repulsed by Marcel Duchamp's equally iconic urinal *Fountain* (1917).

Aesthetic issues have attracted considerable philosophical enquiry to bring them into the Enlightenment worldview.[50] It began much earlier, with the Ancient Greeks, led by Aristotle and Plato who focused on the quality of beauty.[51] During the Enlightenment, aesthetics regained philosophers' interest. In 1725, Francis Hutcheson published *An Inquiry Concerning Beauty, Order, Harmony*, pioneering a systematic theory of aesthetics as a special mode of human cognition.[52]

---

[47] UNESCO – United Nations Educational, Scientific and Cultural Organization (2013), 'Fujisan, Sacred Place and Source of Artistic Inspiration', http://whc.unesco.org/en/list/1418.

[48] D Bird Rose, *Nourishing Terrains: Australian Aboriginal Views of Landscape and Wilderness* (Australian Heritage Commission, 1996).

[49] *Ktunaxa Nation v British Columbia (Forests, Lands and Natural Resource Operations)* [2017] 2 SCR 386.

[50] For an introduction, see JW Manns, *Philosophy and Aesthetics* (Routledge, 2016).

[51] MC Beardsley, *Aesthetics from Classical Greece to the Present: A Short History* (Macmillan, 1966).

[52] F Hutcheson, *An Inquiry Concerning Beauty, Order, Harmony, Design* (Springer, 1973).

In the 1750s, Alexander Baumgarten wrote his major tome on aesthetics, a field that he called 'the science of perception'.[53] Beauty was of much philosophical interest, often defined with reference to geometric concepts, such as William Hogarth's theory that correlated beauty with principles of uniformity, simplicity and variety.[54] By contrast, David Hume shifted the focus from objective beauty, or the qualities of a work, to the experience of the viewer; wishing to avoid lapsing into relativism, Hume emphasised the importance of qualified judges of taste.[55] Thus, the development of a science of aesthetics generated an objectivist view focusing on the aesthetic properties of an object, versus a subjectivist or phenomenological view emphasising the qualities of the perceiver.

The most seminal contribution during this formative period was Immanuel Kant's *Critique of Judgement*, published in 1790. Although also preoccupied with understanding natural beauty and appreciation of art, Kant believed that the underlying issue was the need to justify aesthetic judgements because he considered beauty and other aesthetic values not simply as properties of objects but rather emanating from how observers respond to them. While Kant accepted everyone's capacity for personal sensual experiences, he saw them as linked to the ability of individuals to share such experiences and evaluate them communally. Inter-subjective comparisons of aesthetic experiences could be made, believed Kant, if one adopts what he termed a 'disinterested' aesthetic judgement. Disinterestedness means a mental state detached from moral, utilitarian or personal interests, a state of mind potentially available to all.[56]

Kant's theory thus helped to advance the study of aesthetics beyond describing sensual experiences to theorising an objective basis of how one ought to make aesthetic judgements, by treating aesthetic appreciation as an end-in-itself. Scholars have since debated extensively the Kantian legacy that subordinates the sensual experience to rational consideration. His legacy, suggests Jane Kneller, also promotes 'cross-cultural aesthetic recognition and understanding'.[57]

Faith in disinterested aesthetic judgements becomes problematic once we account for everyday activities, including enjoying the natural environment.[58] Many experiences such as hiking through the woods or photographing animals involve acquiring some collateral knowledge or benefit from the natural environment, such as to improve one's physical health (in the first example) or gain knowledge of wildlife (in the second). These engagements lack 'disinterestedness'. Separating aesthetic pleasure from feelings of affection or

---

[53] RA Makkreel, 'Aesthetics' in K Haakonssen (ed), *The Cambridge History of Eighteenth-Century Philosophy* (Cambridge University Press, 2006) 516, 521.

[54] W Hogarth, *The Analysis of Beauty: Written with a View of Fixing the Fluctuating Ideas of Taste* (W Strahan, 1772).

[55] D Hume, *Of the Standard of Taste* (1757).

[56] J Kneller, 'Aesthetics and Communication' in J McMahon (ed), *Social Aesthetics and Moral Judgment* (Routledge, 2018) 213, 218.

[57] Ibid.

[58] Saito, *Aesthetics of the Familiar* (above n 35).

Figure 1.3 *Immanuel Kant*, 1768, Johann Gottlieb Becker (1724–1804), oil on canvas; Schiller-Nationalmuseum, Marbach am Neckar, Germany

moral regard also becomes problematic given that some individuals have strong biophilic affiliations.[59]

With growing scholarly interest in the aesthetics of the familiar or everyday life, as associated with nature walking, gardening, shopping, socialising and other realms, has come a shift from a preoccupation with aesthetic judgements to aesthetic *experiences*. John Dewey's *Art as Experience* made a pioneering scholarly contribution by extending recognition of aesthetics into everyday life and ordinary experience.[60] In his wake, many have deepened our understanding of the importance of aesthetic experiences, such as Gernot Böhme's *The Aesthetics of Atmospheres* that brought to the fore the aesthetic qualities of contexts and spaces that we experience in quotidian life.[61] I will discuss the relevance of everyday aesthetic experiences for environmental values and decisions later in this book.

[59] RG Collingwood, *The Principles of Art* (Clarendon Press, 1938) 39.
[60] Dewey, *Art as Experience* (above n 36).
[61] Böhme, *The Aesthetics of Atmospheres* (above n 33).

Music has received less scholarly attention, as many aestheticians are preoccupied with the visual. Compared to other fine arts, Kant considered instrumental music to be trivial, and only when combined with lyrics did songs acquire aesthetic significance in his opinion. In the early nineteenth century, ETA Hoffmann and Arthur Schopenhauer challenged such views in championing the emotional and conceptual significance of instrumental music. Schopenhauer valued music highly as being not just a representation of emotions but in fact their essence.[62] More ambitiously conceptualising music's significance, Alan Harvey in *Music, Evolution and the Harmony of Souls* identifies it as crucial for telling stories and fostering communal relationships in human evolution: 'music's communal, socializing power acted as an essential counterweight to the individualization experience by increasingly intelligent and articulate members of *"Homo sapientor"*'.[63] The shared emotional experiences of listening to (and playing) music can foster this solidarity, or 'harmony of souls' as Harvey's monograph is entitled. One can extend the foregoing account of 'everyday aesthetics' to the influence of contemporary popular music on mass culture as well.

Others have sought to account for aesthetic experiences through a psychological approach that postulates that sensory stimuli trigger distinct psychological reactions.[64] These researchers felt the need to investigate empirically the reactions of people to colours, shapes, sounds and other aesthetic attributes of art and everyday objects, rather than make determinations based on philosophers' abstract speculation or artists' personal experiences. Hence, the psychological model aspires to establish a rational, objective basis to the study of aesthetics by identifying common factors that shape aesthetic appreciation.

Interest in the psychological effects of sensory stimuli has a long history. Polymath Edmund Burke was enamoured by the nature of beauty, which in his 1757 treatise he associated with certain emotional effects, like pleasurable feelings of tranquillity and euphoria, as contrasted to the discomfort of sublimity from witnessing mighty natural forces.[65] The study of the psychology of aesthetics was more scientifically grounded in the nineteenth century, led by Gustav Theodor Fechner, who attempted to correlate the associations between the physical properties of stimuli and the resulting sensations.[66] Fechner provided evidence to support the 'golden ratio' hypothesis, by which a proportion equal to 0.618 closely relates to perceptions of beauty in the human body, architecture, paintings and the forms of other species and their environments.[67]

---

[62] A Neill, 'Schopenhauer' in T Gracyk and A Kania (eds), *The Routledge Companion to Philosophy and Music* (Routledge, 2011) 339.

[63] A Harvey, *Music, Evolution, and the Harmony of Souls* (Oxford University Press, 2017) 205.

[64] For an overview of the literature, see PL Tinio and JK Smith (eds), *The Cambridge Handbook of the Psychology of Aesthetics and the Arts* (Cambridge University Press, 2017).

[65] E Burke, *Philosophical Inquiry into the Origin of Ours Ideas of the Sublime and Beautiful*, P Guyer (ed) (1757 original, Oxford University Press, 2015).

[66] GT Fechner, *Vorschule der Aesthetik* (Breitkopf and Härtel, 1876).

[67] M Livio, *The Golden Ratio: The Story of PHI, the World's Most Astonishing Number* (Broadway Books, 2003).

Another pioneer was Rudolf Gestalt, who investigated the psychological processes influencing the perceptual system, and why individuals selectively focus on specific elements. One explanation is the degree to which elements fall into a pattern, with a perceptual relationship to one another.[68] This work illuminates the human preference for fractal patterns in nature, as found in the recurrent shapes of plants and clouds.[69]

A third important contributor was Daniel Berlyne, who helped shift preoccupation with the perceptual attributes of artworks to how they arouse viewers.[70] Berlyne measured both the physical characteristics of a stimulus and the resulting physiological effects in viewers, concluding that it is a work's degree of complexity that provides the primary stimulus. Building on this approach recently is Colin Martindale, whose neural network theory of beauty tries to explain our preference for certain colours and shapes on the basis that beauty judgments are closely related to certain states in individuals' sense organs and the brain.[71]

Aesthetic preferences have also been evaluated through the lens of evolutionary psychology, which postulates that some human psychological traits reflect evolved natural selection or sexual selection adaptations to ancestral environments. Although some scholars believe art and aesthetics are 'exaptations' rather than adaptations,[72] in other words side effects of traits that evolved for other purposes, many researchers hypothesise that aesthetic appreciation matters for habitat and mate selection, among a variety of functions. On habitat preferences, Gordan Orians and Judith Heerwagen explain they may have come 'from an evolved psychology that functioned to help hunter-gatherers make better decisions about where to move, where to settle, and what activities to follow in certain localities'.[73] Mate choice has similarly been tied to aesthetic preferences, with certain desirable traits such as body shape and odour correlating with access to procreation opportunities.[74]

Other researchers have explored evolutionary advantages from *Homo sapiens'* art instinct, which include improving one's ability to abstract and convey ideas, to stimulate greater insight and bring meaning to one's life, and to

---

[68] R Arnheim, *Art and Visual Perception: A Psychology of the Creative Eye* (Faber and Faber, 1969).

[69] J Briggs, *Fractals: The Patterns of Chaos. Discerning a New Aesthetic of Art, Science and Nature* (Simon and Schuster, 1992).

[70] D Berlyne, *Aesthetics and Psychobiology* (Appleton-Century-Crofts, 1971).

[71] C Martindale, 'A Neural-Network Theory of Beauty' in C Martindale, P Locher and VM Petrov (eds), *Evolutionary and Neurogocnitive Approaches to Aesthetics, Creativity, and the Arts* (Baywood Publishing, 2007) 181.

[72] Notably, S Pinker, *How the Mind Works* (Norton, 1997).

[73] GH Orians and JH Heerwagen, 'Evolved Responses to Landscapes' in JH Barkow, L Cosmides and J Toby (eds), *The Adapted Mind: Evolutionary Psychology and the Generation of Culture* (Oxford University Press 1992) 556, 557.

[74] G Miller, *The Mating Mind: How Sexual Choice Shaped the Evolution of Human Nature* (Doubleday, 2000).

enrich human imagination including to contemplate alternative realities beyond the present.[75] Art may also give its creators greater influence over others, such as for telling stories to gain attention.[76] Another line of research has examined how the arts, especially music, help to reduce stress and promote more peaceful relationships, as well as to strengthen social bonds through rituals and ceremonies.[77] While evolutionary psychology struggles to empirically verify some of its claims,[78] other research on cognitive explanations has helped. For instance, research on facial attractiveness has identified cross-cultural preferences globally for facial symmetry, averageness and clear skin.[79]

In conclusion at this juncture, the burgeoning study of aesthetics has shifted the understanding of aesthetic appreciation and art from the realm of the subjective and idiosyncratic experiences to one that people can share and from which they can acquire common aesthetic preferences or criteria for aesthetic evaluation. Such preferences should no longer be scorned as relativist tastes, as in the clichéd 'beauty is in the eye of the beholder'. Rather, in the words of British landscape architect Simon Bell,

> any aesthetic response [...] is a complex one, affected by many factors, some of which are uniquely applied to each individual, others more associated with social or cultural groups and yet more that are feature of being human and common to all.[80]

Philosophical and psychological research into aesthetics continues, strengthening our capacity for serious dialogue and making defensible judgements about aesthetic values. Taking aesthetics seriously extends to the law, from providing opportunities for aesthetic experiences to protecting places judged as aesthetically significant. Our capacity to critically assess, share and debate aesthetic values makes them amenable to many of the decision-making processes of the law.

The following pages look specifically at environmental aesthetics so as to connect this enquiry more concretely to this book's principal enquiry.

---

[75] See J Carroll, 'The Adaptive Function of Literature' in C Martindale, P Locher and V Petrov (eds), *Evolutionary and Neurocognitive Approaches to Aesthetics: Creativity and the Arts* (Baywood, 2007).

[76] NE Aiken, *The Biological Origins of Art* (Praeger, 1998).

[77] See E Dissanayake, *Art and Intimacy How the Arts Began* (University of Washington Press, 2000); H Fukui, 'Music and Testosterone: A New Hypothesis for the Origin and Function of Music' (2001) 930 *Annals of the New York Academy of Sciences* 448.

[78] M Nadal and G Gómez-Puerto, 'Evolutionary Approaches to Art and Aesthetics' in P PL Tinio and JK Smith (eds), *The Cambridge Handbook of the Psychology of Aesthetics and the Arts* (Cambridge University Press, 2017) 167, 181.

[79] G Rhodes and L Zebrowitz (eds), *Facial Attractiveness: Evolutionary, Cognitive and Social Perspectives* (Praeger, 2001); K Grammer and R Thornhill, 'Human (*Homo Sapiens*) Facial Attractiveness and Sexual Selection: The Role of Symmetry and Averageness' (1994) 108(3) *Journal of Comparative Psychology* 233.

[80] S Bell, *Elements of Visual Design in the Landscape* (Routledge, 2004) 9.

IV. ENVIRONMENTAL AESTHETICS

A. Bringing Nature into Aesthetic Valuation

When we consider nature, aesthetic appreciation lacks the artistic conventions or contexts that can guide us. As Emily Brady, a leading scholar here explains, 'various natural objects – beetles, butterflies, seascapes or landscapes – lack a human maker, an artist, and also an artistic context in respect of the type of artwork, e.g. a painting'.[81] The study of environmental aesthetics addresses this challenge of understanding what frames our aesthetic interpretation and evaluation of the natural world. It applies not just to so-called 'wilderness', an unpeopled nature, but also environments modified by or including people, even urban settings. And the legal system influences the foregoing, shaping how people perceive and engage with the world aesthetically.

Environmental aesthetics has a long history, well before the ascendency of the global environmental movement. In East Asian cultures, nature has held high aesthetic and spiritual importance in Shintoism and Daoism.[82] Landscape aesthetics for Chinese, Japanese and Koreans was traditionally based on not only an appreciation of scenic panoramas but also the mythology and antiquity of a place associated with its human history (see Figure 1.4).[83] Nature aesthetics among Indigenous peoples also are strongly embedded in a cultural context, as in the 'dreamtime' cosmology of Aboriginal Australians.[84]

In Western cultures, three developments have particularly shaped environmental aesthetics. One comes from philosophical aesthetics. During the early Romanticism, nature was exalted as the model of aesthetic experience. Kant himself, explains Brady in her history of the field, 'privileged nature over art, and interpretations of his aesthetic theory show that the aesthetic appreciation of nature was more significant – even more edifying morally – to human life than the appreciation of the arts'.[85] During the nineteenth century, however, philosophers such as Georg Wilhelm Friedrich Hegel helped shift attention from nature to art because of the latter's perceived greater aesthetic quality. A second seminal influence came from landscape theory and practice, which during the eighteenth century under the auspices of luminaries like William Gilpin and Uvedale Price propagated the notion of the 'picturesque', a model of scenery appreciation that

---

[81] E Brady, 'Imagination and the Aesthetic Appreciation of Nature' (1998) 56(2) *Journal of Aesthetics and Art Criticism* 139, 139.

[82] J Ramsay, *The Aesthetic Value of Landscapes: Background and Assessment Guide* (ICOMOS-IFLA International Scientific Committee on Cultural Landscapes, 2015) 7–9.

[83] B Rowland, *Art in East and West: An Introduction through Comparisons* (Harvard University Press, 1954).

[84] C Hammond and M Fox, *Creation, Spirituality and the Dreamtime* (Millennium Books, 1991).

[85] E Brady, 'Environmental Aesthetics' in J Callicott and R Frodeman (eds), *Encyclopedia of Environmental Ethics and Philosophy*, volume 1 (Macmillan Reference, 2009) 313, 314.

Figure 1.4 *Landscapes with Poems*, 1688, Gong Xian (1619–1689), ink on paper; Metropolitan Museum of Art, New York

informed garden and landscape designs, as well as pictorial art.[86] The third key influence, emerging strongly in the late nineteenth century, was scientific and spiritual interest in nature conservation, epitomised most strongly in appreciation of wilderness aesthetics.

From the 1960s this third prong gained traction in mass society, dovetailing with anxieties about global environmental degradation and decline. During this phase environmental aesthetics emerged as a distinct field of scholarship. Although the national parks movement of the nineteenth century was heavily influenced by aesthetic appreciation,[87] a century later it was heightened public awareness of the negative aesthetics of urban sprawl, industrial pollution and wildlife losses that mattered more. The emergence of explicit environmental art genres in the twentieth century helped to represent these concerns and provide a social space for dialogue about environmental aesthetics even as it was acknowledged that admiring art does not provide the same sensory experience as personal engagement in nature.

These shifts have also reshaped the language by which we conceptualise nature, with relevance for environmental laws and policies. Figurative language itself is an aesthetic medium, notably in poetry and specific literary devices such

[86] Ibid, 315–16.
[87] See T Patin, *Observation Points: The Visual Poetics of National Parks* (University of Minnesota Press, 2012).

as alliteration, metonyms and metaphors. We inhabit a visual-conscious world, being enamoured by the power of images to represent ides and emotions, but figurative language also matters vitally for expressing our evolving relationship with the natural world. Important metaphors include: '*nature as a storehouse*' (denoting its supply of raw materials for human need), '*Mother Earth*' (nature as a giant organism, rather than a machine, as captured by the Gaia theory), the '*web of life*' (the ecological interconnections that bind humans and other species together), 'the *balance of nature*' (ecological systems in a generally stable equilibrium) and '*nature knows best*' (the natural world as a context and measure for ethics).[88] As these environmental linguistic devices become incorporated into our discourse, they can have powerful effects in normalising how we see ourselves with nature, and the ensuing environmental laws and policies adopted.

The increasing association of undamaged nature with positive aesthetic values, as evident in environmentalists' reliance on imagery of beautiful landscapes to attract support, came with the downside of bifurcating nature into 'special' and 'ordinary' aesthetic values.[89] The former, often garnering higher legal protection, might be snow-capped peaks, sun-drenched beaches or cute animals. Emphasising nature's superlative qualities implies another realm derided as ordinary, routine or less interesting, and therefore less deserving of conservation.[90] Such aesthetically mundane or even unsightly places might be monotonous grassland or muddy swamps, despite their possible ecological significance.[91] Even human-dominated landscapes punctuated by billboards and buildings, or golf courses and garbage dumps, can harbour resilient wildlife.[92] Specialness might also be nurtured by the increasing rarity of a species; in this sense, therefore, specialness can dovetail with scientific criteria, as a species judged by scientists as nearing extinction might dovetail with its increasing 'charismatic' appeal compared to common varieties. However, waiting for a species to slip towards extinction hardly offers a useful threshold of aesthetic appreciation to trigger the law's intervention.

We not only bifurcate the natural world into special and ordinary aesthetic values, we divide it into benign and malevolent qualities. Nature was disliked by influential polymath Francis Bacon (1561–1626), who saw it lacking beauty because it was 'the entrance of prevarication and corruption'.[93] Some natural environments have always had a particularly ambivalent cultural status, such as

---

[88] Discussed in FC Verhagen, 'Worldviews and Metaphors in the Human-Nature Relationship: An Ecolinguistic Exploration Through the Ages' (2008) 2(3) *Language and Ecology* 1.

[89] The ideas here draw a little on my article, BJ Richardson, 'Aesthetics and Environmental Law: Valuing Tasmania's "Ordinary" Nature' (2018) 27(1) *Griffith Law Review* 1.

[90] H Doremus, 'The Special Importance of Ordinary Places' (2000) 23(2–3) *Environs* 3.

[91] KJ Willis et al, 'Determining the Ecological Value of Landscapes Beyond Protected Areas' (2012) 147 *Biological Conservation* 3, 3.

[92] T Low, *The New Nature* (Penguin, 2017).

[93] F Bacon and B Montagu, *The Works of Francis Bacon, Lord Chancellor of England*, volume 1 (Carey and Hart, 1844) 290.

swamps and dense jungles associated with supernatural forces or harbouring dangerous beasts.[94] These anxieties about nature's darker side can reverberate in popular culture today, notably Hollywood horror films set in gloomy woods or disaster movies about violent storms, fires or earthquakes – all of which can imbue nature with a negative aesthetic.

The launch of environmental aesthetics into a distinct research field owes heavily to Ronald Hepburn's pioneering 1966 essay, 'Contemporary Aesthetics and the Neglect of Natural Beauty', which explored how aesthetic appreciation of nature differs from that of artworks.[95] He argued that nature provides opportunities for a wider array of sensory experiences and perspectives because environments are not framed in the manner we encounter as when art is displayed in a gallery. Paintings and sculptures showcased in art galleries are generally discrete and independent objects situated for appreciation by passive viewers from particular vantage points, unlike how we commonly appreciate natural beauty walking through the countryside, without being separated by any pre-determined distances, and drawing on a broader array of senses including smell and touch. Unlike art objects, these environmental conditions exist dynamically by their very organic qualities (eg seasonal flowering of vegetation or migration of wildlife) or their context (eg fluctuations in weather). However the actual *practice* of making art, from plein air painting to nature photography, can engage participants intimately in the aesthetic values of the natural world.

Other relevant considerations for differentiating the study of environmental aesthetics are that art works reflect intentional design for presentation in a different curatorial context. Museum and gallery curators place works in historical or thematic categories for viewers to follow a specific narrative. This curatorial context differs from natural environments, even if substantially modified by human activity, as they are not primarily the product of intentional human design. Our aesthetic experiences outside art galleries and museums can also be curated, such as via national park visitor centres, but they exert less control over how people interpret their surroundings.[96] Nonetheless, because many experience natural environments vicariously, through natural history museums or David Attenborough films, we cannot entirely remove the study of environmental aesthetics from the analysis of artworks. The law itself, as well will come to, can also play a curatorial role in shaping appreciation of nature aesthetics.

---

[94] H Selin (ed), *Nature Across Cultures: Views of Nature and the Environment in Non-Western Cultures* (Springer, 2003).

[95] RW Hepburn, 'Contemporary Aesthetics and the Neglect of Natural Beauty' in B Williams and A Montefiore (eds), *British Analytical Philosophy* (Routledge and Kegan Paul, 1966) 285.

[96] G Bateson, *Steps to an Ecology of Mind* (University of Chicago Press, 1972).

B. Theories of Environmental Aesthetics

Hepburn's insight opened the way for others to forge more elaborate philos-ophies of environmental aesthetics, with several distinct theoretical positions emerging. An influential position is the 'aesthetics of engagement'. According to its lead proponent, Arnold Berleant, aesthetics theory must overcome the separa-tion of appreciator and object by affirming the value of the active participation of people in the appreciative process.[97] Aesthetic value thereby emanates not simply in the object or in the observer, but rather inheres in 'a reciprocal process of perceptual participation between appreciator and object'.[98] This approach lends itself particularly to the natural world, be it a rugged wilderness or urban neighbourhood, where one's engaged participation rather than disengaged contemplation should generate richer, more meaningful aesthetic experiences. The Berleantian model also valuably emphasises multi-sensory engagement in contrast to the traditional prioritisation of visual appreciation.

This emphasis on personal engagement dispenses with the ex-ante criteria for aesthetic valuation of nature, yet yields little guidance on 'good' or 'bad' aesthetic appreciation. We may, for instance, admire a bucolic vista without recognising its weeds, invasive species or absent wildlife. The Berleantian model might result in aesthetic judgements that trivialise certain aspects of nature because participants lack insight into their significance on other grounds such as biodiversity rarity. Then again, the cogency of this reservation depends on how one experiences an environment, as putting one's self close to the ground can reveal the aesthetic glory of fungi, insects and other little critters otherwise obscured when one just casually strolls past.

An alternate position on nature aesthetic appreciation known as scientific cognitivism has been forged by Allen Carlson and Glenn Parsons. As Parsons explains, it's 'a normative thesis about aesthetically appreciating nature […] [W]e appreciate nature's aesthetic qualities in the proper manner in so far as we aesthetically appreciate it in light of scientific knowledge'.[99] Just as art historians and museum curators guide our taste in fine art, so too Carlson and Parsons believe the natural sciences, such as botany and zoology, offer resources to inform aesthetic appreciation of nature.[100] Science can steer the perceiver to points of aesthetic significance, such as the botanical knowledge that allows the viewer to fully discern a plant's patterns and colours. Without some expertise,

---

[97] A Berleant, *Living in the Landscape: Toward an Aesthetics of Environment* (University Press of Kansas, 1997).

[98] A Berleant, 'What is Aesthetic Engagement?' (2013) *Contemporary Aesthetics*, https://contempaesthetics.org/newvolume/pages/article.php?articleID=684.

[99] G Parsons, 'Nature Appreciation, Science, and Positive Aesthetics' (2002) 42(3) *British Journal of Aesthetics* 279, 279–80.

[100] A Carlson, *Aesthetics and the Environment: The Appreciation of Nature, Art and Architecture* (Routledge, 2000).

a copse of deciduous trees shedding their leaves in iridescent colours might be viewed adversely as a malady rather than a healthy seasonal cycle.

Importantly, scientific cognitivism supports a 'positive aesthetics' in nature. Earlier, Carlson proclaimed that 'the natural environment, insofar as it is untouched by man, has mainly positive aesthetic qualities: it is, for example, graceful, delicate, intense, unified, and orderly'.[101] In other words, Carlson postulated an aesthetic formalism based on the order, harmony, balance and other integrating properties that he believed flourished in a healthy environment. Following his later awareness that this aesthetic formalism reflected an outmoded understanding of ecology, as scientific knowledge had evolved to characterise nature as complex, chaotic, unbalanced and non-teleological,[102] Carlson with Parsons outlined a modified theory known as 'functional beauty'. They explain:

> our conception of Functional Beauty holds to an 'internal' relationship between function and aesthetic appreciation. It is not merely that certain of the cheetah's features are attractive, and also happen to be functional. Rather, certain of its features are attractive, in part, *because* they possess a particular function. [...] It is in this sense that Functional Beauty, in our sense, 'emerges out of' the function of the object.[103]

Non-living nature can also have functional roles, such as the life-giving properties of water. Hence, acquiring scientific knowledge about the function of natural phenomena can improve one's aesthetic appreciation of it, enabling deeper and more pleasurable insights. It also follows that natural elements that fail this functional test, such as a diseased or wounded animal, may be critically judged as lacking aesthetic significance or appeal.

Scientific cognitivism, unsurprisingly, still has its detractors, owing to its premises about the science of ecology and its attempts to correlate positive aesthetic value in nature's 'ordered' or 'functional' qualities. Others recommend we can find aesthetic pleasure also in nature's disordered and dysfunctional elements,[104] or focus on what is 'interesting' rather than beautiful.[105] Furthermore, the very prerequisite of scientific knowledge unsettles some critics; consider young children who appreciate the aesthetic traits of butterflies and birds in their garden without expert knowledge. Emily Brady, among others, argues that many common aesthetic experiences, like observing a vivid sunset or thunderous waterfall, can appeal to us without prior scientific expertise.[106]

---

[101] A Carlson, 'Nature and Positive Aesthetics' (1984) 6(1) *Environmental Ethics* 5, 5.

[102] J Kricher, *The Balance of Nature: Ecology's Enduring Myth* (Princeton University Press, 2009); SA Levin, 'Towards a Science of Ecological Management' (1999) 3(2) *Conservation Ecology* 6.

[103] G Parsons and A Carlson, *Functional Beauty* (Oxford University Press, 2008) 123.

[104] R Paden, LK Harmon and CR Milling, 'Ecology, Evolution, and Aesthetics: Towards an Evolutionary Aesthetics of Nature' (2012) 52(2) *British Journal of Aesthetics* 123.

[105] E Hargrove, *Foundations of Environmental Ethics* (Prentice Hall, 1989) 88.

[106] E Brady, *Aesthetics of the Natural Environment* (Edinburgh University Press, 2003) 369–70.

Intermediary or modified positions to some of the foregoing major theories of aesthetics have emerged. Emily Brady emphasises the percipient's imagination in amplifying perception alone. Consider her following illustration:

> In contemplating the smoothness of a sea pebble, I visualize the relentless surging of the ocean as it has shaped the pebble into its worn form. I might also imagine how it looked before it became so smooth, this image contributing to my wonder and delight in the object.[107]

To overcome the objection that imagination might engender 'incorrect or inappropriate responses by trivialising the object',[108] Brady advocates aesthetic appreciation of nature that, like Kantian disinterestedness, is coupled with honing the skill of 'imagining well' through practice and discipline. It should enable one to ward off 'shallow, naïve, and sentimental imaginative responses which might impoverish rather than enrich appreciation'.[109]

The Japanese wabi-sabi worldview is also gaining currency for thinking about environmental aesthetics beyond the narrow tropes of the picturesque or sublime. Features of the wabi-sabi aesthetic include imperfection, transience, asymmetry, coarseness and austerity in natural objects and processes.[110] Japanese landscaped gardens can embody the wabi-sabi, with minimal artificial ornamentation, rustic simplicity and use of natural materials such as stones and wood allowed to age naturally. The related concept of shibui, explains author Mari Fujimoto, 'recalls the beauty revealed by the passage of time':

> Inhering in an aesthetic of calm – colours subdued and brightness muted – this word reminds us to appreciate the things that improve with age. There is a grace in maturity, and the experiences of life mark their objects with a pleasant richness. You might experience *shibui* in the colour of leaves in early winter, or an old teacup on a table.[111]

These concepts resonate in the Japanese reverence of the cherry blossom, their most beautiful flowering tree, precisely because of its ephemeral blossoming. These Japanese aesthetic principles can lead people to appreciate the aesthetic qualities of 'ordinary' nature and their everyday surroundings, or to find beauty in transitory, austere or frugal environments, in contrast to the Western adoration of the sublime and spectacular.

Of the variety of other research on environmental aesthetics, one comes out of evolutionary psychology, as encountered earlier in this chapter. To recap, it posits that some of our aesthetic preferences reflect deeply evolved adaptive traits or at least by-products of such adaptation. In other words, the aesthetic qualities people value reflect environmental attributes that facilitated human

---

[107] Brady, 'Imagination' (above n 81) 144.
[108] Ibid.
[109] Ibid, 146.
[110] A Juniper, *Wabi Sabi: The Japanese Art of Impermanence* (Tuttle, 2008).
[111] M Fujimoto, *Ikigai and Other Japanese Words to Live By* (Modern Books, 2019), quoted in F MacDonald, 'Seven Words That Can Help Us to Live a Little Calmer' *BBC News* 25 January 2019, www.bbc.com/culture/story/20190124-seven-words-that-can-help-us-to-be-a-little-calmer.

adaptation, such as for selecting fecund mates or finding suitable habitat for shelter and food.[112] Although not normative, this theory may valuably help identify shared, cross-cultural aesthetic preferences. On visual preferences, it suggests people favour landscapes that resemble *Homo sapiens*' evolutionary cradle: the undulating, and sparsely treed, African savannah. Jay Appleton, Stephen Davies and Denis Dutton, of this view, correlate the appeal of such landscapes to their opportunities for providing 'prospect and refuge' to aid human survival.[113] Some anecdotal evidence points to widely shared visual partialities that may have also an evolutionary basis: photographer Penelope Umbrico's project *Suns from Sunsets*, which harvested images from *Flickr*, found that sunsets were the most widely available image on the photo-sharing website (with 541,795 examples in 2006, and 10 million uploaded to *Flickr* by December 2012).[114] We also evidently have a strong aesthetic affinity for water, such that observing oceans and rivers brings feelings of calm and well-being, confirmed by the higher prices people routinely pay for waterfront property or water views.[115] Other research on the psychology of aesthetic preferences postulates that we prefer fractal geometry in natural scenery, involving patterns recurring at increasingly fine magnifications such as in clouds and sea waves.[116]

Figure 1.5 Nature's fractal patterns; photograph by Benjamin J Richardson

[112] See generally E Voland and K Grammer (eds), *Evolutionary Aesthetics* (Springer, 2003).

[113] D Dutton, *The Art Instinct. Beauty, Pleasure, and Human Evolution* (Bloomsbury Publishing, 2010) passim; J Appleton, *The Experience of Landscape* (Wiley, 1975) 73–74; S Davies, *The Artful Species: Aesthetics, Art and Evolution* (Oxford University Press, 2012).

[114] See www.penelopeumbrico.net/index.php/project/sun.

[115] W Nichols, *Blue Mind: The Surprising Science That Shows How Being Near, In, On, or Under Water Can Make You Happier, Healthier, More Connected, and Better at What You Do* (Little and Brown, 2014).

[116] B Spehar and RP Taylor, 'Fractals in Art and Nature: Why Do We Like Them?' (2013) 8651 *Proceedings of SPIE – The International Society for Optical Engineering* 18.

Our evolutionary endowment also appears relevant to our auditory and olfactory preferences. Music psychologist Patrik Juslin believes 'the survival of our ancient ancestors depended on their ability to detect patterns in sounds, derive meaning from them, and adjust their behavior accordingly'.[117] Alan Harvey adds that music 'was an essential attribute of our early ancestors that has aided human evolutionary success through promotion of mental wellbeing and social bonding.[118] More cautiously, David Huron asserts 'musicality has some adaptive function' but nonetheless contemporary 'music culture and tastes are largely a product of enculturation' whereby the evolutionary endowment probably makes only a 'minimal' contribution.[119] Even more sceptical, Steven Pinker demotes music to a pleasurable by-product of the development of language rather than an evolutionary adaptation itself.[120] Of other senses, John McQuaid's bestseller *Tasty: The Art and Science of What We Eat*[121] shows the strong evolutionary basis to our sense of smell and taste in choosing healthful and safe foods, as well as human beings' own aromatic chemicals that convey sexual compatibility with potential mates.[122]

By linking aesthetic preference to evolved psychology, the foregoing literature may dovetail with the hypotheses of topophilia (instinctive affinities between people and cultural landscapes) and biophilia (between people and nature). The latter idea was pioneered by Edward O Wilson and Stephen Kellert,[123] postulating that human beings' material dependence on nature extends to the 'craving for aesthetic, intellectual, cognitive, and even spiritual meaning and satisfaction'.[124] Honed by long evolutionary development, the biophilic impulse is hypothesised as derived from our ancestors' daily habits that required observing cues from nature, as for finding food, water and shelter, avoiding predators and surviving inclement weather. Of course, not all elements of nature provoke affinity or affection, such as spiders and snakes, suggesting we also have an evolved biophobia. 'Topophilia', shorthand for love of a place, was popularised in 1974 by geographer Yi-Fu Tuan.[125] Although Tuan does not dwell on the type of places we prefer, his insights inform the work of architects and planners

---

[117] PN Juslin, 'From Everyday Emotions to Aesthetic Emotions: Towards a Unified Theory of Musical Emotions' (2013) 10(3) *Physics of Life Reviews* 235.

[118] Harvey (above n 63) 8.

[119] D Huron, 'Is Music an Evolutionary Adaptation' (2006) 930(1) *Annals of New York Academy of Sciences* 43, 61.

[120] S Pinker, *How the Mind Works* (Penguin, 1999) 524.

[121] J McQuaid, *Tasty: The Art and Science of What We Eat* (Simon and Schuster, 2016).

[122] K Grammer, B Fink and N Neave, 'Human Pheromones and Sexual Attraction' (2005) 118(2) *European Journal of Obstetrics, Gynecology and Reproductive Biology* 135.

[123] EO Wilson, *Biophilia* (Harvard University Press, 1984); SR Kellert and EO Wilson, *The Biophilia Hypothesis* (Island Press, 1993).

[124] Kellert and Wilson, *Biophilia* (above n 123) 20.

[125] YF Tuan, *Topophilia: A Study of Environmental Perceptions, Attitudes, and Values* (Columbia University Press, 1974).

in designing aesthetically pleasing structures and settings, and perhaps explain how homeowners diligently embellish their properties and gardens. The sense of place is postulated as strongest where people have cultural or familial ties to a site.[126]

The foregoing discussion roams across a variety of bases for environmental aesthetics, and now needs some synthesis and clarification for thinking about the implications for environmental law. These theoretical perspectives are not necessarily antagonistic, though potential conceptual and practical difficulties arise in aligning them. A participatory, engagement approach does not preclude aesthetic appreciation via the resources advocated by the cognitive model, while scientific cognitivism does not necessarily rule out the value of participatory engagement to enrich one's knowledge of the aesthetic properties of specific places. However, presuppositions about the objectivity of science and expertise as a portal for 'correct' aesthetic experiences sits uneasily with a participatory model that privileges direct sensory engagement available to anyone. As participatory engagement prioritises lay people's experience and interpretation in aesthetic judgements, a tension can arise if individual taste leads to trivialisation of serious problems such as those associated with global warming or species extinctions. As many environmentalists use the natural sciences to bolster their cause, especially climate science and conservation biology, not to mention their salience in the law, the sciences will invariably influence our engagement with nature aesthetics.

Evolutionary psychology suggests we share a consistent aesthetic preference that environmental law can accommodate, but it accounts only for our evolutionary 'base' rather than the diversity of cultural layers that embellish humankind's final landscape and seascape preferences. Different artistic expressions and preferences flourish both between and within cultures, and in today's art world. When such variability applies to natural elements, it might be difficult to reach agreement on their aesthetic values to protect: some people prefer anthropomorphic landscapes such as gardens and rural idyll while others desire rugged wilderness.

Theories of environmental aesthetics carry normative implications for environmental policy and law. They can provide criteria for determining how people should experience nature, which regulators can adapt for managing national parks or planning land use. They could help delineate aesthetic criteria for protection of specific landscape features and wildlife deemed of high aesthetic value. Conversely, environmental aesthetics can help identify adverse or negative attributes, such as 'ugly' pollution, for heightened legal control. Yet, if aesthetic

---

[126] KM Korpela et al, 'Stability of Self-reported Favourite Places and Place Attachment Over a 10-month Period' (2009) 29(1) *Journal of Environmental Psychology* 95.

judgements shape environmental law only according to what people love or loathe, they can have troubling consequences, suggests geographer Jonathan Prior, if not aligned with 'healthy, functioning landscapes'.[127] The following chapters of my book, with their case studies and examples, must be considered to understand properly the strengths and weaknesses of the foregoing accounts of environmental aesthetics for environmental law. It would be premature for me to prescribe a 'correct' theoretical perspective, and indeed I will not advocate a specific or particular position but rather a combination of considerations.

At this juncture, however, we can at least take away the following considerations from the foregoing commentary. Firstly, if we expect environmental lawmakers to take aesthetics seriously, then aesthetic appreciation should have some correlation to the quality of environmental conditions. If aesthetics is to contribute to robust environmental policy that tackles climate change or the biodiversity crisis, we need to engage with more aesthetically ambiguous or diverse experiences beyond the simple beauty/ugly dichotomy, and carefully consider the implications of our aesthetic preferences for environmental behaviour. If people admire the sight of a polluted landscape over a healthy ecosystem, then scientific knowledge – as Carlson suggests – may need to play a formative role in fostering appropriate aesthetic appreciation. Secondly, as human interventions into nature such as construction of wind farms introduce aesthetic changes, their aesthetic valuation may need to incorporate utilitarian criteria such as the contribution of renewable energy to fighting climate change. Conversely, depiction of appealing environmental imagery in corporate marketing might be problematic if it serves to mask dubious practices that the law should curb. Thirdly, as modern environmental law commonly emphasises the value of public participation in decision-making, the Berleantian theory of aesthetics of engagement would seem relevant to understanding how promotion of civic environmentalism can dovetail with appreciation of nature aesthetics. The closing chapter will build on these considerations in arguing for a critical aesthetics to guide environmental law.

Moreover, given that many environmental permutations transcend our direct sensory experience, especially those discernable only over long timescales or by travel to distant lands, the arts will acquire a seminal role mediating some realms of nature aesthetics. Additionally, the arts can provide a social practice for civic environmentalism, communicating or critiquing environmental science, and arousing public attention to environmental issues for actions. We thus cannot, in the context of environmental law, easily separate aesthetics and the arts. We can now consider this issue more closely.

---

[127] J Prior, 'Sonic Environmental Aesthetics and Landscape Research' (2017) 42(1) *Landscape Research* 6, 10.

V. ART AND THE ENVIRONMENT

A. The Arts and Nature Aesthetics

In our dominant urban demography, knowledge of nature aesthetics outside one's local environs is often accessible just vicariously – through David Attenborough films, National Geographic magazines, nature coffee-table books, bird call CDs and so forth. Artistic depictions of nature have ancient roots: renderings of wildlife are among humankind's earliest cultural artefacts, such as the 20,000 year-old Palaeolithic paintings adorning the Lascaux Caves in France or Australian Aboriginal rock art of even older vintage. Today, the arts have cultural currency worldwide: art galleries and museums are the preeminent cathedrals for aesthetic appreciation and social communion; people flock to the Guggenheim, Louvre and MOMA, as well as arts festivals from Dark Mofo to the Venice Biennale. In the aestheticised, postmodern culture of the West, with its ubiquitous consumer marketing, art has never been more pervasive in history.

In our globalising world ravaged by destructive permutations, the visual, musical and performative interpretations of nature matter increasingly. With the expanding spatial and temporal scales of anthropogenic upheaval, from global warming to marine plastic debris, far from the environs most of us inhabit, the arts can help make us aware of environmental change. Some of NASA's earliest photographs of Earth – most famously, the iconic *Earthrise*, taken in December 1968 by the Apollo 8 crew, and the *Blue Marble*, captured in December 1972 by the Apollo 17 crew (see Figure 1.6) – were such formative influences.[128] Their social importance was foreshadowed in 1948 by astronomer Fred Hoyle, who remarked:

> once a photograph is taken of Earth taken from outside, is available, we shall, in an emotional sense, acquire an additional dimension [...] once let the sheer isolation of the Earth become plain to every man, whatever his nationality or creed, and a new idea as powerful as any in history will be let loose.[129]

These NASA images of Earth spurred the global environmental movement with a new aesthetic of our beautiful yet isolated and vulnerable planet in an unlimited void.

The arts engage with environmental issues eclectically, from decorative representation to critical commentary, and thus their potential to appropriately engage the public in environmental aesthetics varies greatly.[130] Distinctive genres

---

[128] R Kelsey, 'Reverse Shot: Earthrise and Blue Marble in the American Imagination' in EH Jazairy (ed), *Scales of the Earth* (Harvard University Press, 2011) 10, 12.

[129] From V Goldberg, *The Power of Photography: How Photographs Changed Our Lives* (Abbeville Publishing, 1991) 52.

[130] JA Fisher, 'Environmental Aesthetics' in J Levinson (ed), *The Oxford Handbook of Aesthetics* (Oxford University Press, 2005) 667, 674–76.

Figure 1.6 *Blue Marble*, Apollo 17 crew, December 1972; NASA

of landscape art have flourished for centuries, emerging in East Asia from at least 900 CE and in Western Europe more evidently since the Renaissance.[131] They helped render a more benign view of nature through pictorial styles, which became well established during the Romanticism movement in the West at its height from about 1780–1840.[132] The 'picturesque' iconography denoted the 'picture-like', where the environment appears as if partitioned into art-like scenes, such as a painting of a beautiful valley flanked by rolling hills and illuminated by a golden sunrise. The 'sublime' – a concept introduced by Edmund Burke in 1757 – represented nature's most unruly dimensions such as stormy seas, roaring waterfalls and deep canyons, as evoked by Casper David Friedrich's *Wanderer Above the Sea of Fog* (1818). While the sublime could suggest terror, when observed through the 'disinterested' perspective it can be calmly appreciated. Alternatively, artists might celebrate the 'pastoral': the bucolic landscapes that imply benevolent human domination, with manicured gardens and peaceful rural scenes adorned with shepherds tending flocks of sheep. Consider, for instance, Claude Lorrain's seventeenth century landscape paintings of Italian countryside dotted with crumbling Roman ruins, a common leitmotif then. These traditions still impress some contemporary art, such as

---

[131] M Sullivan, *The Birth of Landscape Painting in China* (University of California Press, 1962); N Tsuda, *History of Japanese Art: From Prehistory to the Taisho Period* (Tuttle Publishing, 2009); B Novak, *Nature and Culture: American Landscape and Painting, 1825–1875* (Oxford University Press, 2007).

[132] C Casaliggi and P Fermanis, *Romanticism: A Literary and Cultural History* (Routledge, 2012) 119–20.

landscape photography that accentuates untroubled, gorgeous scenery.[133] They remain as problematic, however, projecting sanitised imagery of landscapes that omit socially or politically problematic or controversial details. Take John Constable's iconic *The Hay Wain* (1821), a canonical image of bucolic England that 'belies the exploitative labour relations, and the rural unrest and extreme poverty that was sweeping the countryside in that era'.[134]

Art in the so-called 'New World' often additionally mediated the colonisers' experience with unfamiliar places by rendering the 'alien' landscape seemingly more habitable.[135] Such art could concomitantly be complicit in the extinguishment of the original Indigenous inhabitants. In Tasmania, Australia, invaded by the British in the early 1800s, the commissioned art of the early colonising period omitted acknowledgement of the Indigenous inhabitants that the British persecuted. According to art historians Greg Lehman and Tim Bonyhady, Tasmanian landscape paintings were implicitly propaganda pieces, portraying an idyllic, pastoral existence in order to entice free settlers.[136] When, in 1831, the 'Black War' was over, and the vanquished Aboriginal people exiled, influential painter John Glover began to inscribe them back into the landscape, perhaps as a way to 'memorialise' their former presence. The foregoing artistic traditions continue to leave another legacy in the form of the national parks that lawmakers started to set aside from the late nineteenth century owing to impressions about their scenic splendour or unpeopled wilderness.

B. Contemporary Environmental Art

During the twentieth century, environmental art evolved in new directions that coincided with societal anxiety about our degraded planet. In the 1960s a genre called 'Land Art' (or Earth Art) emerged, particularly in the United States, as artists sought to 'enter' nature rather than merely depict it.[137] Sculptural earthworks have an ancient lineage, such as the Nazca Lines in Peru as old as 500 BCE, and the prehistoric White Horse at Uffington, England, providing inspiration for Land artist notables Michael Heizer and Robert Smithson. The latter's iconic *Spiral Jetty* (1970), sculptured into a Utah lake, resembles rock petroglyphs carved by prehistoric Native Americans. The earthworks, however, have an ambiguous relationship with their land; their geometrical,

[133] D Bright, 'The Machine in the Garden Revisited: American Environmentalism and Photographic Aesthetics' (1992) 51(2) *Art Journal* 60.

[134] H Hawkins, 'Picturing Landscape' in P Howard, I Thompson and E Waterton (eds), *The Routledge Companion to Landscape Studies* (Routledge, 2013) 190, 193.

[135] E Johns et al, *New Worlds From Old: 19th Century Australian and American Landscapes* (National Gallery of Australia, 1998).

[136] T Bonyhady and G Lehman, *The National Picture: The Art of Tasmania's Black War* (National Gallery of Australia, 2018).

[137] J Kastner (ed), *Land and Environment Art* (Phaidon, 1998).

minimalist style, coupled with the emphasis on scale and space, smacks of the 'antithesis of the accidental, free, organic shapes of nature'.[138] The engineering skills and technologies to reshape the landscape may remind us of industrial mining: Heizer's *Double Negative* (1968) gouged 218,000 tonnes of earth from the cliff-sides of a Nevada desert. Unsurprisingly, some environmental groups complained.[139]

Also courting controversy are the arts duo Christo Vladimirov Javacheff and Jeanne-Claude, gaining notoriety for 'wrapping' islands, cliffs and buildings. *Wrapped Coast* (1969) was one of their most audacious efforts, applying 100 million square feet of polypropylene and 59 kilometres of rope to wrap one linear mile of 80-foot high coastal cliffs at Sydney. One commentator observed, 'the wind, by swelling and rippling the fabric, introduced movement and became an important adjunct in informing the wrapped coast with a breath of prime-val life'.[140] Another behemoth project, *Running Fence* (1976), placed an 18-foot high, curtain-like fence meandering through 38 kilometres of Californian coun-tryside. The project's threat to migratory wildlife led authorities to require an environmental impact study as a condition of regulatory approval. Further controversy ensued when Christo breached the project approval conditions by allowing the 'fence' to extend into the sea.[141]

Over the past half-century, environmental art has flourished into other styles and agendas that reflect wider societal concerns and practices. Eschewing the grandiose, muscular temperament of Land Art, some artists enter nature with a spiritual reverence, seeking to leave no permanent mark. 'Walking artists' Hamish Fulton and Richard Long, and sculptor and photographer Andy Goldsworthy, all from Britain, exemplify this oeuvre.[142] Long documented his patient perambulations through nature, where he might make a path through the terrain by walking back and forth for hours (eg *A Line in the Himalayas*, 1975). Goldsworthy uses natural materials including stones and sticks to fash-ion appealing geometrical arrangements; generally ephemeral, they gradually dissipate by the actions of the wind, rain or tide. His works evoke a ritualistic engagement with the sites and their progressive dislocation through the vagaries of weather becomes a symbolic statement of the non-possessiveness of nature.

Another genre has embraced the aesthetics of environmental restoration in which the art not only depicts recovering ecologies but also actively partakes in their restoration, as explored further in Chapter 6. Archetypical examples

---

[138] E Baker, quoted in S Boettger, *Earthworks: Art and the Landscape of the Sixties* (University of California Press, 2002) 216.

[139] M Auping, 'Earth Art: A Study in Ecological Politics' in A Sonfist (ed), *Art in the Land: A Critical Anthology of Earth Art* (Dutton, 1993) 92, 96.

[140] A McCulloch, 'Letter from Australia' (1970) 14(10) *Art International* 44.

[141] Auping, 'Earth Art' (above n 139) 92.

[142] See R Long, *From Time to Time* (Ostfildern-Ruit (Cantz Verlag, 1997); A Goldsworthy, *Wood* (Viking, 1996).

include Alan Sonfist's *Time Landscape* (1965–1978), Agnes Denes's *Wheatfield – A Confrontation* (1982) and Joseph Beuys's *7000 Oaks* (1982). Sonfist erected numerous natural monuments to commemorate and restore their lost ecology. His seminal work *Time Landscape*, located in New York, began in cooperation with the Metropolitan Museum of Art and municipal planners.[143] Here it recreated the original indigenous vegetation of New York (eg oak and beech trees), with the project representing nature reclaiming itself and evoking memories of the revegetated site. Another notable practice has come from Newton and Helen Harrison, who often collaborate with ecologists, urban planners and local communities to produce functional art that contributes to watershed restoration, sustainable agriculture and urban renewal.[144] Their initiatives incorporate maps, photographs, drawings and poetic texts, as well as spoken performances. Their *Lagoon Cycle*, created over 12 years and first shown at the Los Angeles County Museum of Art in 1987, is a narrative installation comprising seven lagoon projects created by the artists. The Harrisons do not see their art as a 'product', but rather a discourse that tells the story of ecological places, aiding public awareness about threatened ecosystems and their recovery.

Making art itself often affords aesthetic engagement with nature, dovetailing with Berleant's message.[145] Plein air painting, nature photography, walking art and eco-restoration works enable their protagonists to engage intimately with sites that enrich their ecological literacy and ethical valuation of nature. Art practice also contributes to place-based, lived connections to nature that serve as sites of artistic composition. This may involve developing a consciousness of the geography, learning the history and local culture embedded in specific places. The resulting art objects can also touch audiences, albeit usually without the same intimacy. The difference is sharpest where art is experienced within walled galleries and museums, unlike the open world at large that engages us through our panoply of senses.

Art also aids environmental knowledge and policy by revealing information about historical conditions relevant to understanding ensuing changes to the climate or biodiversity. For eras before comprehensive records were kept, art can be a barometer for measuring climatic shifts through depictions of previous weather. Researchers have studied winter landscapes depicted in the Netherlands several centuries ago for clues as to former climatic conditions, such as images of frozen canals and lakes, as portrayed in Hendrick Avercamp's *Winter Landscape near a Village* (1610) (see Figure 1.7).[146] Delving more deeply into the past, marine biologists have examined ancient Roman mosaics to understand the

---

[143] J Kastner and B Wallis (eds), *Environmental and Land Art* (Phaidon, 1998) 50.

[144] As detailed in their website, http://theharrisonstudio.net.

[145] A Berleant, 'The Aesthetics of Art and Nature' in S Kemal and I Gaskell (eds), *Landscape, Natural Beauty and the Arts* (Cambridge University Press, 1993) 228.

[146] PJ Robinson, 'Ice and Snow Paintings of Little Ice Age Winters' (2005) 60(2) *Weather* 37.

Figure 1.7 *Winter Landscape near a Village*, 1610, Hendrick Avercamp (1585–1634), oil on canvas; Rijksmuseum, Amsterdam

typical size of Mediterranean fish before the advent of large-scale commercial fishing, and thereby gauge the success of new marine protected areas for recovery of fisheries.[147]

Environmental art lately has become more closely intertwined in the political, cultural and economic dimensions of environmental upheaval. Rather than objectifying nature 'as an ontology divorced from social, political and technological processes',[148] art is aiding dissent and social change. The arts 'can play a central transformative role' believes TJ Demos, a leading 'eco-arts' commentator, in leveraging 'creative perceptional and philosophical shifts' that challenge the 'destructive traditions of colonizing nature'.[149] Concurring, Timothy Morton contends that people's image of nature hinders progressive environmental behaviour, and he champions the arts for their power to help us reimagine a more environmentally benign future.[150] Artists can also help express that which might be hidden or obscured from our sensory perception; in *Slow Violence*, environmental humanities scholar Rob Nixon encourages artists to deploy 'their imaginative ability and worldly ardour to help amplify the media-marginalized causes of the environmentally dispossessed'.[151] Alan Braddock recommends

[147] M McClure, 'Stanford Researcher Turns to Roman Art for Marine Conservation' *Stanford News* 7 September 2011, https://news.stanford.edu/news/2011/september/grouper-art-research-090211.html.

[148] Demos (above n 30) 44.

[149] Ibid, 19.

[150] Morton, *Ecology Without Nature* (above n 28).

[151] R Nixon, *Slow Violence and the Environmentalism of the Poor* (Harvard University Press, 2011) 5.

an 'eco-critical' approach that emphasises 'environmental inter-connectedness, sustainability, and justice in cultural interpretation' in our evaluation of art.[152] The eco-critical stance challenges the 'anthropocentrism of art history'[153] to expose the misguided assumptions behind the construction of 'nature' in art and to re-interpret environments in more diverse ways that respect ecological integrity and social justice. This message is also being propounded by arts-based activist networks, such as the CLIMARTE group in Australia,[154] which uses art for educating the public on climate change issues, as well as protest artists engaged in 'culture jamming' to challenge corporate or government environmental practices.[155] I examine these strategies in Chapters 7 and 8.

It would be grossly misleading, however, to imply that artists have only recently served political ends. From the 1930s American photographer Ansel Adams deployed his wilderness imagery to rally support for more national parks, and he personally lobbied with some success, notably with the Sierra Club to protect Kings Canyon in 1940. Art has also been conscripted by environmental non-governmental organisations (NGOs) as a campaigning tool; in Tasmania, the sublime photograph *Morning Mist, Rock Island Bend, Franklin River* (1979) by Peter Dombrovskis was used in the early 1980s by the Wilderness Society in their successful campaign to prevent the impoundment of the Franklin for a hydro-power scheme.

Yet, whereas the latter artists' photographs perpetuated the trope of an unspoiled wilderness needing protection, a newer generation of artists has interrogated the forces of environmental destruction. Many involve site-based performances. Tue Greenfort's *Diffuse Deposits* (2007) had a manure truck spraying iron chloride (a chemical that prevents algae blooms in waterways contaminated with agricultural runoff) into an artificial lake in Münster, Germany. His message: such treatment offers only a cosmetic solution, alleviating the symptoms without removing the underlying threat. Another practice subverts the idealised landscapes associated with the Romantics. One target was John Constable's bucolic *The Hay Wain* (1821); collaborating with the Campaign for Nuclear Disarmament, Peter Kennard's photomontage *Haywain with Cruise Missiles* (1980) abruptly disrupts Constable's blissful idyll with three superimposed American nuclear warheads. By his irreverent recasting of one of Britain's most cherished paintings, Kennard's gesture made a cutting denunciation of Anglo-American foreign policy. Another theme of Romantic art, the 'sublime', has been redefined with reference to frightening industrial landscapes. Israeli artist Nadav Kander's photography explores the ecological

---

[152] AC Braddock, 'Ecocritical Art History' (2009) 23(2) *American Art* 24, 26.
[153] TJ Demos, *Against the Anthropocene: Visual Culture and Environment Today* (Sternberg Press 2017) 27.
[154] See www.climart.info.
[155] M DeLaure and M Fink (eds), *Culture Jamming: Activism and the Art of Cultural Resistance* (New York University Press, 2017).

toll of Chinese industrialisation: his series *Yangtze: The Long River* captures the magnitude of unstoppable economic and technological transformation that overwhelms the environment. Edward Burtynsky's images of dams, mines and factories, notably his 2012 exhibition *The Industrial Sublime*, typify this oeuvre too. Another contrast to the romanticised representation of nature is the 'new topographic' photography that emerged in the United States in the mid-1970s, such as the work of Joe Deal and Art Sinsabaugh, who confronted the iconography of landscape representation by shifting to the mundane and ordinary, such as suburbia, parking lots, gas stations and other artefacts of the sprawling urban landscape.[156]

The Global South has numerous artists critically engaging with these themes. Some evoke their concerns through a return to traditional, eco-friendly materials (eg bamboo poles, coconut husk and forest vines) for the construction of tapestries, sculptures and installations. Roberto Villanueva, from the Philippines, has erected bamboo-walled installations that evoke holy grounds containing deities (eg *The Dream Weaver*, 1992), while Ghanaian El Anatsui's wall hangings and sculptures made from recycled materials such as discarded bottle caps, fabrics, copper wire and anything else he finds highlight both the tide of waste in his country with limited recycling capabilities and the beauty from remaking 'ugly' detritus.[157] South African painter Hanien Conradie focuses on exploring themes of environmental damage and responsibility in her homeland. Some artists collaborate to provide both practical and aesthetic responses to environmental issues, such as Hong Kong's ArtVplastic project tackling plastic waste in its waters.[158]

I should also comment briefly about music's contribution. Although it hasn't attracted as much scholarly attention as lavished on the visual arts, music is as culturally pervasive.[159] It's socially valuable as entertainment, creating solidarity, conveying ideas and enabling emotional release. The discipline of eco-musicology focuses scholarly enquiries into the intersections between music and the environment,[160] with researchers investigating how melodies nurture empathy and foster a sense of place,[161] and music's ability to educate as much as entertain.[162] Music valuably provides a mnemonic framework that facilitates

---

[156] D Bright, 'Of Mother Nature and Marlboro Man: An Inquiry into Cultural Meanings of Landscape Photography' in R Bolton (ed), *The Contest of Meaning: Critical Histories of Photography* (MIT Press, 1993) 124.

[157] B Pollock, 'El Anatsui, a Sculptor Who Starts From Scrap' *Washington Post* 23 March 2008, MO6.

[158] Plastic Free Seas, http://plasticfreeseas.org/artvplastic.html.

[159] J Wilford, 'Flutes Offer Clues to Stone-Age Music' *New York Times* 24 June 2009.

[160] AS Allen and K Dawe (eds), *Current Directions in Ecomusicology: Music, Culture, Nature* (Routledge, 2015); M Pedelty, *Ecomusicology: Rock, Folk and the Environment* (Temple University Press, 2012).

[161] T Edensor (ed), *Geographies of Rhythm: Nature, Place, Mobilities and Bodies* (Ashgate, 2010).

[162] JL Publicover et al, 'Music as a Tool for Environmental Education and Advocacy: Artistic Perspectives from Musicians of the *Playlist for the Planet*' (2017) 24(7) *Environmental Education Research* 925.

memory and learning; we commonly teach children through nursery rhymes because they find learning and remembering songs and verses easier than prose due to the predictable rhyme and rhythm.[163] And because of the participatory nature of many music activities, such as concerts and choruses, they can foster social cooperation.[164] Of course, these conclusions depend on the type of music and context;[165] think of songs with violent lyrics or sexist messages, as well as patriotic national anthems harnessed for dubious causes.

Sound itself crucially mediates our experience of nature, yet only a handful of scholars, notably Jonathan Prior, prioritise nature soundscapes in their theorisation of environmental aesthetics.[166] Nature's acoustics are also studied by scientists to help decipher wildlife behaviour and ecological processes,[167] such as recordings of melting glaciers and ice calving to ascertain their effects on marine life.[168] While vision acuity enables our spatial perception of our surroundings, in ecological settings our auditory (and olfactory and tactile) senses can make us aware of other objects and activities beyond one's line of sight, and sound is crucial for navigating in darkness. Many of nature's soundscapes offer immense aesthetic pleasure, as evident in the numerous websites and playlists catering to enthusiasts of nature's melodies.[169] Bird songs, for affirming territory and attracting mates, provide among the most beautiful tunes we hear outdoors. Chirping crickets and croaking frogs also delight many. The physical forces of nature, such as steady rainfall and alternating ocean waves, likewise often feature in nature soundscapes that relax listeners. The aesthetic pleasure of what we hear and see in nature, however, are not always aligned; Australia's koalas are widely admired for their cute appearance, in contrast to their coarse bellowing or grunting vocalisations less commonly encountered.

Musicians sometimes incorporate sounds of nature to compose their work, as done by the bands Gondwanaland and Tribes of Neurot. The term 'biomusic' was invented to describe such compositions, which blend in birdcalls or whale vocalisations. A variety of popular music also evokes environmental concerns via their lyrics or tones, such as Joni Mitchell's *Big Yellow Taxi* (relating to insecticide DDT), Michael Jackson's *Earth Song* (protesting against environmental injustice), Julian Lennon's *Saltwater* (bemoaning environmental degradation), Orbital's *Impact: The Earth is Burning* (about climate change) and Pixies'

---

[163] V Bower and S Barrett, 'Rhythm, Rhyme and Repetition' in V Bower (ed), *Developing Early Literacy 0–9: From Theory to Practice* (Sage, 2014) 118.

[164] S Kagan and V Kirchberg, 'Music and Sustainability: Organizational Cultures Towards Creative Resilience' (2016) 135(1) *Journal of Cleaner Production* 1487.

[165] D Ingram, *The Jukebox in the Garden: Ecocriticism and American Popular Music Since 1960* (Rodopi, 2010) 69.

[166] Prior, 'Sonic Environmental Aesthetics' (above n 127).

[167] BC Pijanowski et al, 'Soundscape Ecology: The Science of Sound in the Landscape' (2011) 61(3) *Bioscience* 203.

[168] See the work of Alaskan glaciologist Erin Pettit, https://glaciers.gi.alaska.edu/people/pettit.

[169] Eg 'Wild Ambience': https://wildambience.com.

Monkey Gone to Heaven (touching on the ozone layer and climate change). Mega-music festivals also unite eco-conscious musicians and raise publicity for their causes, including the Sunstock Solar Festival (California), Destination Moon (New York), Baltic Sea Festival (Stockholm), Woodford Folk Festival (Queensland), Green Man (Wales) and the Roskilde Festival (Denmark). Climate change dominates some of these collaborations: one continuing initiative since 2016 is 'Music for a Warming World'.[170] According to Simon Kerr, one of its creators, it uses 'both large scale immersive visuals, live music (broadly drawing on folk, reggae and world-music), and a narrative arc that takes audiences on a guided journey through the climate challenge'.[171] Some aspects of the music industry, we should note, exert their own toll on nature, from celebrities' extravagant lifestyles to the large eco-footprint of major concerts; U2's 360 Degrees world tour from 2009 to 2011 featuring 44 concerts incurred criticism in the press for its 'staggering' carbon impact estimated as 'equivalent to the annual waste produced by 6,500 British people'.[172]

Theatre and performance art also deserve a few remarks here. In Ancient Greece, political discourse and story-telling were commonly expressed through theatre. It has a long tradition of serving political dissent, notably in the former Soviet Union and its eastern bloc allies, where activists had to rely on subtle or covert means of expressing opposition in order to avoid arrest or censorship. During the struggle against South Africa's apartheid regime, the Black Consciousness Movement collaborated with playwrights and poets in expressing dissent in a climate of severe political censorship.[173] A niche genre known as 'eco-theatre' has emerged too, such as Cherrie Moraga's *Heroes and Saints* (1992) play that revolves around the struggle of Californian farm workers exposed to dangerous pesticides.

Theatre's potential to transform society is perhaps limited in countries where theatre-going caters mainly to the socially privileged as a recreational pleasure, while radical fringe theatre is confined, a small enclave lacking social visibility. Some theatre commentators suggest street performance art offers a more accessible mode for engaging with more diverse audiences and challenging their comfort zone.[174] Street performance has already demonstrated its value to activists who engage in 'culture jamming' to challenge corporate and political malfeasance, often using humour and pranks to attract public interest (as I will explore in the closing chapter).

Much art, of course, will not make these positive contributions, and indeed the arts industry generally is afflicted by a degree of consumerism at odds with

[170] See www.musicforawarmingworld.org.

[171] S Kerr, 'Climate, Culture and Music: Coping in the Anthropocene' (2019) *University of Tasmania Law Review* forthcoming.

[172] S Michaels, 'U2 Criticised for World Tour Carbon Footprint' *The Guardian* 10 July 2009.

[173] R Kavanagh, *Theatre and Cultural Struggle in South Africa* (Zed Books, 1985).

[174] P Barclay, 'Theatre for Dissent and Opposition' *ABC Radio National 'Big Ideas'* 19 December 2019, www.abc.net.au/radionational/programs/bigideas/summer-dissent/10209954.

environmental values. Hal Foster, a leading critic of this trend, excoriates art practitioners who valorise wealth and fame over artistic skill and message.[175] The 2018 documentary film *The Price of Everything* voices a similar concern. Professional art markets, emerging in Europe from the seventeenth century onwards, have surged since the 1950s to become popular with vain, cashed-up investors.[176] The global art market reached a hefty US$45 billion in sales in 2016.[177] The rise of celebrity artists raking in the millions, notably Damien Hirst and Jeff Koons, may skew attention from creative work that seeks to draw attention to social and environmental problems.[178] Contrariwise, a few art movements have sought to resist commodification: Italian Arte Povera (meaning 'poor art') inspired artists to disdain consumerism by reusing everyday found objects,[179] while Land Art and Conceptual Art helped to dematerialise the art object in order to circumvent the commercial gallery culture.[180] These concerns should not imply that the sale of art is intrinsically problematic: full-time practitioners can hardly support themselves otherwise, and art sales can directly support progressive politics, such as environmental NGOs' retailing coffee-table books, calendars, posters, music CDs and other aesthetic paraphernalia.

VI. LEVERAGING CHANGE

A. The Power of Aesthetics

That aesthetic appreciation indulges us instead of other species because it is anthropogenic does not necessarily mean that it is anthropocentric. We may value aesthetic experiences for their potential not only to gratify our minds but also to foster attitudinal and behavioural changes that promote nature conservation, reduce pollution and deliver other eco-benefits. The prevalent appeal to aesthetic values in environmentalists' campaigns to save nature, especially via imagery of scenic landscapes and charismatic wildlife, stems from a widely held assumption about the power of aesthetics to shape public opinion and, ultimately, legal and policy decisions. This faith has been affirmed at the highest

---

[175] H Foster, 'The Medium is the Market' in N Degen (ed), *The Market* (Whitechapel Gallery, 2003) 198.

[176] N Horowitz, *Art of the Deal: Contemporary Art in a Global Financial Market* (Princeton University Press, 2011).

[177] 'Welcome to the $45 Billion Art Market' *Artnet News* 4 March 2017, https://news.artnet.com/market/tefaf-2017-art-market-report-880727.

[178] F Jameson, *Postmodernism, or, the Cultural Logic of Late Capitalism* (Duke University Press, 1991).

[179] C Cerny and S Seriff (eds), *Recycled Re-Seen: Folk Art from the Global Scrap Heap* (Museum of International Folk Art, 1996).

[180] T McEvilley, *The Triumph of Anti-art: Conceptual and Performance Art in the Formation of Post-modernism* (McPherson and Company, 2005).

levels, as when the United Nations (UN) hosted the seminal 'Transformative Power of Art' exhibition in 2015 at its New York headquarters.[181]

The power of images to influence public opinion and politics is evident in many realms, especially depictions of violence and suffering. The saturated televised coverage of the Vietnam War broadcast graphic images of the conflict into Americans' living rooms, thereby helping to galvanise opposition to US involvement. One dramatic moment was the close-up footage of the summary execution by General Nguyễn Ngoc Loan of a Vietcong prisoner on the streets of Saigon on 1 February 1968, a scene that shocked global audiences such that historian Alan Brinkley concluded that 'no single event did more to undermine support in the United States for the war'.[182] Not surprisingly, in subsequent hostilities the US military has vigilantly reduced journalists' access to the conflict zones, albeit with mixed results. During the 2003 Iraq War, the Abu Ghraib torture and prisoner abuse committed by US soldiers went largely unnoticed by the mass media despite reports from Amnesty International, until shocking imagery of the scandal aired in April 2004 on *60 Minutes* and a story in *The New Yorker*.[183] Thereafter some of the offenders were successfully prosecuted.

Positive sensory experiences, especially concerning beauty, also leverage change. Beauty has a ubiquitous hold in human culture, being valorised in romantic courtship, fashion, housing design and recreational pursuits.[184] It has also been connected to morality.[185] Although Kant's affirmation of 'disinterested' appreciation divorces the viewer from making associations between beauty and ethics, he acknowledged that when a person is engaged with beauty, 'we have cause to suppose that he has at least a pre-disposition to a good moral attitude'.[186]

Appreciation of nature's aesthetic values has been hypothesised as nurturing environmental ethics and correlating with sustainable lifestyles. Aldo Leopold famously remarked, 'we can only be ethical in relation to something we can see, feel, understand, love, or otherwise have faith in'.[187] Green architect Lance Hosey argues that natural beauty 'is inherent in sustainability' because of its association with healthy ecosystems and its ability to encourage people to admire and

---

[181] General Assembly of the United Nations, President of the 69th Session, 'President Kutesa Commissions "The Transformative Power of Art" exhibition', press release, 12 June 2015, www.un.org/pga/120615_press-statement-art-exhibit.

[182] Quoted in D Culbert, 'Television's Visual Impact on Decision-Making in the USA, 1968: The Tet Offensive and Chicago's Democratic National Convention' (1998) 33(3) *Journal of Contemporary History* 419, 422.

[183] HJ Weil, 'Review: The Aesthetics of Abu Ghraib' (2012) 71(2) *Art Journal* 123.

[184] R Plum, *The Evolution of Beauty: How Darwin's Forgotten Theory of Mate Choice Shapes the Animal World – and Us* (Doubleday, 2017); A Marwick, *A History of Human Beauty* (Bloomsbury, 2007).

[185] D Whewell, 'Aestheticism' in S Davies et al (eds), *A Companion to Aesthetics* (Wiley-Blackwell, 2009) 128, 130.

[186] I Kant, *Critique of Judgment*, s. 42, 167, quoted in R Ronen, *Art Before the Law: Aesthetics and Ethics* (University of Toronto Press, 2014) 45.

[187] A Leopold, *A Sand County Almanac* (Oxford University Press, 1949) xxvi.

care for nature'.[188] It wasn't always so believed, however, but changing conceptions of natural beauty have helped to align it with pro-environmental positions. Nature was once more commonly associated with malevolent supernatural forces and 'untidy' features defying traditional formulae of beauty based on symmetry or proportionality. In Western culture, the Romantics helped to shift such attitudes as the aesthetic of the 'picturesque' and the 'sublime' took hold, with painters and poets coming to rejoice in the irregular, coarse and dynamic qualities of nature, such as the torrid waterfall or variegated foliage of a tree. Further permutations in conceptions of natural beauty have ensued recently, as earlier canvassed.

In non-Western cultures, aesthetics has been more explicitly associated with morality. Japanese aesthetics, explains Yuriko Saito, has a 'long tradition of regarding moral virtues and aesthetics as inseparable'.[189] She gives the example of the tea ceremony, an artistic practice dating from the sixteenth century with scrupulous attention by the host for the feelings of the guests, becoming 'the model for civilised behaviour and rules of etiquette that are still alive and well in Japan today'.[190] Also illustrative of this oeuvre is Japanese garden design, in which the arrangement of stepping stones, juxtaposition of rocks, positioning of paths and other aesthetic features serve to stimulate the visitor's experience with humble respect for the natural materials. Japanese culture especially appreciates natural phenomena that evoke qualities of fragility and transience, such as cherry blossoms, snowflakes and bird songs.[191]

Faith in the proselytising power of aesthetics and the arts, however, must be reconciled with how these realms have also been harnessed to brainwash people with destructive ideologies associated with government propaganda, business marketing or religious indoctrination. They can manipulate aesthetics for unscrupulous ends at odds with maintaining environmental sustainability or social justice. Racism has manipulated people's perception of human beauty, such as the Nazi regime's attempts to breed an Aryan master race. Patriarchal cultures have imposed cruel stereotypes of beauty, like foot binding of young girls in pre-communist China or corset wearing in Victorian Britain.[192] Naomi Wolf's *The Beauty Myth* argued that idealistic social standards of physical beauty persist because of commercial influences through the 'beauty industry'.[193] Business also uses artful marketing to promote environmentally degrading consumerism, and many companies cultivate an image of being socially responsible using aesthetic techniques including logos, advertisements and product packaging to sway public opinion. Thus, if we accept the power of aesthetics,

---

[188] L Hosey, *The Shape of Green* (Island Press, 2012) 8, back cover.
[189] Saito, *Aesthetics of the Familiar* (above n 35) 150.
[190] Ibid, 151.
[191] S Odin, *Tragic Beauty in Whitehead and Japanese Aesthetics* (Lexington Books, 2016) 275.
[192] L Frost, '"Doing Looks": Women, Appearance and Mental Health' in J Arthurs and J Grimshaw (eds), *Women's Bodies: Cultural Representations and Identity* (Bloomsbury, 1999) 117, 119.
[193] N Wolf, *The Beauty Myth* (Chatto and Windus, 1990).

we must recognise its power to induce not only positive environmental practices but also to motivate undesirable ones. Such is why societal institutions, including the laws by which we govern ourselves, matter: because they can influence the direction in which this power flows.

B. Changing Environmental Attitudes and Behaviours

Environmental aestheticians' belief that our sensory experiences associated with nature can stimulate ethics and eco-friendly behaviour have backing by a variety of theoretical models, although the field remains subject to some modelling uncertainty and gaps in empirical evidence. This chapter earlier canvassed some of the extensive literature on the psychology of art and aesthetics, which has helped to empirically test hypotheses about reactions to sensory stimuli. This scholarship has advanced so strongly that a niche known as 'neuroaesthetics' has established itself, devoted to understanding the cognitive and neural processes induced by aesthetic experiences.[194] Much of this research dwells on sensory responses to visual art, without addressing how environmental aesthetics affects ethics and behaviour, such as whether aesthetic appreciation encourages audiences to stop littering or vote for green political parties.

Quite a few studies confirm that aesthetic stimuli associated with the colours, complexity or fragrance of nature offer therapeutic benefits, including lower stress and quicker recovery from illness.[195] The Health Council of the Netherlands found the health of people living near greenery improved faster.[196] Research has also found psychological benefits associated with a variety of outdoor experiences, including visiting city parks,[197] gardening[198] and exploring wilderness.[199] Conversely, the depletion of environmental ambience can bring mental anguish, as many know from inhabiting crowded, noisy cities with bustling traffic. Our digital world – computer games, television, Internet and smartphones – can similarly corrode our health as we shirk time outdoors.[200] Some of these findings

---

[194] MT Pearce et al, 'Neuroaesthetics: The Cognitive Neuroscience of Aesthetic Experiences' (2016) 11(2) *Perspectives on Psychological Science* 265.

[195] D Franklin, 'How Hospital Gardens Help Patients Heal' *Scientific American*, 1 March 2012, www.scientificamerican.com/article/nature-that-nurtures/#.

[196] Health Council of the Netherlands, *Nature and Health: The Influence of Nature on Social, Psychological and Physical Well-Being* (Health Council of the Netherlands and Dutch Advisory Council for Research on Spatial Planning, 2004).

[197] RA Fuller et al, 'Psychological Benefits of Greenspace Increase with Biodiversity' (2007) 3(4) *Biology Letters* 390.

[198] N Dunnett and M Qasim, 'Perceived Benefits to Human Well-being of Urban Gardens' (2000) 10 *HortTechnology* 40.

[199] S Kaplan and JF Talbot, 'Psychological Benefits of a Wilderness Experience' in J Altman and JF Wohlwill (eds), *Behavior and the Natural Environment* (Plenum, 1983) 163.

[200] OR Pergams and PA Zaradic, 'Is Love of Nature in the US Becoming Love of Electronic Media? 16-year Downtrend in National Park Visits Explained by Watching Movies, Playing Video Games, Internet Use, and Oil Prices' (2006) 80 *Journal of Environmental Management* 387.

already influence landscape management[201] and urban planning,[202] and indeed the associations have been advocated far longer. Ebenezer Howard's prescient book *Garden Cities of Tomorrow*, published in 1902, argued that 'human society and the beauty of nature are meant to be enjoyed together',[203] and his advice spurred British authorities to designate greenbelts near urban areas. In the 1970s, another milestone came with visual impact assessment methods in landscape research, which would help regulators to identify and protect elements of landscapes (eg tree canopy and water features) considered the most appealing for people.[204] In recent times, the health sector has also responded, redesigning hospitals to improve their aesthetic ambience, including wards offering tranquil soundscapes and more views of greenery.[205]

Another body of aesthetics research scrutinises the impact of business marketing on consumers. Companies invest substantially in embellishing their advertising, packaging and product design for competitive differentiation and profitability. Substantial anecdotal evidence confirms such efforts shape consumer acceptance and business success.[206] Famously, Apple triumphed with its colourful iMac, offering similar functional features as other personal computers but with a strikingly different visual appearance. Some research has also focused on the effect of eco-marketing on green consumerism.[207] While no comprehensive theoretical framework for this field of enquiry has emerged, it nonetheless provides a relevant perspective to this book because corporate marketing illustrates how some can manipulate aesthetics to undermine environmental standards, as Chapter 5 investigates.

Aesthetic experiences associated with nature, as well as the role of art supplementing or mediating such experiences, have also been investigated for their capacity to generate pro-environmental behaviour. A variety of theoretical models identify causal relationships or predict responses. In the 1970s, a knowledge-attitude-practice model suggested that providing environmental education, both academic and experiential learning, would generate useful knowledge, thereby engendering attitudinal shifts and corresponding behavioural changes.[208] Subsequent theoretical models and empirical research suggest

---

[201] M Conan (ed), *Environmentalism in Landscape Architecture* (Dumbarton Oaks, 2000).

[202] AR Beer, 'Urban Design: The Growing Influence of Environmental Psychology' (1991) 11 *Journal of Environmental Psychology* 359.

[203] E Howard, *Garden Cities of Tomorrow* (Faber and Faber, 1946, original 1902) 48.

[204] EH Zube, JL Sell and LG Taylor, 'Landscape Perception: Research, Application and Theory' (1982) 9 *Landscape and Urban Planning* 1.

[205] H Moss and D O'Neill, 'The Art of Medicine: Aesthetic Deprivation in Clinical Settings' (1994) 383 *Lancet* 1032.

[206] Eg Y Mumcu and HS Kimzan, 'The Effect of Visual Product Aesthetics on Consumers' Price Sensitivity' (2015) 26 *Procedia Economics and Finance* 528; PH Bloch, 'Seeking the Ideal Form: Product Design and Consumer Response' (1996) 59 (July) *Journal of Marketing* 16; R Batra et al (eds), *The Psychology of Design: Creating Consumer Appeal* (Routledge, 2016).

[207] Eg AM Todd, 'The Aesthetic Turn in Green Marketing: Environmental Consumer Ethics of Natural Personal Care Products' (2004) 9(2) *Ethics and the Environment* 86.

[208] CE Ramsey and RE Rickson, 'Environmental Knowledge and Attitudes' (1976) 8 *Journal of Environmental Education* 10.

more complex variables and pathways by accounting for situational contexts, cultural norms and individuals' resource constraints or opportunities.[209] Already it's clear that considerable dissemination of the findings of climate change science into the mass media has failed to convince hardened global warming sceptics.[210]

Theorising from environmental psychology and sociology, researchers such as David Curtis have sought to delineate key factors by which aesthetics and the arts may positively influence human attitudes and behaviour.[211] They emphasise individuals' existing personal values as predictive of responses.[212] Personal values may shift where individuals feel emotional indignation about an issue triggered by a powerful aesthetic experience. Individuals' self-identity is a related variable, being amenable to change through ongoing social interactions. Eleonora Belfiore and Oliver Bennett suggest exposure to music and visual arts in social settings, from city murals to community concerts, can help mould individuals' self-identity.[213] Making art may also contribute, explain Curtis and others, because the 'research and reflection that are part of the creative process help one develop or consolidate ideas and knowledge about a topic'.[214] Moreover, the *type* of art appears to matter in influencing audiences; the Climate Visuals project, which researches the effect of climate change imagery in engaging audiences, has found that images with people more effectively elicit responses from audiences, such as photographs of victims of catastrophic floods or storms.[215] Empirical research by some academics concurs in the importance of choosing the right images to convey the salience of climate change or to encourage audiences to act positively.[216]

The cultivation of new social norms on the environment can also be shaped by communal activities that involve aesthetic or artistic dimensions.[217]

---

[209] JM Hines, HR Hungerford and AN Tomera, 'Analysis and Synthesis of Research on Responsible Environmental Behavior: A Meta-Analysis' (1987) 18 *Journal of Environmental Education* 1.

[210] R Manne, 'Diabolical. Why Have We Failed to Address Climate Change?' *The Monthly* December 2015, www.themonthly.com.au/issue/2015/december.

[211] This discussion partially draws on DJ Curtis, N Reid and I Reeve, 'Towards Ecological Sustainability: Observations on the Role of the Arts' (2014) 7(1) *Sapiens*, http://journals.openedition.org/sapiens/1655. Also, see R De Young, 'Changing Behaviour and Making it Stick – the Conceptualization and Management of Conservation Behaviour' (1993) 25(3) *Environment and Behavior* 485.

[212] T Jackson, *Motivating Sustainable Consumption: A Review of Evidence on Consumer Behaviour and Behavioural Change* (University of Surrey, 2005); B Devall and G Sessions, *Deep Ecology: Living as if Nature Mattered* (Gibbs Smith, 1985).

[213] E Belfiore and O Bennett, *The Social Impact of the Arts: Intellectual History* (Palgrave Macmillan 2008) 10.

[214] Curtis, Reid and Reeve, 'Towards Ecological Sustainability' (above n 211); and also DJ Curtis, 'The Arts and Restoration: A Fertile Partnership?' (2003) 4 *Ecological Management and Restoration* 163.

[215] Climate Visuals, www.climatevisuals.org.

[216] S O'Neill et al, 'On Use of Imagery for Climate Change Engagement' (2013) 23(2) *Global Environmental Change* 413.

[217] B Szerzynski, 'Ecological Rites: Ritual Action in Environmental Protest Events' (2002) 19(3) *Theory, Culture and Society* 51; L Meekison and E Higgs, 'The Rites of Spring (and Other Seasons): The Ritualising of Restoration' (1998) 16(1) *Restoration and Management Notes* 73.

Curtis and others explain: 'the celebratory aspects of the visual and perform-ing arts have the effect of affirming pro-environmental behaviour by signalling social approval'.[218] From their empirical studies, they discern that 'the arts can synthesize and convey complex scientific information, promote new ways of looking at issues, touch people's emotions, and create a celebratory atmosphere'.[219] Music may have similar effects. Alan Harvey argues that music offers a communal, shared experience that can foster solidarity and stimulate listeners' emotional engagement.[220] Eric Clarke and others identify music's capacity for nurturing empathy, a critical building block for effective social cooperation.[221]

Making people more aware of the consequences of their actions can also drive behavioural changes, suggest Paul Stern's value-belief-norm[222] and Shalom Schwartz's norm-activation theory.[223] The arts can have such a pedagogic role, sensitising audiences to the environmental ramifications of their behaviours.[224] Imagery and sounds can convey ideas and build awareness of the impacts of one's behaviour, such as how carbon-intensive lifestyles fuel climate change, as Chapter 7 explores. Yet, merely augmenting people's knowledge about their environmental profligacy will generally not alone alter their conduct unless audiences feel emotionally engaged.[225] One conceptual response to this lacuna is the Mehrabian-Russell model, which depicts how emotional reactions such as arousal or pleasure triggered by specific environmental contexts can influence human behaviour.[226]

Some research also identifies constraints to changing environmental attitudes and behaviours. Evolutionary psychology suggests personal choice is less decisive because some human values and behaviours, including those tied to landscape aesthetic preferences, reflect deeply-rooted predilections shaped by ancestral environments.[227] This implies that sociocultural interventions that

---

[218] Curtis, Reid and Reeve, 'Towards Ecological Sustainability' (above n 211).

[219] DJ Curtis, N Reid and G Ballard, 'Communicating Ecology Through Art: What Scientists Think' (2012) 17(2) *Ecology and Society* 3.

[220] Harvey, *Music* (above n 63).

[221] E Clarke, T DeNora and J Vuoskoski, *Music, Empathy and Cultural Understanding* (Arts and Humanities Research Council, 2014).

[222] P Stern et al, 'A Value-Belief-Norm Theory of Support for Social Movements: The Case of Environmentalism' (1999) 6(2) *Research in Human Ecology* 81.

[223] SH Schwartz, 'Normative Influences on Altruism' in L Berkowitz (ed), *Advances in Experimental Social Psychology* (Academic Press, 1977) 221.

[224] B Carruthers, *Mapping the Terrain of Contemporary EcoART Practice and Collaboration: Art in Ecology – A Think Tank on Arts and Sustainability* (Canadian Commission for UNESCO, 2006); SK Jacobson, MD Mcduff and MC Monroe, 'Promoting Conservation through the Arts: Outreach for Hearts and Minds' (2007) 21(1) *Conservation Biology* 7.

[225] JA Pooley and M O'Connor, 'Environmental Education and Attitudes: Emotions and Beliefs are What is Needed' (2000) 32(5) *Environment and Behavior* 711.

[226] A Mehrabian and JA Russell, *An Approach to Environmental Psychology* (MIT Press, 1974).

[227] JH Cartwright, *Evolutionary Explanations of Human Behaviour* (Routledge, 2001).

advocate practices at odds with our evolutionary endowment will have less traction. Another body of enquiry on 'confirmation bias' has become influential in understanding barriers to changing individuals' values merely through exposure to new information. Confirmation bias is the propensity to accept factual evidence that confirms one's existing beliefs and to dismiss evidence that contradicts them.[228] Confirmation bias may equally influence individuals' aesthetic preferences, such as tastes in music and art.[229] But aesthetic experiences may counterbalance confirmation bias if they work through a different psychological mode. The Gates Foundation's 'The Art of Saving Life' project takes this approach in commissioning art works to overcome the bias against vaccinating children due to (asserted) unfounded fears that vaccinations cause autism or other bodily harms.[230]

The foregoing research reveals the influence of aesthetics and the arts at the level of individuals and even communities, and suggests plausible causal relationships and opportunities or barriers for leveraging change,[231] but these conclusions do not necessarily hold for *institutions* including business corporations, governments and international organisations. We should be careful about assuming that mere changes in public opinion will translate into policy and governance changes. Even in the most democratically governed societies, mass public opinion rarely translates exactly into corresponding environmental policies and laws.

Research on this broader context of institutions and social systems nonetheless suggests aesthetics matter, and increasingly so. Political scientists such as Kevin DeLuca have observed a marked growth in our media-saturated culture of the phenomenon of 'image politics', in which images have become crucial for more impactful political discourse.[232] Mazyar Lotfalian speaks of an era of 'aestheticized politics' that have, with the aid of new digital technologies, transformed the public sphere.[233] Aesthetics has similarly influenced the symbols and rituals of the nation-state, as the following chapter explains, as evident in states' coats-of-arms, bank notes, flags, national anthems and other artful insignia of sovereign authority. Likewise, international organisations including the UN and its specialist agencies articulate their identity through aesthetic artefacts including institutional logos, colourful webpages, ceremonies and rituals as associated with staging global conferences, and figurative language in their publications.

---

[228] H Mercier and D Sperber, *The Enigma of Reason* (Harvard University Press, 2017) 213–18.

[229] S McNerney, 'Confirmation Bias and Art' *Scientific American*, 12 July 2011, https://blogs.scientificamerican.com/guest-blog/confirmation-bias-and-art.

[230] See http://artofsavingalife.com.

[231] See eg PC Wang and CY Yu, 'Aesthetic Experience as an Essential Factor to Trigger Positive Environmental Consciousness' (2018) 10 *Sustainability* 1.

[232] KM DeLuca, *Image Politics: The New Rhetoric of Environmental Activism* (Routledge, 2005).

[233] M Lotfalian, 'Aestheticized Politics, Visual Culture and Emergent Forms of Digital Practice' (2013) 7 *International Journal of Communication* 1371.

In sum, aesthetics helps express and legitimise the workings of international and domestic governance in environmental issues and other policy realms.

Equally so, aesthetic factors have demonstrated importance for non-state actors in their political campaigning, public discourse and alternative governance regimes. This applies to both the private sector (business corporations and industry groups) and non-profit sectors (community groups and environmental NGOs). Corporate brands and marketing are deeply embedded in aesthetic paraphernalia, while activist NGOs engage the public through catchy rhetoric, artful banners and billboards, sensational imagery and performance theatrics that clamour for our attention in a media-obsessed culture.[234] Aesthetic activism especially permeates environmental politics, with artists playing an increasingly strategic role in governance struggles, such as that over climate change.[235] Taking account of this institutional and political context does not displace the importance of individual psychology. As later parts of this book show, much environmental governance that engages with aesthetics takes place at the level of individuals and their communities: from local involvement in ecological restoration projects to the responses of individual consumers to business advertising. Ultimately, therefore, we should evaluate the influence of aesthetics holistically from the behaviour of individual persons to group institutions.

VII. CONCLUSION

To recap, through this chapter I have begun to lay the foundations for my argument that scholars and practitioners of environmental law should take aesthetics seriously. For their benefit, I have introduced key themes and contentions in the background literature about aesthetics and the arts, and explained their relevance to our environmental challenges. Seasoned scholars of aesthetics and arts probably would find that coverage unnecessary, but it matters for a readership unfamiliar with this field.

Specifically, I have grappled with three fundamental issues. Firstly, the debate about the subjective nature of aesthetic appreciation, and whether and how rational and defensible positions can be taken that could then inform governance decisions from nature conservation to resources management. Secondly, I have considered the role of arts in mediating aesthetic experiences associated with the natural world, and thus the role of the arts as a key governance stakeholder. Thirdly, I have canvassed the influence of aesthetic experiences and the arts on our environmental attitudes and behaviours, which of course also matters greatly for governance.

[234] See FA Vlavo, *Performing Digital Activism* (Routledge, 2018); www.aestheticsofprotest.com.
[235] B Cozen, 'Mobilizing Artists: *Green Patriot Posters*, Visual Metaphors, and Climate Change Activism' (2013) 7(2) *Environmental Communications* 297.

This chapter rejects the idea that we should reduce aesthetics to pure subjectivity or cultural variation, as that might denigrate the aesthetic experience and discourage 'citizens from carefully examining the grounds and value of such an experience and from taking public measures to protect it'.[236] Although individuals' perceptions of beauty and other aesthetic qualities comprise diverse emotional sentiments and moral acuities, such reactions matter because they shape our environmental attitudes and behaviours, and public participation has become a formative influence in law making in this field.

This chapter thus has seminal implications for environmental decision-making, which the following pages explore. Aesthetics and art should not be seen as fundamentally at odds with the scientific and economic methodologies and knowledge systems that dominate environmental governance, but rather as vital additions. These disciplines can provide potent intellectual representations of the stress of the Anthropocene, but human environmental behaviour equally comes from sensory experiences that environmental governance must reckon with. Aesthetics can contribute to closing this deficit, providing creative and participatory experiences to build people's sense of place in nature and to expand their imaginations for dealing with environmental damage. Aesthetic experiences introduce additional values and feelings into environmental decisions beyond scientific facts or economic calculations. Art practice itself can engage with environmental values, and communicate them to a wider audience.

Equally, where the appeal to aesthetics has blindspots, such as the tendency to accentuate the charismatic or picturesque over the aesthetically mundane, science can help illuminate the ecological value of these other natural elements. Likewise, science can help counteract aesthetically driven environmental destruction. We kill animals for their fur, feathers or skins, capture and cage birds as household companions, and design gardens full of exotics to maximise their sensory appeal. And science, along with democratic checks and balances, can help ensure that aesthetics is grounded in an ethical compass, for without reference to an ecologically compassionate stance some may harness aesthetics for unscrupulous commercial and political ends.

Environmental aesthetics should be understood as a way of relating to nature, of looking, hearing and touching within a social context. Being engaged with nature intimately, as part of our world not as a separate 'other', is crucial. I am reminded here of a *BBC* story in 2018 about Switzerland's Lake Geneva, remarking that what from afar looked mesmerisingly beautiful, on close-up inspection was revealed to be stained by ugly pollution from plastic debris accumulating along its foreshores.[237] Nature and our assaults on it will be sensed differently

---

[236] R Brooks and P Lavinge, 'Aesthetic Theory and Landscape Protection: The Many Meanings of Beauty and their Implications for the Design, Control and Protection of Vermont's Landscape' (1985) 4(2) *UCLA Journal of Environmental Law and Policy* 129, 131.

[237] M Hogenboom, 'Why Pristine Lakes are Filled With Toxins' *BBC News*, 30 April 2018, www.bbc.com/future/story/20180426-why-plastics-are-not-just-an-ocean-problem.

depending on the context and relationship. And as the following chapters explore, the law is sometimes crucial to that interpretative context. We need greater aesthetic literacy and intimacy, to recognise how 'our seemingly innocuous and inconsequential aesthetic tastes, judgements, and decisions significantly affect the state of the world and the quality of life, for better or worse', explains aesthetician Yuriko Saito.[238] The following chapter explores how environmental law has considered this advice.

---

[238] Saito, *Aesthetics of the Familiar* (above n 35) 186.

2

Aesthetics and Environmental Law

I. LAW AND AESTHETICS

WHAT DOES ENVIRONMENTAL law have to do with aesthetics? For the many scholars and practitioners attuned to the scientific, economic and ethical doctrine that informs environmental decisions, the answer would be not very much. This chapter shows otherwise, as aesthetic issues materially shape environmental law from the politics of its making to the adjudication of its application. Aesthetics matter because our appreciation of the natural world is as much a sensory experience as an intellectual rendition of it. I do not suggest that aesthetics should trump other values or knowledge in environmental policy, but we should respect it as indispensable to sound governance. Taking a broad definition of environmental law to encompass its institutional and symbolic characteristics, in addition to formal legal doctrine, this chapter investigates the interface between aesthetics and environmental law in three principal domains.

Firstly, it considers aesthetics in the making of environmental law. Civil societal groups often appeal to natural beauty in rallying community support to save endangered species, old growth forests and many other biosphere values. Equally, they may highlight aesthetic qualities at risk from 'unsightly' development. In these guises, aesthetics provides criteria for identifying environmental issues or places that the law should address, as well as contributing a political resource for motivating action.

Secondly, this chapter considers the status of aesthetic values or criteria in substantive environmental law. It begins with the literary qualities that express the seminal concepts of environmental policy underpinning the law – relating to sustainability, the circular economy and other figurative language that renders complex and abstract ideals into an accessible narrative for the mass public. Turning to regulation and case law, we find that they recognise aesthetic factors haphazardly and ambiguously. Aesthetic criteria relating to visual, acoustic and other sensory triggers permeate resource management, land-use planning, pollution control and nature conservation governance. Such aesthetic considerations are sometimes formulated in language that speaks of 'public health' or 'amenity' values. Moreover, some laws' terminology specifies spiritual and recreational considerations, which can also imply aesthetic values. Whatever the vocabulary, environmental legislation tends to lack clear definitions about the substance of such values or operational directions about how to protect or manage them.

The third interface between law and aesthetics is the symbolic incarnations of governmental authority that contribute to societal understandings of the characteristics and purposes of the nation-state. The emotive paraphernalia of the nation-state, such as flags, monuments, national anthems and insignia, can unleash the potential of aesthetics to shape social attitudes. Environmental themes can be harnessed as symbols of national culture or sovereign identity, especially where these environmental motifs uniquely relate to a country, as with China's panda bear or Australia's kangaroos. These symbols do not directly regulate environmental behaviour, but still matter for nation building and legitimating the authority of the state. These practices feed off the broader aestheticisation of politics in our era, in which political struggles are fought with images as much as words.

Before examining these issues in environmental law, let's begin with the aesthetic dimensions of the legal system at large, as they illuminate some underlying issues and trends observable in environmental law itself.[1] The current scholarship on law and aesthetics, of modest extent, falls into three main clusters. I will also identify a fourth important dimension for law and aesthetics, yet hardly identified in this literature, because of its particular relevance to environmental law.

To start with, researchers have evaluated the law in regulating aesthetic issues that arise in a variety of policy contexts.[2] Although the law may present itself as a realm of clinical and abstract decision-making, standing above the emotions and theatre of other domains of society, including the aesthetic, 'the law has always had an aesthetic policy, an attitude of policing images and licensing pleasures', explains Desmond Manderson.[3] Likewise, in *Law and Image* Costas Douzinas and Lynda Nead show that throughout history many nation states have used and governed aesthetic phenomena with great interest.[4] Today, authorities regulate them not only in environmental management, as we will consider shortly, but across numerous domains from intellectual property rights to cultural heritage protection. Illustratively, aesthetic issues enter medical malpractice suits for botched cosmetic surgery; sexual discrimination cases based on the complainant's appearance; copyright infringement claims relating to works of arts; anti-drug laws in the name of promoting cleanliness; and public order regulations policing obscenity and indecencies. Lawmakers may also regulate or use art as means of political control, as Oren Ben-Dor and others investigate in *Law and Art*.[5] Fascist and communist regimes during the twentieth century had a particularly intense interest in both controlling art and harnessing it for propaganda and social discipline.

---

[1] D Manderson, *Songs Without Music* (University of California Press, 2000) 181–82.

[2] R Kevelson, 'Introduction: Dialectic, Conflicts in Cultural Norms, Laws and Legal Aesthetic' in R Kevelson (ed), *Law and Aesthetics* (Peter Land, 1992) 1, 6.

[3] Ibid, 5.

[4] Ibid, 9.

[5] O Ben-Dor, 'Standing Before the Gates of the Law?' in O Ben-Dor (ed), *Law and Art: Justice, Ethics and Aesthetics* (Routledge, 2011) 1, 2.

Secondly, the interface between law and aesthetics has excited the so-called 'law and literature' school. While some of its researchers examine law *in* literature, others focus on law *as* literature, evaluating legal texts using the methods and insights of literary critics. This field thus 'deals with the question of form and contributes to law a depth of understanding about language and a variety of analyses of the problematic relationship of text and meaning', explains Manderson.[6] By conceptualising the law as a performative language, the law is recast as an avenue for story-telling and rhetorical devices rather than exclusively a mechanism for adjudicating disputes or enforcing rules. This methodology has had some traction among environmental law scholars specifically, highlighting the narratives and literary devices that inform the field as evident in court judgments, pleadings and other law-related texts.

This research field's staple is analogy or metaphor for drawing connections between law and literature. Famously, Ronald Dworkin's 'chain novel' metaphor characterised the decisions of courts as an ongoing, collectively authored novel. He explained: 'in this enterprise a group of novelists writes a novel seriatim; each novelist in the chain interprets the chapter he has been given in order to write a new chapter, which is then added to what the next novelist receives'.[7] Ed Morgan's *Aesthetics of International Law* also fits this genre, arguing that 'the aesthetic qualities of [international] law mirror similar qualities in literature', as he compares international legal discourse with sampled Western literature from Franz Kafka to Kurt Vonnegut.[8] As 'the meaning of the law has long been exhausted', Moraga argues, the expression and presentation of the law matters more.[9]

The aesthetic of legal argument has especially fascinated some. Ernest Weinrib valorises the law for evoking beauty through its proportion, coherence and unity, as derived from the law's internal ordering based on legal reasoning and fidelity to precedent.[10] In *Law and Aesthetics*, Adam Gearey also unveils the law as a literary language.[11] Influenced by critical legal studies, Gearey explains that 'just as the image represents and distorts reality by making what is fluid appear fixed and unchanging, law is criticised as a reification of the world'.[12] Gearey uses insights from aesthetics to empower critical perspectives in legal discourse.[13] Martha Nussbaum also believes that scholars should investigate the law as a form of literature, and she encourages use of narratives in legal reasoning that evoke sympathy for the cause that she believes is lacking in other models of legal reasoning stultified by abstract or technical formulae.[14]

---

[6] Manderson, *Songs Without Music* (above n 1) 30.
[7] R Dworkin, *Law's Empire* (Harvard University Press, 1986) 229.
[8] E Morgan, *The Aesthetics of International Law* (University of Toronto Press, 2007) 29.
[9] Ibid, 169.
[10] EJ Weinrib, *The Idea of Private Law* (Harvard University Press, 1993).
[11] A Gearey, *Law and Aesthetics* (Hart Publishing, 2001).
[12] Ibid, 25.
[13] Ibid, 31.
[14] M Nussbaum, *Poetic Justice: The Literary Imagination and Public Life* (Beacon Press, 1997).

To the extent that the law and literature movement treats each 'as subjects for comparison not of interaction', observes Manderson, it fails to capture the legal system's own aesthetic properties in its modes of legal reasoning, rituals and symbols of authority.[15] In this third perspective on the aesthetics of law, which he favours, the law is imbued and alive with aesthetic qualities rather than just means to regulate the aesthetic of art or as a point of intellectual comparison with literature. This approach thus starts from the assumption that 'aesthetics is already in the law' rather than the law being 'about' aesthetics or 'compared' to aesthetics.[16] This perspective can draw on postmodern legal theory because it takes us beyond a literal understanding of the expression of the law.

This third scholarly approach thus considers how legal texts and institutions have sensory significance. In *Law and Image*, Douzinas and Nead observe 'the law arranges, distributes, and polices its own images through icons of authority and sovereignty, tradition and fidelity'.[17] Concurring, Piyel Halder argues 'the law continues to be structurally dependent upon aesthetic principles and remains grounded in the rhetoric of the image. This is manifest most explicitly in the physical architecture of the legal environment'.[18] These material aesthetics include courts, legislatures, prisons, presidential palaces and other public buildings connected with the authority of the nation state.

Courts have particular interest for these scholars. Halder argues that the 'tropes and figures of courtroom design'[19] are a rhetorical ornament of importance because the 'law needs to stand out from the mundanity of other institutions and therefore needs an ornate architecture'.[20] Courtroom architecture symbolises the tradition and majesty of the law, and insinuates an exclusive or special space that demarcates and articulates the authority of the law and how people should behave.[21] The spectacle, solemnity, rituals of litigation buttress courts' authority and facilitate the public's 'subordination' to it.[22] In recent decades authorities have moderated some of the ornamentation, such as removal of art works from courtrooms, the robing of judges in sober black and white, and the replacement of colourful seals by simple signatures on legal documents. This may reflect a trend to present the law and justice as more 'neutral', according to Martin Jay.[23]

---

[15] Manderson, *Songs Without Music* (above n 1) 30–31.

[16] Ibid, 31.

[17] Ibid, 9.

[18] P Haldar, 'The Function of the Ornament in Quintilian, Alberti and Court Architecture' in C Douzinas and L Nead (eds), *Law and the Image: The Authority of Art and the Aesthetics in Law* (University of Chicago Press, 1999) 117, 117.

[19] Ibid, 121.

[20] Ibid, 135.

[21] Z Bankowski and G Maugham, *Images of Law* (Routledge, 1976).

[22] Ibid, 136.

[23] M Jay, 'Must Justice be Blind? The Challenge of Images to the Law' in Douzinas and Nead, *Law and the Image* (above n 18) 19, 24.

A preeminent aesthetic symbol of Anglo-American legal systems is the goddess Justitia (the Roman deity of justice), often represented in statues and fountains fronting civic buildings and public spaces. Known today as Lady Justice, and commonly depicted as blindfolded, holding a balance and sword, it's an allegorical personification of the moral force in judicial systems. Her aesthetic qualities have changed through history, and only from the late fifteenth century has she tended to be blindfolded.[24] It came to symbolise not helplessness but impartiality and equality before the law.[25] Douzinas and Nead surmise that this involves an anti-aesthetic stance, in that 'justice must be blindfolded', administered in abstract logic without distortion by aesthetic considerations such as the appearance of disputants.[26] In other words, the 'law is presented as the solution to the conflict of values and the plurality of interpretations and is therefore functionally and politically differentiated from art and literature'.[27]

Figure 2.1 *Justice*, 1636, Abraham Bosse (1602–76), etching; Metropolitan Museum of Art, New York

---

[24] Ibid.

[25] Ibid, 20–21.

[26] C Douzinas and L Nead, 'Introduction' in Douzinas and Nead, *Law and the Image* (above n 18) 1, 2–3.

[27] Ibid, 3.

The aesthetic qualities of law extend to its institutional processes, often used in environmental governance, from public inquiries to international treaty-making conferences. The affirmation of public participation in modern regulation has required more imagery and other aesthetic devices to engage the public. These include the distribution of posters and brochures in public information campaigns, and the presentation of scientific evidence in inquiries and tribunals through visual aids including maps and photographs. Public inquiries and environmental assessments sometimes include site visits where participants may engage directly with an environment's aesthetic qualities. New Zealand's Waitangi Tribunal, which considers Maori grievances relating to rights to control natural resources, often makes field trips to sites of significance.[28] Similarly, Australia's former Resource Assessment Commission often sponsored site visits to enable its agents to learn and experience first-hand about the issues in contention.

In *Songs without Music*, Manderson argues that aesthetics permeates all legal practice, not just the foregoing overt examples associated with courtroom architecture, statutes of Lady Justice or public consultation institutions. Law and justice, he explains, are the 'cultural medium of expressive form, through which sense and symbols are combined, communicated and interpreted'.[29] Building on Ronald Dworkin's conceptualisation of judicial precedents as analogous to a 'chain novel',[30] Manderson calls the law 'not so much a novel as a soap opera'.[31] The opera is imbued with 'rhetoric, metaphor, form, images, and symbols'.[32] Literary devices in court judgments, such as proverbs, similes, parallel structures, alliteration and rhyme, can also contribute to its aesthetic persona and public impact.[33] Consider the following animated writing of US Justice Michael Musmanno, a connoisseur of literary devices:

> It is regrettable that the Court should [...] seem to restrict the freedom and the willingness of combatting parties to leave the battlefield of hot contention, repair to a tree of deliberation, and under its comforting shade of mutual ineffectiveness, reach a common understanding of reciprocal benefit.[34]

The law's aesthetic qualities matter because they contribute to the law's influence over our emotions, values and practices. 'A sensitivity to the use of rhetoric and metaphor', Manderson adds, 'can enrich our understanding of the meaning

---

[28] Waitangi Tribunal, 'Tribunal Site Visit, Wairau', https://teara.govt.nz/en/photograph/32499/tribunal-site-visit-wairau.

[29] Manderson, *Songs Without Music* (above n 1) 201.

[30] R Dworkin, 'Law as Interpretation' (1982) 9 *Critical Inquiry* 179.

[31] Manderson, *Songs Without Music* (above n 1) 30.

[32] Ibid, ix.

[33] D Kurzon, 'Poetic Language and Court Opinions' in R Kevelson (ed), *Law and Aesthetics* (Peter Land, 1992) 281, 295–97.

[34] *Schoellhammer's Hatboro Manor Inc v Local Joint Executive Board of Philadelphia*, 426 Pa 53231 A 2d 160 (1967), quoted in Kurzon, 'Poetic Language' (above n 33) 292.

of law, for the style of a legal judgment contributes to both its weight as precedent and its meaning'.[35]

The foregoing accounts of aesthetics and the law must be updated to accommodate some important shifts in how states govern in recent years, a trend especially relevant to environmental law. As governance is increasingly delegated to or shared with non-state actors, such as business corporations and civil society groups, the aesthetics of the legal system change. No longer can we (if ever we could) just dwell on the aesthetic of courtrooms or public monuments, or how states regulate aesthetic issues in society; we must also account for the aesthetic dimensions of governance without government, a milieu where rules and standards that influence social behaviour emanate increasingly from actors and processes beyond the state. Unlike the tidy aesthetics of order, coherence and control associated with modernist legal systems, in our post-modernising world with its cultural pluralism and heterogeneity, as well as transnational qualities, we encounter the aesthetics of fragmentation, disorder and unpredictability.[36]

Environmental law departs strongly from the traditional aesthetic of the law in its diversity, fluidity and plurality beyond the state apparatus. The very making of environmental law, as we will see in this chapter's next section, is stimulated by vibrant civil society groups who appeal to or depict natural beauty as a motivating factor to conserve biodiversity or curb unsightly pollution. Environmental protest actions, from street demonstrations to civil disobedience, also exude distinctive aesthetic atmospheres, and artists assert a crucial role in engaging the public on climate change. Within substantive environmental governance, non-state actors are as active, such as initiating ecological restoration projects that improve the appearance of degraded landscapes. The private sector, specifically business corporations, has also become a seminal governance influence, sequestering a role for itself in environmental decision-making in the guise of 'corporate social responsibility' (CSR), as Chapter 5 explores. The deceptive nature of some corporate marketing, especially on environmental matters, has made the aesthetics of CSR a major battleground for governance where better public transparency and accountability is now sought. In sum, the aesthetic qualities of environmental law and the aesthetic issues it regulates are transformed by a rapidly changing governance milieu that has elevated aesthetics to unprecedented importance.

II. THE MAKING OF ENVIRONMENTAL LAW

A. The Aestheticised Politics of Law Reform

Proponents of stronger environmental laws often appeal to natural beauty or other aesthetic attributes in seeking to influence public sentiment and pressure

---

[35] Manderson, *Songs Without Music* (above n 1) 42–43.
[36] See M Davies, 'The Ethos of Pluralism' (2005) 27(1) *Sydney Law Review* 87.

lawmakers.[37] Exalting attractive scenery and charismatic animals can also directly benefit such proponents, often environmental NGOs, by attracting financial donations. Because the general public may not be able to directly experience places advocated for legal protection, the arts have been enlisted to bring natural beauty to a wider audience. Artists collaborate with environmental activists to creatively highlight the animals, landscapes and impacted human communities they wish to protect.

Aesthetics has intertwined with nature conservation for ages. In the United States, landscape paintings created by the nineteenth century Hudson River School introduced to the public awe-inspiring images of the American wilderness increasingly under threat from the axe or plough, thereby helping to cultivate the public's taste for the aesthetic, spiritual and recreational benefits of nature.[38] In Australia, the Heidelberg School in the 1890s played an equivalent role, painting evocative images that forged a new visual aesthetic of the Australian landscape that helped redeem the 'bush' from its intimidating image. These efforts began to influence the setting aside of natural areas as national parks or forestry reserves. The establishment of the world's first national park at Yellowstone in 1872 is owed partly to the efforts of painter Thomas Moran and photographer William Henry Jackson, whose enticing images of the area's majestic scenery helped win Congressional support.[39] In the twentieth century, US wilderness photographer Ansell Adams continued this tradition, collaborating with the Sierra Club to lobby for expansion of national parks. Rebranding wilderness aesthetics to promote national identity and pride, however, had negative consequences for Indigenous peoples bleached out of these landscapes and displaced from their traditional territories.

Europe has an even longer history of nature conservation, predating the concept of national parks, as found in the management of forest estates in private and public hands. As in the so-called New World, during the late nineteenth century natural beauty garnered greater political concern in some European countries, with growing appreciation of the scenic values of their pastoral landscapes. It led to greater protection of existing forests and promotion of afforestation, such as in the Netherlands via the Nature Scenery Act 1928.[40] Only in Scandinavia did wilderness-like country remain in Western Europe, and as in the United States the tourist industry championed some of the first

---

[37] KK Smith, 'Mere Taste: Democracy and the Politics of Beauty' (2000) 7 *Wisconsin Environmental Law Journal* 151, 154.

[38] JK Howat, *American Paradise: The World of the Hudson River School* (Metropolitan Museum of Art, 1987).

[39] N Strochlic, 'We Have a Painter to Thank for Yellowstone' *National Geographic Magazine* April 2016, www.nationalgeographic.com/magazine/2016/05/explore-thomas-moran-yellowstone-paintings.

[40] Discussed in SW Verstegen, 'The Nature Scenery Act of 1928' (2015) spring/fall *Forest History Today* 4.

Figure 2.2 *The Grand Canyon of the Yellowstone*, 1872, Thomas Moran (1837–1926), oil on canvas; Smithsonian American Art Museum

conservation laws to safeguard these areas, for instance Norway's Nature Preservation Act 1910.[41]

Another pioneer is Japan, which in 1919 enacted the Law for the Preservation of Historic Sites, Places of Scenic Beauty and Natural Monuments, thereby providing a national regime for legal designation of places of, inter alia, aesthetic significance.[42] Japanese cultural scholar Emiko Kakluchi explains what this meant: 'financial support was provided by the government, while any actions which might affect their condition were to be subject to permission by the government'.[43] The legislation protected a variety of natural places including volcanoes and mountains, as well as urban parks and gardens. Since 1950, these protections have operated via the Law for the Protection of Cultural Properties,[44] and it is notable that Japan has integrated natural and cultural heritage protection into a single legal regime.

Non-governmental organisations have also starred in this history. The New Zealand Native Bird Protection Society, established in 1923, was instrumental in campaigning for conservation of the country's birds that were (and remain) menaced by exotic pests such as stoats, and Figure 2.3 shows one of

---

[41] LH Frivold and A Svendsrud, 'State Forestry in Norway' in KJ Oosthoek and R Hölzl (eds), *Managing Northern Europe's Forests* (Berghahn, 2018) 201, 220.

[42] Act no 44 (1919).

[43] E Kakluchi, *Cultural Heritage Protection System in Japan: Current Issues and Prospects of the Future* (National Graduate Institute for Policy Studies, 2014) 3.

[44] Bunkazai Hogo-ho (Law for the Protection of Cultural Properties) Cultural Affairs Protection Department, 1950.

its eye-catching posters distributed for public education. In 1935 the Society was renamed Forest and Bird Protection Society, which endures as one of New Zealand's premier NGOs for protecting wildlife habitat and educating the public.[45]

Figure 2.3 *New Zealanders! Protect your native birds. Cherish your heritage!* 1926, CM Banks, offset lithographers; New Zealand Native Bird Protection Society; Alexander Turnbull Library, Wellington

Promotion of the aesthetic of nature conservation matters more than ever in our media-saturated culture. Campaigns to stop dams and mines frequently appeal to the sensuous imagery and sounds of the imperilled. In Australia, artist and conservationist Kathleen McArthur applied her skills in wildflower painting to launch a campaign in 1969 against sand mining in the Cooloola region of Queensland.[46] She distributed her wildflower postcards to educate the community about the environmental threat, and achieved success, with the area protected since 1971 as the Great Sandy National Park. Another triumph from Australia was activists' use of Peter Dombrovskis' Tasmanian wilderness

---

[45] Forest and Bird, www.forestandbird.org.nz.
[46] S Davis, 'Hidden Women of History: Kathleen McArthur, the Wildflower Woman Who Took on Joh Bjelke-Petersen' *The Conversation* 31 January 2019, https://theconversation.com.

photographs to challenge the proposed impoundment of the Franklin River.[47] His iconic *Morning Mist. Rock Island Bend, Franklin River* (1979) was later displayed in full-page advertisements in national newspapers commissioned by the Wilderness Society, with the blunt caption: 'Could you vote for a party that will destroy this?'. The tactic helped win support for anti-dam political candidates in the Australian parliamentary elections in 1983. As a remote wilderness that very few Australians will ever visit, this artistic intervention was politically astute.

Figure 2.4 'Could you Vote for a Party that will Destroy this? *Morning Mist Rock Island Bend', Franklin River*, 1983, photograph by Peter Dombrovskis 1979; advertisement by Tasmanian Wilderness Society

Nature soundscapes and music have also enlivened this agenda. The songs of Sirocco, an Australian folk band, have been identified by researchers as 'influential in bringing to people's attention, and giving value to, the Macquarie Marshes, a New South Wales ecosystem under threat'.[48] In 1993 the band even held a concert in these awesome wetlands, and its music incorporates some soundscapes from the site now protected under the Ramsar Convention.[49]

---

[47] T Bonyhady, 'No Dams: The Art of Olegas Truchanas and Peter Dombrovskis' in R Butler (ed), *The Europeans: Émigré Artists in Australia 1930–1960* (National Gallery of Australia, 1990) 236.

[48] DJ Curtis, 'Creating Inspiration: The Role of the Arts in Creating Empathy for Ecological Restoration' (2009) 10(3) *Ecological Management and Restoration* 174, 182.

[49] Convention on Wetlands of International Importance especially as Waterfowl Habitat (1971) 996 UNTS 245.

Incorporation of bird songs, waves, weather and other natural ambiences into musical compositions particularly benefits mass audiences unlikely to ever visit the source environments remote from their lives. American composer Douglas Quin has compiled a substantial sound library of the polar regions, travelling under the sponsorship of the National Science Foundation's Artists and Writers program.[50] Quin incorporates sounds from the natural world in composing music, as in his intriguing piece with David Rothenberg called *Toothwalking* (2001) that integrates noisy Alaskan walruses, a keyboard bass and clarinet. Quin's work also yields bioacoustic data of scientific value; for instance, he assisted Conservation Research New Caledonia in protecting the endangered kagu bird (*Rhynochetos jubatus*). Sound and music also aid the fight against global warming. The Climate Music Project declares its mission to 'communicate a sense of urgency about climate change by combining climate science with the emotional power of music to drive meaningful action'.[51] Musicians have composed protest songs to arouse public concern, such as Orbital's song *Impact* (1994) and Brandon Flowers' *Still Want You* (2015).

Such efforts have not always prevailed. Iceland's infamous Kárahnjúkar hydropower dam, located in previously unspoilt terrain on the edge of the Vatnajökull National Park, is one tale. Construction of the massive dam that began in 2002 and inundated two wild rivers, aroused intense opposition focused on the landscape's stunning scenery. Photographic representation of the area was placed on a website, as well as shown in a major Icelandic newspaper and a shopping mall, which gave the campaign extensive publicity. Importantly, the photography not only showcased the typical motifs of Icelandic dramatic scenery, but also enlivened the public 'to beauty of a more delicate nature: to small-scale artworks of rocks, water, plants, birds and animals'.[52] Nonetheless, the dam went ahead, despite being rejected by the Icelandic Planning Committee, as local political forces favoured the economic benefits the project was perceived to bring in powering an aluminium smelter. Tasmania has also suffered similar ignominy from hydropower, when its Lake Pedder in the southwest wilderness, where the Franklin River flows, was dammed in 1972 despite being within a national park gazetted in 1955. Olegas Truchanas, who fought to save Lake Pedder by impressing Tasmanians with its grandeur depicted through his sublime photography, poignantly asked 'is there any reason why, given enlightened leadership, the idea of beauty could not become an accepted goal of national policy?'.[53]

Environmental activists can equally cite negative imagery to challenge ugly activities: hunting, pollution and deforestation. The World Wide Fund for

[50] P Samartzis, 'The Nature of Sound and the Sound of Nature' in B Hince, R Summerson and A Wiesel (eds), *Antarctica: Music, Sounds and Cultural Connections* (ANU Press, 2015) 139, 143–45.

[51] See www.theclimatemusicproject.org.

[52] K Benediktsson, 'Moving Places: The Emotional Politics of Nature' in B Granås and JO Bærenholdt (eds), *Mobility and Place: Enacting Northern European Peripheries* (Ashgate, 2008) 205, 212.

[53] O Truchanas, '"Shining Beacon" Speech, at the Opening of the Exhibition "Lake Pedder 1971"', Saddlers Court Gallery, Richmond, 19 November 1971. See further Bonyhady, 'No Dams' (above n 47).

Nature (WWF), a lobbyist for stronger environmental laws, publicises the menace of land clearing for palm oil plantations, cattle ranching and other threats through photographs and videos posted on its website.[54] The Sea Shepherd Conservation Society uses images taken by its seafaring activists and brings the bloody business of Japanese whaling to a global audience, as part of its ongoing campaign to challenge the legality of so-called 'scientific research' whaling.[55] Its 2019 film, *Defend, Conserve and Protect*, which premiered in my hometown of Hobart, brought to mass audiences the grisly business of Japanese whaling. Likewise, Greenpeace's campaign to save cetaceans has relied on close-up footage of the unlucky creatures harpooned.[56] With invisible environmental threats, notably nuclear radiation, activists rely on artistic means to evoke their concerns, such as colourful posters, banners and other paraphernalia. Protestors have reconfigured the well-recognised nuclear radiation symbol, comprising a circle divided into six equal sections, three of which are black and three yellow.

Lately plastic waste, especially in the oceans, has galvanised many as an urgent priority, with some successes such as the agreement reached in January 2019 to adopt a new EU directive to curb single-used plastics including coffee cups and drinking straws.[57] Many consumers witness this problem in their daily lives, but the distant impacts on marine life such as seabirds and turtles that ingest or become entangled in plastic waste have been brought to the public's attention through film and photography. The UK-based Surfers Against Sewage released a film in 2017 with chilling imagery of the magnitude of the problem as part of their campaign for legal action on throwaway plastics.[58] Similar aesthetic strategies feature in the activism of a growing throng of other anti-plastic groups, many of which collaborate in the Plastic Pollution Coalition, whose website contains upsetting imagery.[59]

The aestheticised character of political activism and discourse has attracted scholarly interest, notably Kevin DeLuca's seminal *Image Politics: The New Rhetoric of Environmental Activism*.[60] The trend is tied to the wider hyper-aesthetic leanings of our culture saturated with mass television and Internet communications. In *Picture Theory*, William Mitchell captures Western culture's 'pictorial turn' in which images have become key means of social and political communication.[61] Concurring, Mark Taylor and Esa Saarinen in *Imagologies* contend that 'in our era, we must philosophize with images

---

[54] WWF, www.worldwildlife.org/media?threat_id=deforestation.

[55] Sea Shepherd, https://seashepherd.org.

[56] A Kalland, *Unveiling the Whale: Discourses on Whales and Whaling* (Berghahn Books, 2009) 42.

[57] Council of the European Union, Proposal for a Directive of the European Parliament and Council on the Reduction of Certain Plastic Products on the Environment, 5483/19, 18 January 2019.

[58] S Laville, 'Surfers Against Sewage Urge MPs to Make Parliament Plastic-Free' *The Guardian* 1 February 2018.

[59] See www.plasticpollutioncoalition.org.

[60] KM DeLuca, *Image Politics: The New Rhetoric of Environmental Activism* (Routledge, 2005).

[61] WJT Mitchell, *Picture Theory: Essays on Verbal and Visual Representation* (University of Chicago Press, 1995).

rather than concepts'.[62] Image-based politics feeds off wider cultural trends; Jean Baudrillard critiques our growing culture of spectacle, in which the public assumes the role of enfeebled spectator and consumer of a commodified 'hyper-reality'.[63] In this milieu, critical public debate succumbs readily to seductive corporate marketing and government propaganda.

The solution, suggests social theorist Guy-Ernest Debord, is for citizen activists to transform the same aesthetic tools into retaliatory means of protest.[64] In a media-inebriated culture, parading images aids social mobilisation and advocacy, supporting traditional means of civic activism such as street marches, petitions and rallies. Art can communicate dissent on its own or in combination with verbal and textual communication. In *The Art of Moral Protest*, James Jasper depicts artists on the 'cutting edge of society's understanding of itself as it changes' by putting 'into concrete form new ways of seeing and judging the world, new ways of thinking and feeling about it'.[65] Images can enable esoteric discourses and ideas to be materially visible and knowable to a wider societal audience, injecting greater political salience into their concerns. Aesthetic activism however, cannot replace a role for conversation and consultation, because a discourse of images needs to accommodate a space for audiences to respond and debate rather than just receive artistic statements.

B. New Environmental Visualisations

New visualisations of nature enabled by technological innovations have created unprecedented perspectives of both aesthetic and governmental significance. The advent of photography, and later satellite and drone imagery, has upended how we see and understand landscapes and seascapes, providing a bird's eye panorama that reveals their holistic character. Before the early twentieth century, maps and ground-level photographs were the primary visual aids through which geographical data was communicated by land surveyors and planners. Once aeroplane technology took off after the First World War, the vantage for gathering knowledge about the planet dramatically changed, as high altitude cameras enable the depiction of shifting environmental conditions over vast spatial and temporal scales. This yielded benefits inter alia for forest management, urban planning and agriculture. Geographical mapping could be assembled from pictures taken at regular intervals by aircraft from controlled heights, and the outputs, detached and panoramic, created a more

---

[62] M Taylor and E Saarinen, *Imagologies: Media Philosophy* (Routledge, 1994) 15.

[63] J Baudrillard, *Simulacra and Simulation*, translated SF Glaser (University of Michigan Press, 1994).

[64] GE Debord, *The Society of the Spectacle* (Black and Red, 1970).

[65] J Jasper, *The Art of Moral Protest: Culture, Biography, and Creativity in Social Movements* (University of Chicago Press, 1999) 13 and 369.

objective visualisation of the landscape than previously possible from ground-level surveyors and explorers.[66]

Aerial photography for environmental management blossomed from the 1930s. An early pioneer, the US Soil Conservation Service and Agricultural Adjustment Administration employed aerial photographers to monitor soil erosion and farmers' compliance with regulatory prescriptions.[67] Such practice has come a long way since with the aid of computer technologies to enhance and analyse the data. They can assist monitoring tree canopy coverage, biodiversity habitat and water runoff, thereby enabling authorities to devise better-tailored land use plans and regulations.[68] Aerial photography also helps detect oil spills, illegal fishing, weed infestations and unauthorised building. As the composition of vegetation is often a reliable indicator of the animal species supported, images of forest cover and species type contribute to mapping biodiversity. Further, drone technology can offer close-up images to identify and document environmental changes, especially in remote and inaccessible terrain, for wildlife identification, spotting forest fires and vegetation removals or additions. Aerial photography can also assist EIAs and generate baseline data for future monitoring, and in urban landscapes too it enables planners to better visualise and manage the layout of settlements.

With the advent of satellite imagery in the 1970s, much greater visual representation of the planet became possible, with further ramifications for our sensory perception of nature. Unlike photographs, computers must first process satellite imagery to generate meaningful visual data, such as mapping vegetation and soil patterns. In 1990, US environmental scientist Paul Uhlir predicted:

> remote sensing data will promote a more profound understanding of our planet's ecosystems and improve our predictive capabilities for better environmental management on national, regional, and international levels. Such information will challenge world leaders to establish appropriate environmental legislation and treaties.[69]

His faith has been validated, as the masses can now access satellite imagery through online, open-access programs such as Google Earth. Offering time-lapsed, bird's-eye panoramas of many areas of the planet over recent decades enables one to see environmental conditions changing rapidly and often adversely.[70]

---

[66] M Dyce, 'Canada Between the Photograph and the Map: Aerial Photography, Geographical Vision and the State' (2013) 39 *Journal of Historical Geography* 69.

[67] G Parak, 'Picturing the State of the Nation's Environment: Early Aerial Photography in the United States from the 1930s to the Late 1960s' in B Schneider and T Nocke (eds), *Image Politics of Climate Change* (Transcript Verlag, 2014) 325, 332.

[68] D McFarlane and P Caccetta, 'The Planner's New Best Friend: We Can Now Track Land-use Changes on a Scale of Centimetres' CSIROscope, 28 January 2016, https://blog.csiro.au/the-planners-new-best-friend-we-can-now-track-land-use-changes-on-a-scale-of-centimetre.

[69] PF Uhlir, 'Applications of Remote Sensing Information in Law: An Overview' in *Earth Observation Systems: Legal Considerations for the '90s* (American Society for Photogrammetry and Remote Sensing, and the American Bar Association, 1990) 8, 16.

[70] See http://earthengine.google.org/#intro. Users can also view some images on Time Magazine, at http://world.time.com/timelapse.

Google Earth users can zoom into virtually any spot to watch time-lapsed sequences of images since 1984. Taken from Landsat satellites, they evoke a dramatic retrospective of permutations in the planetary landscape over a mere few decades. One time-lapse series reveals Dubai mushrooming into a mega-metropolis, with artificial islands; another tracks the carcinogenic-like sprawl ringing Las Vegas; while a further depicts the ravenous deforestation of the Amazon. We could not glean the spectacle of planetary decline through these panoramas so easily from the vantage of the present or a single image of the past. We struggle to perceive aesthetically the enormity of our eco-footprint without sensing changes over time, which such imagery can enable by capturing evidence of pollution, deforestation and other visible declines for lawmakers to act on.[71]

Technology has not only altered the public's visualisation of the planet's environment, it has spawned a variety of practical applications for decision-making. Remote sensing technology has enabled the development of geographic information systems (GIS) to store, manipulate and analyse geographic data for land use planning and regulation. GIS mapping can aid forestry, soil conservation, wildlife management and numerous other uses of relevance to environmental decision-making. Users may also manipulate GIS data to show not only current patterns but also relationships between past data and future projections to depict environmental changes over time. Equally valuable, NGOs wishing to challenge environmentally damaging development can use GIS data; the US-based Earth Justice prepared a 'Fraccidents map' to allow concerned communities to identify the risks to themselves from hydraulic fracturing projects.[72]

In the latest advance, satellite-based spectrometer technologies have been harnessed to assist monitoring greenhouse gas (GHG) emissions regulated under international law. The Tropospheric Monitoring Instrument, launched by the European Space Agency in 2017, maps plumes of methane, carbon dioxide, nitrogen oxides and other emissions over industrial facilities and cities across the globe. This technology can also help pinpoint emission leaks from, inter alia, pipelines and oil wellheads. Other remotely sensed data-gathering facilities are Japan's Greenhouse Gases Observing Satellite and the NASA Orbiting Carbon Observatory 2, operational since 2009 and 2014 respectively.[73] As these technologies become refined, satellite-based monitoring and mapping will provide far more efficient and large-scale monitoring to improve compliance with GHG emissions regulation than that attainable by haphazard, ground-based monitoring.

---

[71] C Davies, S Hoban and B Penhoet, 'Moving Pictures: How Satellites, the Internet and International Environmental Law Can Help Promote Sustainable Development' (1999) 28 *Stetson Law Review* 1091.

[72] Earth Justice, 'Fracking Across the United States', https://earthjustice.org/features/campaigns/fracking-across-the-united-states.

[73] S Hardwick and H Graven, *Satellite Observations to Support Monitoring of Greenhouse Gas Emissions* (Grantham Institute Briefing paper no 16, Imperial College London, 2016) 5.

Advances in data-gathering technologies also yield unprecedented images of the ocean depths. The advent of remotely operated underwater vehicles (ROVs) in the 1960s has transformed ocean exploration for scientific research.[74] An ROV is an underwater robot equipped with a video camera, steered remotely by a person on a ship or offshore platform. Unlike manned submersibles, ROVs can remain underwater for ages to conduct extensive surveys, opening new vistas for oceanographic research and generating scientific knowledge to improve marine conservation. ROV technology also enables greater exploitation of deep-sea natural resources, including offshore hydrocarbon exploration and seabed mineral exploitation. The biotechnology industry deploys ROVs to explore the biogenetic attributes of deep-sea life for their potential commercialisation, including for cosmetic and pharmaceutical products. While international law does not regulate ROVs in the high seas beyond national jurisdiction, it provides some constraints on end-use exploitation of deep seabed and living resources, principally under the UN Convention on the Law of the Sea[75] and supplementary instruments.[76]

One legal intervention to improve the quality and accessibility of GIS data is the EU's INSPIRE (INfrastructure for SPatial InfoRmation in Europe) Directive of 2007.[77] It requires EU Member States to share such data on 34 designated themes through a network that gives public authorities efficient access to the necessary information to support their environmental policies and laws, as well as access for third parties such as business enterprises. The network promotes harmonious standards for posting, finding and exchanging GIS data for information generators and users in relation to hydrography, natural hazard zones, soil, agriculture, population and numerous other issues. These provisions enable sharing and comparison of spatial data covered by the Directive across EU Member States into integrated governance schemes. Yet the INPSIRE Directive is more than just a means for efficient communication of spatial information, argue Lasse Baaner and Line Hvingel; it expands environmental legislation beyond written norms to spatially-conceived norms that depend on their representation in digitised GIS formats.[78] They argue for a distinction, for instance, between watercourses shown on maps generated by public authorities pursuant to water quality legislation, whereby the maps in themselves constitute legal norms, and conversely, GIS representation of watercourses, which are 'spatial

---

[74] PI Macreadie et al, 'Eyes in the Sea: Unlocking the Mysteries of the Ocean Using Industrial, Remotely Operated Vehicles (ROVs)' (2018) 634 *Science of the Total Environment* 1077.

[75] (1982) 21 ILM 1245.

[76] V Wyssbrod, *L'exploitation des ressources génétiques marines hors juridiction nationale* (Brill, 2017).

[77] Directive 2007/2/EC of the European Parliament and of the Council of 14 March 2007 establishing an Infrastructure for Spatial Information in the European Community, OJ L 108, 25 April 2007, 1.

[78] L Baaner and L Hvingel, 'Spatiality of Environmental Law' (2015) 12 *Journal of European Planning and Environmental Law* 173, 175.

representations of the norms only, with errors and inaccuracies, as all representations are, and are not legally valid'.[79]

The foregoing observation identifies potential problems of legal accountability in using visual representations of spatio-legal data to govern environmental activities. Furthermore, photographs may be digitally manipulated or the raw data processed by erroneous techniques, and viewers may interpret the imagery divergently.[80] Thus, high-tech imagery cannot assure unquestioned objectivity to the sensory perception of environmental conditions. When used to aid environmental governance, follow-up site visits by officials sometimes may be necessary to verify GIS data or high altitude images. New visual technologies sometimes also aid this ground-level assessment, such as the increasingly ubiquitous CCTV cameras that can capture individuals' movements.

The law may also mediate the reception of new photographic and digital imagery by determining when it can assist compliance proceedings. The use of aerial photographs and satellite mapping in prosecuting landowners who illegally clear vegetation, dump waste or commit other offences has required the courts to rule on the admissibility of such imagery as evidence. It can help judges and juries understand the issues more clearly, and indeed sometimes it may be the only evidence that captures the offence. On the other hand, privacy considerations from unauthorised photography may arise that cause courts to rule such evidence inadmissible.

Still, the overall trend shows judicial receptiveness to aerial photography and remote sensing data increasing. One early breakthrough in US law was the 1989 Texan case, *ANR Production Co v M/V Mekhanik Dren*, where satellite photographs taken shortly before and after the collision of the ship and the oil platform were accepted as evidence because they showed local weather conditions at the time of the event.[81] European regulators are also using satellite images to investigate potential breaches of environmental law. However, often the technology is not able to provide sufficiently accurate data to support a prosecution without the need for supplementary research, such as with the identification of ships responsible for pollution spills.[82] Illegal forest clearing cases prosecuted in Australia regularly rely on aerial imagery, but they may need additional ground-based site evidence to determine the species of tree removed and whether it was regrowth or old growth, as such variables are relevant to the applicability of the legislative protections.[83]

---

[79] Ibid, 184.

[80] CA Guilshan, 'A Picture is Worth a Thousand Lies: Electronic Imaging and the Future of the Admissibility of Photographs into Evidence' (1992) 18 *Rutgers Computer and Technology Law Journal* 365.

[81] 1989 AMC 2299 (SD Texas).

[82] CM Billiet, 'Satellite Images as Evidence for Environmental Crime in Europe: A Judge's Perspective' in R Purdy and D Leung (eds), *Evidence from Earth Observation Satellites* (Brill, 2012) 321.

[83] R White, 'Experts and Expertise in the Land and Environment Court' (2017) 49(4) *Australian Journal of Forensic Sciences* 392.

Another aesthetic tool that relies on digitised mapping to communicate data about environmental changes and impacts is the cartogram, a type of picto-gram. Used increasingly by environmental NGOs and educational institutions to engage both lay people and policy makers, the cartogram provides a diagram-matic presentation of statistical data on a map base. It enables audiences to visualise the relative size of different countries', cities' or other geographical units' environmental activities or impacts, such as deforestation, GHG emissions and other eco-footprint indicators, wherein both colour and area are displayed as a function of the relative values.

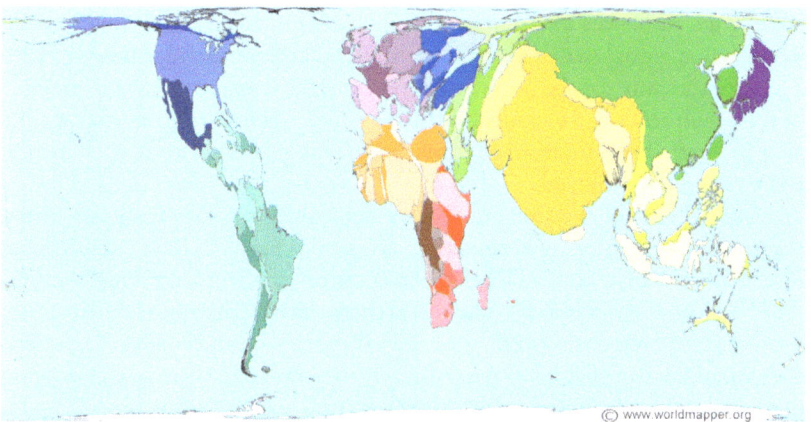

Figure 2.5 World Population Cartogram Map 2002, cartogram; Benjamin Hennig and Worldmapper Project; licensed under Creative Commons

Cartograms provide vivid representation of global environmental trends, issues and impacts. The organisation Population Education created a World Popu-lation Map, which scales the size of each country relative to the size of its population rather than its land mass.[84] Its sponsor explains, the 'map is a power-ful tool for examining how population data can be visually represented and what trends affect population size and growth in countries worldwide'.[85] Another popular use of the cartogram is depicting countries' CO_2 emissions, which show the United States and China dominating the world map while shrinking Africa's stature. The website carbonmap.org displays many climate-related cartograms, such as current and historic GHG emissions, fossil fuel reserves, as well as risk exposures to sea level rise and other climate-related adversities. Meat consump-tion, another driver of global warming, has been rendered into a cartogram to show disparities in countries' meat diets relative to the global average.[86]

---

[84] See http://populationeducation.org.

[85] Population Education, *World Population Map Activity Guide* (2014) 1, http://populationeducation.org/sites/default/files/pepwomtbya2_0.pdf.

[86] Meat Eaters, www.viewsoftheworld.net/?p=4876.

Marine fisheries catch data have been converted into cartograms, with countries depicted 'proportional to the magnitude of the annual catches and fishing effort by their fleets'.[87] The most comprehensive library of environmental cartograms is the 2010 published *Real Atlas of the World*, whose authors provide maps on food consumption, pollution, resource depletion and numerous other environmentally salient trends.[88] Of several online sites, the Worldmapper project and Views of the World host numerous cartograms displaying current and historic data about social and environmental issues, such as poverty and distribution of natural resources.[89]

In sum, cartograms offer a unique aesthetic device for researchers and activists to engage audiences in visualising major environmental trends and impacts, especially on a global scale. A single cartogram can provide a far more efficient and memorable way for the public to appreciate the enormity of environmental upheavals than reading a technical scientific paper. Some cartograms are accompanied by textual information to provide curious readers with deeper insights into the visualised problems.

To finish, I should mention another, rather quirky type of pictogram known as the 'horrendogram', a term coined by academics Suzanne Boyes and Michael Elliott in their article about visual representation of the horrendous complexity in EU marine governance.[90] The researchers devised their horrendograms to assess the adequacy and coverage of a multiplicity of international, regional and national laws in this field. After Brexit, they updated their horrendograms to depict the additional complexity facing marine governance as the UK faces a post-EU future.[91] The terminology of horrendograms and cartograms in themselves convey a certain aesthetic, which takes us into the next topic on figurative language in environmental policy discourse.

III. ENVIRONMENTAL POLICY DISCOURSE

Environmental law is tethered to a rich discourse of policies and principles that puts the meat on the bones of legal rules and standards. It is legally salient because these ideals and concepts guide regulators in their exercise of discretionary powers and specify desired environmental outcomes. This realm also has powerful aesthetic qualities in the figurative language that expresses policy

---

[87] R Watson and D Pauly, 'The Changing Face of Global Fisheries – the 1950s vs the 2000s' (2013) 42 *Marine Policy* 1, 1.

[88] D Dorling, M Newman and A Barford, *The Real Atlas of the World* (Thames and Hudson, 2010).

[89] See https://worldmapper.org; www.viewsoftheworld.net.

[90] SJ Boyes and M Elliot, 'Marine Legislation – The Ultimate "Horrendogram": International Law, European Directives and National Implementation' (2014) 86(1) *Marine Pollution Bulletin* 39.

[91] SJ Boyes and M Elliot, 'Brexit: The Marine Governance Horrendogram Just Got More Horrendous' (2016) 111 *Marine Pollution Bulletin* 41.

norms, environmental challenges or governing principles, enabling the public to comprehend abstract concepts and relate them to more familiar dimensions of their world. Readers of this book will already know many basic norms of environmental governance, which do not need further explanation, but their literary character does. One is the notion of 'sustainability' or 'sustainable development', the conceptual ballast of modern environmental law.[92] It conveys a journey, never ending, and a self-renewing quality. Sustainability also evokes the ideal of living within nature's means, a goal captured by the nearly equally well-known metaphor of 'eco-footprint', which appeals because it's so personal and instantly comprehensible.[93] The footprint metaphor has in turn spawned derivatives, such as 'carbon footprint', and the design of environmental footprint calculators for airline travellers and other purposes. 'Resilience' has also entered the policy idiom to express the importance of ecosystems and societies being able to withstand adversity and change,[94] and like sustainability it's increasingly acknowledged in legislative texts.

This policy-related vernacular also enlivens an extensive scholarly literature and public discourse about our environmental challenges and aspirations.[95] The narratives that frame environmental law, be it wilderness conservation or apocalyptic climate change, resonate through such vivid rhetoric.[96] The metaphor in particular, giving a poetical or rhetorical description of one thing as something else, helps people to efficiently understand phenomenon by relating it to another, more familiar experience or object. It and other literary devices can powerfully convey environmental issues, impacts and behaviours: 'web of life', 'food chain', 'tragedy of the commons', 'spaceship Earth' and 'lifeboat' resonate easily with many lay people.[97] The 'spaceship Earth' metaphor conveys our planet as a fragile life-support biome, while 'lifeboat' alludes to Earth's finite capacity to support a burgeoning humanity.

This aesthetic language predates the advent of modern environment law. As literary critic MH Abram explains, the 'Romantic poets, at the turn of the nineteenth century, introduced into the literary realm an extraordinary emphasis on the natural world and an unprecedented set of concepts, attitudes, and

---

[92] C Voigt, *Sustainable Development as a Principle of International Law* (Martinus Nijhoff Publishers, 2009).

[93] M Wackernagel and W Rees, *Our Ecological Footprint: Reducing Human Impact on Earth* (New Society Publishers, 1996).

[94] S Carpenter et al, 'From Metaphor to Measurement: Resilience of What to What? (2001) 4 *Ecosystems* 765.

[95] E Scotford, *Environmental Principles and the Evolution of Environmental Law* (Hart Publishing, 2017).

[96] H Doremus, 'The Rhetoric and Reality of Nature Protection: Toward a New Discourse' (2000) 57 *Washington and Lee Law Review* 11; MA Burke, 'Klamath Farmers and Cappuccino Cowboys: The Rhetoric of the Endangered Species Act and Why it (Still) Matters' (2004) 14 *Duke Environmental Law and Policy Forum* 441.

[97] For more examples, see B Larson, *Metaphors for Environmental Sustainability* (Yale University Press, 2011).

feelings with reference to that world'.[98] Of this genre, Samuel Coleridge's famous poem, *Kubla Khan; Or a Vision in a Dream* describes 'Alph, the sacred river [...] through caverns measureless to man, down to a sunless sea'.[99] The same oeuvre flourished over the following century in writings about environmental ethics and nature conservation; Aldo Leopold wrote evocatively that we need 'to think like a mountain', or what we would more prosaically say as to perceive our lives holistically within our whole ecosystem.[100] Rachel Carson's *Silent Spring*, published in 1962, similarly exudes poetic language serving to evoke not so much of nature's beauty but to sharpen our awareness of its degradation.[101]

Contemporary political oratory, legislative texts and judicial writings can provide colourful and evocative descriptions of environmental values or issues. Former South African leader Thabo Mbeki's 'I am an African' speech, made on 8 May 1996 on the adoption of the nation's new constitution when he was vice-president, begins 'I owe my being to the hills and thee valleys, the mountains and the glades, the rivers, the deserts, the trees, the flowers, the seas and the ever-changing seasons that define our native land'.[102] Of legislative text examples, New Zealand's Te Urewera Act 2014, which affirmed the legal personality of a region formerly of national park status, describes the entity as 'ancient and enduring, a fortress of nature, alive with history; its scenery is abundant with mystery, adventure, and remote beauty'.[103]

Judicial prose, often considered solemn and impersonal, can also both excite the intellect and enthuse the heart. A master of it, the British judge Lord Denning sometimes embellished his legal analyses with iconic visions of bluebell woods and English summertime.[104] Denning's judgments also often began with a simple but compelling story, in which adjectives and verbs were at a premium. He began one 1982 judgment: '[t]he coast of Cornwall is beautiful. Much of the inland is ugly. It is despoiled by china clay workings. Not far from them is open farmland with small villages dotted around'.[105] Australia's Lionel Murphy, who sat on its High Court, also cultivated a distinctive style of writing that departed from the austerity of some of his peers. In the famous Tasmanian Dam case of 1983, Murphy wrote:

> The preservation of the world's heritage must not be looked at in isolation but as part of the cooperation between nations which is calculated to achieve intellectual

---

[98] MH Abrams, 'This Green Earth: The Vision of Nature in the Romantic Poets' 1999 William H and Jane Torrence Harder Lecture, Cornell Plantations.

[99] ST Coleridge, 'Kubla Khan: a Vision in a Dream' in M Drabble, J Stringer and D Helm (eds), *The Concise Oxford Companion to English Literature* (Oxford University Press, 2007; original 1816).

[100] A Leopold, *A Sand County Almanac* (Oxford University Press, 1949) 132.

[101] R Carson, *Silent Spring* (Houghton Mifflin, 1962).

[102] The full speech can be read at www.soweto.co.za/html/i_iamafrican.htm.

[103] Section 3(1).

[104] *Hinz v Berry* [1970] 2 QB 40; *Miller v Jackson* [1977] 1 QB 966.

[105] *R v Chief Constable Devon and Cornwall, ex parte Central Electricity Generating Board* [1982] QB 458, 465.

and moral solidarity of mankind and so reinforce the bonds between people which promote peace and displace those of narrow nationalism and alienation which promote war.[106]

Another pertinent example, from South Africa, is judge PLA Gamble's opening remarks in a case about a development affecting Cape Town's famed Table Mountain:

> There can be no doubt that Table Mountain is an imposing edifice which people all over the world associate with the Mother City, its breathtaking natural beauty is there for all to behold. [...] From sunrise to sunset it changes hue as the day progresses, at all times offering a beacon to those who may have lost direction.[107]

American jurist Benjamin Cardozo was renowned for his engaging rhetorical skills, although himself urging caution against reliance on literary devices that can oversimplify complex legal issues and encourage uncritical thinking, as epitomised in his admonition that '[m]etaphors in law are to be narrowly watched, for starting as devices to liberate thought, they end often by enslaving it'.[108]

You may be surprised to learn that the natural sciences also embrace figurative language, such as 'greenhouse effect', 'sinks' and 'keystone species' – contradicting the belief one might have that the scientific vernacular is just verbose jargon. Environmental economics, sometimes often assumed as offering similarly dry, mechanical parlance, in fact carries metaphors such as 'natural capital', 'ecosystem services' and 'ecological debt'.[109] When such evocative language gains traction in the mass media and popular discourse, it can influence public debates and policy choices on the environment.

Environmental activists, unsurprisingly, especially embellish their language, including in the very names of their organisations. The Earth Liberation Front, which favours economic sabotage to ignite change, has a name conjuring up a war-like campaign waged to free nature from human dominion.[110] Contrary to this militant overtone, Greenpeace, established in 1971 and now one of the world's preeminent environmental NGOs, has a brand name that immediately invokes an ethos of non-violence. A similarly peaceful message is associated with Friends of the Earth, a major global NGO for four decades. In the field of ecological restoration, 'rewilding' has become a slogan for some environmental groups seeking to heal past damage, and indeed it's incorporated into the very name of one – Rewilding Europe.

Some vocabulary can ascribe problematic ways of thinking about the natural world that we might assume as common sense. 'The terms employed

---

[106] *Commonwealth v Tasmania* (1983) 158 CLR 1, 176.

[107] *Parkscape v MTO Forestry and South African National Parks*, Case No 15910.2016, High Court, 1 March 2017, para 1.

[108] *Berkey v Third Avenue Railway Co*, 244 NY 84, 94, 155 NE 58, 61 (1926).

[109] B Coffey, 'Unpacking the Politics of Natural Capital and Economic Metaphors in Environmental Policy Discourse' (2016) 25(2) *Environmental Politics* 203.

[110] See the film *If a Tree Falls: The Story of the Earth Liberation Front* (2011), www.ifatreefallsfilm.com.

in environmental sciences do more than merely describe', explains one critic, 'they also guide attitudes, frame discussions, and shape policy. In short, they have in them the power to prescribe'.[111] Seemingly innocuous terms as natural 'resources' or environmental 'services' can insinuate the perception of nature as of value just for meeting human needs. 'Wilderness' is also dodgy, for its connotations of an unpeopled landscape, ignoring the Indigenous peoples who may have shaped its ecology over millennia. Habituation to such language in turn can influence environmental laws and policies without close scrutiny.

Critical discourse theory can valuably sharpen our awareness of how language can privilege ways of thinking about nature and its exploitation or conservation, and the need for a better vocabulary to shift our perceptual orientation as a precondition of respecting nature.[112] The critique of metaphors is particularly relevant to discourse analysis because of the power of this literary device to influence how we conceive of the world.[113] We must critically reflect on our environmental discourses and policy language for their normatively laden metaphors and other literary devices to ensure they convey appropriate meanings. I am not implying that we can reduce solving environmental governance challenges to our vernacular, as though if only we changed metaphors our policy responses would succeed, because numerous other factors from allocation of resources to political courage also matter. But equally true is the fact that the latter decisions occur not in isolation from our aesthetic representation of, or engagement with, nature.

IV. ENVIRONMENTAL REGULATION

A. Scenic Beauty

Ostensibly, quite a few environmental regulations acknowledge aesthetic factors, including for landscape management, biodiversity conservation, ecological restoration and pollution control.[114] They may direct regulators to protect extraordinary natural beauty, reduce eyesores or remove odorous pollution. Legislation may also include hortatory statements about the lofty status of such aesthetic considerations. The core purposes of the US National Environmental Policy Act (NEPA) 1969 include ensuring '*esthetically* and culturally pleasing surroundings' (emphasis added) and preserving 'important historic, cultural,

---

[111] MS Carolan, 'The Values and Vulnerabilities of Metaphors Within the Environmental Sciences' (2006) 19 *Society and Natural Resources* 921, 929.

[112] CS Brown, 'The Real and the Good' in CS Brown and T Toadvine (eds), *Eco-phenomenology: Back to the Earth Itself* (State University of New York Press, 2003) 3.

[113] M Hajer and W Versteeg, 'A Decade of Discourse Analysis of Environmental Politics: Achievements, Challenges, Perspectives' (2005) 7 *Journal of Environmental Policy and Planning* 175.

[114] Some parts of this section draw on my publication, BJ Richardson, E Barritt and M Bowman, 'Beauty: A Lingua Franca for Environmental Law?' (2019) 8(1) *Transnational Environmental Law* 59.

and natural aspects of our national heritage'.[115] NEPA-style laws at the state level similarly have affirmed the relevance of aesthetic values; the Californian statute introduced the stipulation to maintain an environment 'pleasing to the senses and intellect of man'.[116]

Aesthetic values may also feature in the statutory definitions of key terms such as 'environment' or 'natural heritage'. South Africa's lodestar National Environmental Management Act 1998 defines 'environment' as 'the physical, chemical, *aesthetic* and cultural properties and conditions [...] that influence human health and well-being' (emphasis added).[117] New Zealand's lead law, the Resource Management Act 1991, defines 'environment' to include 'the social, economic, *aesthetic*, and cultural conditions' which affect or are effected by 'ecosystems', 'all natural and physical resources' and '*amenity* values' (emphasis added).[118] Sometimes, however, legislation simply identifies the importance of aesthetic values: Mexico's General Law of Ecological Balance and Environmental Protection 1998 acknowledges 'beauty' and 'aesthetics' as relevant factors for the establishment of national parks and national monuments respectively.[119] And some core legislation may omit any reference to aesthetic factors, such as the Netherlands' Environmental Management Act 2004.[120]

That aesthetic values influence the making of environmental law does not mean they are routine priorities for regulators. Such values compete with other policy considerations. Scientific and economic dogma can weigh more heavily on decision-makers, perhaps due to their seeming objectivity and rationality, and the political influence of those who promote such disciplines. Clues to this bias may be apparent from the legislation itself. Australia's premier environmental statute, the Environment Protection and Biodiversity Conservation Act 1999 (Cth), refers to 'aesthetics' (or related concepts) just once compared to 29 entries for 'economics' and 223 for 'science' or 'scientific'. Under this legislation, the listing of threatened species commonly reflects scientific advice on their conservation status, while pollution standards generally derive from scientific evidence of potential hazards and the economic costs of alleviating them. Even in legislation explicitly dedicated to protecting aesthetic qualities, notably in land use planning, non-aesthetic criteria can readily prevail, as researchers have found with British legislation.[121]

Bias also affects which aesthetic values sway regulators. Marine areas tend to be under-acknowledged relative to terrestrial landscapes for their aesthetic values – odd, given our deeply evolved attraction to water. The UNESCO

---

[115] Section 101(b).
[116] California Environmental Quality Act, Stats 1970, Ch 1433. s 21000(b).
[117] Act 107 of 1998, s 1(1)(iv).
[118] Section 2(1).
[119] Articles 50 and 52.
[120] Eg s 1.2.
[121] P Selman and C Swanwick, 'On the Meaning of Natural Beauty in Landscape Legislation' (2010) 35(1) *Landscape Research* 3.

Convention on Protection of the Underwater Cultural Heritage 2001 omits any reference to this realm, despite the obvious relevance of aesthetics to shipwrecks and seabed relics that attract intrepid scuba divers.[122] The UN Convention on the Law of the Sea also ignores aesthetics, although its provisions for controlling pollution and promoting sustainable use of marine living resources could at least protect natural elements of aesthetic value.[123] Unusually, Iceland's Nature Conservation Act 1999 has specific provision for identification and protection of scenic sites in its coastal waters.[124] South Africa's Integrated Coastal Management Act also explicitly affirms the need to safeguard aesthetic values in designated coastal protection zones.[125] The scale at which aesthetic values are discernable in marine and terrestrial areas differs, with implications for their governance. A 2013 report prepared for Australian authorities on managing the Great Barrier Reef remarked: 'in terrestrial properties aesthetic value is almost always associated with appreciation of the large scale, grandeur or diversity of a landscape [whereas …] underwater aesthetic values are associated with attributes visible within a confined or relatively small space'.[126] In this ecosystem it is beautiful coral reefs, admired up close, that attract regulators' interest, rather than the overall appearance of the ocean. This preference, however, is increasingly at risk as global warming contributes to the bleaching and death of corals.

Affirmation of aesthetic values in environmental law has been facilitated by courts' willingness to recognise them as grounds to accord standing to public interest litigants. The US case of *Scenic Hudson Preservation Conference v Federal Power Commission*, brought in the mid-1960s by an NGO challenging a hydropower monstrosity in rural New York, affords one seminal example. The Second Circuit Court of Appeals affirmed the group's standing because of their 'special interest in aesthetic […] aspects of the mountain'.[127] As Justice Hays explained: 'the cost of a project is only one of several factors to be considered', in addition to concerns about 'the preservation of natural beauty and national historic sites'.[128] Although the court didn't halt the dam project, its 1965 ruling helped consecrate the legitimacy of aesthetic issues in environmental cases and empowered the judiciary to play a greater role in supervising aesthetic impacts. The US Supreme Court, as well as state courts, have gone on to approve natural beauty and other scenic values as legitimate considerations in land use management. *Scenic Hudson* also contributed to the 1966 decision to establish the Commission on Natural Beauty for the state of New York to sensitise land use planning to aesthetic factors.[129]

---

[122] (2002) 41 ILM 40.
[123] (1982) 21 ILM 1261.
[124] Act No 44 of 1999, art 54.
[125] Act 24 of 2008, s 17.
[126] Context, *Defining the Aesthetic Values of the Great Barrier Reef: Final Report prepared for DSEWPaC* (Context, 2013) 15.
[127] 354 F2d 608 (2d Cir, 1965) para 30.
[128] Ibid, para 92.
[129] D Riesel, 'Aesthetics as a Basis for Regulation' (1981) 1(3) *Pace Law Review* 629, 632.

Nature conservation law affirms aesthetic criteria more commonly than other realms of environmental law, albeit typically in a cursory manner. New Zealand's National Parks Act 1980 defines its purpose as including to preserve in perpetuity for public benefit areas 'that contain scenery of such distinctive quality, ecological systems, or natural features so beautiful […] that their preservation is in the national interest'.[130] In Australia, the state of Victoria's National Parks Act 1975 specifies that parks serve the public's 'inspiration, solitude and appropriate self-reliant recreation'.[131] The UK's Countryside and Rights of Way Act 2000 provides for the designation of 'Areas of Outstanding Natural Beauty' (AONB), but it does not define the term.[132] This task has shifted to supplementary policy guidance as developed through public consultation, the result of which is that 'natural beauty' has predominantly been defined by the 'character' of the landscape as delineated by hedgerows, mature trees, archaeological ruins, topography and so forth.[133] As of June 2019, there were 46 AONB in the UK (excluding Scotland) covering about 20 per cent of its land.[134]

Figure 2.6 The 'picturesque': Blue Mountain View nature reserve, Tasmania, 2015, from where I wrote much of this book; photograph by Benjamin J Richardson

American nature conservation legislation also implicitly or explicitly identifies aesthetic values. The Antiquities Act 1906 enables the President by proclamation to create national monuments from federal lands to safeguard notable cultural and natural features.[135] While it does not overtly authorise protection of lands for their scenic beauty, its implementation has accommodated such a goal.[136]

---

[130] Section 4(1).

[131] Section 4(ab)(iii)).

[132] 2000, c 37, ss 82–89.

[133] Selman and Swanwick, 'On the Meaning of Natural Beauty' (above n 121) 13–15.

[134] Statistics from Landscapes for Life: www.landscapesforlife.org.uk.

[135] Public Law 59-209, 34 Stat 225.

[136] See further, CA Klein, 'Preserving Monumental Landscapes Under the Antiquities Act' (2002) 87 *Cornell Law Review* 1333.

Legislation that does explicitly recognise aesthetics includes the Wilderness Act 1964[137] and the Wild and Scenic Rivers Act 1968.[138] The latter defines 'scenic rivers' with reference to their lack of human modification, namely: 'rivers or sections of rivers that are free of impoundments, with shorelines or watersheds still largely primitive and shorelines largely undeveloped, but accessible in places by roads'.[139] In designating 'scenic rivers', this Act stipulates 'primary emphasis shall be given to protecting [their] esthetic, scenic, historic, archeologic, and scientific features'.[140] The Federal Land Policy and Management Act 1976[141] also cites scenic values as worthy of its protection.

Reference to scenic beauty punctuates the environmental laws of many other countries. China's lodestar Environmental Protection Law 1989 specifies 'scenic spots' as among places deserving 'special protection'.[142] Curiously, the 1994 Regulations of the People's Republic of China on Nature Reserves, used for protecting some of the country's scenic gems including the Lijiang River picturesque zone, listed under the World Heritage Convention, lack explicit reference to scenic values; it does, however, stipulate that natural areas of 'cultural value' are worthy for protection in a nature reserve.[143] Nepal's National Parks and Wildlife Conservation Act 1973 declares in its preamble the goal of conserving 'natural beauty', and the definition of national park is an area set aside, inter alia, for conservation of its 'scenery'.[144] Kenya's Wildlife Conservation and Management Act 2013 provides for issuance of 'wildlife conservation orders' to protect, inter alia, 'scenic views, topographical features and landscapes'.[145] Iceland's Nature Conservation Act 1999 contains numerous similar references: the design of new developments should be adapted to 'the appearance of the land'; billboards are banned in rural areas and any other advertisements must be 'unobtrusive'; and buildings and vessels must not 'fall into disrepair so that they can be considered as eyesores'.[146]

The beauty of individual species also can elicit legal protection. The US Bald Eagle Protection Act 1940 protects a creature chosen as America's national emblem in 1782,[147] while the Endangered Species Act 1973 protects threatened species for reasons that include to preserve their 'esthetic [...] value to the Nation and its people'.[148] In Australia, the NSW government's Kosciuszko Wild Horse

---

[137] Public Law 88-577, 78 Stat 890.
[138] Public Law 90-542, 16 USC 1271.
[139] Section 2(b)(2).
[140] Section 10(a).
[141] 43 USC, ss 1701–84.
[142] Article 18.
[143] Promulgated by Decree No 167 of the State Council of the People's Republic of China on October 9, 1994, art 10(4).
[144] Preamble and s 2.
[145] Section 65(4)(f).
[146] Act no 44 of 1999, arts 35, 43 and 44.
[147] The Act was later amended to include another species, and is now known as the Bald and Golden Eagle Protection Act, 16 USC 668-668c.
[148] Public Law 93-205, 87 Stat 884, 16 USC s 1531(a)(3).

Heritage Act 2018 seeks to sustainably manage the aesthetically and culturally prized wild horses that roam that state's alpine region, a controversial law examined in more detail in Chapter 3.

Equally, examples of nature conservation and wildlife legislation silent on aesthetic issues abound. India's Wildlife Protection Act 1972 provides for the declaration of parks and sanctuaries 'by reason of [their] ecological, faunal, floral, geomorphological, or zoological association or importance'.[149] Likewise, Canada National Parks Act omits explicit reference to aesthetic values, instead emphasising scientific management in the stipulation that 'maintenance or restoration of ecological integrity [...] shall be the first priority of the Minister when considering all aspects of the management of parks'.[150] Australia's Great Barrier Reef Marine Park Act 1975 (Cth), which protects the planet's largest coral reef systems, and of significant aesthetic value to the tourism industry, surprisingly omits any overt reference to aesthetic concepts. Instead, they are subsumed within more generic statutory criteria of 'cultural systems and value' and 'public enjoyment and appreciation'.[151]

Forestry legislation occasionally acknowledges aesthetic values, either for the purpose of designating areas of high scenic value that should be excluded from logging[152] or for managing harvesting operations so as to minimise visual impacts, such as by retaining tree lines along road sides and other areas accessible to public viewing. Some forestry authorities also have policies to protect individual trees of distinctive aesthetic and biological significance. In Tasmania, home to the world's second tallest tree species (*Eucalyptus regnans*), the forestry authority in 2002 adopted a 'giant trees' policy that seeks to identify and protect behemoths in the 800,000 hectares it manages, with such giants defined as at least 85 metres tall and 280 cubic metres in stem volume (which translates into a minimum tree girth of five metres). The policy also protects a 100-metre radius around each giant tree.[153] At least 100 trees now benefit from this policy, in addition to many others in national parks.

Conservation of nature aesthetics is sometimes comingled with laws to protect cultural heritage. Reference was made earlier in this chapter to Japan's Law for the Protection of Cultural Properties 1950, as used to protect scenic natural places. South Africa's National Heritage Resources Act 1999 serves to protect heritage resources of 'cultural significance', defined as including aesthetic value.[154] A place or object forms part of South Africa's national estate

---

[149] Section 35(1).
[150] SC 2000, c 32, s 8(2).
[151] Section 2A(2)(a).
[152] The Forestry Act 1920 of Tasmania was amended in 1975 to specify that forestry reserves may be established for the 'protection of any features of the land of aesthetic [...] value': s 20(1)(b).
[153] J Balmer, J Hickey and T Leamen, *Management of Tasmania's Giant Trees* (Department of Primary Industries and Water, undated).
[154] Sections 2(vi) and 3(1).

if it has 'importance in exhibiting particular aesthetic characteristics valued by a community or cultural group'.[155] One key governance tool in the South African legislation for safeguarding such values is the requirement for development proponents to undertake a heritage impact assessment as part of the regulatory approval process.[156]

International law also responds to such values. Some of the earliest treaties in the environmental field, such as the Convention on Nature Protection and Wild Life Preservation in the Western Hemisphere of 1940,[157] were inspired by aesthetic appreciation of nature. The preambles of several more recent treaties evoke a similar sentiment. The 1973 Convention on International Trade in Endangered Species of Flora and Fauna declares that its state parties are 'conscious of the ever growing value of wild fauna and flora from aesthetic [...] points of view'.[158] The Convention on Biological Diversity 1992 acknowledges the 'aesthetic values of biological diversity'.[159] Similar considerations also figure in the Antarctic Protocol on Environmental Protection 1991,[160] as well as in a variety of regional nature conservation treaties,[161] such as the Convention on the Conservation of European Wildlife and Natural Habitats 1979.[162] The European Landscape Convention, prepared by the Council of Europe in 2000, also acknowledges in its preamble the status of landscapes of 'outstanding beauty'[163] and it defines landscape as 'an area, as perceived by people, whose character is the result of the action and interaction of natural and/or human factors'.[164] This definition thus implies an aesthetic assessment of landscapes. The Convention introduced two important concepts in landscape governance: that landscapes need to be protected and managed, as opposed to left alone. Thus, governance of landscapes including their aesthetic properties required planning through strategies and programs for restoring, enhancing, conserving and other outcomes.

The foremost international instrument for protecting natural beauty is the World Heritage Convention of 1972.[165] Its criteria for inclusion of places in the illustrious World Heritage List encompasses 'superlative natural phenomena or areas of exceptional natural beauty and aesthetic importance'.[166] However, the

---

[155] Section 3(3)(e).
[156] Section 38.
[157] (1940) 161 UNTS 193.
[158] (1973) 13 ILM 1088.
[159] Preamble, 31 ILM 818 (1992).
[160] Article 3.
[161] Preamble.
[162] 1 June 1979, European Treaty Series, No 104.
[163] 20 October 2000, European Treaty Series, No 176.
[164] Ibid, art 1(a).
[165] 11 ILM 1358 (1972). art 2.
[166] World Heritage Committee, *Operational Guidelines for the Implementation of the World Heritage Convention* (UNESCO, 2016) 17; see further A Palmer, 'Legal Dimensions to Valuing Aesthetics in World Heritage Decisions' (2017) 26(5) *Social and Legal Studies* 581.

Convention's pivotal criterion of 'outstanding [...] natural beauty' remains largely undefined. UNESCO, which administers the treaty, has offered no formal criteria of 'natural beauty', and its Operational Guidelines explain no more than that the term means 'exceptional natural beauty and aesthetic importance'.[167] Of some relevance is that properties inscribed on natural criteria must also satisfy conditions of integrity. On this point, the Operational Guidelines explain that listed properties should:

> include areas that are essential for maintaining the beauty of the property. For example, a property whose scenic value depends on a waterfall, would meet the conditions of integrity if it includes adjacent catchment and downstream areas that are integrally linked to the maintenance of the aesthetic qualities of the property.[168]

UNESCO's World Heritage Committee, which makes decisions on inclusion of properties in the World Heritage List, has tended to evaluate the aesthetic values of nominated sites in conjunction with other criteria rather than on aesthetic values alone; and with the Committee's growing interest in 'cultural landscapes', it has increasingly interpreted aesthetic values in the natural world with a strong connection to human culture.[169]

Artistic depictions of landscapes can also influence decisions on their inclusion in the World Heritage List. Alice Palmer, who has analysed this issue, cites evidence of Peter Dombrovskis' photographs of Tasmania's southwest wilderness being used by the Australian government in its nomination of this area for World Heritage status in 1982, and that the IUCN, an important stakeholder in World Heritage governance, has commented that 'sources of evidence that demonstrate aesthetic landscape values at an international level include works of art, literature, cinema, and music'.[170]

B. Wild Soundscapes

Natural soundscapes, the totality of ambient sounds in an area, are a vital element of the aesthetic appreciation of nature and a perspective of growing interest to many nature enthusiasts.[171] The sounds of wildlife, from singing birds to stridulating insects, and the resonances of inorganic matter such as

---

[167] World Heritage Committee, *Operational Guidelines*, ibid, 21.

[168] Ibid, 24.

[169] UNESCO, *Cultural Landscapes: The Challenge of Conservation* (World Heritage Papers No 7, UNESCO, 2002).

[170] Palmer, 'Legal Dimensions' (above n 166) citing Australian Government (1982), *World Heritage Nomination: Tasmanian Wilderness* (1982) 23; N Mitchell et al, *IUCN Study on the Application of Criterion (vii)*, Report for the International Union for the Conservation of Nature, World Heritage Study No 10 (IUCN, 2013) 39.

[171] B Krause, *Wild Soundscapes: Discovering the Voice of the Natural World* (Yale University Press, 2016).

the trickle of flowing streams, wind rustling in the trees and waves breaking on the seashore, contribute to the aural qualities of natural landscapes. These soundscapes can also sometimes be very quiet, such as in deserts, thus offering visitors solitude. The US National Park Service's acoustic monitoring program has found that some parts of its estate, as in the Haleakala National Park in Hawaii, are so quiet that the natural ambient sound level does not register on its monitoring equipment.[172] While complete silence can make some individuals feel uneasy and disoriented, loud and prolonged sounds can be very stressful. We often encounter them in urban landscapes, dominated by noises issuing from motor vehicles, machinery and crowds gathered in streets, sports events and shopping malls.

The sounds of nature have become a seminal element in environmental policy. Since Rachel Carson's bestseller *Silent Spring* (1962), the presence or absence of sound has been identified as a key indicator of the health of ecological systems. The absence of birdcalls owing to the decimation of avifauna by agri-chemicals was brought to global attention by Carson as a sign of a lethal threat to biological systems. The increasing loss of wild soundscapes in a world crowded with anthropogenic noise is a serious impoverishment of the aesthetic character of the natural world, and impairing our own psychological well-being.[173]

Growing awareness of the importance of sound in ecological processes has spawned a new field of research known as 'soundscape ecology' or 'ecoacoustics'.[174] Sound has long been an important tool for studying nature and ecosystem management. Wildlife researchers use a range of technologies to record and analyse acoustic data, such as for monitoring wildlife populations.[175] Echo-location technologies now also allow for recording the presence of bats, whose calls are mostly inaudible to the human ear. Some artists also use field recordings as the basis of their work, composing soundscapes offering both aesthetic and scientific benefits.[176] Researchers suggest that unnatural sounds, especially loud and recurring noises, can adversely affect wildlife, such as interfering with breeding cycles, navigation and detecting predators.[177] A 2015 study

[172] B Janiskeem, 'Got Quiet? Great Sand Dunes National Park and Preserve has Plenty' *National Parks Traveller*, 22 November 2008, www.nationalparktraveler.org/2008/11/got-quiet-great-sand-dunes-national-park-preserve-has-plenty.

[173] B Krause, 'Mourning the Loss of Wild Soundscapes: A Rationale for Context When Experiencing Natural Sound' in A Cunsolo and K Landman (eds), *Mourning Nature: Hope at the Heart of Ecological Loss and Grief* (McGill-Queen's University Press, 2017) 27.

[174] BC Pijanowski et al, 'Soundscape Ecology: The Science of Sound in the Landscape' (2011) 61(3) *BioScience* 203; A Farina and SH Gage (eds), *Ecoacoustics: The Ecological Role of Sounds* (Wiley, 2017).

[175] MA Acevedo and LJ Villanueva-Rivera, 'Using Automated Digital Recording Systems as Effective Tools for the Monitoring of Birds and Amphibians' (2008) 34 *Wildlife Society Bulletin* 211.

[176] C Lane and A Carlyle, *In the Field: The Art of Field Recording* (Uniformbooks, 2013).

[177] JR Barber, KR Crooks and KM Fristrup, 'The Costs of Chronic Noise Exposure for Terrestrial Organisms' (2010) 25 *Trends in Ecology and Evolution* 180; CL Brown, 'The Effect of Human Activities and Their Associated Noise on Ungulate Behavior' (2002) 7 *PLoS One* e.40505.

found that noise pollution in many parts of the world has interfered with birds' abilities to receive and respond to acoustic signals.[178]

Such knowledge has begun to feed into the law's greater vigilance against noise pollution. Legal standards range from controls on anthropogenic noise to management of natural soundscapes. Noise pollution control is now a well-established facet of environmental law worldwide, targeting innumerable sources from the noisy neighbour to music concerts. In urban landscapes, where residents have to endure the perpetual and changing din of city living, the law tends to prescribe abatement measures rather than demand silence. Thus, airports are not closed but their noise may be mitigated through curfews, and preferential runways and flight routes. Street traffic noise may similarly be abated, through speed limits and installation of roadside walls. In controlling noise, the law is also capable of prescribing precise technical rules with the aid of acoustic technologies that measure decibels. Much has already been written about noise pollution law,[179] which does not need to be reviewed here, as our principal focus in this section is the aesthetics of natural soundscapes.

National park authorities may adopt measures to limit anthropogenic noises, including road traffic and tourism infrastructure, that may interfere with natural soundscapes.[180] Yet, the concomitant legislative policy to promote public access to and enjoyment of parks has resulted in compromises in which outright bans on anthropogenic noise are generally not sought or attainable. Aircraft overflight is one special problem where these tensions arise, as intrepid visitors' contemplative solitude in seemingly remote locations can be spoiled by the whirl of helicopters catering to tourists with limited time or preferring an aerial vista. United States authorities enacted the National Parks Overflights Act 1987 to tackle this problem.[181] It codified minimum height limits for helicopters and other aircraft in national parks, such as prohibiting them from flying 'at an altitude of less than 2,000 feet over the surface of Yosemite National Park', with exemptions for emergencies and search and rescue operations.[182] The policy of the US National Park Service aims to 'restore to the natural condition wherever possible those park soundscapes that have become degraded by unnatural sounds (noise), and will protect natural soundscapes from unacceptable impacts'.[183] Supplementary controls exist in the enabling legislation for some individual national parks. The Grand Canyon Enlargement Act of 1975, to illustrate, requires authorities to respond to any aircraft activity that is likely to 'cause a significant adverse effect on the natural quiet and experience of

---

[178] C Francis, 'Vocal Traits and Diet Explain Avian Sensitivities to Anthropogenic Noise' (2015) 21(5) *Global Change Biology* 1809.

[179] E Murphy and EA King, *Environmental Noise Pollution* (Elsevier, 2014).

[180] NP Miller, 'US National Parks and Management of Park Soundscapes: A Review' (2008) 69(2) *Applied Acoustics* 77.

[181] Public Law 100-91, 16 USC 1-1a.

[182] Ibid, s 2(a) and 2(d).

[183] National Park Service (NPS), *National Park Service Management Policies* (NPS, 2006) 56.

the park'.[184] A 1998 federal court decision relating to the Grand Canyon's soundscape upheld the US National Park Service's definition of natural quiet as the absence of aircraft noise.[185]

Concomitantly, natural soundscapes can influence human well-being, including recreational, therapeutic and aesthetic values, which the law can similarly protect. A survey of visitors to US national parks revealed that they came to enjoy the natural soundscape (91 per cent) nearly as much for the scenic views (93 per cent).[186] The US Wilderness Act 1964 defines 'wilderness' as including a place with 'outstanding opportunities for solitude',[187] and that areas of wilderness designated by the Act for protection 'shall be devoted to the public purposes of recreational, scenic, scientific, educational, conservation, and historical use'.[188] Iceland's Nature Conservation Act 1999 similarly explicitly links 'wilderness' conservation to places of 'solitude [...] without disturbance from man-made structures or the traffic of motorised vehicles'.[189] The US Fish and Wildlife Service's policy for management of wilderness elaborates that the statutory reference to 'solitude' means 'a state of mind, a mental freedom that emerges from settings where visitors experience nature essentially free of the reminders of society', which the Service suggests 'is enhanced by the absence of distractions, such as large groups, mechanization, unnatural noise and light'.[190] How authorities dampen noisy distractions is illustrated by the following anecdote from the *Washington Post* about a wilderness area in Virginia:

> few fallen trees block the steeply ascending trail, but when Forest Service maintenance crews come through, they won't bring chain saws and bulldozers. No motorized equipment is permitted, so they will use the two-handled crosscut saws they call 'misery whips'.[191]

Unnatural noise has become a target for litigants seeking tranquillity in America's national parks. The US Fish and Wildlife Service in 2009 was enjoined by a court to withhold permits for a company's oil and gas drilling operations in the Great Sand Dunes National Park in Colorado because, in the words of the presiding judge, of the likelihood that 'the drilling would not only disturb wildlife but also impair the refuge's 'significant "sense of place" and quiet'.[192]

---

[184] Public Law 93–620, s 8.
[185] *Grand Canyon Air Coalition v Federation Aviation Authority* [1998] USCADC 194;154 F 3d 455, 459 (DC Circuit, 1998).
[186] National Park Service (NPS), *Report on Effects of Aircraft Overflights on the National Park System: Report to Congress* (NPS, 1995), cited in M Jensen and H Thompson, 'Natural Soundscapes in the National Park System' (2004) 21(1) *The George Wright Forum* 14, 14.
[187] Section 2(c).
[188] Ibid, s 4(3).
[189] Article 3(4).
[190] US Fish and Wildlife Service, *Natural and Cultural Resources Management* 610 FW 1 (2008) 4.
[191] S Nash, 'Wilderness Areas Studies in Solitude' *Washington Post* 28 July 1988.
[192] Quoted in S Streater, 'Solitude Becomes Exhibit A in Battle Over National Parks Management' *New York Times* 8 October 2009.

Another case brought by environmental groups in relation to Yellowstone National Park over recreational snowmobiling, resulted in a landmark ruling in 2008 that park managers' stewardship of park resources 'apply equally to the conservation of the parks' natural soundscapes'.[193] This interpretation of the law is not because the governing legislation, the National Park Service Organic Act 1916,[194] mentions aesthetic values but because the National Park Service interprets the legislation as requiring prohibition of 'unacceptable impacts' that would interfere with 'the natural soundscape maintained in wilderness and natural, historic, or commemorative locations within the park'.[195]

Some other jurisdictions have taken comparable measures. In New Zealand, with about 30 per cent of its landmass managed for nature conservation, protection of tranquillity is a policy goal tackled through legislative measures. The Waitakere Ranges Heritage Area Act 2008, which protects the forested water catchment of the city of Auckland, identifies the protected heritage values of the ranges as including 'the quietness and darkness of the Waitakere Ranges'.[196] This acoustic value is managed through enabling land use plans developed by local government. New Zealand authorities have also applied bespoke legislative measures to protect specific fauna populations from anthropogenic noise. Aircraft flight restrictions have been implemented under the Civil Aviation Act 1990 to protect colonies of gannets and albatrosses.[197] The National Parks Act 1980 bans 'motorised vessels (including hovercraft and jet boats)' from 'embarking or disembarking passengers or goods in a wilderness area'.[198] The management plan for Fiordland National Park, New Zealand's largest, acknowledges the problem of aircraft noise as at odds with the goal of Fiordland wilderness experience to provide 'solitude, peace and natural quiet'.[199]

Some World Heritage areas protected for their exceptional natural beauty have been identified as at risk of being impaired by anthropogenic noise. The International Union for Conservation of Nature (IUCN) has recommended that helicopter flights to access the Putorana Plateau in Russia be minimised in order to reduce the acoustic impacts on wildlife.[200] In Australia, approval for a fly-in-fly-out luxury resort on Halls Island/Lake Malbena, has outraged Aboriginal and environmental groups and has been challenged in court, for

---

[193] *Greater Yellowstone Coalition, et al, v Dirk Kempthorne, et al, National Parks Conservation Association v United States Department of Interior; National Park Service*, 577 F Supp 2d 183 (2008).

[194] 39 Stat 535.

[195] Section 1.4.7.1 of the NPS Policies.

[196] Section 7(2)(e).

[197] A Tal, '"Naturally Quiet": Towards a New Legislative Strategy for Regulating Air Space Above Conservation Areas in New Zealand' (2004) 10 *Otago Law Review* 537.

[198] Section 14(2)(d).

[199] Department of Conservation (DoC), *Fiordland National Park Management Plan* (DoC, 2007) 120–22.

[200] IUCN, *IUCN Evaluation of Nominations of Natural and Mixed Properties to the World Heritage List* (IUCN, May 2008) 73.

inter alia, the projected acoustic impacts on the aesthetic values of this piece of Tasmanian World Heritage.[201]

Anthropogenic noise is not only a powerful sensory pollutant in terrestrial landscapes; in can affect aquatic life as well.[202] Unlike the title of Jacques Cousteau's famous documentary film *The Silent World*, released in 1956, the oceans are increasingly noisy environments, much to the detriment of marine life. A group of NGOs federated as the Ocean Noise Coalition calls for greater international regulation to curb 'noise proliferation [that] poses a significant threat to marine ecosystems'.[203] These threats include disruption to species' navigation and swimming behaviour as animals are disoriented or stressed. Sources of anthropogenic noise in the oceans include seismic exploration and testing, military vessels' sonar, and ship traffic. Cetaceans in particular seem to be vulnerable to such acoustic pollution, which probably contributes to mass beach strandings.[204]

As a substantial majority of the oceans are high seas, outside of the jurisdiction of coastal states, the presence of international rules on marine noise pollution is obviously important. The UN Convention on the Law of the Sea, the primary treaty governing the high seas, lacks explicit provisions on marine noise although the Convention's definition of pollution is broad enough to compass anthropogenic noise.[205] The EU Marine Strategy Directive of 2008 was the first international legal instrument to explicitly include anthropogenic underwater noise within the definition of pollution,[206] which the Directive seeks to reduce in order to achieve its aspiration of the 'good environmental status' of European marine waters by 2020.[207] The Directive lists 'the introduction of energy, including underwater noise, at levels that do not adversely affect the marine environment' among the criteria to achieve the good environmental status.[208]

Antarctica is one of the quietest places you can imagine, apart from the periodic howling winds. Mining is banned on the continent and relatively few ships are equipped for the oceans around it, though summer tourism is rapidly increasing. Yet such quietness also means that any human disturbances will seem more noticeable. The Protocol on Environmental Protection to the Antarctic Treaty 1991 is playing a role in encouraging more attention by states active in Antarctica to reduce noise pollution from their activities.[209] In 2009 the

---

[201] Environmental Defenders Office Tasmania, 'Protecting Wilderness Values: Halls Island' (November 2018), www.edotas.org.au/about-edo/significant-cases/protecting-wilderness-values-halls-island.

[202] AN Popper and A Hawkins (eds), *The Effects of Noise on Aquatic Life II* (Springer, 2016).

[203] Ocean Noise Coalition, *Drowning in Sound* (brochure, undated) 1.

[204] Whale and Dolphin Conservation Society (WDCS), *Oceans of Noise* (WDCS, 2004).

[205] (1982) 21 ILM 1261, art 1(1) and (4).

[206] Directive 2008/56/EC of the European Parliament and of the Council of 17 June 2008 establishing a framework for community action in the field of marine environmental policy, OJ L 164, 25 June 2008, art 3(8).

[207] Ibid, art 1.

[208] Ibid, Annex I, cl 11.

[209] (1991) 30 ILM 1455.

German government commissioned EIA studies in connection with a permit for the use of noisy seismic airguns for exploration of the seabed.[210] In national law, too, measures have been taken covering both coastal waters and vessels on the high seas under the jurisdiction of such states. The US National Oceanic and Atmospheric Administration has formulated acoustic guidelines to assist with implementation of the Marine Mammal Protection Act and the Endangered Species Act in protecting whales from harmful sound.[211]

C. Regulating the Unsightly

Regulators target a wide array of activities that offend our senses. Officialdom has a long history of supervising the visual, acoustic and olfactory impacts of private land use, targeting eyesores such as billboards and junkyards, smelly piggeries, noisy factories, and in recent years even environmentally beneficial wind turbines that some perceive as a blight on the landscape.[212] Just as importantly, the law can oblige the restoration of degraded environments in order to improve their appearance, as well as for ecological and economic benefits, a theme explored further in Chapter 6. In this section I will canvass some examples of regulation of aesthetic impacts to illustrate the range of issues and assess law responses.

Lighting in excessive or inappropriate locations is sometimes considered aesthetic pollution. Sources of artificial light pollution include advertising, residential lighting, commercial offices, streetlights and floodlit sporting venues. They may be regulated for a variety of reasons including to minimise unnatural interferences with the movement of nocturnal bats and owls, to protect astronomical facilities that depend on unobscured skies for star gazing, to safeguard navigation of planes and ships, or just to maintain a desired light ambience for residential communities. In an increasingly climate-conscious world, reducing energy waste provides further reason to control light pollution.

The problem of light pollution is sufficiently serious that an International Dark-Sky Society exists for 'combatting light pollution worldwide' by working with 'the public, city planners, legislators, lighting manufacturers and park' managers to 'provide and implement smart lighting choices'.[213] Most

---

[210] Bewertung der Risikoanalyse, *Strategic Assessment of the Risk Posed by the Use of Airguns in the Antarctic Treaty Area* (2011).

[211] National Oceanic and Atmospheric Administration (NOAA), *Technical Guidance for Assessing the Effects of Anthropogenic Sound on Marine Mammal Hearing: Underwater Acoustic Thresholds for Onset of Permanent and Temporary Threshold Shifts* (NOAA, 2016).

[212] Eg *In re Halnon*, 811 A 2d 161 (Vt 2002) (the court upheld denial of approval to build a wind turbine because of its aesthetic effects); *John Donnelly and Sons v Roger L Mallar*, 453 F Supp 1272 (D Me 1978) (court upholding a law to restrict unsightly billboards); and *Brophy v Town of Castine*, 534 A 2d 663 (Me 1987) (court upheld municipality's rule obliging on location of satellite dishes to preserve the community's aesthetic welfare).

[213] International Dark-Sky Society, 'Who We Are', www.darksky.org/about.

light pollution regulation comes locally through municipal authorities. The UK's Clean Neighbourhoods and Environment Act 2005 extended the earlier statutory nuisance regime to include artificial light.[214] Thousands of US local governments have outdoor lighting regulations. One from California is the Ojai Valley municipality's Dark Sky Ordinance, whose environmental goals include: to 'protect and reclaim ability to view the night sky and stars'; 'greater tranquillity and maintenance of the rural ambiance' and to 'promote safe, energy-efficient and cost effective outdoor lighting'.[215] Turning lights down or off is not feasible in all situations, such as along highways or in city parks where public safety considerations may matter more.

Visual pollution, from light or other sources, sometimes gets assessed by the law through the lens of 'amenity values', a term related to aesthetics but encompassing broader considerations relating to public health and convenience. To illustrate, New Zealand's Resource Management Act 1991, described by one court as making 'the aesthetic an indispensable concern in every planning regime and for every consent authority',[216] obliges regulators to consider 'the maintenance and enhancement of amenity values'.[217] The Act defines amenity value (but not aesthetic value) as the 'natural or physical qualities and characteristics of an area that contribute to people's appreciation of its pleasantness, aesthetic coherence, and cultural and recreational attributes'.[218] Local planning authorities have developed a variety of policies and rules to protect such amenity values.[219] The Wairoa District Council's land use plan explains that an acceptable level of amenity will depend on the type of local context, and gives this example: 'noisy agricultural machinery is accepted as part of the rural environment, yet would be totally unacceptable in an urban residential situation'.[220]

The courts may intercede in disputes over aesthetic or amenity impacts, especially where regulation lacks clear standards or precise terminology.[221] The judiciary's traditionally hesitant embrace of this role reflects its assumptions about the subjective or arbitrary nature of the aesthetic, and the difficulty of formulating intelligible standards. Case law from the United States illustrates such trends. In the early 1900s, its courts regularly barred municipal ordinances that attempted to curb development on the basis of mere unsightliness.[222]

---

[214] 2005, c 16, s 102.

[215] Ojai Valley Dark Sky Ordinance, https://vcrma.org/ojai-valley-dark-sky-ordinance.

[216] *Society for the Protection of Auckland City and Waterfront v Auckland City Council* [2005] NZRMA 155, para 73.

[217] Section 7.

[218] Section 2.

[219] J Barrett, 'Law, Aesthetics and the Environment: Some Thoughts on Sustaining Natural Beauty in New Zealand' (2013) 1(1) *New Zealand Online Journal of Interdisciplinary Studies* 1, 4.

[220] Wairoa District Council, *Wairo District Plan* (2005) 10–11.

[221] 870 A 2d 566 (2005), discussed in N Walworth, 'Regulating Aesthetics of Coastal Maine: Kroeger v Department of Environmental Protection' (2005) 11 *Ocean and Coastal Law Journal* 99, 112–16.

[222] Eg *City of Passaic v Patterson Bill Posting Co*, 62 A 267 (NJ 1905); *Crawford v Topeka*, 33 P 476 (Kan 1893); *Commonwealth v Boston Advertising Co*, 74 NE 601 (Mass 1905).

A New Jersey court declared in 1905 that it was not 'aware of any case which holds that a man may be deprived of his property because his tastes are not those of his neighbors. A[e]sthetic considerations are a matter of luxury and indulgence rather than of necessity'.[223] This court elaborated that 'it is necessity alone which justifies the exercise of [governmental] power to take private property without compensation'.[224] In rejecting a municipal ordinance that would restrict apartment blocks in a residential neighbourhood, an Ohio Supreme Court in 1925 commented:

> certain legislatures might consider that it was more important to cultivate a taste for jazz rather than Beethoven, for posters than for Rembrandt and for limericks than for Keats. The world would be at continual seesaw if aesthetic considerations were permitted to govern the use of [governmental] power.[225]

In 1954 the US Supreme Court finally affirmed that land use regulators could consider aesthetic issues, on the basis that they fell within the public welfare goals that the legislature should protect.[226] Even with this precedent, courts continued to handle aesthetic issues uneasily. One judge bemoaned in a 1983 case that 'aesthetic considerations are fraught with subjectivity. One man's pleasure may be another man's perturbation. [...] Judicial forage into such a nebulous area would be chaotic'.[227] Similarly, academic commentators have wrestled with the difficulties of how courts and regulators should define or apply aesthetic criteria in land use planning.[228] Sometimes the judiciary has drawn on diverse considerations such as community opinion, property values and economic impacts to rationalise its rulings. Aesthetic values have tended to be most explicitly defended by US courts in designated scenic landscapes, especially on protected conservation lands. In *State of Minnesota, ex rel Drabik v Martz*,[229] the Minnesotan judges ruled that its state's Environmental Rights Act 1971,[230] which explicitly protects natural resources that include 'scenic and esthetic' places, precluded the erection of a radio tower on privately-owned land that would 'materially adversely affect' nearby protected scenic and aesthetic assets.[231]

---

[223] *City of Passaic v Patterson Bill Posting, Advertising and Sign Painting Co*, 62 A 267, 268 (NJ 1905), quoted in Simon Eisner, Arthur Gallon and Stanley Eisner, *The Urban Pattern*, 6th edn (John Wiley and Sons, 1993) 229.

[224] *City of Passaic v Patterson Bill Posting, Advertising and Sign Painting Co*, (1905) 72 New LJ 267, 268.

[225] *City of Youngetown v Kahn Building Co*, 112 Ohio St 654 (1925) 661–62.

[226] *Berman v Parker*, 348 US 26, 33 (1954).

[227] *Ness v Albert*, 665 SW 2d 1, 4 (1983).

[228] See eg M Bobrowski, 'Scenic Landscape Protection Under the Police Power; (1995) 22 *Boston College Environmental Law Review* 697; BA Rowlett, 'Aesthetic Regulation Under the Police Power: The New General Welfare and the Presumption of Constitutionality' (1981) 34 *Vanderbilt Law Review* 603.

[229] 451 NW 2d 893 (Minn Ct App 1990).

[230] Minnesota Statutes (1990) ss 116B.02, subdiv 4.

[231] T Murphy, 'Environmental Law – Protection of Scenic and Aesthetic Resources Under the Minnesota Environmental Rights Act – State ex rel Drabik v Martz, 451 NW 2d 893 (Minn 1990) (1991) 17(4) *William Mitchell Law Review* 1190, 1204–1208.

Such rulings may be influenced by the outcomes of environmental impact assessments (EIA) of proposed developments. Most EIA laws cover a range of ecological and social effects, with the primary determinant of the scope of an assessment being the statutory definition of the 'environment'. The NSW Environmental Planning and Assessment Act 1979 defines it very broadly as including 'all aspects of the surroundings of humans, whether affecting any human as an individual or in his or her social groupings',[232] which would enable assessment of diverse aesthetic effects. The EU's Directive on EIA implies aesthetic considerations in its reference to 'cultural heritage and the landscape' as relevant factors.[233] Guidance from a South African provincial government on assessment of visual impacts acknowledges 'a significant change to the fabric and character of the area', a 'visual intrusion in the landscape' and 'obstruction of views of others'.[234] The regulator's guidance also recommends respect for the 'need to preserve the special character or "sense of place" of a particular area'.[235] Assessment of environmental aesthetic impacts is recognised by the South African authority as difficult however, because 'unlike water quality or air quality, thresholds for visual or scenic quality cannot be easily quantified, as they tend to be abstract, and often relate to cultural values or perceptions'.[236]

The principal technique to depict potential visual impacts is the photomontage, which can help land use planners and courts perceive the probable changes from a proposed development. A photomontage is 'a superimposition of an image onto a photograph for the purpose of creating a representation of potential changes to any view', and it can represent visually a development in the landscape from a variety of vantage points.[237] A developer may be required to create photomontages as part of its licence application and consultation with affected communities. Acoustic impacts are not represented in photomontages, but may be forecast using decibel readings of comparable sources of noise.

Photomontages help communities to visualise potential impacts but in themselves do not resolve the underlying differences in stakeholders' aesthetic preferences, as disputes over wind farms show.[238] Climate-conscious activists advocate wind farms for their renewable energy, and welcome legislation to fast-track project approvals, as has occurred in some jurisdictions, notably Ontario's

---

[232] Section 1.4(1).

[233] Directive 2011/92/EU of the European Parliament and of the Council of 12 December 2011 on the assessment of the effects of certain public and private projects on the environment, OJ L 26, 28.2.2012, as amended, art 3(c).

[234] Department of Environmental Affairs and Development Planning, *Guideline for Involving Visual and Aesthetic Specialists in EIA Processes* (Provincial Government of the Western Cape, 2005) 5.

[235] Ibid, 11.

[236] Ibid, 20.

[237] Landscape Institute and Institute for Environmental Management and Assessment, *Guidelines for Landscape and Visual Impact Assessment* (Routledge, 2011) s 8.18.

[238] J Good, 'The Aesthetics of Wind Energy' (2006) 13(1) *Human Ecology Forum* 76; SL Martin, 'Wind Farms and NIMBYs: Generating Conflict, Reducing Litigation' (2009–10) 20 *Fordham Environmental Law Review* 427.

Green Energy Act 2009.[239] A few jurisdictions, including the Australian state of Victoria, have gone the other way, to put the brakes on these development applications by giving more scope for impacted communities to assert any aesthetic concerns.[240]

The Taralga wind farm litigation in NSW, Australia, illustrates the difficulties of adjudicating wind farm disputes. Decided by the NSW Land and Environment Court, the bitter dispute pitched the public benefits of green, renewable energy against the aesthetic impacts on the township of Taralga to host 62 turbines.[241] In approving the development, Chief Justice (CJ) Brian Preston cited the principle of intergenerational equity as a prevailing consideration in a project that would help address climate change. In gauging the aesthetic impacts on the historic township and its vicinity, the court reviewed five photomontages depicting the turbines from different locations. It also gathered evidence from site inspections and heard from three 'visual impact assessment experts'. All this was in addition to the assessment of the aesthetic issues during the government's initial approval of the project, which included an EIA report that attracted 218 submissions from the public, with 165 opposing the project and 23 raising some concerns.

The court grappled at great length with how to comprehend the visual and sonic impacts in legally cognisable language. CJ Preston began, noting that 'insertion of wind farms into a rural landscape involves interrupting the rural and natural cohesion of that landscape'.[242] He found the evidence of the 'visual impact assessment experts' to 'ultimately [be] of little assistance as there was no agreement between [them]'.[243] He then considered whether the project could be modified, such as by allowing fewer turbines or repositioning them, but concluded that this might render the project 'uneconomic'.[244] The judge also rejected requests for monetary compensation for property owners affected by the 'blight' of the wind farm, concluding that the claim would 'strike at the basis of the conventional framework of landuse planning'.[245] The noise impacts, by contrast, were much easier to adjudicate because technology allows for precise quantification of noise levels, and the availability of governance standards such as the *South Australian Environmental Noise Guidelines: Wind Farms*, which the court considered.

In sum, the Taralga case shows that the toolbox for adjudicating aesthetic concerns – site visits, commissioning expert evidence, receiving public submissions, etc – encounter major difficulties generating decisive and legitimate

---

[239] SO 2009, c 12, Sch A.

[240] E de Wit and A Guild, 'Winds of Change: Wind Farm Amendments to Victorian Planning Schemes' (Norton Rose Fulbright, 17 March 2011).

[241] *Taralga Landscape Guardians Inc v Minister for Planning and RES Southern Cross Pty Ltd* [2007] NSWLEC 59 (12 February 2007).

[242] Ibid, para 116.

[243] Ibid, para 123.

[244] Ibid, para 136.

[245] Ibid, para 160.

decisions. Interestingly, the extensive evidence about the climate change benefits of the renewable energy project appeared to have little effect in shifting community opinion. In another Australian case, Tasmania's Resource Management and Planning Tribunal once remarked that a community's perception of an environment 'as aesthetically pleasing or otherwise, could be affected by the extent to which the community understood [... its] ecological significance'.[246] The Taralga case, however, does not appear to corroborate such confidence.

Aesthetic criteria are sometimes also referenced in pollution control, though such regulation is primarily based on bio-chemical criteria. Recreational and potable water standards can include aesthetic criteria expressed in terms of 'transparency, odour and colour'.[247] Thus, the presence of pollutants detectable by sight or smell can be thresholds for determining whether a body of water is safe for swimming. Visible litter provides another indicator on which to base pollution regulation. The famous Keep American Beautiful campaign, launched in 1953 as a reaction to the growing problem of highway litter, has encouraged community clean-up programs that target rubbish as an eyesore and legacy of anti-social behaviour.

Some aspects of the aesthetics of pollution are distilled into highly specific, technical criteria. The Queensland government has issued guidelines under its Environmental Protection (Air) Policy 2008, providing that: 'the environmental values to be enhanced or protected under this policy are [...] the qualities of the air environment that are conducive to protecting the aesthetics of the environment, including the appearance of buildings, structures and other property'.[248] According to the policy's implementation guidance, an applicant for an air pollution licence:

> must describe how emissions from the proposed development will be managed to ensure they do not affect aesthetic values. [...] The general aesthetics of the environment can be expressed using measurable parameters such as: odour, dust, visibility reducing particles [or] light.[249]

The guidance offers further details on quantifying unacceptable levels for each of these variables, such as an odour-rating spectrum and dust deposition limits in excess of '120 milligrams per square metre per day, averaged over 1 month'.[250] Of course, some might view these considerations as matters of amenity rather than aesthetic values. Distillation of aesthetic impacts into conventional pollution control metrics also overlooks the relevance of, and

---

[246] *Tasmanian Conservation Trust v Assessment Committee for Dam Construction and Latrobe Council* [2005] TASRMPAT 90 (27 April 2005) para 10.

[247] National Health and Medical Research Council, *Guidelines for Managing Risks in Recreational Water* (Australian Government, 2008) 159.

[248] Clause 7(c).

[249] Queensland Department of Environment and Science, *Guideline: Application Requirements for Activities with Impacts to Air* (2015) 11.

[250] Ibid, 11, 13.

variations in, the cultural salience of a place that influences a community's sense of attachment to it.

Private law can also mediate disputes over unsightly activity. The tort of private nuisance protects a property owner's use and enjoyment of her land and requires courts to balance aesthetic considerations, community interests and utility, in deciding whether to prohibit nuisances. Generally, common law courts are unwilling to accept mere unsightliness as an actionable wrong.[251] This is exemplified in a 2017 decision of the Supreme Court of Vermont, where the impact of a commercial solar array on an area's 'rural aesthetic' was deemed insufficient to constitute an actionable nuisance.[252] Instead, private nuisances more commonly centre on olfactory and aural criteria, which can supposedly be more objectively quantified and thus enable courts to avoid the uneasy role of 'arbiters of style and taste'.[253] Nonetheless, occasionally courts foray into adjudicating visual nuisances. A 2004 decision of the High Court of South Africa elevated the aesthetic complaint to one about the value of the property, which enabled them to find that the installation of an unsightly thatched roof amounted to a private nuisance.[254] And US courts have adjudicated claims about the beauty of a particular area in relation to zoning decisions and/or challenges to the exercise of the government power of eminent domain.[255] Thus, judicial confidence in introducing aesthetic criteria into legal doctrine is mixed.

To recap at this juncture, the foregoing pages show that the law acknowledges aesthetic criteria in environmental conservation and control of threatening activities. Such acknowledgment, ranging from hortatory statements about the value of natural beauty to technical standards for mitigating visual and acoustic impacts, does not suggest that aesthetic issues have special priority in governance, but at least have legitimate status. Aesthetic values trouble regulators for a host of reasons including that the significance of such values cannot usually be formally quantified, variability in community aesthetic preferences, and competition from other policy considerations as derived from scientific data, economic costs or sheer political advantages. Thus, legal doctrine struggles to formulate environmental aesthetics into a priori models for governance. As Manderson concluded in his own account of a related subject, 'the meaning of the aesthetic may [...] be sensed, but [it] can never be codified or entirely understood'.[256] Aesthetic values manifest through specific relationships and contexts rather than as general propositions.

---

[251] GP Smith II, 'The Price of Beauty: An Economic Approach to Aesthetic Nuisance' (1991) 53(15) *Harvard Environmental Law Review* 53, 66–75; however, visual aesthetics have been found relevant for access to natural light (*Regan v Paul Properties DPF No 1 Ltd* [2006] EWCA Civ 1391) and the notorious 'sight' of sex workers (*Thompson-Schwab v Costaki* [1956] 1 WLR 335 (CA)).

[252] *Myrick v Peck Electrical Company* [2017] VT 4.

[253] Ibid.

[254] *Waterhouse Properties v Hyperception Properties* [2004] ZAFSHC 97.

[255] Smith, 'The Price of Beauty' (above n 251) 73–80.

[256] Manderson, *Songs Without Music* (above n 1) 195.

V. NATIONALISING NATURE

A. Symbolising the Sovereign

Nature and nationalism often come together in forging the cultural identities of countries and symbolising governmental authority. The pioneering political theorist Eric Voegelin explains, 'the self-illumination of society through symbols is an integral part of social reality' because through it citizens experience 'more than an accident or convenience; they experience it as of their human essence'.[257] The symbolisation of societal values and identities has a particularly strong association with the nation state. In *Sensing the Nation*, Stefan Huygebaert and others show that the democratic legitimacy of political and legal orders must be 'sensed' by the public, analogously to the aphorism 'not only must justice be done; it must also be seen to be done'.[258] The sensory manifestation of the nation acquires legal salience through particular symbolic representations of sovereign authority, notably in official coinage, stamps, flags, monuments, national anthems and coats-of-arms, which serve to etch in the public conscious-ness certain idealised national values and histories. Although such symbols may not be explicitly associated with formal law, they acquire legal salience through what Sarah Marusek describes as a 'folk legality' that insinuates sanitised narra-tives about legal policy or values into everyday cultural usage.[259] Equally, the potency and visibility of these insignia can make them targets for subversive challenges to the authority of the state, for instance flag burning or refusing to stand for the national anthem.

Environmental motifs feature in many of these aestheticised nation-state identities. 'National identity', observed Simon Schama in his masterful analysis of landscape aesthetics, 'would lose much of its ferocious enchantment without the mystique of a particular landscape tradition'.[260] Thus, certain landscapes, wildlife and other natural icons have been leveraged for nation-forming and nationalism. Orvar Löfgren explains that in North America, lacking Europe's rich historical ruins, countries turned to their natural heritage as markers of national identity.[261] Animals and plants featured in these sovereign symbols may have been selected for their actual geographical presence in the country or because they evoke distinctive aesthetic qualities such as grace and beauty that a nation wishes to affirm as part of its character. Mark Sagoff suggests a deep association in US history between the ideals of the new republic (eg valour,

---

[257] E Voegelin, *The New Science of Politics* (University of Chicago Press, 1952) 27.

[258] S Huygebaert et al (eds), *Sensing the Nation's Law: Historical Inquiries Into the Aesthetics of Democratic Legitimacy* (Springer, 2018).

[259] S Marusek, 'The Crafting of Law and the Coining of Culture: Legal Semiotic of the American Quarter' (2015) 11 *Law, Culture and the Humanities* 110.

[260] S Schama, *Landscape and Memory* (HarperCollins, 1995) 15.

[261] O Löfgren, 'The Nationalization of Culture' (1989) 19 *Ethnologia Europaea* 5.

freedom and strength) and wilderness, including wild animals such as the bald eagle (which in 1782 became its national symbol).[262]

Animals feature in many countries' national iconography. Many sovereign flags depict natural elements distinctive to their country, such as the maple leaf (Canada), condor (Ecuador), raggiana bird (Papua New Guinea) and turtle (Cayman Islands). Similarly, government-issued stamps can serve to forge national identities around particular natural elements, such as the huia birds (since extinct) on the New Zealand stamp depicted in Figure 2.7. Many countries have also proclaimed official animal and floral emblems to symbolise links between their national geography and character: Thailand's national flower is the golden shower tree, while Israel's is the poppy anemone, and of animal emblems, the Congo has the okapi and Colombia the Andean condor. Relatedly, from the nineteenth century some governments started to proclaim annual national days for similar purposes. In 1872, Nebraska began a tree-planting holiday called 'Arbor Day', resulting in the planting of one million trees, and inspiring many other jurisdictions to proclaim similar festivals.[263] Libby Robin suggests that national nature days were particularly important in the settler colonies and implicitly served to foster civic-mindedness by associating nature with a moralising influence and fostering community cooperation through tree planting and other group activities.[264]

Figure 2.7 New Zealand government stamp, Huia birds, 1907

[262] M Sagoff, 'On Preserving the Natural Environment' (1974) 84 *Yale Law Journal* 205, 243.

[263] DR Hickey, SA Wunder and R Wunder, *Nebraska Moments* (University of Nebraska Press, 2007) 121.

[264] L Robin, 'Nationalising Nature: Wattle Days in Australia' (2002) 26 *Journal of Australian Studies* 13.

In some cases, this cultural nationalism has become harnessed for political nationalism, occasionally with sinister aims. Japanese culture is sometimes associated with the aesthetic of cherry blossom trees, which during the Second World War were, according to Yuriko Saito, 'appropriated by the military for uniting Japanese citizens in their war-time efforts', such as by planting the trees on colonised territory in Korea and Manchuria.[265] Today, the panda bear assists Chinese elites' international practice of 'panda diplomacy' for courting favours.[266] Political parties may also associate themselves with specific environmental imagery: the UK Conservative Party has the oak tree as its official logo, while its main rival, the Labour Party, adopted the red rose, while the logos of the two major US political parties feature a donkey (Democrats) and elephant (Republican), these being odd choices for those unfamiliar with the history of American politics.

Official coinage and bank notes also symbolise national values, and frequently harness environmental themes. Many African nations, whose identity is sometimes closely associated with their impressively large fauna, include animals in their currency, such as the elephants and giraffes on Zimbabwe's bank notes and the zebra on Rwanda's currency. Such seemingly benign imagery can also serve to obfuscate or sanitise unsavoury aspects of a country's history. In her analysis of US coinage, Sarah Marusek observes that 'national events involving racial violence [...] and the domestic elimination of native peoples are dimmed against such picturesque images as palm trees, Magnolia blossoms, and sailboats'.[267] She goes on to explain in her analysis of the quarter-dollar coin, that they are 'visual artifacts of an American past of imperialism and injustice that may be dismissed against the depiction of the bucolic and trivial characterizations of American history'.[268]

One prominent motif in US coinage, along with that of some other national currencies associated with settler colonialism such as South Africa and New Zealand, is the harnessing of natural resources for farming, mining and other economic 'progress'. Australia's former two-dollar banknotes featured images of sheep and wheat with the faces of John Macarthur and William Farer, who were leading protagonists in these industries' development. Official currency thereby serves to figuratively convey a mythology that links national identity to the subjugation of nature, and through this aesthetic backdrop government authority is more legitimated in regulating natural resources and their exploitation.

---

[265] Y Saito, *Aesthetics of the Familiar: Everyday Life and World-making* (Oxford University Press, 2017) 145.

[266] H Nicholls, *The Way of the Panda. The Curious History of China's Political Animal* (Pegasus, 2011).

[267] S Marusek, "Appreciation or Appropriation? An Indigenous Moment in the American Numismatic Narrative (1999–2009)' in S Huygebaert et al (eds), *Sensing the Nation's Law: Historical Inquiries into the Aesthetics of Democratic Legitimacy* (Springer, 2018) 170, 172.

[268] Ibid.

Individual government or international agencies sometimes adopt their own logos as a unique visual identifier. The Commission for the Conservation of Antarctic Marine Living Resources (CCAMLR) has one displayed on its website and publications (see Figure 2.8). The compact logo reflects an ocean around the Antarctic continent.[269] The International Whaling Commission's logo, unsurprisingly, features a whale against a blue background.[270] The UNESCO Convention on the Protection of the Underwater Cultural Heritage 2001 is accompanied by an official logo adopted in 2015 that represents waves rolling over a submerged cultural heritage site.[271] The emblem of the UN Environment (formerly UN Environment Programme), modified from the general UN emblem, is a person standing in cross-position surrounded by a wreath. An enveloping wreath also features in the logo of the International Maritime Organization, a specialised UN agency responsible for ship safety and prevention of maritime pollution.[272] Of national examples, the US Environmental Protection Agency's logo and seal comprises the two-leaved flower, with stem, encircled by the name of the agency.[273] The logo of the German equivalent authority, the *Umwelt Bundesamt*, features a person standing cross-armed against a green background with the name of the organisation.[274] These visual brandings serve to raise the public profile of environmental agencies, as they have become more sensitive to public opinion as a result of governance changes since the 1970s in which the law has accorded greater opportunities for public consultation in environmental decision-making. Well-designed logos and emblems may help to project a more pleasing, friendly image of an agency that wishes to be seen as committed to public service rather than red tape.

The nation-state itself commonly has its own visual branding, often with reference to environmental themes. Historically this practice has been associated with official seals and coats-of-arms. The official seal of the United States, used since 1792 to authenticate documents issued by the federal government such as passports, is most easily recognised by its bald eagle, clutching an olive branch in its right talon and arrows in its left (symbolising respectively the power to make peace and war). The Australian coat-of-arms depicts a shield, with symbols of Australia's six states, held up by the kangaroo and the emu – incongruously, both species were heavily persecuted when and since the coat-of-arms was adopted. Similarly incongruous, India's official state emblem, adopted in 1950, centres on an image of three lions, a species so heavily hunted that its lions are now confined to single national park.

---

[269] See www.ccamlr.org/en/organisation/ccamlr-logo.
[270] See https://iwc.int/home.
[271] See www.unesco.org/new/en/culture/themes/underwater-cultural-heritage/2001-convention/the-logo-of-the-convention.
[272] See www.imo.org.
[273] See www.epa.gov/stylebook/using-epa-seal-and-logo.
[274] See www.umweltbundesamt.de.

Figure 2.8 Official logo of the Commission for the Conservation of Antarctic Marine Living Resources

In recent decades a trend has emerged towards more commercial designs in tandem with governments' growing online presence and reliance on marketing like business corporations. Canada's logo features 'Canada' written in a serif font with the national flag, the small maple leaf symbol, sitting over the final letter. The New Zealand government has adopted an all-of-government logo, which in some forms includes the silver fern, which serves, according to the government's explanatory guide, to 'show a unity of purpose across' government services, to improve their 'visibility', and promote 'credibility and trust' by the public.[275]

Another means of visually projecting the authority of the nation is via monuments and memorials. Many states favour the large, imposing monolith or sculptural figure erected in prominent public spaces such as in civic parks or along major thoroughfares. They have existed for eons, as demonstrated by Rome's triumphal arches. Monuments may also be projected in a more ephemeral condition, such as festivals and rituals that commemorate a society's heritage. A public space itself may be the monument: Andrew Shanken identifies how societies increasingly supplement sculptural monuments with utilitarian 'living memorials', such as concert halls and parks, in acknowledging their history and culture.[276] These government-sponsored monuments honour persons and

---

[275] State Services Commission, *All of Government Brand Policy and Guidelines* (Government of New Zealand, 2007) 2.
[276] AM Shanken, 'Planning Memory: Living Memorials in the United States During World War II' (2002) 84(1) *The Art Bulletin* 130.

events, notably 'heroic' military victories and famous politicians. The former Soviet Union produced some of the most spectacular examples, such as the gigantic 1949 Soviet War Memorial in Berlin (Yakov Belopolsky, *Soviet War Memorial*). The tropes sometimes also depict environment-related themes, such as intrepid explorers who discovered new lands or slayed ferocious beasts.

Their grandeur, ornamentation and public prominence can make these monuments not only aesthetically prominent but also tools to suppress memories or erase history's 'losers'.[277] Memories are not merely personal archives, but include the culturally-mediated narratives of history that chronicle, exalt, commiserate, ignore or take other responses that reflect the biases and prejudices of society.[278] The limitations of such monuments are not merely their narrow, one-dimensional view of history; they do little to engage viewers about their future, such as the importance of avoiding future wars and enabling peace. I return to this theme in the closing chapter in its exploration of the alternative of 'counter monuments'.

Music also expresses state authority. The national anthem, which first became widespread in Europe during the eighteenth century, is a potent expression of national identity that evokes and commemorates the history, character and achievements of a society.[279] The communal singing of the anthem is a patriotic ritual in politics and public life, and is done in a wide variety of contexts, including major sporting events such as the Olympic Games, school assemblies, and an assortment of official rites such as new citizenship ceremonies. As a symbol of state authority, the national anthem serves to nurture a sense of patriotic belonging, and its contribution to public rituals helps to legitimate the authority of states.

Nearly all anthems have lyrics, conveying messages that reinforce national identity. Some refer to military or bloody themes, such as China's 'brave the enemy gunfire' and Portugal's 'to arms, to arms', while others such as Great Britain's 'God Save the Queen' (or King) honour national leaders. The most common leitmotif in anthems, however, is their celebration of the nation's landscape and environment. The Danes sing of their 'lovely land', the Swedes the 'loveliest land on earth', Australians their 'land abounds in nature's gifts', Russians 'our forests and fields', and Brazilians 'clear, pure, beauteous skies'. While the foregoing are in rather generic language, some anthems celebrate terrain emblematic of a country's landscape, such as Austria's 'land of mountains' and Norway's 'rugged, storm-scared o'er the ocean'. Some anthems also refer to specific plants and animals, such as Senegal's 'lion' and Bangladesh's 'mango grove'.

---

[277] JE Young, *The Texture of Memory: Holocaust Memorials and Meaning* (Yale University Press, 1993).

[278] D Lowenthal, *The Past is a Foreign Country–Revisited* (Cambridge University Press, 2015) 13–14.

[279] J Zikmund II, 'National Anthems as Political Symbols' (1969) 15(3) *Australian Journal of Politics and History* 73.

Landscapes and their wildlife play a powerful role in the construction of national identity. Schama observes, 'landscapes are culture before they are nature [...] constructs of the imagination projected onto wood and water and rock'.[280] Thus to fervent nationalists, showing the geographical unity of a people and the land they occupy is a powerful way to portray the innate nationhood to which they belong. Nationality is thus to be felt as 'natural'. Landscape features, aesthetically mundane or otherwise, thus become tied through anthems to narratives about national identity and belonging. References to rivers, mountains and forests are means for the constructed 'representations of places' in the national psyche that link a society to the qualities of specific environments.[281] Even if a community does not feel that their connection to a specific geographical place is sufficient to arouse nationalist sentiment, undoubtedly 'sovereignty implies space'.[282]

Governments may also sponsor propaganda through the mass media for similar ends. Consider the New Zealand government's tourism campaign slogan '100% Pure New Zealand'. It peddles a picture-postcard image of a clean, green country; the reality differs remarkably.[283] Aotearoa, as the native Maori call the place, has the world's worst record of bird extinctions, having lost 42 per cent of its terrestrial avifauna since human beings arrived at least 800 years ago, with many of the survivors still menaced with extinction, and losing about 90 per cent of its wetlands and 60 per cent of its forests.[284] Yet, without an appreciation of the islands' deep ecological history and the ensuing spatial changes, the casual visitor today might indeed be misled into thinking that much of New Zealand resembles an unadulterated ecological paradise. Some visitors, however, aren't; the *New Zealand Herald* reported in April 2018 of a disappointed US backpacker complaining that 'the country's environment did not live up to the advertising campaign'.[285]

B. Mapping Landscapes, Cultures and Nations

Cartography has also contributed to the figurative representation of national authority.[286] The symbolic and metaphorical power of maps to define people's

---

[280] Schama, *Landscape and Memory* (above n 260) 61.

[281] GJ Ashworth and BJ Graham (eds), *Senses of Place: Senses of Time* (Ashgate, 2005) 3.

[282] H Lefebvre, *The Production of Space*, translated D Nicholson-Smith (Blackwell, 1991) 280.

[283] See NJ Morgan, A Pritchard and R Piggott, 'New Zealand, 100% Pure: The Creation of a Powerful Niche Destination Brand' (2002) 9(4/5) *Journal of Brand Management* 335.

[284] See New Zealand's *Fifth National Report to the United Nations Convention on Biological Diversity: Reporting Period: 2009–2013* (Ministry for the Environment, 2014); TerraNature, 'New Zealand's Ecology: Extinct Birds', http://terranature.org/extinctbirds.htm.

[285] 'US Backpacker Blasts "Pure New Zealand" as a "Myth"' *New Zealand Herald* 25 April 2018.

[286] See especially J Branch, *The Cartographic State: Maps, Territory and the Origins of Sovereignty* (Cambridge University Press, 2014); K Miles, 'Insulae Moluccae: Map of the Spice Islands, 1594' in IJ Homhann and D Joyce (eds), *International Law's Objects* (Oxford University Press, 2018) ch 15.

places and relationships in landscapes has been observed by geographers and artists.[287] The curator of the 1999 art exhibition *Mapping Our Countries*, Paul Tacon, observed:

> Maps may have scientific or mythological characters but they always do the same thing – they tell stories of relationships to geographic locations that are important to the individuals and groups doing the story telling. They are artefacts that embody, reaffirm and publicize the personalisation of place. Without maps we would exist in totally different, unimaginable ways.[288]

Maps also matter to legal governance of landscapes. They are pictorial devices that not only represent space but also influence how we perceive it by emphasising or obscuring topographical and cultural elements. Medieval European maps, with their elaborate ornamentation, served to symbolise and impress viewers with the reification of space under sovereign dominion. Contemporary global maps, less embellished but no less influential, reshape space by distorting the size or position of countries and thereby privileging particular geo-political realms. Along with delineating frontiers, maps also name places, and thus have inclusive and exclusive properties; the naming of topographical features such as mountains and rivers can reify and legitimate the presence of colonisers while erasing the history of their original inhabitants.

Environmental law, with strong territorial dimensions, functions within this cartographic aesthetic. By demarcating boundaries and dividing geographies, maps aid in excluding or granting access to natural resources, and shaping how they will be governed. Maps delineate the international boundaries of governmental jurisdiction, which for coastal states can include a valuable 'exclusive economic zone' of up to 200 nautical miles seaward that gives control over fisheries and seabed minerals. In disputes over maritime jurisdiction, maps can assist in adjudicating the claims, as has occurred in some decisions of the International Court of Justice.[289] Within nation-states, maps can likewise delineate jurisdiction among provinces or regions, and demarcate land use management through zoning regimes. Environmental and topographical features can influence mapping decisions, such as the direction of rivers or the edges of watersheds.[290] Equally though, maps can be complicit in the spatial representation and governance of nature that violates underlying ecological relationships, a problem that so-called 'bioregional' planning seeks to overcome.[291]

---

[287] Eg JB Harley, 'Deconstructing the Map' (1989) 26(2) *Cartographica* 1; D Woods, *The Power of Maps* (Guilford Press, 1992).

[288] P Tacon and J Watson, *Mapping Our Countries* (Djamu Gallery/Australian Museum, 1999) unpaginated.

[289] Eg *Territorial and Maritime Dispute* (Nicaragua v Colombia) [2012] ICJ Reports 624.

[290] K Gardner, 'Moving Watersheds, Borderless Maps and Imperial Geography in India's Northwestern Himalaya' (2018) 62(1) *The Historical Journal* 149, https://doi.org/10.1017/S0018246X18000146.

[291] DJ Brunckhorst, *Bioregional Planning: Resource Management Beyond the New Millennium* (Routledge, 2000).

With the aid of computer software and data storage technologies, environmental regulators can develop intricate online maps with multiple layers of authoritative information about land use zoning, property tenure, wildlife habitat, geology, soils and numerous other variables relevant to management of natural values. Tasmania's Natural Values Atlas, maintained by the Department of Primary Industries, Parks, Water and Environment, is a particularly comprehensive example, which 'informs planning and decision making processes across all levels of government, industry and the general public, assisting to improve conservation outcomes for natural values in the State'.[292] Lay people can access the Atlas to generate multiple data sets into a single report for the natural values of specific areas, such as locations of endangered species, weeds, biosecurity risks and other data to assist land managers. Importantly, the Atlas provides a citizen science tool that allows any member of the public to submit data, such as sightings of significant wildlife. On a far grander scale, Google Earth has evolved into a sophisticated mapping database to identify and monitor environmental changes. Developed from remote sensing technology, Google Earth now offers the most accessible geographic information systems for the world, and amateur enthusiasts such as I can use it easily without training.

Mapping is also an instrument of colonisation and social injustice, with further implications for management of natural resources. The delineation of boundaries and ownership, along with toponyms, can override the history and presence of historic communities such as Indigenous peoples who are thereby aesthetically marginalised. Maps thus can have serious implications for their struggle to gain legal recognition of their traditional territories.[293] As Alexander Reilly explains, 'maps use a particular iconography, scale and projection that mask innumerable alternative readings of the areas represented on the map'.[294] In Canada's Arctic frontier, maps have become politically salient to control over natural resources, with contrasting maps developed by the government and the Inuit Tapiriit Kanatami, the organisation representing Inuit living in the Canadian north.[295]

World maps also project distortions, a challenge that arises because any such map tries to represent a round planet on a flat surface. Cartographers thus have choices, which can reflect biases about what they consider important to represent. The traditional global atlases tended to show countries incorrectly in proportion to one another, exaggerating the size of high-latitude countries such as in Scandinavia and making the equatorial regions appear much smaller. The most

[292] DPIPWE, 'Natural Values Atlas', https://dpipwe.tas.gov.au/conservation/development-planning-conservation-assessment/planning-tools/natural-values-atlas.

[293] A Reilly, 'Cartography, Property and the Aesthetics of Place: Mapping Native Title in Australia' in AT Kenyon and PD Rush (eds), *An Aesthetics of Law and Culture: Texts, Images and Screens* (Elsevier, 2004) 221.

[294] Ibid, 228.

[295] MM Bennett et al, 'Articulating the Arctic: Contrasting State and Inuit Maps of the Canadian North' (2016) 52(6) *Polar Record* 630.

widely used of these maps is the 'Mercator projection', named after Gerardus Mercator, a Flemish engraver and globe-maker, who developed his map in 1569 as a seafaring navigational tool. By exaggerating the size of the Earth around the poles while shrinking the equatorial regions, his map makes much of the developed world, in Europe and North America, appear far larger than their actual size relative to the Global South. The Mercator projection depicts Greenland as about the same size as Africa, although Africa is 14 times larger.

Figure 2.9 *Colton's Illustrated and Embellished Steel Plate Map of the World on Mercator's Projection*, JH Colton, 1854; US Library of Congress

Cartographers have devised other maps that challenge the northern hemisphere bias. The Peters Projection map, now adopted by some UN agencies and many educational institutions, gives an accurate representation of the size of countries, but sacrifices shape because land masses around the equator are stretched while those towards the poles are squashed.[296] Invented by German cartographer Arno Peters in 1973, the Peters map has been useful for proponents of an anti-colonial view that restores the geographic prominence of the Global South. The distortion of countries' shapes created by the Peters World Map has itself encouraged the development of alternate maps, such as non-rectangular maps like that devised by the Robinson or Winkle Tripel projects, which purport to provide a batter balance between the size and shape of landmasses.

---

[296] See http://petersmap.com.

Other ways to represent the world to challenge the biases of traditional maps include to reverse the hemispheres so that the south is up, which like the Peters map can bring the generally poorer southern hemisphere into greater prominence. Another convention of world maps open to challenge is their centring on the prime meridian, or zero degrees longitude. Like the north up convention, this choice is also scientifically arbitrary, derived from the location of the Royal Observatory in Greenwich, London. It results in Europe (though Africa too) being the centre of the world map. The Pacific-centred map, increasingly popular, elevates Asia while displacing Western Europe to the edge. The UN flag depicts another, completely different view of the world, using what is known as the Azimuthal polar projection. It represents the world from the vantage of looking down on the North Pole, which distorts both the area and shape of landmasses while Antarctica is pushed to the edges and almost obscured from view. Finally, as noted earlier in this chapter, environmentalists are reconfiguring maps into cartograms that display environmental data about natural resource consumption and impacts, which can aid in shaping public debate and policy reform.

VI. CONCLUSION

This chapter has hopefully put to rest any scepticism readers might have had about the need to take aesthetics seriously in environmental law. From protection of scenic landscapes to pollution control, aesthetic criteria habitually show their relevance to decision-making. The inception of many environmental laws also reflects forceful appeals to aesthetic values in a political culture where imagery has become as important to dialogue as the written word. Furthermore, the very authority of the state itself is enveloped in aesthetic symbols referencing environmental motifs that help define national culture and identity. Official maps, monuments, flags and coinage articulate an aestheticised national character that helps to legitimate the state's authority over places and landscapes, though in practice more commonly they serve exploitation rather than conservation of natural resources.

While these aesthetic qualities are evidently distillable into visual or acoustic symbols of national authority, in the law itself they have tended to defy codification into precise legal formulae. Legislative or judicial recognition of aesthetic values, as in statements of statutory purposes for instance, is generally not matched by detailed standards. But that should not imply that aesthetics are unimportant to governance. Indeed, as the following chapter explores, it might not be possible or even desirable to codify. Beauty, explained John Dewey, 'is at the furthest remove from an analytic term, and hence from a conception that can figure in theory as a means of explanation or classification'.[297]

---

[297] J Dewey, *Art as Experience* (Balch, 1934) 129.

Still, the ambiguity or open-endedness of aesthetic qualities creates challenges for accountability in legal governance, necessitating greater reliance being placed on the integrity of decision-making at the outset, including public consultation. John Costonis observes that 'how individuals or groups respond to an environmental feature [is] profoundly shaped by the conventions of culture and time' and thus 'if there is a case for aesthetic regulation', he believes 'it must be fashioned from intersubjective patterns of communal aesthetic response'.[298] His observation strikes a chord with this and other chapters' references to public participation, but we will also see later in this book that it is not enough to ensure that aesthetics is taken seriously in environmental law.

---

[298] J Costonis, *Icons and Aliens: Law, Aesthetics and Environmental Change* (University of Illinois Press, 1999) 358.

3

Governance Challenges

I. ORIENTATION

T HE PRECEDING CHAPTER mapped the interactions between aesthetics and
environmental law, and identified the law in some guises as an aesthetic
phenomenon itself. Yet, what challenges come with governing with
aesthetics? This chapter explores them and some opportunities to overcome
them. This broad synopsis informs the detailed case studies in Part Two, where
I probe some of these challenges in specific realms including climate change and
ecological restoration.

The following pages navigate through five specific challenges. I begin by
considering whether and how legal governance can codify environmental
aesthetics into workable legal standards or rules to inform land use planning,
nature conservation and other domains where environmental decision-making
encounters aesthetics. Codification may matter if environmental law is to protect
aesthetic values and adjudicate disputes. Secondly, I consider how aesthetic and
non-aesthetic values (especially from the natural sciences and economics) interact and sometimes conflict in the making of environmental decisions, and how
the law mediates such tensions.

Moving on, 'biased aesthetics' constitutes a third challenge, namely that
the appeal to environmental aesthetics can result in decisions that differentiate
nature aesthetically into extraordinary and ordinary categories to the detriment
of both. An aesthetically mundane landscape may nonetheless still harbour rich
biodiversity or vital ecosystems, and thus policy makers must grapple with how
to promote appreciation of natural beauty without creating collateral damage
for places or species judged as aesthetically inferior. Biased aesthetics may even
designate some aspects of nature as ugly or aesthetically disagreeable, and thus
earmarked not for neglect (as for the aesthetically mundane) but active persecution. What we demonise as 'ugly' may become legally classified as vermin
or weeds. Equally, our bias to the beautiful can bring harm, as evident in the
destructive exploitation of animal furs and feathers.

Two further challenges occupy this chapter. One I call 'absent aesthetics',
denoting the unseen or unheard environmental impacts of humankind. Time
and space distort many environmental upheavals and damage that transcend our
sensory awareness, be it to distant lands or future eras. As aesthetics underpin
our emotional and moral engagement with nature, the law must take seriously

the gaps posed by absent aesthetics. The chapter closes by focusing on the seductive allure of some sensory experiences manipulated for unscrupulous purposes. The aesthetics of commerce and politics are sometimes associated with corporate greenwashing and state propaganda respectively, and can mislead the public and foster complacency about the governance of environmental problems. Dissident 'counter aesthetics' have become brazen means by which environmental activists challenge political and commodity aesthetics.

II. CODIFYING BEAUTY

Environmental law has little apparent difficulty acknowledging aesthetic factors in its statutory objects or regulatory criteria but struggles to translate them into intelligible standards by which regulators can be held measurably accountable. Statutory references to 'natural beauty' or 'scenic attraction', among the most commonly affirmed terms, typically remain undefined, with government agencies thus resorting to supplementary guidance if possible. As conceded by Natural England, the agency responsible for protecting natural beauty under Britain's National Parks and Access to the Countryside Act 1949 and Countryside and Rights of Way Act 2000:

> Natural beauty is not exhaustively defined in the legislation. It is also a very subjective characteristic of a landscape and ultimately involves a value judgment. In deciding whether an area has natural beauty, Natural England must therefore make a judgment as to whether people are likely to perceive a landscape as having sufficient natural beauty.[1]

The difficulties of codifying 'beauty', as explained earlier, are multi-faceted, including the psychological and cultural differences of perceivers, as well as the variable contexts in time and space by which we experience nature. The Australian-American comedy film *Babe* (1995) enamoured audiences with a cute, pretty piglet while Islamic societies traditionally disavow pigs as dirty and impure. While virtually all appreciate the sight and sound of running water, we may not when associated with mosquitoes, floods or other discomforts. Apart from such contextual differences, legal institutions themselves can lack the expertise or tools to decipher natural beauty, as Linda Pinkerton has examined in urban heritage conservation.[2] The very language of the law itself may struggle to convey intelligibly that which satiates our senses, a deficit related to the wider problem that Critical Legal scholars have critiqued about legal terminology.[3]

---

[1] Natural England, *Guidance for Assessing Landscapes for Designation as National Park or Area of Outstanding Natural Beauty in England* (Natural England, 2011) 11.
[2] L Pinkerton, 'Aesthetics and the Single Building Landmark' (2013) 15 *Tulsa Law Journal* 610, 612.
[3] RM Unger, *Law in Modern Society* (The Free Press, 1976).

The broader language of 'aesthetics' offers challenges of equal complexity for lawmakers. The term is occasionally defined in legislation dealing with protection of intellectual property rights but not environmental law.[4] Aesthetic impairment, such as relating to acoustic or olfactory impacts, can prove troublesome for legal adjudicators to disentangle, as in development proposals subject to Environmental Impact Assessments (EIAs) that reveal sensory impacts of community concern. In some instances they can comprise the dominant impacts, as in the dispute over South Africa's Gauteng Rapid Rail Link, a public works project initiated in 2002 that was challenged by affected local residents on grounds that rested heavily on the detrimental noise and vibrations from the 80-km rail link. Yet, the High Court of South Africa adjudicated the case not on the substantive merits of these concerns but rather on the administrative law principles relating to the government authorisations granted.[5]

Thus, the integrity of the decision-making processes that assess aesthetic values has become the primary way by which the law seeks to achieve legitimate decisions on aesthetics. Legitimacy hinges on two elements in particular: that aesthetic judgements are accepted as objective, and that such judgements ensue from consultative and transparent decisions. Additionally, legitimacy can be bolstered by accountability through judicial review, such as by courts ensuring that regulators took only relevant considerations into account, acted intra vires and for a proper purpose.

Objective aesthetic judgements, as discussed in Chapter 1, do not mean a consensus of opinion, but rather relate to how aesthetic appreciation is rendered, such as by 'disinterested' observation, engaged participation or scientifically knowledgeable appreciation. As philosopher Janna Thompson explains:

> The mere fact that people have different opinions about what is especially beautiful in nature does not mean that aesthetic judgments about nature are not objective [...] It does mean that we have to consider what reasons people can give for their preferences [and] ... be able to make and justify, however tentatively, comparative evaluations of natural beauty.[6]

Knowledge of the natural sciences can decisively assist, suggests Allen Carlson, in justifying aesthetic value in nature.[7] Other aestheticians including Arnold Berleant and Emily Brady, however, postulate that aesthetic appreciation hinges more on emotions, imagination and multi-sensory engagement with nature.[8]

---

[4] Eg, South Africa's Designs Act 1993, s 1.

[5] *Muckleneuk/Lukasrand Property Owners and Residents Association v MEC Department of Agriculture Conservation and Environment Gauteng Provincial Government and Others* [2006] ZAGPHC 86, [2007] 4 All SA 1265.

[6] J Thompson, 'Aesthetics and the Value of Nature' in A Carlson and S Lintott (eds), *Nature, Aesthetics, and Environmentalism: From Beauty to Duty* (Columbia University Press, 2008) 254, 257.

[7] A Carlson, *Aesthetics and the Environment: The Appreciation of Nature, Art and Architecture* (Routledge, 2000).

[8] A Berleant, *Living in the Landscape: Toward an Aesthetics of Environment* (University of Kansas Press, 1997); E Brady, *Aesthetics of the Natural Environment* (Edinburgh University Press, 2003).

So too in the realm of environmental policy, where numerous challenges from climate change to wildlife management defy political consensus, defensible policies based on diverse scientific, economic and ethical criteria can still be generated.

On the second legitimating criterion, the process of codifying preferred aesthetic values must include public consultation and transparency. This criterion is not separate from the objectivity requirement but integral to it, given that objectivity claims hinge on reasoned decisions. The UK's Royal Commission on Environmental Pollution in its 1998 report on environmental standards noted the importance of accommodating the diversity of cultural values involved in environmental behaviour, and that decision-makers should adopt 'more rigorous and wide-ranging exploration of people's values [through] discussion and debate' than allowed by 'traditional forms of consultation'.[9]

Yet whose views should count in assessing aesthetic merit? Answering this question begins by ascertaining who belongs to the decision-making community. American legal scholar Timothy Murphy identifies affected private landholders as foremost members of such a community.[10] This however, offers a too restrictive view: who for instance has a stake in the aesthetics of climate change? In our Anthropocene and more globally inter-connected societies, the notion of affected 'community' must broaden to take account of the changing temporal and spatial dimensions of environmental problems.

The question of whose voice counts also involves the relative importance of expert professionals and lay people. Carlson and Glenn Parsons believe scientific knowledge helps validate aesthetic judgements, which implies that the views of the more educated matter more. Yet, basing aesthetic judgements on the determinations of skilled planners or landscape architects creates 'risks of powerful professional groups usurping democratic decision-making'.[11] Modern environmental law straddles this often unresolved tension, with key decisions sometimes having to be made by elected officials answerable to their constituents. In my home town of Hobart, Tasmania, municipal affairs have become dominated by residents' concerns about the proposed lifting of building height limits in an urban landscape so far largely saved from the high-rise blight that afflicts numerous metropolises. Whether the maximum height should be 45 metres or 55 metres ultimately is not just about expert judgements of the shadowing effects of taller structures but the overall aesthetic character of the urban morphology that residents find tolerable.

---

[9] Royal Commission on Environmental Pollution, *Twenty-first Report: Setting Environmental Standards*, Cm 4053 (October 1998) 136.

[10] TS Murphy, 'Environmental Law – Protection of Scenic and Aesthetic Resources under the Minnesota Environmental Rights Act – State ex rel. Drabik v Martz, 451 NW 2d 893 (Minn 1990)' (1991) 17(4) *William Mitchell Law Review* 1190, 1212–13.

[11] J Barrett, 'Law, Aesthetics and the Environment: Some Thoughts on Sustaining Natural Beauty in New Zealand' (2013) 1(1) *New Zealand Online Journal of Interdisciplinary Studies* 9.

Environmental law worldwide now commonly mandates some public input into decision-making. The European Landscape Convention 2000 advocates it, including an obligation that government 'undertakes to define landscape quality objectives for the landscapes identified and assessed, after public consultation'.[12] Some environmental laws identify specific stakeholders for consultation or consideration. New Zealand's Resource Management Act 1991 obliges authorities to respect the cultural values and interests of the indigenous Māori people,[13] for whom the environment is conceived foremost as a cultural and historical landscape associated with spiritual (wairua), sacred (tapu) and authority (mana) values.[14] Canadian law imposes a duty on governments to consult with Indigenous First Nations in numerous contexts that may impinge on their interests, including in environmental management.[15]

The costs and delays accompanying the foregoing processes should be preferable to the neoliberal alternative of the 'free' market determining what is protected or exploited. One advocate of the latter deplores the prospect of aesthetics regulation by 'unqualified' judges and bureaucrats, instead preferring the marketplace to resolve such choices.[16] I find this option unpalatable and unpersuasive: the market may price the value of fine art, but it cannot determine the complex aesthetic values of landscapes or wildlife, nor provide the means to prevent externalities imposed on wider society from unsympathetic use of their aesthetic properties. Moreover, because market wealth is skewed unevenly, the 'free' market ideology brings freedom to control aesthetic properties only to the financially prosperous.

A process for defensible aesthetic judgements must also accommodate changes in societal values, as well as changes to the natural environments to which such values relate. Natural beauty is not a fixed, enduring object of admiration, analogous to a masterpiece in an art gallery. The forces of entropy and evolution continually mould nature, and likewise human culture – including environmental attitudes shifts – as history shows. Consider the evolving perceptions of wilderness in American culture. The first English settlers found it alienating: William Bradford, governor of the fledgling Plymouth Colony from 1620 to 1657, condemned his new environs as 'a hideous and desolate wilderness, full of wild beasts and wild men'.[17] By the mid-nineteenth century, wilderness was symbolising American courage and pride. In 1853, Henry David Thoreau,

---

[12] European Landscape Convention, 2000, CETS No 176, art 6.2.D. See further M Jones and M Stenske (eds), *The European Landscape Convention: Challenges of Participation* (Springer, 2011).

[13] Sections 7–8.

[14] GR Harmsworth and S Awatere, 'Indigenous Māori Knowledge and Perspectives of Ecosystems' in JR Dymod (ed), *Ecosystem Services in New Zealand – Conditions and Trends* (Manaaki Whenua Press, 2013) 274, 281.

[15] DG Newman, *Revisiting the Duty to Consult Aboriginal Peoples* (Purich Publishing, 2014).

[16] Pinkerton, 'Aesthetics' (above n 2) 641–42.

[17] W Bradford, 'A Hideous and Desolate Wilderness (1647)' in CJ Magoc (ed), *Nature and the Environment in American History and Culture* (SR Books, 2002) 24, 25.

the pioneering naturalist and philosopher, wrote in his journal, 'I long for wildness, a nature which I cannot put my foot through, woods where the wood thrush forever sings, where the hours are early morning ones, and there is dew on the grass'.[18] A similar story perhaps could be told about the Eurasian wolf (*Canis lupus lupus*), now enjoying a renaissance in some countries where it was persecuted as vermin until recently, as Europeans come to appreciate in new ways the aesthetic and ecological values of their fauna.[19]

Of course, changes in our adoration of nature may occur unevenly across society: not everyone welcomes wolves in their neighbourhood. Eagles as well, considered by philosopher Glenn Parsons to be 'paradigms of aesthetic excellence in Western culture',[20] as corroborated by their status as national symbols of the United States and Germany. Yet farmers often despise them as a predatory threat to their livestock. Sadly, in 2018 Australian media reported that over 400 dead wedge-tail eagles (*Aquila audax*, the country's largest bird of prey) were found on farms in the state of Victoria, the victims of illegal poisonings and shootings.[21] The conflicts between aesthetic and non-aesthetic values occupy this chapter as a further governance challenge.

Codification of aesthetic values at the international level would appear to raise additional hurdles because of the greater cultural variation on a global scale, along with the inevitable geo-political considerations. Encouragingly, some researchers give reasons for optimism. According to Russ Parsons and Terry Daniel:

> while similarities in landscape preferences tend to be greater among similar cultures […] and less so among dissimilar ones […] even among dissimilar cultures there is evidence of substantial overlap in how people understand and evaluate environments.[22]

Japanese aesthetician Yuriko Saito also sees advantages from globalisation, in that it brings diverse cultural traditions into aesthetics valuation and helps us move beyond the dominant Western paradigm.[23] Also, aesthetics governance in international law rarely confronts the difficulties encountered in the domestic realm because treaties focus more on facilitating rather than regulating behaviour, and nation states have the option to withdraw from regimes not aligned with their interests.

[18] H Thoreau, 22 June 1853, quoted in O Shepard (ed), *The Heart of Thoreau's Journals* (Dover Publications, 1961) 118.

[19] AD Smith, 'On the Trail of the Wolf, Europe's Much Maligned and Misunderstood Predator' *The Guardian* 3 January 2016.

[20] G Parsons, 'The Aesthetic Value of Animals' (2007) 29(2) *Environmental Ethics* 151, 151.

[21] K Lazzaro, 'Farm Worker Who Poisoned 406 Wedge-tailed Eagles in East Gippsland Jailed and Fined' *ABC News* 26 September 2018, www.abc.net.au/news/2018-09-24/man-poisoned-wedge-tailed-eagles-in-gippsland-jailed/10298426.

[22] R Parsons and TR Daniel, 'Good Looking: In Defence of Scenic Landscape Aesthetics' (2002) 60 *Landscape and Urban Planning* 43, 47.

[23] Y Saito, 'Future Directions in Environmental Aesthetics' (2010) 19 *Environmental Values* 373, 385.

Still, we can learn much from international law that is of relevance to codi-fication of aesthetic values anywhere by looking at the practice of the World Heritage Convention 1972, whose goals include protecting outstanding natural beauty of global significance.[24] The 2011 UNESCO manual for *Preparing World Heritage Nominations* provides the following guidance on the interpretation of Criterion (vii) (relating to 'superlative natural phenomena' and 'exceptional natural beauty and aesthetic importance'):

> Two distinct ideas are embodied in [Criterion (vii)]. The first, 'superlative natural phenomena', can often be objectively measured and assessed (e.g. deepest canyon, highest mountain, largest cave system, highest waterfall, etc.).
>
> The second concept, that of 'exceptional natural beauty and aesthetic importance', is harder to assess [...] Merely asserting these qualities without a robust supporting argument is insufficient. The application of this criterion should not be confused with the recognition of the aesthetics of cultural properties and cultural landscapes that is currently expressed through the use of the cultural criteria.
>
> In addition, the nature of this criterion is that the types of properties that are proposed for inscription will have comparable sites distributed on a worldwide, rather than regional basis, so standards applied under this criterion are expected to meet a global standard of proof.
>
> Evaluation in relation to this aspect is based on comparison with properties previously inscribed by the World Heritage Committee under this criterion and, to the extent possible it also involves a comparison of measurable indicators of scenic value.[25]

Unlike the other three natural heritage criteria for nominating properties to the World Heritage List, relating to scientific values of geology (Criterion (viii)), ecosystems (Criterion (ix)) and biodiversity (Criterion (x)), the UNESCO manual thus suggests that the assessment of 'exceptional natural beauty or aesthetic importance' is more subjective and qualitative.

An IUCN-sponsored study in 2013 of implementation of Criterion vii identified some difficulties in articulating natural beauty as a global standard.[26] Very few nominations to the World Heritage List on Criterion vii alone have occurred. The study discerned an unclear relationship between 'superlative natu-ral phenomena' and 'exceptional natural beauty', as both have been interpreted through an aesthetics lens. The IUCN also found that decision makers focus on the visual character of landscapes rather than soundscapes or multi-sensory assessments. Further, natural heritage and aesthetic values have tended to be evaluated under the Convention separately from cultural heritage despite their important interrelationships, and that the Convention's definition of cultural

---

[24] (1972) 11 ILM 1358, art 2.
[25] UNESCO, *Preparing World Heritage Nominations* (UNESCO, 2011) 40.
[26] N Mitchell, *IUCN Study on the Application of Criterion (vii)*, Report for the International Union for the Conservation of Nature, World Heritage Study No 10 (IUCN, 2013).

heritage in Article 1 includes aesthetic factors. The IUCN's study recommended 'improved understanding of the relationship between cultural and natural beauty. [… and to] consider ways of articulating notions of beauty within a wide inter-disciplinary context'.[27]

Another international treaty where even less progress has ensued in defining aesthetic values is the Protocol on Environmental Protection to the Antarctic Treaty 1991. Its guiding environmental principles include '[t]he protection of the Antarctic environment […] including its wilderness and aesthetic values', which are 'fundamental considerations in the planning and conduct of all activities in the Antarctic Treaty area'.[28] The Protocol acknowledges aesthetic values in four other clauses, yet does not define the term, and researchers who have examined implementation of the Protocol since it came into effect in 1998 conclude that the lack of systematic or explicit protection of such values in Antarctica is due in part to this omission.[29] Yet, the literature on Antarctic exploration speaks extensively of the continent's beauty, especially its incredible ice sheets and icebergs.[30] The Protocol's reference to aesthetic values was imported from the environmental provisions of the rejected proposal for a Convention on the Regulation of Antarctic Mineral Resource Activities 1988,[31] where those provisions were intended for regulating the environmental impacts of mining. Today, it is tourists rather than mining that may endanger Antarctica's aesthetic values, and their environmental impacts are ostensibly regulated via the national laws of Antarctic Treaty parties.[32]

Domestic environmental regulation has extensively codified principles and standards relating to its scientific and economic underpinnings, such as on risk assessment, the precautionary principle and cost-benefit analysis. For nature aesthetics, technical indicia such as form and colour have been heavily criticised as a 'shallow and superficial' basis for landscape planning.[33] More acceptable is 'landscape character assessment' (LCA), which attempts to correlate pleasurable aesthetic experiences to specific perceivable characteristics of a landscape.[34] The LCA involves a two-stage process, beginning with characterisation of landscapes into smaller spatial components, followed by judgements about the value of these elements. The process focuses on visual qualities, with only

[27] Ibid, 53.

[28] (1991) 30 ILM 1455, art 3(1).

[29] R Summerson and ID Bishop, 'Aesthetic Value in Antarctica: Beautiful or Sublime?' (2011) 1(2) *Polar Journal* 225.

[30] R Summerson and JL Lieser, 'Opinion: Wilderness and Aesthetic Values in the Antarctic Sea-live Zone' (2018) 8(1) *Polar Journal* 16.

[31] (1888) 27 ILM 868, arts 2.3(d) and 4.2(e).

[32] Eg Australian Antarctic Division, 'Visitor Guidelines', www.antarctica.gov.au/about-antarctica/tourism/visitor-guidelines.

[33] A Carlson, 'On the Possibility of Quantifying Scenic Beauty' (1977) 4 *Landscape and Planning* 131, 158.

[34] G Fairclough, I Herlin and C Swanwick (eds), *Routledge Handbook of Landscape Character Assessment* (Routledge, 2018).

limited attention to aesthetic qualities discerned via other modes such as nature soundscapes.[35]

A number of jurisdictions have developed LCA for land use planning, nature conservation and regulation of development infrastructure. In the United States, a report by Churchward and others for the National Cooperative Highway Research Program advised that the rural landscape characteristics that communities often prefer include: (1) surface water (eg lakes and rivers); (2) variable terrain relief; (3) woodlands occupying some areas; and (4) land use activities that blend into the landscape.[36] In urban settings these considerations will differ. Britain has used LCAs for designating sites of natural beauty pursuant to the National Parks and Access to the Countryside Act 1949 and the Countryside and Rights of Way Act 2000. According to 2011 guidance from Natural England, the main factors relevant to assessing natural beauty are:

> *Landscape quality*: this is a measure of the physical state or condition of the landscape.
>
> *Scenic quality*: the extent to which the landscape appeals to the senses (primarily, but not only, the visual senses).
>
> *Relative wildness*: the degree to which relatively wild character can be perceived in the landscape makes a particular contribution to sense of place.
>
> *Relative tranquillity:* the degree to which relative tranquillity can be perceived in the landscape.
>
> *Natural heritage features*: the influence of natural heritage on the perception of the natural beauty of the area. Natural heritage includes flora, fauna, geological and physiographical features.
>
> *Cultural heritage*: the influence of cultural heritage on the perception of natural beauty of the area and the degree to which associations with particular people, artists, writers or events in history contribute to such perception.[37]

Whereas LCAs focus on positive aesthetic values, regulators use different methods to curb negative aesthetics. These could be permissible noise levels, as measured through acoustic technologies, or water and air pollution tolerances as gauged, inter alia, by reference to visual and olfactory tests.[38] Public health considerations can inform standards developed from such tests.

Regulation of aesthetic issues, both positive and negative, is sometimes tied to 'amenity' values, which include the public's convenience and comfort.

---

[35] See JA Benfield et al, 'Aesthetic and Affective Effects of Vocal and Traffic Noise on Natural Landscape Assessment' (2010) 30 *Journal of Environmental Psychology* 103.

[36] C Churchward et al, *Evaluation of Methodologies for Visual Impact Assessment*, NCHRP report 741 (National Cooperative Highway Research Program, Transportation Board of the National Academies, 2013) 41.

[37] Natural England, *Guidance* (above n 1) 13.

[38] FR Rehm, 'Test Methods for Determining Emission Characteristics of Incinerators' (1965) 15(3) *Journal of the Air Pollution Control Association* 127.

These wider connotations might make amenity values an inappropriate surrogate for nature aesthetics because, for instance, they can fail to conserve a natural environment against certain types of development (eg eco-tourism facilities) that offer visitors convenience and comfort yet impair that environment physically and visually. Amenity has also proved just as tricky to codify because, like the aesthetic, it hinges heavily on context and perception. Consider how the definition of a 'tree' has perplexed UK courts adjudicating on tree preservation orders to protect amenity values. The former Town and Country Planning Act 1947 authorised such orders 'in the interest of amenity', but did not define 'tree'.[39] The issue came up in an action brought by Kent County Council against a landholder accused of illegal felling.[40] Recognising that the legislation aimed to protect amenity values, Lord AT Denning advised:

> Furthermore, I must say that there is an ambiguity in this Act. [...] We are not told what is a 'tree'. Many bushes and saplings are certainly not 'trees'. In woodland like this, it is often, from the agricultural point of view (especially in a derelict area such as this) very important to get out the bushes, scrub and saplings and to replant – as, indeed, Mr Batchelor was doing. There is no definition of 'tree'. I should have thought that in woodland it ought to be something over seven or eight inches in diameter.[41]

This might seem a rather arbitrary conclusion, but the legislation protected trees for their amenity value rather than scientific or conservation reasons. In another English case, in 2009, dealing with tree preservation orders under a later iteration of the legislation, where evidence was received from arborists, Justice R Cranston concluded, contrary to Denning, that the size of the tree did not matter and that a tree could include the smallest sapling, reaching this decision in part because of the importance of protecting 'regeneration or new planting'.[42] He acknowledged the importance of 'amenity' values (a word uttered 17 times in his judgment) but reached a different conclusion from Denning in light of his belief that small trees can grow into larger, more attractive specimens.

Other jurisdictions such as New Zealand have also shown interest in framing aesthetics around amenity value.[43] Its Resource Management Act 1991 obliges authorities to consider 'amenity values' when making decisions, a term it defines as 'those natural or physical qualities and characteristics of an area that contribute to people's appreciation of its pleasantness, aesthetic coherence, and cultural and recreational attributes'.[44] New Zealand courts suggest that

[39] 10 & 11 Geo VI c. 51, s 26(1).

[40] *Kent County Council v Batchelor* (1976) 33 P&CR 185.

[41] Ibid, 189.

[42] *Palm Developments Ltd v Secretary of State for Communities and Local Government* [2009] EWHC 220 (Admin), para 21.

[43] Some of this discussion on New Zealand precedents draws on Barrett, 'Law, Aesthetics and the Environment' (above n 11).

[44] Section 2(1).

judgements about aesthetic and amenity values can be objective. In *Society for the Protection of Auckland City and Waterfront Inc v Auckland City Council* (2005), the High Court observed, in a case involving a proposed 36-storey office tower, that the legislation 'makes the aesthetic an indispensable concern in every planning regime and for every consent authority' and the 'the proposition that aesthetics is taste by another name, and that taste is irretrievably subjective and individual [...] is at odds with the ordinary principles of architecture and design, and of planning'.[45] Perhaps less confident on this view, the New Zealand Ministry of Environment has advised against 'simple "bulk and location" rules to address amenity' because the determination of amenity value is highly place-based, and thus requires careful delineation in local land use plans customised to local community interests.[46]

In closing on this issue, we should recognise that the question whether the law can, and should, codify environmental aesthetic values (or amenity values) does not answer another related consideration, of whether the law should seek to actively shape aesthetic appreciation rather than merely respond to pre-existing community preferences. If we are to channel aesthetic preferences in ways that strengthen environmental governance, and curb environmentally inappropriate tastes, it will surely not suffice for the law to be a bystander. Chapter 8 examines how the law could avoid that situation.

III. COMPETING VALUES

Not only do environmental aesthetics resist distillation into discrete legal formulae, aesthetics must seemingly compete with other fields of knowledge and values that inhabit environmental law, notably from the natural sciences and economics. Their vernacular, associated with influential ideas such as the precautionary principle, financial incentives and cost-benefit analysis, may not only ignore aesthetic values, but sometimes conflict with them.

Environmental law deals infrequently with simple binary choices, like whether to dam or conserve a scenic river.[47] More commonly, it adjudicates disputes where trade-offs can be brokered. Selective cutting rather than mass clearing may mitigate the aesthetic trauma of forestry operations, as also can maintaining tree coverage along roadsides to conceal logging scars. Objections to high-rise towers that would block scenic views may be moderated by reducing the buildings' height or mass, and using different construction materials, although such concessions might make the developments commercially unviable. Mining can be subject to post-project rehabilitation requirements that restore landscape appearance.

---

[45] [2005] NZRMA 155, para 70.
[46] New Zealand, Ministry for the Environment, 'Amenity Findings', www.mfe.govt.nz/publications/towns-and-cities/review-urban-design-case-law/4-amenity-findings.
[47] G Law, *The River Runs Free* (Penguin, 2008).

These options of course don't always succeed. Entrenched community opposition to nuclear power plants and forestry pulp mills can readily lead to an impasse.[48] In Tasmania, where I live, a feisty controversy over a proposed cable car from Hobart to Mount Wellington (Kunanyi) that looms over the city has been fought largely over aesthetics, which the developer has sought to appease by proposing a less visually intrusive route. Some locals remain steadfast against any cable car, which they view as inherently incompatible with the spiritual and aesthetic values they attach to the mountain.[49] Courts sometimes get embroiled in these disputes. In the Taralga wind farm litigation in Australia, as discussed in the previous chapter, the New South Wales (NSW) Land and Environment Court adjudicated over the anticipated aesthetic impacts of the proposed development that required also taking into account biodiversity impacts (eg bird strikes), the provision of renewable energy to combat global warming, and non-environmental policy considerations (notably job creation).

I can canvass a few examples in greater detail to illustrate these challenges. Consider disputes over control of feral horses, known as 'brumbies', in Australia's alpine region straddling the states of NSW and Victoria.[50] Over 6,000 of them roam it, bringing aesthetic and cultural pleasure to their admirers, but they are perceived to be a wrecker of delicate ecosystems and alpine beauty by their opponents. Scientists have blamed the beasts' hooves and grazing habits for damaging terrain supposedly protected in national parks, and in November 2018 the horses were declared by the NSW government's Threatened Species Scientific Committee a 'key threatening process', jeopardising 34 native plant and animal species.[51] Yet, this government's Kosciuszko Wild Horse Heritage Act 2018, enacted a few months earlier, proclaimed the horses' heritage value. According to the NSW Minister sponsoring the legislation:

> Wild brumbies have been roaming the Australian alps for almost 200 years and they are part of the cultural fabric and folklore of the high country. I have said in this House before that nothing is more synonymous with the Australian outdoor lifestyle than the brumby, from *The Man from Snowy River* to the integral role that the Snowy Mountains bush horses played in the Australian Light Horse campaign during World War I. They even featured at the opening ceremony of the Sydney 2000 Olympics.[52]

[48] H Caldicott, *Nuclear Power is Not the Answer* (The New Press, 2006).

[49] T O'Connor, 'Mt Wellington Cable Car: Ups and Downs of Hobart's Most Controversial Development Proposal' *ABC News* 5 April 2017, www.abc.net.au/news/2017-04-04/hobart-cable-car-explained/8389310.

[50] R French, 'Those in Search of Natural Beauty Fear a Land Trampled Under Hoof' *Weekend Australian* 8–9 December 2018, 7.

[51] Australian Associated Press, 'NSW Deems Alpine Brumbies a Threat to Plants After Passing Laws to Protect Them' *The Guardian* 30 November 2018.

[52] J Barilaro, 'Kosciuszko Wild Horse Heritage Bill 2018: Second Reading Speech', NSW Legislative Assembly Hansard, 23 May 2018.

Figure 3.1 Wild Brumbies at Snowy Wilderness retreat in Jindabyne NSW, Australia, 2003; photograph by Claire Charters; licensed under Creative Commons

The legislation allows for managing the brumbies' numbers, without shooting, by mustering and trapping for re-homing.[53] Controversially, it provides for management direction of the horses to shift from the NSW National Parks and Wildlife Service to a Wild Horse Management Community Steering Group, a move that gives less assurance for nature conservation.[54]

In Victoria, where the current government is less enamoured by feral horses, community opposition has grown to its plans to remove over a thousand of them from conservation areas. The Australian Brumby Alliance, in December 2018, applied for a court injunction to stall the plan, asserting that the horses pervade the 'stories, legends and myths of the mountains and mountain lifestyle'.[55] Animal welfare groups also oppose the culling; Save the Brumbies advocates the 'humane, controlled management and the abolition of shooting of wild horses in national parks and public lands Australia wide'.[56] Conversely, the Reclaim

---

[53] NSW National Parks and Wildlife Service, *Kosciuszko National Park Horse Management Plan* (Department of Environment and Climate Change, 2008) 25, 27.

[54] See in particular s 12 and Sch 1.

[55] Australian Brumby Alliance, media release, 7 December 2018.

[56] Save the Brumbies, 'About Us', www.savethebrumbies.org/about-us.

Kosci group wants governments to cull feral horses, which it believes not only harm ecological values but undermine the parks' 'natural beauty' by creating 'degraded and dung fouled picnic and camping areas, polluted and damaged streams'.[57]

Controversy over wild horse management is not unique to Australia, as significant populations, called 'mustangs', inhabit parts of the United States. In 1971 the US Congress enacted the Wild Free-Roaming Horse and Burros Act, which recognised these creatures 'as symbols of the historic and pioneer spirit of the West, which continue to contribute to the diversity of life forms within the Nation and enrich the lives of the American people'.[58] Like the NSW legislation, this statute aims not to exterminate wild horses but to authorise their population control, mainly through humane capture and release into private care. Similar public controversies over the aesthetic, cultural and ecological status of wild horses rage in the United States, although with one key difference from Australia, being that because horses were once native to North America, until going extinct about 12,000 years ago, mustang advocates see their presence today as ecologically benign.[59]

Tenacious conflicts over animal welfare, heritage and aesthetics can overwhelm public consultation and management planning. Conservationists believe that trapping and re-homing are ineffective in controlling booming wild horse populations, which supposedly can only be efficiently done by aerial mass shooting. The thought of dead horses strewn across the landscape aesthetically repulses horse lovers, rivalling conservationists' wish to remove the horses for their aesthetic disfiguration of the landscape. Equally, the pro-horse lobby is enamoured by the aesthetics of the power and grace of *Equus ferus* with its lustrous mane and shimmering coat.

Another telling example of the conflicted aesthetic and non-aesthetic values confronting environmental law concerns cosmetic pesticides. In towns and cities worldwide one encounters the ubiquitous, manicured lawns, some entirely synthetic. The lawn became a potent aesthetic symbol of post-war affluence and domesticity in the West, as home ownership became a reality for the rising middle classes. Lawns have also invaded public spaces including parks, cemeteries, golf courses and along roads. In the United States, researchers in 2003 estimated that 23 per cent of the entire urban land area was covered by lawns.[60] American lawns apparently exceed the land area of any single food crop, yet

---

[57] Reclaim Kosci, 'Feral Horses in Kosciuszko: Busting the Myths', https://reclaimkosci.org.au/myths-v-facts.

[58] Public Law 92–195, preamble.

[59] Saving America's Mustangs, http://savingamericasmustangs.org.

[60] P Robbins and T Birkenholtz, 'Turfgrass Revolution: Measuring the Expansion of the American Lawn' (2003) 20 *Land Use Policy* 181.

provide no sustenance.[61] Lawns have caught on in many other countries; a recent study of Swedish cities found that lawn cover had increased by 50 per cent over 50 years and now occupies 22.5 per cent of the sampled towns.[62] These turfs cost time and money to maintain, requiring frequent watering, spraying, mowing and landscaping. Typically comprising non-native grasses, lawns also contribute 'to the homogenisation of urban landscapes and loss of urban biodiversity'.[63]

Though largely indifferent to the ecological deprivation lawns cause, many municipal authorities cherish the aesthetic protocols of lawns associated with neatness, uniformity and simplicity. Through their bye-laws, they readily oblige householders to prevent dishevelled vegetation. Consider the City of Ipswich in Queensland, which advises its residents that:

> Overgrown vegetation is visible from outside the property and is known to cause a significantly lower visual standard in the area, due to the visible lack of maintenance. Overgrown grass also has the potential to harbour or attract vermin and reptiles.[64]

Stiff penalties can apply for violations; one Australian municipality threatened a local resident with a hefty fine of $A5,890 for an unsightly lawn.[65] Equally vigilant, the township of Markey, Michigan, has enacted a bespoke Tall Grass and Weed Ordinance that declares: 'tall grass and weeds can have a blighting effect on neighbourhoods and can provide a refuge for vermin and insects'.[66] It goes on to oblige landowners to keep lawn grass below eight inches in height.

In recent years the aesthetic aura of tidy lawns has begun to be tested by community anxiety of the hazards of applying pesticides to keep them weed-free. The challenge gathered legal backing when local governments started banning cosmetic pesticide use. In 1999 the small town of Hudson, Quebec led the way, after a local dermatologist raised concerns about the health of her patients that she believed was related to heavy pesticide use on gardens and lawns. Hudson's anti-pesticide bye-law was challenged by two lawn care businesses, Spray Tech and ChemLawn, whose case was eventually decided by the Supreme Court of Canada.

The decision of the Supreme Court to uphold the pesticide bye-law, even if a chemical product or practice is approved by the federal government, inspired many other municipalities and jurisdictions within and beyond Canada to

---

[61] K D'Costa, 'The American Obsession with Lawns' *Scientific American* 3 May 2017, https://blogs.scientificamerican.com/anthropology-in-practice/the-american-obsession-with-lawns.

[62] M Hedblom et al, 'Estimating Urban Lawn Cover in Space and Time: Case Studies in Three Swedish Cities' (2017) 20(5) *Urban Ecosystems* 1109.

[63] M Ignatieva et al, 'Lawn as a Cultural and Ecological Phenomenon: A Conceptual Framework for Transdisciplinary Research' (2015) 14(2) *Urban Forestry and Urban Greening* 383, 385.

[64] City of Ipswich, 'Overgrown and Unsightly Land', www.ipswich.qld.gov.au/residents/nuisances-and-complaints/overgrown-properties.

[65] L Starkey, 'Resident Could've Been Fined $5890 for Overgrown Lawn' *Daily Mercury* 22 March 2016.

[66] Ordinance No 44, 2009, s 2.

follow suit.[67] Some 200 towns in Canada have done so as of 2019, and Ontario instituted a province-wide ban of some 300 lawn and garden products in 2009 with limited exceptions.[68] The pesticide-free movement has spread to other countries, and some have imposed sweeping bans on private and public property. The European Pesticides Free Towns Network is facilitating such actions across Europe.[69] Some US municipalities are doing likewise, such as Richmond (California) and Takoma Park (Maryland), but most US states have a pre-emption law that prevent municipalities from regulating pesticides in their locality, and chemical and lawn-care companies are lobbying and litigating to counter the crusade. In August 2017 a judge struck down a Montgomery County's anti-pesticide bye-law on the ground it was pre-empted by Maryland state law.[70]

The governance of urban lawns thus pitches a variety of stakeholders, including concerned parents, health professionals and environmental activists, against chemical and lawn-care businesses wrestling for control over local environmental policy. For the opponents of change, their arguments revolve around 'nanny-state intrusion', property owners' rights and the aesthetic appeal of the hallowed suburban lawn.[71] While proponents of the pesticide bans rest their case on environmental and health concerns, they have yet to mount any serious alternate to lawn aesthetics. It is sometimes not enough to get rid of lawn care pesticides; the very notion of green lawns needs to be challenged as an ecological barren ideal that hinders the return of biodiversity back to our cities and towns. Lawns also consume much water and require regular trimming with fossil fuel-powered mowers.

The two principal mechanisms by which the law attempts to reconcile competing values and appease opponents are through opportunities for public participation in environmental decision-making, and decision-making informed by scientific evidence, such as that gathered from EIA studies. Community participation is a strongly endorsed value of many environmental law instruments, as affirmed by the Aarhus Convention.[72] Public participation allows for identification and deliberation over contested aesthetic and non-aesthetic values. Participation is also sometimes melded with procedures for science-based decisions, notably in land use planning, risk assessments and EIA studies. While such processes often fail to generate an outcome or compromise that meets everyone's preferences, they can still result in broadly legitimate decisions if the processes are perceived to be fair. Where 'noisy' advocates or well-resourced

---

[67] *114957 Canada Ltée (Spraytech, Société d'arrosage) v Hudson (Town)* [2001] 2 SCR 241.

[68] Ontario Regulation 63/09 and Cosmetic Pesticides Ban Act, 2008, SO 2009, c 11.

[69] See www.pesticide-free-towns.info.

[70] *Complete Lawn Care Inc v Montgomery County*, 427200-V (Md Cir Ct, 3 August 2017).

[71] B Turque, 'Proposed Ban on Cosmetic Pesticides Causes Turf War in Montgomery County' *Washington Post* 8 March 2015.

[72] Convention on Access to Information, Public Participation in Decision-making and Access to Justice in Environmental Matters, (1999) 39 ILM 517.

litigants skew the outcome, the outcome may not however be perceived as fair. The closing chapter returns to these themes.

IV. BIASED AESTHETICS

Like any quality in life, our aesthetic judgements are eclectically diverse, from that we find mesmerisingly beautiful to our distaste of the dull or ugly. In other words, we have aesthetic preferences and biases. Having them isn't objectionable, for to admire everything with the same intensity and feeling would render aesthetics rather unhelpful for guiding sensory appreciation of the world. While these aesthetic biases probably don't matter when it comes to reflecting on what we like or dislike when visiting an art gallery, they do for the natural places and wildlife we encounter.

The history of nature conservation shows that we tend to tend to accord the greatest legal protection to places we admire as scenically spectacular, like Mount Kilimanjaro and the Grand Canyon, and likewise with wildlife, such as elephants and dolphins, that we cherish as charismatic. Conversely, the aesthetically mundane can struggle to gain our attention. The demise of the Australian rodent, *Melomys rubicola*, officially declared in February 2019 as the world's first mammal extinction from human-induced climate change, was aggravated by the failure to implement an earlier prepared recovery plan. According to John Woinarski, a scientist who researched the species, 'it suffered from living a long way away from anywhere else, and being a rat and being not particularly attractive'.[73] A 2006 survey of 20 years of conservation science found that aesthetics bias permeates even among the supposedly most objective of professions: marine, tundra, and desert biomes were least likely to be studied by scientists despite their conservation importance, while amphibians were understudied compared to other, less endangered taxonomic groups.[74]

Today, World Heritage listing affords the premier accolade for nature's aesthetic splendours. Consider the following official statement of the outstanding aesthetic virtues of Australia's Great Barrier Reef, on the World Heritage List:

> From the air, the vast mosaic patterns of reefs, islands and coral cays produce an unparalleled aerial panorama of seascapes comprising diverse shapes and sizes. The Whitsunday Islands provide a magnificent vista of green vegetated islands and spectacular sandy beaches spread over azure waters. This contrasts with the vast mangrove forests in Hinchinbrook Channel, and the rugged vegetated mountains and lush rainforest gullies that are periodically cloud-covered on Hinchinbrook Island.
>
> [...]

---

[73] Quoted in An Australian Rodent Has Become the First Climate Change Mammal Extinction' *ABC (Triple J Hack)*, 20 February 2019, www.abc.net.au/triplej/programs/hack/bramble-cay-melomys-first-climate-change-mammal-extinction/10830080.

[74] JL Lawler et al, 'Conservation Science: A 20-Year Report Card' (2006) 4(9) *Frontiers in Ecology and the Environment* 473.

Beneath the ocean surface, there is an abundance and diversity of shapes, sizes and colours; for example, spectacular coral assemblages of hard and soft corals, and thousands of species of reef fish provide a myriad of brilliant colours, shapes and sizes. The internationally renowned Cod Hole near Lizard Island is one of many significant tourist attractions. Other superlative natural phenomena include the annual coral spawning, migrating whales, nesting turtles, and significant spawning aggregations of many fish species.

Another enclave of World Heritage superlative beauty is Scotland's St Kilda archipelago, whose official statement extols:

> The scenery of the St Kilda archipelago is particularly superlative and has resulted from its volcanic origin followed by weathering and glaciation to produce a dramatic island landscape. The precipitous cliffs and sea stacks as well as its underwater scenery are concentrated in a compact group that is singularly unique.[75]

Impressive descriptions! Yet, this aesthetic accolade implies another realm that's aesthetically ordinary or dull, and thus putatively less deserving of legal protection. How can our aesthetic preferences for extraordinary nature co-exist with ensuring legal protection for the aesthetically 'deprived'? Few laws match the even-handedness of the European Landscape Convention 2000,[76] which extends its protections to 'landscapes that might be considered outstanding as well as everyday or degraded landscapes',[77] a concession that reflects that the aesthetically deprived might have cultural or ecological value on other criteria, or be capable of restoration.

Places of aesthetic grandeur do not necessarily correlate with ecological or biological significance, while places lacking beauty may have it. Australian biologist Tim Low in *The New Nature* explains that wilderness parks – often established for aesthetic reasons – do not necessarily have the greatest reservoirs of biodiversity, while towns and farms can harbour much of it. He remarks that the water ponds around the Olympic Games facilities in Sydney accommodate a thriving colony of rare frogs,[78] and that his own urban backyard and local creek support more reptiles and rainforest species than the 'biodiversity desert' of Tasmania's southwest wilderness.[79] Indeed, the city of Brisbane, Queensland, with 2.5 million residents, has 27 species of snakes compared to just three in all of Tasmania. The Australian brush turkey (*Alectura lathami*) now flourishes in the midst of Brisbane and Sydney, where it benefits from weed-infested gullies that shield young birds from predators.[80] Thus, we should debunk

[75] UNESCO World Heritage Centre, St Kilda, https://whc.unesco.org/en/list/387.
[76] European Treaty Series, No 176.
[77] Ibid, art 2.
[78] T Low, *The New Nature* (Penguin Books, 2017) 23.
[79] Ibid, 41.
[80] A Beaini, 'Why Brush Turkeys are Headed to a Sydney Suburb Near You' *Sydney Morning Herald* 2 January 2018.

the rhetoric that 'nature has to be big and remote and [aesthetically] pristine to count'.[81]

Furthermore, our aesthetic preferences can collide with nature conservationists' advice. One telling example is the furore over the removal of exotic pine plantations fringing Cape Town's famed Table Mountain. Local residents opposed plans of South African National Parks to fell a plantation of pines, which residents wished to retain for their aesthetic and recreational benefits. In 2017 the High Court barred removal of the trees without adequate public consultation, as confirmed by the Supreme Court of Appeal the following year. A local NGO called Parkscape led the challenge to protect the shaded park, in an iconic, World Heritage listed property. Judge PAL Gamble agreed that 'there can be no doubt that there are important ecological issues at play' but 'these need to be balanced against [...] the public's undisputed right of quiet enjoyment of an important public amenity'.[82]

Our love of running water, its sight and sound, also can diverge from nature's natural condition. Authorities managing Australia's largest river system, the Murray-Darling basin, have through dams and weirs reversed the natural cycle – that creates plump, flowing rivers in winter but desiccated, muddy pools over summer. Rivers in southeast Australia tend naturally to run low during the hot, dry summers owing to high evaporation and rainfall patterns, yet for aesthetic and economic reasons, authorities engineered them to stay flowing to appease boaters, fishers and farmers. The recent community uproar over unsightly dry riverbeds during the basin's drought in 2018–19 ignores that these events partly reflect landscape's natural rhythm.[83]

A place of extraordinary aesthetic appeal will also not necessarily maintain such status. The discourse on wilderness, and its frequent association with sublime or picturesque aesthetics, was an artefact of nationalism and cultural identity formation in North America, and later in Australia and New Zealand. Orvar Löfgren explains that lacking Europe's rich historical ruins and cultural past (apart from Indigenous peoples, who were repressed), these 'New World' countries turned to their natural heritage, 'cathedrals of nature', as markers of national identity.[84] While their splendid landscapes have sometimes secured protection in national parks, the aesthetically 'ordinary' remain in private hands, outside of the parks system, and thus at risk from economic exploitation or anti-social behaviour.[85]

---

[81] Low, *The New Nature*, 42.

[82] *Parkscape v MTO Forestry and South African National Parks*, Case No 15910.2016, High Court, 1 March 2017, para 50.

[83] F Rochford, 'The Irrigator's Poet: Henry Lawson and Nature as an "Outside Reality"', Legal Theory and History Seminar Series, University of Tasmania, 28 February 2019.

[84] O Löfgren, 'The Nationalization of Culture' (1989) 21 *Ethnologia Europaea*: 2.

[85] BJ Richardson and T Baxter, 'Governance of Tasmania's Private Bushlands: Artful Ensemble or Hodgepodge?' (2016) 33(1) *Environmental and Planning Law Journal* 47.

We also have aesthetic biases for animals. In their marketing and public outreach, environmental NGOs commonly associate themselves with majestic or endearing creatures, such as panda bears and lions.[86] Scholarly research confirms preferences for certain species, as verified by studies of wildlife tourism, and visits to zoos and aquaria.[87] We particularly prefer animals that are human-like and tame, exhibiting features and behaviour that we more easily understand.[88] Other animals such as: 'penguins, pandas, seal pups, monkeys, dogs, cats and many other "higher" vertebrates also evoke inordinate amounts of sympathy. They are easy to anthropomorphise'.[89] Stephen Kellert, a leading researcher in this field, found public affection for some species of birds, insects and fish species far removed from human characteristics, such as butterflies and tropical fish admired for their beauty.[90] Dangerous creatures, such as tigers, can also be highly appealing to view at zoos. Research on children's books reports that the animals most featured include horses, rabbits, dogs, cats, lions and bears.[91] Conversely, studies show that invertebrates, notably spiders, are widely disliked.[92] So too we loathe snakes.[93] Clearly, our aesthetic preferences for animals are intertwined with a range of non-aesthetic issues, such as their intelligence, threat to people, and cultural and historical significance.

Aesthetic biases also colour our dietary choices. The perceptions of beauty applied to food can levy an ugly price on nature. Consumers, at least according to supermarkets that sell to them, are unwilling to buy fruits and vegetables of the 'wrong' shape, hue or size, resulting in the dumping of much farm produce. Up to 40 per cent of Australia's banana crop is discarded by farmers annually not because the bananas are inedible but because 'they don't fit standards set by supermarkets. Basically they are too bent, too straight, too long, too short, too fat or too thin'.[94] Apart from the loss of food that could support the hungry millions around the world, such waste also degrades nature through deforestation and agri-chemicals to support banana plantations, as well as composting landfills that generate methane, a potent greenhouse gas (GHG).

[86] B Clucas, K McHugh and T Caro, 'Flagship Species on Covers of US Conservation and Nature Magazines' (2008) 17 *Biodiversity Conservation* 1517.

[87] WM Bart, 'A Hierarchy Among Attitudes Toward Animals' (1972) 3(4) *Journal of Environmental Education* 4; SR Kellert, 'Contemporary Values of Wildlife in American Society' in WW Shaw and I Zube (eds), *Wildlife Values* (US Forest Service, 1980) 31; WE Hammit, JN Dulin and GR Wells, 'Determinants of Quality Wildlife Viewing in Great Smoky Mountains National Park' (1993) 21(1) *Wildlife Society Bulletin* 21.

[88] Ibid.

[89] Quoted in J Serpell, *In the Company of Animals: A Study of Human-Animal Relationships* (Basil Blackwell, 1986) 141.

[90] SR Kellert, 'Perceptions of Animals in America' in RJ Hoage (ed), *Perceptions of Animals in American Culture* (Smithsonian Press, 1989) 5.

[91] TA More, 'Wildlife Preferences and Children's Books' (1979) 7(4) *Wildlife Society Bulletin* 274.

[92] SR Kellert, 'Values and Perceptions of Invertebrates' (1993) 7(4) *Conservation Biology* 845.

[93] B Woods, 'Beauty and the Beast: Preferences for Animals in Australia' (2000) 11(2) *Journal of Tourism Studies* 25, 34.

[94] M Lallo, 'War on Waste: Craig Reucassel Confronts Supermarkets Over "Ugly" Bananas' *Sydney Morning Herald* 11 May 2017.

The law can exacerbate misguided food aesthetics. Previous EU market standards stipulated acceptable parameters for the size and shape of many fruits and vegetables sold to consumers, and while law reform has shed some of these standards, aesthetic stipulations remain on ten items. The relevant European Commission regulation decrees that bananas should be 'free from malformation or abnormal curvature', and it classifies bananas into three different categories according to their aesthetic imperfection.[95] The regulation serves not to ban misshapen bananas but rather to set grading standards so that importers and retailers understand what they will receive when ordering them. Yet still, about one-third of fruit and vegetables sold within the EU is discarded annually because it fails aesthetic expectations, according to a 2018 University of Edinburgh study.[96]

Consumers, however, can be educated to accept aesthetically 'disfigured' produce. With increasing awareness of the environmental and health benefits of organic food, some consumers now see imperfectly shaped fruits and vegetables as not only tolerable but a sign of their nutritiousness. The market for 'ugly' food also benefits from its cheaper prices. Some boutique food delivery companies have found demand for cosmetically flawed produce, such as the San Francisco-based Imperfect Produce that sells some of the estimated 20 per cent of US food wasted for aesthetic reasons.[97] In France, supermarket giant Intermarché has launched a commercially successful campaign called 'Inglorious Fruits and Vegetables', in which aesthetic rejects retail at a 30 per cent discount.[98]

Our aesthetic biases also give no assurance for conservation of the most beautiful. Nature's aesthetic gems, including animal furs and feathers, and precious stones, attract exploitation. Mining to extract gems and gold disfigures landscapes and pollutes their soil and water, all with the imprimatur of the law. Animals have long been hunted for their skins, tusks and other aesthetic commodities that we seek for decorating our bodies or homes, sometimes also with the backing of the law. Plants do not escape either, with orchids and other pretty species pillaged by collectors. Taxidermy displays in natural history museums and hunters' trophy lodges memorialise the aesthetics of vanquished wildlife, which Chapter 4 considers.[99] The persecution of the beautiful inhabits many cultures, not just in the West; many Indigenous peoples traditionally adorned themselves with furs and feathers as symbols of

---

[95] EU Commission Regulation No 1333/2011, L 336/23, 20 December 2011, annex I, II.A.

[96] S Porter et al, 'Available Food Losses and Associated Production-phase Greenhouse Gas Emissions Arising from Application of Cosmetic Standards to Fresh Fruit and Vegetables in Europe and the UK' (2018) 201 *Journal of Cleaner Production* 869.

[97] Discussed in J Bhatia. 'Ugly Fruits and Vegetables: Why You Have to Learn to Love Them' *The Guardian* 18 November 2016.

[98] See http://itm.marcelww.com/inglorious.

[99] ST Asma, *Stuffed Animals and Pickled Heads: The Culture of Natural History Museums* (Oxford University Press, 2003).

chiefly status.[100] Beauty can thus serve humanity's desire to dominate nature as much as to protect it.

Likewise, residential development and eco-tourism exerts a heavy toil on nature's most beautiful environments. High-rise, high-density seaside resorts can end up devouring the very aesthetic qualities that motivated their development in the first place; visitors expecting tranquil beaches and panoramic views instead encounter bustling shopping centres, noisy traffic and endless, ugly concrete. The northern and western Mediterranean, such as Spain's Costa del Sol and Italy's Adriatic coastline, epitomises this mania of poorly-regulated development, which not only destroys natural beauty but wrecks coastal ecosystems such as sand dunes and wetlands vital for migratory birds.[101]

This blight afflicts more than just a few touristy enclaves. No part of the planet escapes the eco-tourism industry's reach, with cruises to Antarctica bringing 51,000 tourists in the 2017–18 season, up 17 per cent from the year before.[102] The national parks movement, born in the late nineteenth century, arose as much out of a desire to promote visitor opportunities as to preserve nature on scientific grounds. Yellowstone, the world's first national park, attracted over four million visitors in 2018 compared to just 300 when it was inaugurated in 1872. Government marketing also fuels mass eco-tourism, and some states even go so far as to define their national identity around it, as with New Zealand's '100% Pure' tourism marketing slogan.[103] Eco-tourism can enrich visitors' environmental knowledge and promote sympathetic behaviours, but the industry also brings collateral damage, not only locally from tourist infrastructure, traffic, noise and waste, but also globally from travellers' GHG emissions. A study published in *Nature Climate Change* attributed 8 per cent of world GHG emissions from 2009 to 2013 to the tourist industry (though not all of this is eco-tourism).[104]

Our bias for nature's aesthetic wonders is matched by our desire to destroy its alter ego, the ugly or aesthetically disagreeable. Such 'negative aesthetics' typically co-exist with other issues or concerns, such as economic costs or personal safety, but they can help to reinforce rationales to exterminate wildlife or tame landscapes on these other grounds.

Some natural environments make people fearful or anxious, notably swamps or impenetrable jungles associated with supernatural forces, in contrast to the comfort people find in manicured parks and gardens. Some may also fear the

[100] AM DeMeo, 'Access to Eagles and Eagle Parts: Environmental Protection v. Native American Free Exercise of Religion' (1995) 22 *Hastings Constitutional Law Quarterly* 771.
[101] S Castle, 'Crushing the Costa del Concrete' *The Independent* 25 July 2005.
[102] 'Antarctica Tourism Numbers Surge' *Cruise Industry News* 30 April 2018, www.cruiseindustrynews.com/cruise-news/18920-antarctica-tourism-numbers-surge.html.
[103] See NJ Morgan, A Pritchard and R Piggott, 'New Zealand, 100% Pure: The Creation of a Powerful Niche Destination Brand' (2002) 9(4/5) *Journal of Brand Management* 335.
[104] MF Lenzen et al, 'The Carbon Footprint of Global Tourism' (2018) 8 *Nature Climate Change* 522.

former for harbouring dangerous beasts such as wolves and yetis. These anxieties about nature's forbidding character permeate popular culture. The 1999 horror film *The Blair Witch Project* revolved around a young trio stalked by an unseen terror while lost in the woods. Nature also can evoke violence and fury associated with 'acts of God', as depicted in Hollywood disaster movies like the 2004 blockbuster *The Day After Tomorrow*, which depicts apocalyptic climate change. In literature, Sebastian Junger's *The Perfect Storm*, also made into a film, evokes similar themes about tempestuous natural forces. While fear of some natural phenomena, explains legal scholar Akhtar-Khavari,[105] may have positive benefits in fostering less anthropocentric conceptions of the natural world, by helping people to become more aware of their embedded existence within that world rather than mastery of it, negative aesthetics can also fuel destructive deeds.

The law augments negative aesthetics by singling out the unwanted for persecution, from drainage of swamps to designation of vermin. Although nearly genetically identical to that we affectionately call 'man's (sic) best friend', wolves have been systematically hunted since the Middle Ages, often aided by official bounties. Apart from fear of their predation on livestock, negative perceptions of wolves have been tied up with religious beliefs, fairy tales (*Little Red Riding Hood*) and tropes (eg 'a wolf in sheep's clothing'). In European folklore the wolf was a widespread metaphor for vice, and in the guise of the legendry 'werewolf' was a nocturnal servant of the Devil, a negative mythology that continues in some contemporary horror films such as *Wolves* (2014). By the early twentieth century, wolves had disappeared from much of Western and Central Europe, and by the 1930s bounty hunters had largely extirpated the creature from the continental United States. The aesthetic perception of wolves has been bound up in the war against them; as one avid Alaskan hunter put it, they are a 'stinking dirty cowardly predator'.[106]

In recent decades the wolf's fortunes have been revived for legal, economic and aesthetic reasons. European wolf populations began to recover from the 1960s as traditional farming economies waned, which reduced the need to persecute wolves while allowing wolf prey populations such as deer to increase. Scandinavian wolf populations were some of the first to rebound, aided by legal protection. Wolves have also begun recolonising Germany, France and the Benelux countries. In 1974 the US government gave the grey wolf protected listing under the Endangered Species Act, and in 1995 the US Fish and Wildlife Service began reintroducing wolves to Yellowstone from Canada. As wolf

---

[105] A Akhtar-Khavari, 'Fear and Ecological (In)Justice in Edvard Munch's the Scream of Nature' (2015) 2 *Nordic Journal of Law and Social Research* 130.
[106] P Coates, '"Unusually Cunning, Vicious and Treacherous": The Extermination of the Wolf in United States History' in M Levine and P Roberts (eds), *The Massacre in History* (Berghahn Books, 1999) 163, 179.

Figure 3.2 *Little Red Riding Hood and the Wolf*, 1904, Arpád Schmidhammer (1857–1921), illustration; New York Public Library

populations apparently rebounded, their legal status in the lower 48-states began to be adjusted after 2003 to allow for some management and removal of wolves that kill livestock or deer populations. Yet, with risk of indiscriminate hunting, environmental groups have challenged in court any watering down of the legal protections for wolves, with mixed success. Some 188 wolves were culled in Idaho over its 2009–10 hunting season.[107] Government agencies have also become involved, with the US Forest Service and Idaho Department of Fish and Game exterminating some grey wolf packs in 2014. Authorisation of wolf culling as a population 'management' strategy tends to provide cover for increased illegal poaching and stirs negative public attitudes towards wolves.[108] The aesthetics of wolves are also improving in popular Western culture, acquiring a more majestic and benign reputation. In his book *Wolves of the Shadowlands*, Matthew Manyak describes one: 'its light, understanding gaze cast from its magnificent sapphire eyes, the beauty and grace of its howl as it rose into the night'.[109] But this trend remains work-in-progress, with films such as *The Grey* (2012) doing for wolves what *Jaws* (1975) did for sharks.

---

[107] T Winckler, 'Wolf Hunts End, But Not the Fight' Earthjustice, 2 April 2010, https://earthjustice. org/blog/2010-april/wolf-hunts-end-not-fight.

[108] ER Olson, 'Pendulum Swings in Wolf Management Led to Conflict, Illegal Kills and a Legislated Wolf Hunt' (2005) 8(5) *Conservation Letters* 351.

[109] M Manyak, *Wolves of the Shadowlands* (Lulo.com, 2015) 192.

It's not always easy to differentiate between 'appropriate' (positive) and 'inappropriate' (negative) environmental aesthetics. Even the seemingly innocuous experience of admiring a scarlet sunset can be misleading, as we might be viewing distorted effects of smog rather than unadulterated nature. Meteorologists have found that sunsets can be enlivened by the presence in the atmosphere of the particles and molecules produced by human activity including motor vehicle emissions.[110] Natural events such as major wildfires can also enliven sunsets and sunrises. Clearly, perceptions of natural beauty are not always an assurance that we are admiring a healthy ecosystem.

The philosophy of 'everyday aesthetics' may help moderate the extraordinary/ordinary dichotomy, enabling us to find not necessarily aesthetic appeal but perhaps aesthetically interesting qualities in 'ordinary' nature. Everyday aesthetics refers to the sensory modes of experience people habitually encounter in their daily lives, from cooking a meal to cleaning the home, often experienced without conscious aesthetic attention. Through spiritual discipline, artistic vision or other strategies, philosopher Yuriko Saito believes it is possible to find 'aesthetic richness normally hidden behind the mundane façade of the everyday'.[111] Finding aesthetic pleasure or interest in quotidian life is a cultivated skill and attitude, including sharpened attention, Zen-like contemplation and creative imagination, but these skills are not the preserve of an epicurean elite.

Accounting for everyday aesthetics, however, confronts a paradox, namely to 'appreciate the everyday as something standing out is to negate the very everydayness that needs to be captured and appreciated', reflects Saito.[112] She sees the solution as simply to shift from living our daily lives on 'autopilot', by putting something on our 'conscious radar' through mindful attention.[113] Positive aesthetic values in one's familiar surroundings may also flow from cultivating a 'sense of place' to a particular locality or context, such as the feelings of comfort and warmth from being within one's home or neighbourhood, explains Yi-Fu Tuan.[114] Artists also have a role in overcoming biased aesthetics, by helping people to re-imagine aesthetic values and relationships in their environs: some artists photograph amazing beauty in obscure fungi on the forest floor,[115] while others enlighten us about the character of humble marine invertebrates rather than majestic whales,[116] or reveal the evocative details of insects in blown-up photos.[117]

---

[110] C Ballantyne, 'Fact or Fiction? Smog Creates Beautiful Sunsets' *Scientific American* 12 July 2007, www.scientificamerican.com/article/fact-or-fiction-smog-creates-beautiful-sunsets.

[111] Y Saito, *Aesthetics of the Familiar: Everyday Life and World-Making* (Oxford University Press, 2017) 13.

[112] Ibid, 21.

[113] Ibid, 24.

[114] YF Tuan, *Topophilia: A Study of Environmental Perception, Attitudes, and Values* (Prentice-Hall, 1974) 99.

[115] Eg work of Stephen Axford: discussed in J Davis, 'Micro Fungi of Australia – in Pictures' *The Guardian* 23 June 2014.

[116] See the artistic portrays of coral reefs by Alex McKenzie and Miranda Lowe: Royal Museums Greenwich, 'Who Are the Radical Fun Advisors', 27 September 2017, www.rmg.co.uk/discover/behind-the-scenes/blog/who-are-radical-fun-advisors.

[117] Eg E Daley, *An Introduction to Tasmania's Winged Insects* (Riffles, 2007).

Governments can also play a curatorial role to rebalance aesthetic preferences. A simple gesture might be to pick 'ordinary' plants and animals for symbolising national identity and legal authority, as the South Australian government did in declaring the leafy seadragon (*Phycodurus eques*), which resembles a piece of floating weed, as its official marine emblem. The closing chapter will delve more deeply into how the law can curate aesthetic preferences.

The Leafy Seadragon looks just like the weed it hides in.

This amazing animal is the official marine emblem of South Australia.

Figure 3.3 *Leafy seadragon*, official marine emblem of South Australia; photograph by Benjamin J Richardson; Art Gallery of South Australia

V. ABSENT AESTHETICS

Some environmental change or decline is imperceptible – unseen and unheard, other than perhaps the occasional glimpse or murmur. The attritional decay of ecosystems, the invisible GHG emissions, or the toxic chemicals wafting through the food chain, are among the environmental scourges beyond our sensory faculties. Of course, we may know about them vicariously from scientific research or media stories, but these environmental problems are aesthetically absent and thus not registering within part of our mind.

Our incomplete sensory perception of nature owes much to the effects of time and space. Nature is dynamic, in constant flux, and anthropogenic influences accelerate the tempo of change. Some of the anthropogenic upheavals such as climate change are temporally displaced into the future, beyond our current sensory appreciation. Concomitantly, many adverse environmental legacies emanate from the deep past, before our lives, for which there may be no tangible traces to see or hear, such as extinct wildlife, other than memories preserved in museums or history books. Likewise, many environmental disturbances are displaced spatially far from the originating cause, beyond our direct sensory realm. Marine plastic pollution disseminates via ocean currents, sometimes concentrating in huge gyres (aka garbage patches) remote from land where 80 per cent of such debris comes. Some of the detritus eventually disintegrates into tiny microplastics, undetectable to casual observation yet just as harmful to aquatic life ingesting them. Industrial fishing presents another spatial distortion: we may consume seafood harvested oceans away, with no sensory appreciation of how the fish once lived or were caught, and thus underestimating the gravity of the plundering of the oceans. Animal rights advocate Jonathan Safran Foer gives a telling example relating to a popular seafood dish: 'imagine being served a plate of sushi. But this plate also holds all of the animals that were killed for your serving of sushi. The plate might have to be five feet across'.[118]

Absent aesthetics affects legal governance because to the extent that adverse environmental changes transcend our sensory appreciation we may be insufficiently aroused to demand action. Many of these environmental permutations can be represented intellectually through scientific studies, such as the forecasting work of the Intergovernmental Panel on Climate Change, but the lack of direct sensory engagement may dull our emotional and ethical concern. As the adage says, 'out of sight, out of mind'. And of those unsightly impacts readily observable, such as the mountains of noxious e-waste (eg computers, smart phones and televisions), Westerners have a habit of removing them as quickly as possible from their sensory realm, usually by exporting the waste to China or Nigeria.

Climate change, a projected future menace, also figures largely outside our sensory realm, although it's beginning to surface via the forest fires, droughts, floods and other calamities becoming more intense and frequent in a rapidly warming planet. Media images of scorched landscapes, dry riverbeds or drowned townships that bear the fingerprints of climate changes resonate increasingly with an agitated public in the affected places.[119] Many dimensions of climate-related adversity, though, remain in our imagination as impending or possible scenarios including ocean acidification and species extinctions. Climate mitigation measures prescribed by the law to forestall such dangers thus face difficulties winning public acceptance in the absence of tangible or direct sensory appreciation, in addition to some such measures such as wind

---

[118] JS Foer, *Eating Animals* (Penguin, 2010) 50.
[119] O Milan, 'California Fires: What is Happening and is Climate Change to Blame?' *The Guardian* 13 November 2018.

farms arousing opposition because they generate unwelcome aesthetic effects. Chapter 7 explores this theme further.

The prevalence of absent aesthetics contrasts to the previous generation of environmental problems from which many of our laws sprung. These were far more perceptible problems, such as the belching factory smoke, the mass wildlife culling, such as the American bison skulls depicted in Figure 3.4, or the rivers so polluted that they became flammable, as when fire erupted on Ohio's filthy Cuyahoga River in 1969. The presence of an environmental problem could also be discerned by the absence of a familiar sound or look: Rachel Carson's *Silent Spring* rallied the public's attention to the absence of bird sounds as agri-chemicals decimated their populations.[120]

Figure 3.4 American bison skulls, 1870; Burton Historical Collection, Detroit Public Library

I wish to explore in more detail here one specific dimension of absent aesthetics, relating to *past* environmental damage, so as to illustrate this theme more explicitly and provide some background to the case studies in Chapters 4 and 7.

Nature's past losses are both aesthetically challenging and ethically confusing because they often leave traces, a residual presence that reminds us of what once was. It could be the extinct species now memorialised as taxidermy specimens in natural history museums, such as the dodo (*Raphus cucullatus*), Tasmanian

---

[120] R Carson, *Silent Spring* (Houghton Miffin, 1962).

thylacine (*Thylacinus cynocephalus*) or great auk (*Pinguinus impennis*). They can be disarming experiences for viewers – we encounter a visually life-like presence, yet one that is eerily inert, silent and without an ecology.

One may also find memories of a vestigial nature in toponyms – the place names that acknowledge animals, plants or other natural features, some of which have disappeared. In the Tasmanian official place names database, 25 entries record the emu, a large flightless bird extinct on the island since about 1870. In Britain, the Wildlife and Wetlands Trust lists some 270 toponyms that allude to cranes that once graced the Isles in large flocks: names containing 'cran' such as Cranbourne, Cranhill and Cranley.[121] Researchers have also identified some 200 places in England named after wolves, extirpated by about 1500.[122] The Canadian city of Saskatoon is named after the Aboriginal Cree word for 'early berries', which once grew in its riparian enclaves. Many people, however, hardly give a second thought to the origins of the places they inhabit. How many residents of the English village of Sevenoaks Weald (in Kent) appreciate that 'weald' is an Old Saxon word for forest, a feature of the countryside now scarce in its vicinity?

As human memory of nature fades with the passage of time, amidst a continually degrading environment, we may come to accept its aesthetically and ecologically depleted condition today as natural, as though it is a permanent state. Marine biologist Daniel Pauly calls this trend the 'shifting baseline syndrome'.[123] This lowered reference point can in turn diminish what we expect of environmental law. Responding to the gravity of the Anthropocene requires our attention to environmental history to grasp the full magnitude of decline and the challenges for sustaining what remains. Although ocean fisheries are Pauly's focus, shifting baselines apply to numerous environmental changes. George Monbiot finds them in Wales and Scotland, whose residents have become naively accustomed to viewing their treeless mountains as 'natural', seemingly unaware that they were formerly logged or grazed to destruction.[124]

Occasionally, but less commonly, environmental baselines may improve owing to timely legal interventions or technological innovations. One renowned success in many Western countries is improved urban air quality; London was once regularly enveloped by lethal smog until the Clean Air Act 1956 transformed its skies and those of other British cities.[125] Another positive baseline shift is the return of wolves to Western Europe, as hunting pressures have subsided and

---

[121] See www.thegreatcraneproject.org.uk/cranes/crane-history.

[122] C Aybes and D Yalden, 'Place-name Evidence for the Former Distribution and Status of Wolves and Beavers in Britain' (1995) 25(4) *Mammal Review* 201.

[123] D Pauly, 'Anecdotes and the Shifting Baseline Syndrome of Fisheries' (1995) 10(10) *Trends in Ecology and Evolution* 430.

[124] G Monbiot, *Feral. Searching for Enchantment on the Frontiers of Rewilding* (Penguin, 2013) passim.

[125] 1956, 4 and 5 Eliz 2, c 52.

forests expanded amidst declining rural populations.[126] These changes can bring aesthetic improvements, such as cleaner skies and the thrill of observing majestic animals.

The arts can help bring environmental changes, past or present, far or near, within our sensory faculties. As Chapter 1 introduced, artists engage with myriad ecological upheavals, from climate change to marine plastic pollution, and increasingly collaborate with politically active NGOs such as 350.org to help reshape the public consciousness. The arts can convey an aesthetic language that transcends time and space, cutting across geographies and histories to not only represent environmental mayhem though music, paintings and other media but also through the very practice of art to provide novel and rich forms of aesthetic engagement for its practitioners. These efforts, of course, need to ultimately influence environmental governance.

Ultimately, then, some level of legal regulation must ensue so that governments and non-state actors are accountable for achieving environmental performance expectations relating to absent aesthetics. These measures can range from healing degradation to preventing future losses such those as associated with climate change. To render the invisible visible, the silent auditable, environmental law should promote what some call the 'proximity principle'. It expects communities to live sustainably within the resources and means available within their local environment, generating their food and disposing of their waste within what the environment can renewably provide. No longer should waste be shipped abroad, as though out of sight and out of mind, or resources plundered from distant lands to feed another. By putting our senses in proximity to our environmental burden, we may better trigger the cognitive and emotional responses that fuel moral responsibility and practical response. Of course, this is an ideal never fully realisable, for because of geographical constraints, economic inefficiencies or social inequities, but it would provide a goal to aim for as far as practical.

Some legislated progress towards realisation of local self-sufficiency exists, notably the EU Treaty's stipulation 'that environmental damage should as a priority be rectified at source'.[127] This agenda could be implemented through a variety of measures. The law could support local, sustainable agriculture through land use planning requirements, consistent with the 100-Mile Diet (eating only farm produce from within a 100-mile radius of one's home).[128] Export of toxic e-waste should also be banned, with requirements for its processing or safe disposal from the originating source. The EU's End of Life Vehicles Directive implements a related policy goal of extended producer responsibility, and

---

[126] A Trouwborst, 'Managing the Carnivore Comeback: International and EU Species Protection Law and the Return of Lynx, Wolf and Bear to Western Europe' (2010) 22(2) *Journal of Environmental Law* 347.

[127] Treaty Establishing the European Community, art 174(2), 2006 OJ (C 321E) 37, 68.

[128] JB MacKinnon, *The 100-Mile Diet: A Year of Eating Locally* (Random House of Canada, 2009).

includes obligations that manufacturers must design vehicles to facilitate their proper dismantling and allowing reuse of their components.[129]

The figurative concept of the 'circular economy' (as against a 'linear economy', where things get made, used and then discarded) also expresses this imperative. The concept can also apply at the level of individual companies, wherein it is known as the 'circular business model', aiming to minimise the resource inputs into and the waste releases out of the organisational entity. Thus, an economy or business would need, for instance, to achieve zero net carbon emissions in order avoid contributing to global warming. Some governments ostensibly acknowledge the concept seriously. The NSW government adopted a policy in 2018 to promote product longevity and greater repairing, upgrading or recycling of goods.[130] The EU's plans for a circular economy are outlined the 2018 'Circular Economy Package', which aims to 'close the loop' of product life-cycles through, inter alia, better eco-design innovation, waste minimisation and developing markets for recycled materials.[131] Curbing plastic waste is a touted priority, with a supplementary EU strategy for a circular economy for plastics.[132]

The foregoing measures can also contribute to a larger agenda for reforming the governance of environmental aesthetics, which I take up in the final chapter, around the necessity of having an aesthetics of vulnerability. Making ourselves more vulnerable to nature through more direct or vicarious sensory engagement with it matters for building the emotional and ethical respect to live sustainably. Having proximity to our environmental impacts, being more aware of our degrading legacies, informs part of this vulnerability.

VI. ART OF SEDUCTION

Seductive aesthetic pleasure may not only stimulate eco-friendly behaviour; one can manipulate it to encourage the contrary. Corporate marketing and political propaganda use imagery, music and other artistic techniques to shape public opinion and behaviour, whether it be shopping or voting. Problematically, these aestheticised communications can serve to mask dubious environmental practices, and thereby lull the public into complacency about the adequacy of corporate or government policies. In this section, therefore, we will canvass this

---

[129] Directive 2000/53/EC of the European Parliament and of the Council, 18 September 2000, on End of Life Vehicles, OJ L 269/34.

[130] NSW Government, *Circular Economic Policy Statement: Too Good to Waste* (NSW Environment Protection Authority, 2018).

[131] European Commission, '2018 Circular Economy Package', http://ec.europa.eu/environment/circular-economy/index_en.htm.

[132] European Commission, 'A European Strategy for Plastics in a Circular Economy', COM/2018/028 final.

dyadic character of aesthetics, and come to appreciate that it can hurt as much as help environmental governance.

The concept of 'aesthetic atmosphere', theorised by Gernot Böhme, aids in capturing the character and proselytising influence of political and commodity aesthetics.[133] An atmosphere refers to a kind of aesthetic ambience, commonly associated with discrete spatial realms with affective powers over people's moods and feelings created by the mix of visual and acoustic elements. These atmospheric realms might be encountered in shopping centres, work offices or even websites. An aesthetic atmosphere might also be defined by a specific event, such as a wedding, sports game or, closer to our subject matter, a courtroom hearing or parliamentary debate. The atmospheric perspective appropriately broadens our understanding of aesthetic experiences from that associated with discrete objects to their wider contexts infused with a variety of aesthetic elements. This perspective helps to illuminate how aesthetics can insidiously domesticate workers and consumers. Shopping experiences are stimulated through retail environments made appealing through store design and piped music.[134] Corporate offices and factories also present distinctive aesthetic atmospheres emanating from their architectural layout, dress codes and so forth to boost workers' loyalty and productivity.

The aesthetics of business reverberate strongly through corporate marketing encountered on websites, newspapers, television and other media. Major global 'brand' companies can spend as much on advertising their wares as their basic production costs. One effect of these aesthetic tools is to make 'new' product lines appear different so as to induce shoppers to upgrade. Many goods have planned, in-built obsolescence or become socially obsolete as fashion dictates that 'newer' is 'better'.[135] Most new motor vehicles differ only in their design and style rather than in any fundamental improvement to their engineering and technology. The aestheticised consumer culture that seduces shoppers to replace perfectly functional appliances, clothes or other wares purely for reasons of style and fashion, levies a heavy toll on nature through depletion of natural resources, transportation of goods and disposal of waste.

Aesthetic factors also serve to promote the name of companies that explicitly brand themselves as environmentally or socially responsible, seeking benefits for their financial bottom line and social licence. In the name of 'corporate social responsibility' (CSR), businesses embellish their marketing, product packaging and logos to tout their green credentials, as well as create favourable impressions with their stakeholders including employees, suppliers, local communities,

---

[133] G Böhme, *The Aesthetics of Atmospheres* (Routledge, 2016).

[134] R Gagnier, *The Insatiability of Human Wants: Economics and Aesthetics in Market Society* (University of Chicago Press, 2000); Saito, *Aesthetics of the Familiar* (above n 111) 147–48.

[135] G Slade, *Made to Break: Technology and Obsolescence in America* (First Harvard University Press, 2006).

regulators or others who may affect business success. Thus advertisements for cars, which may highlight their fuel efficiency or other 'eco-benefits', typically show drivers cruising through magnificent, unhurried countryside as though the motor vehicles innately belong with the trees and animals rather than the congested, polluted highways. Companies may also issue colourful environmental reports to boast about their performance, with appealing pictures of verdant scenery. 'Greenwashing', as some call such hubris, isn't confined to selling corporate wares, as Toby Miller shows in *Greenwashing Culture*.[136] It could characterise the jet-setting lifestyles of Hollywood's so-called 'green celebrities', or corporate sponsorship of museums and art galleries. Where uncontested, greenwashing can impair environmental law by encouraging complacency among regulators or the general public about the adequacy of existing standards, or enable companies to gain greater control over them through permission to 'regulate' their own environmental performance.

Governments have also been complicit in the aestheticised religion of consumerism; during the Cold War, the West stimulated mass consumption as a way to 'prove' capitalism's economic superiority, and since the 1970s consumerism has been reinforced by neoliberal ideologies that accentuate individual choice through the 'free' market.[137] Tellingly, immediately after 9/11 President George W Bush exhorted Americans to 'go shopping' as part of his appeal not to be intimated by terrorism.

Furthermore, aesthetics is just as important to political activity as the market economy. The phenomenon of 'political aesthetics' was coined in a niche field of scholarship to account for the relevance of aesthetics to political experiences and events.[138] A pioneer in this field, Jacques Rancière showed that politics and aesthetics are intimately connected rather than inhabiting autonomous realms.[139] For Rancière, politics is not the struggle for power, but 'the configuration of a particular space, the framing of a particular sphere of experience' that results in a 'distribution of the sensible'.[140] These are sensual realms, or aesthetic atmospheres, marked by what is visible or heard and what remains invisible or silent in the jostle for power.

These aesthetic qualities include forms of political mobilisation, whether orchestrated by the state or in defiance of it; political rituals and ceremonies such as the inauguration of presidents and monarchs; press conferences and important public speeches; and the design of government buildings including

[136] T Miller, *Greenwashing Culture* (Routledge, 2013).

[137] MS Rosenberg, 'Consumer Capitalism and the End of the Cold War' in MP Leffler and OR Westad (eds), *The Cambridge History of the Cold War*, volume III (Cambridge University Press, 2010) 489.

[138] Eg A Virmani (ed), *Political Aesthetics: Culture, Critique, and the Everyday* (Routledge, 2016); R Baker, *Aesthetics and World Politics* (Palgrave Macmillan 2009).

[139] J Rancière, *The Politics of Aesthetics: The Distribution of the Sensible*, translated by G Rockill (Bloomsbury 2004).

[140] J Rancière, *Aesthetics: and its Discontents*, translated by S Corcoran (Polity Press, 2009) 24.

courthouses and legislatures. Political activity is mediated through aesthetic and performative techniques such as Twitter messages, television advertisements and live-streamed speeches, 'forming the contours of what is sensible, legible, and visible. In doing so, they define the terms of political possibility and create terrain for political acts', explain the editors of *Sensible Politics*, which examines the power of visual culture in political theatre.[141]

With the advent of mass communication technologies, notably cinema, radio, newspapers and now the Internet, governments have gained unprecedented means to corral public opinion. Propaganda, the epithet for such government messaging, is often embellished with artistic presentation to help sway the *hoi polloi*, such as found in posters, films, theatre and monuments. Propaganda mobilises public support for government goals, be it encouraging volunteers to join the army or assisting with criminal investigations. The aesthetics of persuasion is tied to visual imagery in cartoons and posters, public performances, as well as the acoustics of national anthems and patriotic songs. Equally, propaganda can serve to arouse antipathy to 'othered' groups such as refugees, homosexuals or Indigenous peoples. Former fascist movements in Germany, Italy and Spain, and communist regimes in Eastern Europe and the Soviet Union, took artful propaganda to unprecedented heights, while imposing pervasive censorship of aesthetic practices deemed contrary to their ideologies.[142]

Monuments present one of the most tangible symbols of nation-states, erected to commemorate their history and successes, or at least selective renditions of it. Governments raise monuments to their leaders, famous citizens, military triumphs and other achievements that aid in nation-building and ideological indoctrination. The conquest of nature through 'heroic' explorers is one such leitmotif. The *Brigham Young Monument*, also known as the *Pioneer Monument* (1893), located in Salt Lake City, Utah, exemplifies this reverence for the 'heroic' colonisers of landscapes, depicting a rugged, bearded fur trapper. Nature itself has been physically manipulated to create some such monuments, such as the faces of four US presidents carved into South Dakota's Mount Rushmore.[143]

Our memories of colonisation, war or environmental transformation, as codified in monuments or museums, of course are never a facsimile of the past.[144] Rather, the aesthetic conventions of these memorials insinuate the biases and prejudices of their creators and curators.[145] Traditional public monuments, defined by their grandeur, ornamentation and austere detachment from viewers,

---

[141] M McLagan and Y McKee (eds), *Sensible Politics: The Visual Culture of Nongovernmental Activism* (MIT Press, 2012) cover abstract.

[142] T Clark, *Art and Propaganda in the Twenty-first Century* (Harry N Abrams Publisher, 1997) 47–102.

[143] G Borglum and L Borglum, *Mount Rushmore National Memorial*, South Dakota, 1941.

[144] S Groes (ed), *Memory in the Twenty-first Century* (Palgrave Macmillan, 2016); D Lowenthal, *The Past is a Foreign Country – Revisited* (Cambridge University Press, 2015).

[145] Lowenthal, ibid, 113–14.

Figure 3.5 Brigham Young Monument, Salt Lake City, Utah; photograph by Ben PL; licensed under Creative Commons

such as the statutes of famous military generals mounted on tall plinths, offer a sanitised record of history that suppresses memories or at least distorts the record to erase history's 'losers' – the colonised and vanquished.[146]

Music, like the pictorial arts, is also conscripted for propaganda. Think of national anthems and government-endorsed patriotic songs performed on public holidays, at sports events and on special commemorative occasions, rousing national pride and solidarity. Equally, some states keenly censure certain musical genres or events to suppress 'decadent' or 'subversive' forces. Sarah Kagan and Volker Kirchberg suggest:

> music may be employed as an anaesthetic means to numb and manipulate. It can operate as a device to control social behaviour, promoting solidarity within groups while reinforcing hostility towards others, and as an emotive manipulator that influences attitude, motivation and behaviour in unethical ways.[147]

---

[146] Q Stevens and KA Franck, *Memorials as Spaces of Engagement: Design, Use and Meaning* (Routledge, 2016) 11.
[147] S Kagan and V Kirchberg, 'Music and Sustainability: Organizational Cultures Towards Creative Resilience' (2016) 135(1) *Journal of Cleaner Production* 1487, 1494.

The acoustics of political speeches and radio broadcasts, without musical backdrops, are just as relevant to this agenda. In analysing this realm, John Street quips 'that Adolph Hitler's rise to power owed much to the invention of the loudspeaker'.[148] The same could be said of some other zealots or totalitarian regimes.[149]

Government propaganda can reshape the aesthetic presentation of environmental activities and impacts. An ignominious example worth commenting on was the drowning of Tasmania's Lake Pedder for a massive hydropower impost. Seemingly protected within a national park gazetted in 1955, the remnant glacial lake was flooded in 1972.[150] Then Tasmanian Hydro-Electric Commissioner, Alan Knight, dismissed Pedder as 'just a bog hole',[151] and his ally, Tasmanian Premier Eric Reece, retionalised: 'there was a national park out there, but [...] it wasn't of substantial significance [...] [t]he thing that was significant was that we had to double the output of power in this state in ten years'.[152] Environmentalists such as nature photographer Olegas Truchanas tried unsuccessfully to halt the dam by impressing Tasmanians with its grandeur and beauty.[153] After its completion, the Hydro-Electric Commission continued its cunning publicity campaign by depicting the new Lake Pedder, now enlarged from 10 to 240 km², as more beautiful. Brazenly, in 1973 it issued Christmas cards showing before and after images of Lake Pedder, with the intent of portraying the damming as an improvement on the area's appearance (see Figure 3.6). The photographs on the card were a swindle because neither image showed the original lake, one of breath-taking beauty with its dazzling, pink quartzite beach.

Forestry, mining and oil development, all equally disfiguring of landscapes, have attracted similar interest from government agencies keen to extol the benefits of harnessing natural resources for economic progress. Canada offers a pertinent example: to sway public opinion about its tar sands industry, one of the most polluting activities ever devised, the provincial government of Alberta, where the industry is centred, established a 'Public Affairs Bureau' with 117 staff (circa 2008) devoted to 'convincing both Alberta's citizens and US oil

---

[148] J Street, 'Music as Political Communication' in K Kenski and KH Jamieson (eds), *The Oxford Handbook of Political Communication* (Oxford University Press, 2017) 885, 885.

[149] S Mikkonen, *State Composers and the Red Courtiers: Music, Ideology, and Politics in the Soviet 1930s* (University of Jyväskylä, 2007).

[150] K Crowley, 'Lake Pedder's Loss and Failed Restoration: Ecological Politics Meets Liberal Democracy in Tasmania' (1999) 34(3) *Australian Journal of Political Science* 409.

[151] Quoted in 'Lake Pedder' *ABC*, 1 May 1997, www.abc.net.au/science/kelvin/files/s18.htm.

[152] Ibid.

[153] O Truchanas, 'Shining Beacon' speech, at the opening of the exhibition 'Lake Pedder 1971', Saddlers Court Gallery, Richmond, 19 November 1971. Also, see the beautiful commemoration of his work in N Cica, *Pedder Dreaming: Olegas Truchanas and a Lost Tasmanian Wilderness* (University of Queensland Press, 2011).

Figure 3.6 Lake Pedder Christmas Card, 1973, Hydro-Electric Commission Tasmania; National Archives of Australia and Hydro Tasmania

consumers that the tar sands are greener than Kermit the Frog'.[154] On 14 April 2014 the Canadian government, also supportive of the industry, sponsored a full-page photo in *The New Yorker* showing an unspoiled river winding through a verdant valley in an effort to convince Americans that the proposed Keystone XL pipeline – to transport Canadian oil south to larger markets – would be environmentally benign.[155]

Political agendas and prejudices can also be veiled through neighbourhood aesthetic standards that serve as means of social control. Municipal bye-laws and residential condominium rules can set aesthetic protocols that have the tacit effect of discriminating against certain groups less able to comply. One seemingly innocuous example is ordinances that prohibit hanging laundry to dry on balconies and windows. Ostensibly, such regulations assist to uphold the decor of buildings and public streets, and appear socially neutral. In practice, they can penalise poor people who lack electric clothes dryers or space inside their homes to dry their laundry. Illustratively, bye-laws enacted by South Africa's eThekwini Municipality forbid any person to 'dry, spread or hang washing, bedding, carpet, rags, or any other item [...] on premises in such a manner that is visible from

---

[154] A critic quoted in R Smandych and R Kueneman, 'The Canadian-Alberta Tar Sands: A Case Study of State-Corporate Environmental Crime' in R White (ed), *Global Environmental Harm: Criminological Perspectives* (Routledge, 2010) 87, 99.

[155] Discussed in E Reguly, 'Canada's $207,000 Oil Sands Ad: Putting a Price on Deception' *Globe and Mail* 9 May 2014.

a public road'.[156] Upmarket, gated communities and homeowner associations can help maintain their exclusivity through such rules enacted under their own self-governing authority.[157] For similar purposes, they may also enact bye-laws that prescribe aesthetic standards for maintenance of lawns, choice of building colours and other favoured elements of the environmental character of their communities. Violators can be fined or evicted. We should thus be able to appreciate how environmental aesthetic preferences can work to surreptitiously manipulate and control social behaviour.

Political aesthetics is just as relevant to understanding dissident activity, street rallies, blockades, social media, photojournalism and other aestheticised mediums that help to reframe the political discourse around sustainability, social justice, poverty and other contested issues. The political power of what I call 'counter aesthetics' to sway public opinion was acknowledged in the examples from Chapter 1 about the images of atrocities in the Vietnam and Iraq wars that helped sap American popular support for these campaigns. Counter aesthetics can also challenge corporate malfeasance, through strategies known as 'culture jamming', which artistically expose the realities of environmental pollution, sweatshops and other abuses. The final chapter examines culture jamming further, including its potential to forge environmental aesthetics in new directions. It also explores in detail how the aesthetic conventions of public monuments have become a ley target for counter aesthetics, seeking to stimulate alternative narratives about national history and culture.[158] Analysing Holocaust memorialisation in Germany, cultural theorist James Young identifies a dissident artistic style away from heroic, figurative monuments towards humble and ephemeral installations that by their very aesthetic qualities challenge the values embodied in traditional memorials to wars, conquests and other distasteful aspects of history.[159]

Counter monuments exist for the natural environment as well. Some have been fashioned not only to renew memories of nature's former riches, but also – literally – to restore nature. One example, discussed further in Chapter 6, is Alan Sonfist's *Time Landscape*, begun in 1965 to commemorate and restore the lost ecology of a piece of New York. Sonfiist planted the original indigenous vegetation of the city to express nature reclaiming itself and evoking memories of the revegetated site. Japanese artist and trained arborist Tatsuo Miyajima, has created organic monuments to represent peace and regeneration. In atomic

---

[156] eThekwini Municipality: Nuisances and Behaviour in Public Places By-law, 2015, s 7.

[157] MM Ross, LJ Smith and RD Pritt, 'The Zoning Process: Private Land-Use Controls and Gated Communities, the Impact of Private Property Rights Legislation, and Other Recent Developments in the Law' (1996) 28(4) *The Urban Lawyer* 801.

[158] Ibid.

[159] JE Young, 'The Counter Monument: Memory Against Itself in Germany Today' (1992) 18(winter) *Critical Inquiry* 267; JE Young, *The Texture of Memory: Holocaust Memorials and Meaning* (Yale University Press, 1993).

bombed Nagasaki, Miyajima initiated in 1995 his *Revive Time Kaki Tree* project that propagates trees harvested from a single surviving kaki tree from the ruined city. These examples avoid the pitfalls of conventional monuments through unconventional materials, such as living plants that maintain the monument so long as the plants thrive; spaces that allow visitors to enter, touch and engage with the site; choosing unconventional settings, such as an empty side-street or farm field; and, crucially, engaging with a subject matter that speaks for nature, acknowledging not only its past exploitation but its future recovery.

The art of seduction thus plays out in a variety of ways depending on the goals and methods of its protagonists. Whether aesthetics will aid or hurt nature conservation depends partly on the law. Robust controls on corporate advertising can help curb misleading, greenwashed advertising. Generous civil liberties for freedom of association and speech can give voice to dissident, counter-aesthetic strategies. Land use zoning can influence use of public places, be it for edifying monuments or empowering rallies. Environmental law operates in an aesthetic milieu in which the art of seduction can foment changes that help strengthen it, such as through counter aesthetic strategies that raise public awareness of environmental threats needing action, or weaken it through corporate marketing or political propaganda that lull the masses into complacency.

Part II

Stories

4

Vanquished Nature

I. FAKING NATURE

A T AMSTERDAM'S BUSTLING Schiphol airport travellers may find respite in a quiet, eco-themed lounge. In the 'airport park', as it's known, restless jetsetters can put aside their smart phones and laptops to relax on fake tree stumps while listening to the calming chirpings of birds piped through speakers concealed in real or fake greenery, and watching digital images of butterflies fluttering on the walls.[1] This synthetic nature is far more common in our lives than you might realise: hotel lobbies adorned with artificial shrubs and miniature waterfalls; pigeon-deterring, imitation raptors perched on buildings; fake lawn turf covering our cities; artificial snow groomed onto ski resorts; and the ubiquitous food colourants and sweeteners. With the prospect of climate geo-engineering, we may one day routinely encounter fake trees designed to sequester carbon dioxide more 'efficiently' than the real ones.

The prospect of this synthetic caricature was discerned in 1974 by legal scholar Lawrence Tribe in his prescient essay 'Ways Not to Think About Plastic Trees'. He saw 'the perpetually green lawn and the plastic tree, far from representing the outcroppings of some inexplicable human perversion' as expressive of 'a view of nature fully consistent with the basic assumptions of present environmental policy'.[2] Those assumptions include environmental decisions based on 'satisfaction of individual human wants as the only defensible measure of the good',[3] whether determinable by 'objective' cost-benefit analyses or pushy property owners and business moguls. The plastic nature we encounter is a creation licensed by the law to meet human needs, be it decoration, shade or ambience, in place of a real nature increasingly removed from our everyday lives.

Our synthetic world not only replaces nature, it degrades it. Plastic debris has within a mere few decades become identified by scientists as an insidious threat, especially to the oceans where fish, sea mammals and birds ingest or become entangled in it. Half of all the plastics in human history were produced

---

[1] D Netburn, 'Amsterdam: Schiphol's New "Airport Park" Alive with Greenery, Chirping Birds' *Los Angeles Times* 12 May 2011.

[2] LH Tribe, 'Ways Not to Think about Plastic Trees: New Foundations for Environmental Law' (1974) 83(7) *Yale Law Journal* 1315, 1317.

[3] Ibid, 1325.

in just the last 13 years, since 2006.[4] In 2015, some 322 million tonnes of plastic were manufactured worldwide, of which an estimated 6 to 20 million tonnes entered the oceans.[5] Experts predict these numbers to get worse, perhaps doubling by 2050.[6] Without any break-through in clean up technologies, this problem will also endure because petroleum-based plastics degrade very slowly. Synthetic lawns, increasingly used for children's playgrounds, sport fields and suburban gardens, are also made from plastic composites, and they leave a biological desert in their wake that threatens 'butterflies, bees and garden birds as well as creating waste which will never biodegrade'.[7] Plastics are not the only menace; with the propagation of genetically modified organisms (GMOs), some of it aimed at enhancing aesthetic elements such as colour and aroma that appeal to human enjoyment, we have entered the realm of synthetic biology. It poses risks to the wider web of life if altered species breed with unmodified creatures in their natural environment and thereby alter the balance of nature. Clearly, the synthetic hell that Lawrence Tribe warned of has become diabolical in extent in a mere few decades.

We might view the foregoing as merely an extension of a habit deeply etched in human history to remake nature for our comfort, convenience and aesthetic pleasure. The declaration of the Anthropocene represents the culmination of a long history of anthropogenic environmental change. Not only did the advent of agriculture, and later the urban and industrial revolutions, dramatically reshape the biosphere, even hunter gatherer livelihoods precipitated major ecological changes as mega fauna were killed off.[8] When Robert Elliot argued in his 1997 book that environmental restoration projects are morally troubling for 'faking nature',[9] because human ingenuity could not recreate the 'original' state of nature, he was rightly criticised for assuming the existence anywhere of a pristine, unadulterated nature. Yet while we should recognise that that our planet has long been domesticated by *Homo sapiens*, this of course does not morally justify it, nor make further onslaughts acceptable.

We can now look more closely at a variety of realms where aesthetics is implicated in our domination and exploitation of nature. Firstly, this chapter considers the domestication of nature through colonial acclimatisation societies, as well as persecution of aesthetically 'disagreeable' wildlife. Next, we consider the exploitation of natural beauty itself, such as for furs, feathers

---

[4] J Buffington, *Peak Plastic: The Rise or Fall of Our Synthetic World* (ABC CLIO, 2019) 43.

[5] M Landon-Lane, 'Corporate Social Responsibility in Marine Plastic Debris Governance' (2018) 127 *Marine Pollution Bulletin* 310, 310.

[6] N Simon and ML Schulte, *Stopping Global Plastic Pollution: The Case for an International Convention* (Heinrich-Böll-Stiftung, 2017).

[7] S Laville, 'Growth in Artificial Lawns Poses Threat to British Wildlife, Conservationists Warn' *The Guardian* 4 July 2016.

[8] SL Lewis and MA Maslin, *The Human Planet: How We Created the Anthropocene* (Yale University Press, 2018).

[9] R Elliot, *Faking Nature: The Ethics of Environmental Restoration* (Routledge, 1997).

and gemstones. Thirdly, we turn to the role of natural history museums in institutionalising memories of vanquished nature. The final theme of this chapter is contemporary factory farms and the role of the law in supressing sensory awareness of their horrors, a case study that illustrates how vanquishment of other species may sometimes necessitate concealing the aesthetic horrors that would repulse many.

II. DOMESTICATING NATURE

A. A Long History

Nature has been heavily customised for human convenience and aesthetic preference – indeed its reconfiguration has a much deeper history than our recent synthetic, ersatz nature. It's this history that occupies this chapter's opening story about how our aesthetic predilections, with the complicity of the law, have shaped the exploitation and domestication of nature. It thus helps illuminate the dyadic character of environmental aesthetics, which contribute to harmful practices with sometimes an intensity equal to their positive benefits.

The looting of nature because of economic greed has dominated accounts of environmental history. In this narrative, environmental damage has ensued because of a desire to transform nature, even its most beautiful places, into practical economic benefits. Consider the following evocative description penned by an intrepid explorer of the island of Tasmania in the 1830s:

> The path they now pursued was one of exceeding grandeur – fine open forest-land, studded with lofty trees of stupendous growth. [...] Who can tread the wilds of unfettered nature, and contemplate her in all her desolate grandeur, without feeling impressed how insignificant an atom he is amid her glorious works – and how utterly dependent upon his kind? The floral mead – the pearly stream – the godly grove, however they delight the eye, or ravish the imagination – what are they all? A worthless waste, until the genius and industry of man converts and fits them for the welfare and improvement of his kind.[10]

This lyrical account, by settler David Burn from Scotland, illuminates how many of his (and later) generations viewed their new surroundings: despite obviously awed by the landscape's grandeur, he took for granted it was destined for the axe or plough. The same attitude could be found throughout much of Australia, and indeed the domestication of nature was often celebrated with its own aesthetic, as depicted in Figure 4.1 showing a Christmas card rejoicing in the felling of behemoth forests.

---

[10] D Burn, *Pictures of Van Diemen's Land* (Cat and Fiddle Press, 1973) 126–27; original in *The Colonial Magazine*, volume III (Fisher, Son and Co, 1840) 353, 363–64.

Figure 4.1 *Christmas in the Colonies, an Australian Giant, Cutting Him Down and Cutting Him Up*, 1869; Edward Roper (1832–1909), engraving; National Library of Australia

While economics is crucial to understanding the vanquishment of nature, the role of aesthetics in this story is less well known. Aesthetic factors have incited people to degrade or transform nature, from the extermination of 'unattractive' wildlife to the domestication of landscapes through the introduction and breeding of more congenial plants and animals.[11] Species have been bred for selective traits that people find more agreeable and attractive; and the fate of some species has hinged on how well they appeal to our aesthetic taste; consider that some 500 million dogs populate the world relative to just 300,000 gray wolves (*Canis lupus*).[12] Nature's beauty itself has been coveted for exploitation, often with results just as destructive as those wreaked on that designated as more aesthetically disagreeable. Such wantonness has a long, sordid history.

[11] S White, 'British Colonialism, Australian Nationalism and the Law: Hierarchies of Wild Animal Protection' (2013) 39(2) *Monash University Law Review* 452, 461–62.

[12] RK Wayne and C Vila, 'Molecular Genetic Studies of Wolves' in LD Mech and L Boitani (eds), *Wolves: Behaviour, Ecology and Conservation* (University of Chicago Press, 2010) 218, 230.

The Roman emperors enthralled their vulgar subjects with shows in amphi-theatres featuring exotic animals slaughtered in fights with one another or human combatants. The menagerie of exotic beasts captured from the vast reaches of the Imperium Romanorum included panthers, lions, bears, crocodiles and even elephants. The scale of the blood sports is shocking: the Emperor Titus inaugurated the Colosseum with a 100-day festival in which about 5,000 beasts were slaughtered. The practice has survived into the present era in the less gruesome form of the Spanish bullfight. Reflecting Romans' aesthetic awe of

Figure 4.2 Zliten mosaic, Roman Empire (Zilten, Libya), second century CE; Archaeological Museum of Tripoli

butchered fauna, scenes of hunters capturing or killing them in 'heroic' combat were a common motif of Roman mosaics, vases and other art forms. The spec-tacular second century CE Zliten mosaic, found in the town of Zliten in modern Libya, depicts such blood scenes (see Figure 4.2).

Grisly blood sports have retained a place in our history. In *Macbeth*, William Shakespeare included a scene where the protagonist exclaims that his enemies 'have tied me to a stake; I cannot fly. But, bear-like, I must fight the course'; a line that refers to a popular pastime of this era, where crowds flocked to watch bear-baiting and other deadly jousts involving animals.[13] The practice

[13] W Shakespeare, *Macbeth* (c 1606) Act V, scene 7.

in England continued until banned in 1835 by the Cruelty to Animals Act.[14] Bullfighting remains popular entertainment in modern day Spain and Portugal where many consider it an art form. In 2010 the Madrid municipal government declared bullfighting a legally protected piece of its region's cultural patrimony, defying calls by animal welfare campaigners to ban it.[15]

Persecution of fauna was also pursued with gusto because the activity of hunting wildlife brought much aesthetic pleasure. In many parts of the world, hunting has long been revered as a noble pleasure of aesthetic elegance, and even prized as a way to be 'closer' to nature despite the paradox of subjugating it.[16] The tradition of organised fox hunting in rural Britain with hounds and horses was defended as a 'central element' of the 'fabric of British life' before the law severely restricted it in 2004.[17] Not surprisingly, hunting has been a staple subject for many artists since time immemorial, such as Paolo Uccello's exquisite painting *The Hunt in the Forest*, 1470.

Figure 4.3 *The Hunt in the Forest*, 1470, Paolo Uccello (1397–1475), oil on canvas; Ashmolean Museum, Oxford

An aesthetic by-product of hunting is the trade in animal fur, feathers and other accoutrements. The North American fur industry, beginning in the sixteenth century and peaking in the nineteenth, was driven by the economic opportunities from the market for warm and attractive animal pelts. Millions of beavers, bears, wildcats and other fur-bearing creatures were slaughtered to meet the aesthetic tastes of consumers. The fur trade was legalised through licences and concessions issued to the trappers and retailers. A few companies operating under royal charter and collaborating with Native Americans who undertook

[14] 5 and 6 Will 4, c 59.

[15] G Tremlett, 'Madrid Protects Bullfighting as an Art Form' *The Guardian* 7 March 2010.

[16] N Wolloch, *Subjugated Animals: Animals and Anthropocentrism in Early Modern European Culture* (Humanity Books, 2006) passim.

[17] S Moss, 'Hunting the Hunters' *The Guardian* 13 June 2000. See further Hunting Act 2004, c 37, which does not ban all forms of fox hunting.

most of the harvesting, dominated the industry. The British chartering of the Hudson's Bay Company in 1670 created, with the imprimatur of the law, one of the most dominant participants in the fur trade for two centuries.[18]

The Victorian-era penchant for souveniring eggs and feathers, and creating taxidermy trophies for exhibit in natural history museums, sometimes with the blessing of the law in an era where wildlife conservation law was rudimentary,[19] also levied an onerous burden on the prized species. Some became extinct, such as the great auk, a large flightless bird whose soft down was coveted by textile makers. The taxidermy collections and dioramas of natural history museums today are memorials to a vanquished nature, lost to a perverse aesthetics.[20] The exploitation of natural beauty persists today on a large scale, notably the poaching of mega fauna for their prized horns and tusks, but it mostly occurs illegally despite a raft of legal controls such as the 1973 Convention on International Trade in Endangered Species of Wild Fauna and Flora (CITES).[21]

B. Acclimatisation Societies

Aesthetics has an unsavoury history implicated in colonisers' efforts to civilise and tame 'alien' landscapes and creatures, particularly to make settlers feel more at home. Such 'ecological imperialism', as Alfred Crosby labels the export of plants and animals to far-flung colonies, has, along with the imposition of foreign environmental husbandry practices, left a terribly legacy. Fugitive exotics are recognised by the IUCN as one of the leading, systemic drivers of biodiversity loss around the world,[22] causing the demise of 91 (54 per cent) of 170 extinct birds and mammals.[23] These grim numbers are not generally the result of careless mishaps that allowed rogue species to escape but ensued from orchestrated campaigns to disseminate fauna and flora internationally.

So-called 'acclimatisation societies' were created in a number of countries during the nineteenth century to formally facilitate the introduction of plants and animals for reasons of sport, commerce and aesthetic pleasure. It was a 'conquest by assimilation', as Harriet Ritvo characterised the assault.[24] Acclimatisation societies became means for 'civilising' the landscape with

---

[18] RS Mackie, *Trading Beyond the Mountains: the British Fur Trade on the Pacific 1793–1843* (UBC Press, 1997) 31.

[19] For a detailed history of these practices in the UK, see R Lovegrove, *Silent Fields: The Long Decline of a Nation's Wildlife* (Oxford University Press, 2008).

[20] ST Asma, *Stuffed Animals and Pickled Heads: The Culture and Evolution of Natural History Museums* (Oxford University Press, 2003).

[21] TIAS 8249; 993 UNTS 243.

[22] IUCN, 'Invasive Species', www.iucn.org/theme/species/our-work/invasive-species.

[23] N Sodhi, BW Brook and CJA Bradshaw, 'Causes and Consequences of Species Extinction' in SA Levin et al (eds), *The Princeton Guide to Ecology* (Princeton University Press 2009) 514, 516.

[24] H Ritvo, *The Animal Estate: The English and Other Creatures in the Victorian Age* (Harvard University Press, 1987) 241.

domestic livestock and plants and 'securing the land from native incursions of all kinds',[25] while also for sentimental or nostalgic reasons bringing comfort to homesick settlers by importing familiar song birds and ornamental plants.[26] Very occasionally, their focus was importing wildlife from the foreign periphery to the imperial metropole. The first acclimatisation society was La Société zoologique d'acclimatation, founded in France in 1854 as an offshoot of Paris' Muséum national d' histoire naturelle, with the belief that animals could adapt to new habitats.[27] Its original goal was to introduce and adapt foreign animals, and later plants, to France, and in 1861 it established the Jardin d'acclimatation in Paris to showcase the exotica to the French public.

More commonly, however, acclimatisation societies served to export European species abroad. While most efforts were intended to be somehow beneficial or economically valuable, such as crops and livestock to support agriculture, some were proposed on aesthetic grounds such as songbirds and flowers to remake nature in the image of the settlers' ancestral homes. The following observations by natural historian George Thomson, writing in 1922 about the New Zealand experience, capture well this sentiment:

> Here in a land of plenty, with few wild animals, few flowers apparently, and no associations with streams almost destitute of fish, with shy songbirds and few game birds … it seemed to them [early settlers] that it only wanted the best of the plants and animals associated with these earlier memories to make it a terrestrial paradise. So with zeal unfettered by scientific knowledge, they proceeded to endeavor to reproduce – as far as possible – the best-remembered and most cherished features of the country from which they came.[28]

These acclimatisation associations, though privately initiated and operated, operated within state-backed regulatory regimes. Governments supported acclimatisation programs through a variety of techniques including: official registration of acclimatisation societies; provision of financial benefits such as duty-free imports of animals and plants; allocation of property to manage to facilitate establishment of imported species, such as trout and salmon farms; and legislative protection to the most desirable imports against uncontrolled hunting or other threats. Thereby, acclimatisation groups functioned as important agents of governance in the environmental agendas of the settler states.

The American Acclimatization Society was founded in 1871 for introducing European fauna and flora into North America for economic and cultural reasons.

---

[25] H Rangan, A Wilson and C Kull, 'Thorny Problems' in J Frawley and I McCalman (eds), *Rethinking Invasion Ecologies from the Environmental Humanities* (Routledge, 2014) 116, 118.

[26] C Lever, *Naturalised Birds of the World* (T and AD Poyser, 2005) 15.

[27] M Osborne, 'The Société Zoologique D'acclimatation and the New French Empire: Science and Political Economy' in P Petitjean, C Jami and AM Moulin (eds), *Science and Empire* (Springer, 1992) 299.

[28] GM Thomson, *The Naturalisation of Animals and Plants in New Zealand* (Cambridge University Press, 1922) 21–22.

Among the introductions it undertook were European songbirds such as blackbirds and skylarks, 'which were useful to the farmer and contributed to the beauty of the groves and fields' according to reporting of the time.[29] Some of these introductions devastated native flora and fauna across landscapes often far from the originating release sites.[30] The European starling is one such culprit, whose release into the United States in the late nineteenth century was allegedly because the then chairman of the American Acclimatization Society believed that 'any bird worthy of inclusion in Shakespeare's works deserved a place in North America'.[31]

The acclimatisation agenda was particularly common in the British Empire. The British Acclimatisation Society, founded in 1860, undertook to disseminate the country's wildlife across the Commonwealth, in partnership with locally established acclimatisation clubs in each colony.[32] While the transmission of animals was supposed to be reciprocated, it was largely a one-way process with far fewer animals brought from the colonies, and they 'were mostly treated as curiosities for exhibit, dead or alive'.[33] Australia, with its own regional acclimatisation societies established between the 1850s and 1890s, received numerous imports. Christopher Lever explains that 'members of the societies looked on Australia as a country bereft of such attractions as melodious songbird and animals of the chase – omissions which they sought to remedy.'[34] The first of such local societies, the NSW Acclimatisation Society, founded in 1852, declared that its objects:

> shall be the introduction, acclimatisation, and domestication of all innoxious animals, birds, fishes, insects, and vegetables, whether useful or ornamental; the perfection, propagation and hybridisation of races newly introduced or already domesticated; the spread of indigenous animals from parts of the colonies where they are known to localities where they are not known.[35]

Fortunately, most such introductions – many of which would have been particularly pernicious to Australia's native fauna such as monkeys, mongooses and raccoons – never established self-sustaining wild populations.

Of those that did, the red fox (*Vulpes vulpes*) became the most destructive, spreading to occupy about 70 per cent of Australia and devastating its

[29] 'American Acclimatization Society' *New York Times*, 15 November 1877, 2.

[30] AW Crosby, *Ecological Imperialism: The Biological Expansion of Europe, 900–1900* (Cambridge University Press, 1986).

[31] D Taft, 'European Starling, the Bard's Bird' *New York Times* 8 January 2016.

[32] C Lever, *The Naturalised Animals of the British Isles* (Hutchinson, 1977).

[33] G Moore, 'Beasts, Birds, Fishes, and Reptiles: Anthony Trollope and the Australian Acclimitization Debate' in LW Mazzeno and RD Morrison (eds), *Animals in Victorian Literature and Culture: Contexts for Criticism* (Palgrave Macmillan 2017) 65, 72.

[34] C Lever, *They Dined on Eland: The Story of the Acclimatisation Societies* (Quiller Press, 1992) 100.

[35] Quoted in P MacInnis, 'When Learned Men Schemed to Create a Land of Alien Species – The Acclimatisation Societies of the Late 19th Century' (1996) 18(3) *Geo: Australasia's Geographical Magazine* 68, 71.

small marsupials, many becoming extinct.[36] The beautifully coloured North American monarch butterfly has also established virulent populations in Australia since the 1870s, and unlike the fox has become widely admired as a 'romantic addition' to Australian ecosystems despite its invasive reach.[37] Numerous plants came too, often for ornamental reasons, and later spreading as noxious weeds: plants introduced to decorate Australian gardens now account for 72 per cent of its environmental weeds and 69 per cent of its agricultural weeds.[38] One of the most noxious is *Lantana camera*, introduced to decorate gardens with its vivid red-orange flowers, and now occupying about 4 million hectares of the continent. Another menace is bridal creeper (*Asparagus asparagoides*), a South African species introduced in the nineteenth century as a garden plant for use in wedding bouquets, but since spreading to become one of southern Australia's most virulent of invaders. The Jacaranda (*Jacaranda mimosifolia*), admired for its violet-blue flowers, was imported from Brazil in large numbers. The gardening correspondent for the *Sydney Morning Herald* in 1868 explained: '[t]he most beautiful flowering tree is a native of Brazil, and no garden of any pretentions can be said to be complete without a plant of it. [...] Its beautiful rich lavender blossoms, and in light feathery foliage, render it the gem of the season'.[39] Some Australian authorities now regard the Jacaranda as a weed.

In the United States, the terrible beauty of invasive plants has also stirred public controversy. Take purple loosestrife (*Lythrum salicaria*), a lovely but aggressive invader, introduced by settlers in the early 1800s. It poses a particular threat to wetlands, choking off native plants where fish and wildlife would feed and spawn. Although its environmental impact is now well publicised, some local communities still resist eradication efforts because they associate the beautiful flower with a positive presence in nature.[40] The same dilemma arises with deer, which although native to the United States, have increased in plague proportions owing to the removal of their predators such as wolves, coupled with a public that attaches far greater aesthetic pleasure from deer owing to the influence of popular culture, such as the Disney 1942 animated film *Bambi*, a touching tale of a fawn's life in the forest.[41] Amusingly, perhaps, in 2018 a Missouri court that

---

[36] On the fox and other exotic pests brought to Australia, see EC Rolls, *They All Ran Wild: The Story of Pests on the Land in Australia* (Angus and Robertson, 1969).

[37] A Jones, 'The Bitter Taste of the Monarch Butterfly' *ABC (Off Track)*, 27 October 2018, www.abc.net.au/radionational/programs/offtrack/the-bitter-taste-of-the-monarch-butterfly/10391428.

[38] J Virtue, S Bennett and RP Randall, 'Plant Introductions in Australia: How Can We Resolve "Weedy" Conflicts of Interest?' in BM Sindel and SB Johnson (eds), *Weed Management: Balancing People, Planet, Profit: 14th Australian Weeds Conference, Papers and Proceedings* (Weed Society of New South Wales, 2004) 42.

[39] *Sydney Morning Herald* 3 December 1868, quoted in G Greer, *White Beach: The Rainforest Years* (Bloomsbury, 2013) 84.

[40] Y Saito, *Aesthetics of the Familiar: Everyday Life and World-Making* (Oxford University Press, 2017) 142.

[41] MM Eaton, *Merit, Aesthetic and Ethical* (Oxford University Press, 2001) 182.

sentenced a deer poacher to one-year's imprisonment added the stipulation that the offender must watch *Bambi* every month.[42]

Deer are also a prevalent exotic in New Zealand, now overrun with invasive species that have devastated the country's endemic avifauna, and making a mockery of the country's tourist slogan of '100 per cent pure'.[43] The acclimatisation process became institutionalised there in the 1860s, with the tone set by one tabloid article in 1861 that complained 'there is perhaps no country in the world the natural zoology of which supplies so little to the subsistence or enjoyment of its inhabitants, as New Zealand'.[44] What followed has left a terrible legacy. Mustelids imported to control rabbits – another ill-considered import, later declared as 'vermin' – soon turned on New Zealand's native birds, rendering many extinct. Also, Australian brush-tailed possums introduced in 1837 to start a fur industry – another aesthetic-driven folly – decimated the native vegetation that birds feed on. Of the approximately 130 birds brought to New Zealand, 39 species established themselves including the melodious blackbird.

The first introductions into New Zealand, in the 1840s, were privately sponsored without legislative controls, although Governor George Grey himself set an example by importing zebras and monkeys. Regulations enacted in 1846 incentivised such activities by giving duty-free status to all live animal and plant imports.[45] Acclimatisation societies established in the 1860s engendered a more orderly process with official blessing, and legislation passed in 1867 with the purpose of 'encouragement of acclimatisation societies in New Zealand' helped leverage substantial public money to spur the imports.[46] While it had previously been tacitly lawful for anyone to introduce any species, the 1867 legislation tightened controls and barred introduction of 'any fox, venomous reptile, hawk, vulture or other bird of prey'.[47] By 1894 the local press were voicing the need for greater governmental oversight to prevent importation of 'animals or birds that might become nuisances to the community'.[48] It was not until the early twentieth century, with the Animals Protection Act of 1907,[49] that a comprehensive ban on the introduction of any animal without a permit was introduced with the belated aim to safeguard the rapidly dwindling native biodiversity. In sum, the work of acclimatisation societies in New Zealand, more than any other factor, has been responsible for the country's recent ecological upheavals and biological losses.[50]

[42] CR Wootson Jr, 'A Poacher Who Killed Hundreds of Deer was Sentenced to Repeatedly Watch "Bambi"' *Washington Post* 17 December 2018.

[43] RB Allen and WG Lee (eds), *Biological Invasions in New Zealand* (Springer-Verlag, 2006).

[44] Quoted in 'Acclimatisation' *The Press* 17 August 1861, 1.

[45] An Ordinance to Alter Certain Duties of Customs, No XIV 1846, table of duties of customs.

[46] Protection of Animals Act 1867, 31 Victoria 1867, No 35, long title.

[47] Ibid, s 28.

[48] 'The Wood Pigeon Question' *The Press* 23 May 1894, 5.

[49] 7 EDW VII 1907, No. 66.

[50] N Pears, 'Familiar Aliens: The Acclimatisation Societies' Role in New Zealand's Biogeography' (1982) 98(1) *Scottish Geographical Magazine* 23.

Not all settlers shared the aesthetic criteria of the acclimatisation societies. James Cook who 'discovered' Australia for Great Britain, named Botany Bay, near where the colony began, after the large variety of plants collected there by his companion Joseph Banks. In the ensuing years numerous acknowledgements to Australia's native biodiversity and topography were memorialised as toponyms on maps, such as 'kangaroo point', 'emu plains' or 'cockatoo island', although frequently the Aboriginal place names were erased in the effort to build the new national identity.[51] In *The Colonial Earth*, Tim Bonyhady traces a more environmentally sensitive aesthetic taste in some of the early settlers to Australia who came to admire, not destroy, the sights and sounds of their new environs.[52] One example is Eugene von Guérard, who was painting Australian landscapes in the 1850s and 1860s. In seeking to transcend the aesthetic landscape tropes of European art, von Guérard tried to evoke the grandeur of his new surroundings untainted by human interference. His iconic painting *Ferntree Gully in the Dandenong Ranges* (1857) was so masterful in evoking the beauty of the place that the national publicity caught the attention of timber-cutters and fern-collectors who invaded to plunder its riches.[53]

Despite the twentieth-century shift in sentiment to safeguard native biodiversity, plus the advent of extensive biosecurity laws in recent decades to exclude potential pests, many exotics persist with official tolerance. In Australia, known environmental weeds are commonly available in nurseries,[54] and about 10 million ornamental, aquarium fish are imported annually with risk of carrying pathogens and parasites that could devastate local aquatic life.[55] In the United States, hundreds of known weeds have yet to be listed and banned by authorities under the Noxious Weeds Act 1975.[56] Even the UK, historically an exporter of destructive plants and animals, is itself now under siege as global trade brings pests to its own shores.[57] Gray squirrels (*Sciurus carolinensis*), native to North America, were introduced to Britain in the 1870s as fashionable additions to the landed estates, but now threaten the smaller red squirrels (*Sciurus vulgaris*).

Established exotic species may also be pardoned because of their aesthetic values or cultural significance. In Canberra, Australia's capital city, authorities had to abandon a plan to cull a feral population of peafowls (*Pavo cristatus*) after local residents clamoured for the colourful birds originating from India

---

[51] See H Koch and L Hercus (eds), *Aboriginal Placenames: Naming and Re-naming the Australian Landscape* (ANU E-Press, 2009).

[52] T Bonyhady, *The Colonial Earth* (Melbourne University Publishing, 1998).

[53] Ibid, 106.

[54] R Groves, R Boden and M Lonsdale, *Jumping the Garden Fence: Invasive Garden Plants in Australia and their Environmental and Agricultural Impacts* (WWF-Australia, 2005).

[55] A Sallem, 'Aquarium. Fish "Threaten Biodiversity"' *ABC Science* 18 May 2007, www.abc.net. au/science/news/stories/2007/1925566.htm.

[56] Public Law 93–629, 88 Stat 2148, 1975; see US Congress, Office of Technology Assessment, *Harmful Non-Indigenous Species in the United* States (US Government Printing Office, 1993) 26–27.

[57] CM Braiser, 'The Biosecurity Threat to the UK and Global Environment from International Trade in Plants' (2008) 57(5) *Plant Pathology* 792.

to be spared.[58] In New Zealand, conservation authorities' efforts to eradicate the egg-eating kiore rat (*Rattus exulans*) from areas set aside for the recovery of endangered birds have clashed with the desires of some Māori people to protect the cultural icon, which arrived in New Zealand with their Polynesian ancestors.[59]

C. An Ugly Truth: Persecuting the Unsightly

The influx of exotica is only part of the story of the domestication of nature; the other is the persecution of native wildlife. The war waged against creatures branded as vermin, varmint, pest or similar epithet is bound up in a mix of scientific, economic and aesthetic factors. Evolutionary psychologists suggest human beings retain a deep-seated loathing of certain hostile species once frequently encountered in our ancestral environments, such as spiders and snakes.[60] Some of these fears have been stoked by religious dogma; the Christian New Testament in the *Book of Revelation* associates the serpent with Satan, while the Jewish *Book of Genesis* depicts a serpent as a trickster who seduces Eve into eating the forbidden fruit in the Garden of Eden.

Ostensibly, the law delineates the status of wildlife on more rational or objective grounds, such as rarity or ecological significance. Abundant species might exist without legal protection, and thus be open to exploitation, while those considered threatened or endangered will usually be prioritised for conservation. Some societies also use the law to encourage extermination of unwanted species, through legal duties on landowners to remove designated vermin or offering bounties that give a financial incentive for so doing. Classification of vermin may reflect scientific advice about species' threat to other wildlife, or economic considerations such as the impact of pest insects and rodents on agricultural production. Species offering lucrative returns as food, clothing or other benefits will rarely be spared from exploitation, but licensing schemes control harvesting at 'sustainable' levels.

Importantly too, the foregoing decisions can reflect aesthetic preferences. Just as charismatic animals tend to receive additional legal protection, the reviled are readily marked out for persecution, especially where they conjure up negative emotions associated with pestiferous or fearsome traits. Campaigns to exterminate vermin or predators may be embellished by depicting the targeted species as having undesirable aesthetic qualities or effects. The same tactic can validate destruction of vegetation or entire ecosystems.

[58] S Groch, 'Proposed Peacock Cull Cancelled After "Overwhelming" Community Outcry' *Canberra Times* 20 June 2018.
[59] K Chanwai and BJ Richardson, 'Re-working Indigenous Customary Rights? The Case of Introduced Species' (1998) 2 *New Zealand Journal of Environmental Law* 157.
[60] On this deep-rooted fear, see D Quammen, *Monster of God: The Man-Eating Predator in the Jungles of History and the Mind* (WW Norton, 2004).

Swamps have a particularly poor image, with many destroyed in the name of economic progress. When Donald Trump was bidding for the US presidency, he promised to 'drain the swamp' in Washington DC to rid it of corruption and cronyism. He could assume that voters understood the slogan without explanation, as a swamp, in the English language at any rate, represents a dark, dirty and dismal place. In Western folklore, swamps have been a caricature for the obstacle to the domestication of nature, an unruly and even haunted place that needs subduing.[61] Much 'progress' has been made in clearing swamps and other types of wetlands, with scientists estimating that one-third of the planet's wetlands have been lost.[62] Despite an international treaty in place since 1971 to protect wetlands,[63] in recognition of their significant value for providing wildlife habitat and services like water purification and protection from coastal flooding, swamps continue to suffer pollution or drainage for economic development.[64] So long as swamp loathing remains a cultural pastime, nourished by films and novels about swamp monsters and bog beasts, the draining and filling of wetlands will probably persist.

Unappealing wildlife have also suffered. Australia has a sordid history of exterminating wildlife. In the nineteenth century so-called 'Marsupial Destruction Acts' were enacted to facilitate removal of wildlife for economic and aesthetic reasons. Queensland's efforts, beginning with the 1877 Act to Facilitate and Encourage the Destruction of Marsupial Animals, paid professional 'scalpers' who helped with the ensuing destruction of at least 27 million animals such as kangaroos and wallabies, and non-marsupial dingoes and foxes, over 54 years.[65] The parliamentary debates reveal the passion of the law's sponsors, and their vivid language, with the grass-devouring marsupials excoriated as 'pests' or 'vermin', swarming in 'plague' proportions, and causing great 'evil', 'ruin' and 'waste' to the detriment of farmers.[66] Though the animals' appearance themselves could not easily be characterised as unattractive, their environmental and economic effects certainly were in the eyes of many landholders.

Tasmania also used bounties to persecute native fauna threats, focusing on its unique marsupial carnivores. The thylacine (*Thylacinus cynocephalus*) was the most despised. In 1805, two years after the Van Diemen's Land colony was founded (as Tasmania was then known), Governor William Paterson set the

---

[61] A Wilson, *Swamp: Nature and Culture* (University of Chicago Press, 2018).

[62] S Hu et al, 'Global Wetlands: Potential Distribution, Wetland Loss, and Status' (2017) 586 *Science of the Total Environment* 319.

[63] Convention on Wetlands of International Importance especially as Waterfowl Habitat, (1972) 31 *ILM* 963.

[64] See eg M Hettiarachchi, TH Morrison and C McAlpine, 'Forty-three Years of Ramsar and Urban Wetlands' (2015) 32 *Global Environmental Change* 57.

[65] FC Hrdina, 'Marsupial Destruction in Queensland 1877–1930' (1997) 30(3) *Australian Zoologist* 272.

[66] Queensland Parliamentary Debates [Hansard], 'Devastation by Marsupials', Legislative Assembly, 16 November 1876, 953–54; 'The Marsupial Pest', Legislative Assembly, 23 November 1876, 1374–75.

tone when he penned the first account of 'an animal of a truly singular and nouvel description' and 'destructive [...] in the form of a hyaena'.[67] Over the next century, salacious press and mythologising demonised the creature colloquially known as the 'tiger': it was branded a 'mischievous and rapacious carnivorous brute',[68] 'vermin'[69] and 'cowardly in proportion to its size'.[70] After sheep farming came to the island in the 1820s, the thylacine was scapegoated as a bloodthirsty sheep killer, and mercilessly persecuted through various government and private bounty schemes until the early 1900s.[71] On 10 July 1936, shortly before the last known specimen died in a Hobart zoo, the thylacine received complete legal protection under the Animals and Birds Protection Act because of its value to science.[72]

Scientific rarity, it would seem, can shift aesthetic appreciation. Fascination with the thylacine has grown with alleged sightings,[73] and the public has come to appreciate the animal as 'majestic'[74] and a 'rare beauty'.[75] It has now become a 'potent cultural icon' for Tasmania with increasing nostalgic representations in its tourism and travel literature.[76] The thylacine room at the Tasmanian Museum and Art Gallery is its most popular attraction, displaying a taxidermy specimen, film clips and other memorabilia that evoke the aesthetics of an animal now admired for its uniqueness.

Owls are another interesting example of ambivalent aesthetics and variable legal status. In many cultures owls foment superstitious beliefs of death and bad omens, perhaps because the creature is mostly a bird of the night, when such fears are heightened. John Lewis-Stempel describes some of these beliefs in his exploration of *The Secret Life of the Owl*: 'a Suffolk superstition which lingered into the Victorian era held that an owl flying past the window of a room in which a sick person lay meant that death was near'.[77] He also cites how 'Chinese children born on the day of the owl, the summer solstice, were considered to have a matricidal personality (... from the Taoist belief that young owls would

---

[67] Papers of Sir J Banks, 'Description of a Tasmanian Tiger Received by Banks from William Paterson, 20 March 1805', quoted in P Olsen, *Upside Down World: European Impressions of Australia's Curious Animals* (National Library of Australia, 2010) 30.

[68] 'The Kangaroo Bill (to the editor) *Mercury* 21 October 1873, 2.

[69] 'Tiger' (to the editor) *Tasmanian News* 6 September 1887, 4.

[70] 'The Royal Society of Tasmania' *The Courier* 16 June 1858, 2.

[71] R Paddle, *The Last Tasmanian Tiger; The History and Extinction of the Thylacine* (Cambridge University Press, 2000).

[72] 1928, 19 Geo V, No 51.

[73] Eg A Park and R Scott, 'Tasmanian Tiger. Extinct or Merely Elusive' (1986) 1(3) *Australian Geographic* 67; 'Thylacine Tracks Found, Cast' *Mercury* 12 January 1953, 6; '"Phantom" Animal May be Tasmanian Tiger' *Mercury* 1 June 1949, 5.

[74] 'Scientists Search for Extinct Tasmanian Tiger After Sightings in Australia', *Inquirer* 27 March 2017, http://technology.inquirer.net.

[75] S McGrath and A Darlison, *Stripes of the Forest: Story of the Last Wild Thylacine* (Big Sky Publishing, 2016).

[76] SS Turner, 'Negotiating Nostalgia: The Rhetoricity of Thylacine Representation in Tasmanian Tourism' (2009) 17 *Society and Animals* 97.

[77] J Lewis-Stempel, *The Secret Life of the Owl* (Transworld Publishers, 2018) 64.

Figure 4.4 Thylacine gallery; collection of Tasmanian Museum and Art Gallery

pluck out their mother's eyes or even devour her)'.[78] Yet, with their human-like face, large eyes and solitary existence, owls are sometimes also equated with wisdom. In many cultures, such as Native American tribes, owls invoke beauty and spiritual power.[79]

Snakes and spiders are among the most despised creatures of all. The antipathy stirs from an early age. A British study in the 1960s found that 27 per cent of the children surveyed identified snakes as their least liked animal.[80] Andrew Knight tested undergraduate students whether species such as snakes and spiders are perceived differently based on aesthetic preferences and other attitudes, and how this correlated with their legal status, finding that aesthetics is an important variable.[81] Periodic community-run, rattlesnake roundups in the

---

[78] Ibid, 65.
[79] L Calvez, *The Hidden Lives of Owls* (Sasquatch Books, 2016) xii.
[80] R Morris and D Morris, *Men and Snakes* (Hutchison, 1965).
[81] AJ Knight, '"Bats, Snakes and Spiders, Oh My!" How Aesthetic and Negativistic Attitudes, and Other Concepts Predict Support for Species Protection' (2008) 28(1) *Journal of Environmental Psychology* 94.

southern United States result in tens of thousands of snakes being displayed and then slaughtered for public entertainment. Although snakes themselves conjure negative aesthetics, their skins are prized for their beauty and many are killed in countries such as Indonesia to make designer handbags, belts and shoes.[82] Official legal protection given to snakes in many jurisdictions is poorly enforced because of the exemption for killing a snake in self-defence.

Even environmental organisations supposedly more attuned to appreciating wildlife on scientific grounds rather than folklore or aesthetic appeal, show a bias against the unattractive. Charismatic, 'flagship' species such as the panda bear, gorilla, dolphin and elephant appear often in the logos and marketing for environmental NGOs, and government agencies too, while amphibians, reptiles or spiders are not.[83] The WWF symbol displays the panda bear, while the Kenyan Wildlife Service has the elephant. But a few exceptions break this pattern: the Rainforest Alliance logo features a frog. Curiously, in 2012 the Ugly Animal Preservation Society was established, using comedy and theatre 'to raise the profile of some of nature's more aesthetically challenged creatures'.[84]

The aesthetic disparagement of animals can also aid environmental policy when applied to invasive species that are truly destructive to biodiversity. Consider the cane toad (*Rhinella marina*), a native of South America, disseminated during the past century to various Pacific islands and Australia to control pest insects but becoming pests themselves. The media has thrown much vitriol against the toads, and militaristic jargon such as 'frontline' and 'invasion' to stoke anxiety about their 'march' across Australia. Many 'toad busting' community groups wage 'war' against the 'ugly beasts'.[85] The cane toad is a declared pest under legislation such as Western Australia's Biosecurity and Agriculture Management Act 2007 and New South Wales' (NSW) Biosecurity Act 2015.

In sum, adverse environmental aesthetics are complicit in a variety of environmental practices and regulations that aim to domesticate wildlife or biomes. The unappealing imagery of some species that pose genuine environmental threats can assist with governance actions, but more commonly these culturally constructed aesthetics can be counter-productive. Folklore has sometimes not kept pace with the development of environmental laws to protect swamps or owls, creating an impediment to their implementation.

III. LOOKS THAT KILL: PERSECUTING THE BEAUTIFUL

Beauty affords no assurance for nature's legal protection either. Indeed, its most beautiful features have sometimes suffered more than its ugly ones.

---

[82] T Thornhill, 'Inside the Indonesian Slaughter House Where Snakes are Killed and Skinned to Make Designer Handbags, Jackets and Shoes' *Daily Mail* (UK) 4 March 2014.

[83] R Home et al, 'Selection Criteria for Flagship Species by Conservation Organizations' (2009) 36(2) *Environmental Conservation* 139.

[84] See https://uglyanimalsoc.com.

[85] See eg Kimberley Toad Busters, www.canetoads.com.au/hewslet21.htm.

Animals coveted for their attractive feathers, furs, skins, horns and tusks have been slaughtered on industrial scales to satisfy the aesthetic tastes of men and women, with the horrors peaking in the late nineteenth and early twentieth centuries before the advent of environmental law controls. Plants too, such as precious orchids and other ornamentals prized for their fragrance or colour, have also been plundered through both legal and illegal trade.

Of numerous examples, birds offer a particularly telling story. The brutal millinery industry from the nineteenth century intensified as global trade in the imperialist economies expanded access to sources of exotic feathers. Much of the horror was documented in William Hornaday's *Our Vanishing Wildlife: Its Extermination and Preservation*, published in 1913 at the height of the slaughter.[86] Hornaday was an American taxidermist, zoologist and prescient conservationist who sought to raise awareness of endangered wildlife. The plumage trade continues to haunt us, with contemporary writers and artists seeking to maintain a vigil about the atrocities, as for instance documented in the 2011 exhibition *Fashioning Feathers: Dead Birds, Millinery Crafts and the Plumage Trade*, curated with the Material Culture Institute of the University of Alberta.[87]

The imperial trade centered on London, while its manufacturing hubs were in Paris and New York. The trade catalogues document the extent of the sordid business: one covering December 1864 to April 1885 recorded '404,464 West Indian and Brazilian birds of various descriptions, 356,389 East Indian birds, 6,828 Birds of Paradise, 4,974 Impeyan pheasants and 770 Argus pheasants'.[88] Fashionable woman would wear hats adorned with not merely feathers but wings and even entire taxidermied specimens. Many live specimens were also poached from the wild to supply the growing demand for pet birds; one consignment that left Australia for London in the 1860s carried 5,000 pairs of cockatoos, according to Jon Simon's account of the then fauna trade.[89]

The feather fashions drove the extinction of several species: the coveted New Zealand huia (*Heteralocha acutirostris*) and the US Carolina parakeet (*Conuropsis carolinensis*) disappeared in the early twentieth century. Many others such as the snowy egret (*Egretta thula*) and the great egret (*Ardea alba*) veered close to decimation: Hornaday, calculated that over one nine-month period the London market had traded feathers from nearly 130,000 egrets.[90]

Agitation about the carnage and cruelties of the millinery trade contributed to the creation in Europe and North America of conservation societies such as

[86] WT Hornaday, *Our Vanishing Wildlife: Its Extermination and Preservation* (Charles Scribner's Sons, 1913).

[87] See https://fashioningfeathers.info.

[88] M Patchett, 'Murderous Millinery', https://fashioningfeathers.info/murderous-millinery.

[89] J Simons, 'The Scramble for Elephants: Exotic Animals and the Imperial Trade' in M Boyde (ed), *Captured: The Animal within Culture* (Palgrave Macmillan, 2014) 26, 34.

[90] W Souder, 'How Two Women Ended the Deadly Feather Trade' *Smithsonian* March 2013, www.smithsonianmag.com.

Figure 4.5 Head and shoulders of model wearing 'Chanticleer' hat of bird feathers, 1912; US Library of Congress

the Audubon, who sought to ban the plumage trade and change ladies' fashion. Although women were the wearers of bird millinery, some were also the leading protesters against it. On 22 May 1875 *Harper's Bazaar* (a popular fashion magazine for well-to-do women) published an article by Mary Thatcher (later Higginson) entitled 'The Slaughter of the Innocents', which fuelled increasing public debate about the ethics of the plume trade and contributed to its eventual demise with shifts in ladies' fashion and law reform. The Audubon Society, established in 1905, had its roots in the Massachusetts Audubon Society founded in in 1896 by Harriet Hemenway and Minna B Hall. Audubon supporters helped secure a variety of government-backed conservation measures, including the first National Wildlife Refuge, at Pelican Island in Florida, in 1903, the Lacey Act 1900[91] that prohibited interstate commerce in birds taken in violation of state laws, and of the Migratory Bird Treaty Act 1918.[92] In the UK, similar legislative protections to curb the worst excesses were enacted, such as the Sea Birds Preservation Act 1869 and the Wild Birds Protection Act 1872, and even more importantly the foundation of the Royal Society for the Protection of Birds in 1889 (incorporated by royal charter in 1904). The latter body was founded through the efforts of Emily Williamson, who was concerned about plummeting British bird populations and the cruelty of their hunting. Yet, a succession of

---

[91] Ch 553 s 1, 31 Stat 187 (1900).
[92] Ch 128, 40 Stat 703 (1919); see further RW Doughty, *Feather Fashions and Bird Preservation: A Study in Nature Protection* (University of California Press, 1975) 103–15.

'plumage' bills designed to restrict the international trade stalled in the House of Commons until the early 1920s.[93]

The fur industry, still with us although of diminished stature, offers a tale equally barbaric. Wearing of animal furs is probably as old as *Homo sapiens'* evolutionary history, but the modern fur industry took off under the auspices of the imperial trading business, the Hudson's Bay Company, founded in 1670. It established a network of trappers, traders and manufacturers across North America and the UK for some two centuries, catering to the epicurean taste for fur coats and hats fashioned principally from otter or beaver pelts.[94] Established by royal charter, the Hudson's Bay Company enjoyed a privileged legal position to exploit natural resources, with the explicit mandate of 'finding some trade for furs, mineral and other considerable commodities'.[95]

Other corners of the world also got into the business. During the nineteenth and twentieth centuries Australia slaughtered millions of possums, koalas, kangaroos and other fur-bearing marsupials for the global fur trade, and even shipped possums to New Zealand so that it could develop its own fur industry (the imported creatures have now become one of New Zealand's worst pests). To indicate the scale, in Queensland during the first three decades of the twentieth century, between 400,000 to three million possums and between 450,000 to one million koalas were taken annually.[96] While this fur industry declined substantially from the 1930s, it persisted in Tasmania where possum pelts were still harvested for several decades.[97] From around 1920 public opinion began to shift, as evident by letters to newspapers from school children, scientific groups, prominent community members and some farmer groups agitating over fauna population declines and cruel harvesting methods.[98] A newspaper story in 1929 entitled 'The Slaughter of the Innocents' described public opposition to the Queensland government's then recent declaration of an open season against koala, which one group praised as 'one of the most lovable and harmless little animals in the world'.[99]

The rarity or prevalence of a species has had a bearing on the public's valuation of its aesthetic properties. Take the cockatoo, a parrot family comprising 21 species found especially in Australia. During the late nineteenth century, the common sulphur-crested cockatoo (*Cacatua galerita*) was increasingly persecuted as a 'pest' because of its apparently large populations and tendency to

---

[93] Ibid, 117–23.

[94] EJ Dolin, *Fur, Fortune and Empire* (WW Norton, 2010).

[95] The Royal Charter for Incorporating the Hudson's Bay Company, 1670, preamble, http://caid. ca/HubBatCha1670.pdf.

[96] F Hrdina and G Gordon, 'The Koala and Possum Trade in Queensland, 1906–1936' (2004) 32(4) *Australian Zoologist* 543, 571–72.

[97] Department of Primary Industries, Parks, Water and Environment (DPIPWE), *Management Plan for the Commercial Harvest and Export of Brushtail Possums in Tasmania 2010–2015* (DPIPWE, 2010) 7–8.

[98] Hrdina and Gordon, 'The Koala and Possum Trade' (above n 96) 546.

[99] 'The Slaughter of the Innocents' *Telegraph* (Brisbane) 2 May 1929, 8.

Figure 4.6 Truck load of koala skins in the Clermont area, Queensland, 1927; G Pullar; John Oxley Library, State Library of Queensland

browse on farmers' crops; yet, the 'extremely rare' black cockatoo were 'prized as novelties' and sought out for the international pet trade.[100] The New Zealand huia (*Heteralocha acutirostris*), now extinct, was treasured for its feathers and skins, and its growing rarity simply made the species even more coveted. While the bird had legal protection from 1892 under the Wild Birds Protection Act, its feathers could still be traded, thus condoning the illegal hunting.[101] The last huia was seen in 1907.

Natural beauty below the ground is also coveted. Mining of precious metals, such as gold, and gemstones like diamonds and opals, owes to the desire to design jewellery and other works of art, as well to create tangible stores of wealth. Mining has a deep history, with the earliest example in the archaeological records being the 42,000-year-old Ngwenya mine in Swaziland, where red ochre was extracted for use in rock paintings and other purposes.[102] Gold mining is nearly 7,000 years old, as gold artefacts have been found in graves at the 4,600 BCE Varna Necropolis in Bulgaria. Diamonds were perhaps first collected in India about 400 BCE.

Extracting nature's subterranean beauty has wreaked a heavy environmental burden. A miner's description of the onslaught of the Australian gold mining

---

[100] Greer, *White Beach* (above n 39) 308.

[101] M Szabo, 'Huia, the Sacred Bird' *New Zealand Geographic*, October–December 1993, www. nzgeo.com/stories/huia-the-sacred-bird.

[102] The site is now listed under the World Heritage Convention: http://whc.unesco.org/en/ tentativelists/5421.

rush in the 1850s confesses: 'we are horribly destructive of the pictureseque [....]
The trees are felled by thousands; the creeks are laid open in long stretches to the
day, by the tea-trees and scrub being cut down'.[103] Twentieth-century industrial
technologies enabled even greater devastation. American writer Wendell Barry
in 1972 described the ruin brought by strip mining in the Appalachians in his
polemic 'Mayhem in the Industrial Paradise' as follows:

> [i]n some eastern Kentucky counties, for mile after mile, the land has been liter-
> ally hacked to pieces ... Whole mountain tops have been torn off and cast into the
> valleys. ... It is a scene from the Book of Revelation. It is a domestic Vietnam.[104]

In addition to its unsightly scars, mining is sometimes leveraged with toxic chemicals such as arsenic and cyanide that poison the water and soil. Mining sludge
and tailings ponds can leave enduring deathtraps for unwary birds and other creatures that might visit, and occasionally these impoundments break, as occurred
in 2015 at BHP's Samarco mine in Brazil when the collapse of its waste dam wall
released a lethal torrent of sludge that destroyed a village and its environs.[105]
Legal measures to restore mining sites to their former condition are discussed in
Chapter 6 on the aesthetics of ecological restoration.

IV. MUSEUMS FOR NATURE'S RELICS

Natural history museums, often established by governments, have become
prominent forums for demonstrating not only the societal importance of the
natural sciences but also our colonisation of nature. The galleries of taxidermy specimens and landscape dioramas allow museum visitors to encounter
memorials to a vanquished nature that has been souvenired and decorated for
voyeuristic pleasure.[106] Crowds throng to the ghoulish taxidermy displays at
Paris' Le Musée de la Chasse et de la Nature, New York's American Museum of
Natural History or Berlin's Museum für Naturkunde.

Collecting natural ornamentals has a long history. Cabinets of curiosities such as shells and skulls became common among the affluent during the
European Renaissance, while the fashion intensified in the nineteenth century
owing to scientific curiosity and to celebrate the imperial acquisition of exotic
fauna from far-flung colonies. Museums such as King Leopold II's Royal
Museum for Central Africa in Tervuren, Belgium, became imperial archives
complicit with empire-building. Apart from zoos, such collections were (and
remain) sometimes the only means by which the general public could observe

---

[103] Quoted in R Annear, *Nothing But Gold: The Diggers of 1852* (Text Publishing, 1999) 179.
[104] W Berry, *A Continuous Harmony: Essays Cultural and Agricultural* (Harcourt Brace Jovanovich, 1972) 170.
[105] JD Carneiro, 'Brazil Dam Burst: Six Months on, the Marks Left by Sea of Sludge' *BBC News* 6 May 2016, www.bbc.com/news/world-latin-america-36230578.
[106] Asma, *Stuffed Animals* (above n 20).

wild animals 'in the flesh'. While zoos of this era were generally entertainment gardens, museums assumed a more pedagogic role associated with scientific research and educating visitors about the taxonomy of the animal kingdom and species' biogeographical distributions.

Taxidermy itself became a fad in the nineteenth century, coinciding with the height of European empires.[107] The taxidermist removed the decaying parts from dead animal bodies and refilled them with wire and stuffing that recaptured the physicality and even some behaviours of the living original. The display of taxidermic objects commonly comes with information panels about the species' behavioural and geographical traits. The expatriate elite would return home with their spoils and souvenirs to adorn their billiard rooms and hallways, and the zoomorphic craze of the era resulted in many specimens reshaped into footstools, waste bins, walking-stick stands, lamps, ashtrays and other household wares.[108] For specialist game hunters, their country estates bristled with sets of antlers and mounted animal heads as reminders of their 'heroic' subjugation. Though taxidermy no longer is so fashionable, it continues to appeal to hunting enthusiasts; contemporary hunting magazines often feature photographs of trophy heads.[109]

Museums acquired taxidermy collections to appease scientific interest and voyeuristic curiosity, and some specimens were incorporated into substantial three-dimensional dioramas that depicted animals in realistic habitat settings. The word 'diorama', from the Greek for 'to see through', was coined by the French artist Louis Daguerre who in the 1820s began staging theatrical entertainments embellished with realistic scenes painted on background screens. A method transposed to the natural history context in the late nineteenth century, the life-size, three-dimensional environmental diorama added a picturesque backdrop, comprising a painted panoramic setting such as a savannah, or mountain range along with 'foreground' accessories of real-world size such as shrubs, leaf litter and rocks to create a realistic depiction of a large scene in a compact space. Museum curators often perched the animals in action poses, such as birds feeding or a carnivore pursuing its next meal, and the frequent use of dim lighting helped to create a cinematic effect. The moose diorama at Philadelphia's Academy of Natural Sciences, shown below, illustrates how these displays allowed visitors to get tantalising close to the life-like wildlife, offering an intimacy that only zoos could rival. In 2012 the Academy upgraded the dioramas in its North American Hall by adding sound effects including the calls of bears, bison and other creatures to deepen visitors' aesthetic experience.[110]

---

[107] PA Morris, *A History of Taxidermy: Art, Science and Bad Taste* (MPM Publishing, 2010).

[108] A Turner, *Taxidermy* (Thames and Hudson, 2013) 136.

[109] L Kalof and A Fitzgerald, 'Reading the Trophy: Exploring the Display of Dead Animals in Hunting Magazines' (2003) 18(2) *Visual Studies* 112, 115.

[110] 'Unfrozen in Time – New Sound Installation Brings Historic Dioramas to Life at the Academy of Natural Sciences', Drexel NOW, 3 July 2012, https://drexel.edu/now/archive/2012/July/Unfrozen-in-Time-Sound-Installation-Dioramas-Academy.

Figure 4.7 Moose diorama, 1935, with my niece Ramona; Academy of Natural Sciences, Philadelphia; photograph by Tobias Richardson

Carl Akeley pioneered the design of habitat dioramas, beginning at the Milwaukee Public Museum in 1889. Later he worked at the American Natural History Museum in New York, a trailblazer in the art of habitat dioramas of astonishing realism.[111] Typically, scientists, artists and taxidermists organised expeditions to collect specimens and accurately document their habitats for re-creation in the diorama, suggestive of Carlson's ideas about the importance of grounding the appreciation of environmental aesthetics in scientific knowledge. Their techniques were also influenced by the artistic conventions of the picturesque and the sublime that remained influential during this formative period.[112] Ironically, museums displayed animals killed partly in the name of conservation. Carl Akeley himself dispatched many, even gorillas, for his dioramas, and he confessed in 1925:

> I have been constantly aware of the rapid and disconcerting disappearance of African wildlife. [This] gave rise to the vision of the culmination of my work in a great museum exhibit, artistically conceived, which should perpetuate the animal life, the native customs, and the scenic beauties of Africa.[113]

---

[111] SC Quinn, *Windows on Nature: The Great Habitat Dioramas of the American Museum of Natural History* (Abrams, 2006).

[112] C Kamcke and R Hutterer, 'History of Dioramas' in SD Tunnicliffe and A Scheersol (eds), *Natural History Dioramas* (Springer, 2015) 7, 7.

[113] CE Akeley, *In Brightest Africa* (Garden City Publishing, 1925) 251.

Many of the specimens collected by the Smithsonian National Museum of Natural History were provided by former US President Theodore Roosevelt, whose 1909 expedition to East Africa sponsored by the Smithsonian bagged 11,788 animals, many killed by Roosevelt personally who (incongruously) had formerly created the US Forest Service, established five national parks and numerous other wildlife reserves.[114]

Taxidermy and dioramas, it may surprise you at this point, have a variety of connections to the law. As 'a classificatory system through which the natural world was understood',[115] such as cabinets displaying like 'classes' (eg felines, primates, ungulates), taxidermy resembles the law in its approach to bring social order and structure. Natural history museum collections also served to educate the public about natural values and thereby to promote their conservation. Frank M Chapman, the American Natural History Museum's first bird curator, used dioramas for this purpose, with the museum's Pelican Island diorama helping to win federal support for the first national bird reserve.[116] While stuffed specimens and habitat dioramas may be artistic gems, they can make for a poor way for the public to experience nature and promote conservation. As the US Ninth Circuit noted, 'Congress did not mandate that the [National Park] Service preserve the wilderness in a museum diorama [...] that we might observe only from a safe distance, behind a brass railing and a thick glass window'.[117] Environmental law interacts most directly with the taxidermy business through its controls on the trade in endangered species and their parts. The Convention on International Trade in Endangered Species of Wild Fauna and Flora 1973 obliges state parties to restrict trade in species listed under the treaty, covering trade in both live and dead specimens, and their parts such as ivory carvings, animal pelts and taxidermy mountings.[118] Complementary provisions in domestic law, such as licensing of taxidermy practices and prohibitions on stuffing species listed as protected, add to the legal context.

The aesthetics of dioramas and taxidermy became decisively less appealing in the late twentieth century. One turning point might have been the original *Planet of the Apes* film, released in 1968, which shocked audiences with its scene of taxidermied human beings displayed in dioramas for the pleasure of the apes. In one incident the desperate Taylor, the sole surviving astronaut fleeing the apes, stumbles across one of his fellow travellers now rendered into an inert museum exhibit. Interest in dioramas and taxidermy also waned as film itself introduced new, more lifelike perspectives of wildlife.

---

[114] T Roosevelt, *African Game Trails: An Account of the African Wanderings of An American Hunter-Naturalist* (Scribnxer, 1910).

[115] J Philip, 'The Natural Object: Exhibiting the Macleay Museum's Specimen Collections' (2016) 29 *Journal of Museum Ethnography* 11, 15.

[116] A DenHoed, 'The Making of the American Museum of Natural History's Wildlife Dioramas' *The New Yorker* 15 February 2016.

[117] *Wilderness Watch, Inc v U.S. Fish and Wildlife Service*, 629 F 3d (2010) 1024, 1033.

[118] (1973) 12 ILM 1085.

The fetishistic memorialisation of nature has since attracted a range of artistic critiques. One is the travelling show *In Nanoq: The Great White Bear: A Survey of British Taxidermic Polar Bears 2001–2004*, created by Bryndis Snæbjörnsdóttir and Mark Wilson in 2006.[119] Opened at Oslo's Polar Fram Museum, their photography exhibition challenged the mythology of the 'gallant' hunter of the polar bear, an animal now the proverbial 'canary in the coal mine' for global warming. The artists photographed 34 taxidermic *Ursus maritimus* from British collections, with each photograph captioned with details about the bear's biography including where and how it met its demise. The exhibition, which moved through a variety of museums and art galleries over the next three years, sought to celebrate the bear rather than its hunter, taxidermist or collector. For one rendition of their show, ten of the bears were relocated to an art gallery space at Spike Island, England, allowing the specimens to exist on their own terms within viewers' imagination. Snæbjörnsdóttir and Wilson's exhibition gave these animals a new life, and emphasised how symbols and narratives shape our understanding of nature.

Increasingly aware of such sensitivities, some natural history museums have reframed their collections. The Natural History Museum in London informs visitors that: 'the Museum is concerned about the conservation of animals in the natural world and no longer collects skins for taxidermy displays. The specimens in these displays are from the Museum's historical collections'.[120] The curatorial practices of many natural history museums (eg Smithsonian Institution and the Australian Museum) have now transformed these institutions into interactive and educational sites. Inclusion of a 'discovery room', interactive games, a 'live' corner (eg small aquarium), are part of the new generation of curatorial techniques that encourage the audience to question, test and evaluate exhibits.[121]

V. OUT OF SIGHT, OUT OF MIND

This chapter's final story concerns animals whose suffering is kept out of sight, and thus often out of mind. Despite much progress in legislating animal welfare over the past two centuries, as documented in Kathryn Shevelow's masterpiece *For the Love of Animals*,[122] animal abuse continues on a vast scale, with millions of livestock cruelly slaughtered for our food while millions of other creatures are guinea pigs for testing cosmetics or pharmaceuticals. Animal cruelty may

---

[119] M Wilson, *Nanoq: Flat Out and Bluesome: a Cultural Life of Polar Bears* (Black Dog Publishing, 2006). The exhibition was later called *Nanoq: Flat Out and Bluesome*.

[120] Quoted in R Poliquin, *The Breathless Zoo: Taxidermy and the Cultures of Longing* (Pennsylvania State University Press, 2012) 138.

[121] See SM Nair, 'The "Greening" of Natural History Museums' (1996) 48 *Museum International* 8.

[122] K Shevelow, *For the Love of Animals: The Rise of the Animal Protection Movement* (Henry Holt, 2008).

not be as overtly barbaric as in the eighteenth century before legislative reform began, but because of factory farming and the global cosmetics industry it is more prevalent and institutionalised. Not only does the law tolerate the status quo through weak animal 'welfare' standards, it helps conceal it by criminalising covert, unauthorised filming or photography in factory farms or other premises where animals suffer. Censorship has become a powerful tool for lawmakers to control the aesthetics of animal welfare and thus to protect the economically lucrative industries that profit from it.

Historically, animals' misery was much more public and indeed popular entertainment. Using her training as a historian, Shevelow takes us back to eighteenth century England to reveal in livid detail the attitudes and practices under which many animals suffered. Exploited as beasts of burden, horses and donkeys were habitually exhausted to near-death by sadistic stagecoach drivers and haulers. Blood sports were popular with all classes, with bear gardens and cockpits attracting both the *hoi polloi* and the nobility. Shevelow recounts how one such spectacle, involving a tiger pitted against several dogs, caused 'a parliamentary bill concerning the old East India Company to los[e] by ten votes because so many of its supporters in the House of Commons had gone to see the tiger baiting instead'.[123] While wilful ignorance and greed today hinder the humane treatment of animals, two hundred years ago in England it was the belief that cruelty toward animals was not morally wrong.

The focus for animal welfare today has shifted to different contexts. Deploying industrial-like procedures, factory farms maltreat cattle, pigs, poultry and innumerable other creatures in the quest to satiate consumers' desire for convenient, cheap meals and other products such as clothing. Even modest legislative proposals to mitigate abuses face stiff opposition from agricultural businesses and the fast food industry. While many consumers profess empathy for these animals, few will change their dietary preferences or purchase goods certified as 'cruelty free'.

The law is complicit in animal cruelty. Not only may governments appease big business with lax animal welfare standards, or fail to enforce ostensibly stricter ones, they may use the law to conceal the horrors within factory farms and animal testing laboratories. The latter measures are colloquially known as 'ag-gag' laws, serving to gag whistle-blowers by criminalising undercover investigations on farms, especially by film or photography. Ag-gag laws shield the agricultural sector from public scrutiny by concealing abuse such as cramped cages and inhumane slaughtering. Violations of such laws can attract harsh penalties, and thus may deter employees or animal rights activists who wish to publicise animal husbandry malpractices. Activists thus see their most important strategy as not simply theoretical elaboration of their position, as in Peter Singer's ground-breaking work,[124] but to foster social change by making the public more directly and intimately aware of animal suffering.

[123] Ibid, 44.
[124] P Singer, *Animal Liberation: A New Ethics for our Treatment of Animals* (Random House 1975).

As the animal rights group Voiceless explains, 'surveillance footage, which is often graphic and confronting, promotes public awareness of these issues. This in turn leads to open dialogue, which is essential in shaping public opinion and encouraging law reform'.[125] Such surveillance footage may also provide evidence to support prosecution of animal welfare offenders. An example of this strategy is the effort in Australia to curb the live animal export trade. The exposé *A Bloody Business*, aired on national television, showed millions of viewers footage of Australian cattle being abused in Indonesian slaughterhouses. The uproar led Australian authorities to suspend the live animal exports to Indonesia, and introduce the Export Supply Chain Assurance Scheme to improve regulatory oversight of the trade.[126] The issue remains contentious, with covert footage of distressed sheep exported on ships to the Middle East shown on Australian media in 2018 sparking calls for permanent bans of the trade, but resulting only in rules requiring more space be given to shipped sheep to improve ventilation.[127]

Ag-gag laws emerged only recently. Devised in the United States, seven US states had enacted them as of early 2019, although courts struck down two of these efforts because they violated freedom of speech. Idaho's Agricultural Security Act 2014 was ruled unconstitutional in August 2015, and the same fate was met by Utah's ag-gag statute in July 2017.[128] Although the US Congress Animal Enterprise Terrorism Act 2006 does not contain explicit ag-gag provisions, it serves a similar goal to intimidate and stigmatise animal welfare advocates perceived as attempting to disrupt farming operations, even by such innocuous means as leafleting.[129] With similar aims to thwart transparency, so-called food libel laws have been enacted in some US states, and they were sensationally used by the beef industry against Oprah Winfrey in 1998 after her remarks about the 'mad cow' disease scandal.

Ag-gag laws have caught the attention of some Australian legislators, albeit without progress so far. In NSW, the Animal Protection and Crimes Legislation Amendment (Reporting Animal Cruelty and Protection of Animal Enterprises) Bill 2018, which lapsed without being passed in February 2019, envisioned new criminal offences that target the whistle-blowing activities of animal rights activists, and to require any footage of cruelty to animals to be handed over to the police. At federal level, the Criminal Code Amendment (Animal Protection) Bill 2015, which has also lapsed, sought to create new offences in relation to failure to hand over to authorities any visual recording of malicious cruelty to domestic

---

[125] Voiceless, 'Ag-Gag', www.voiceless.org.au/hot-topics/ag-gag.
[126] Australia Department of Agriculture and Water Resources, 'Exporter Supply Chain Assurance System', www.agriculture.gov.au/export/controlled-goods/live-animals/livestock/information-exporters-industry/escas.
[127] G Brown and E Ritchie, 'Call for Live Animal Trade Ban After TV Footage of Dying Sheep' *The Australian* 9 April 2018.
[128] *Animal Legal Defense Fund v Otter*, 118 F Supp 3d 1195 (D Idaho 2015); *Animal Legal Defense Fund et al v Herbert*, 263 F Supp 3d 1193 (D Utah 2017).
[129] Public Law 109-374 (2006).

Figure 4.8 Iowa Ag-Gag protest 2012; Mercy for Animals; licensed under Creative Commons

animals, and interference with the conduct of lawful animal enterprises. Legislative reform has, however, succeeded in the other direction; the Australian Capital Territory's Animal Welfare (Factory Farming) Amendment Act 2017 effectively bans factory farming through prohibitions on certain cruel animal handling facilities and practices. From England, another positive step is an obligation introduced in 2018 on all abattoirs to install CTTV so that veterinarians can monitor how animals are housed and killed to ensure better compliance with animal welfare standards.[130]

Concurrent with efforts to suppress ugly imagery of their operations, food companies peddle a deceptive aesthetic of bucolic farming. Corporate greenwashing is examined in detail in Chapter 5, but a few comments will help here to flesh out this discussion. Food packaging, including for meat products, commonly contains images of serene agrarian farming at odds with industrialised production methods. Images of golden wheat fields, apple-cheeked farmers and rustic barns, accompanied by slogans such as 'humanely raised' and 'family farms', help to seduce shoppers. This pastoral fantasy also helps to dull their awareness of the supermarket milieu itself, disconnected from the sounds and images of the countryside where previous generations lived. The Animal Welfare Institute's review of 25 food labels approved by the US government on meat products found that it 'regularly approv[es] the use of animal welfare and

---

[130] Mandatory Use of Closed Circuit Television in Slaughterhouses (England) Regulations 2018, No 556.

environmental claims with little or no supporting evidence documenting the accuracy of the claims'.[131]

The law also mediates the aesthetics of drug and cosmetic safety testing on animals through similar techniques of criminalising undercover investigations and restricting publication of photographs or films. Ironically, cruelty to animals is often done in the name of beauty, as cosmetics are tested on monkeys or guinea pigs to improve consumers' appearances. Unlike factory farms, however, animal rights are increasingly affirmed in the realm of lab testing. Leading the way, the EU's Cosmetics Directive 2003 introduced bans on testing cosmetic products and their ingredients, and marketing of any such cosmetics tested else-where, which was phased in over the following six years.[132] As of early 2019, four US states have legislated bans on testing cosmetics on animals, beginning with California's decree in 2002.[133]

Animal cruelty and its regulation are thus mired in a political struggle between the food and cosmetic industries and animal welfare proponents over not merely the underlying animal handling standards but also public trans-parency. For the perpetrators, 'out of sight, out of mind' matters. For their opponents, the preferred adage is 'seeing is believing', thus seeking to educate consumers and politicians through not merely reasoned argument but raw images and sounds of animal suffering to provoke empathy.[134] The book's closing chapter examines the animal rights activists' promotion of a counter aesthetic through undercover operations.

VI. CONCLUSION

The aesthetics of colonised nature are increasingly contested socially and legally, as pressures grow for a more enlightened, post-colonial outlook. The penchant for domesticated nature, from the inert museum specimens to the pacified coun-tryside, is challenged by a new politicised aesthetics in which the public has to confront environmental violence and animal cruelty. The law has already shown considerable evolution in responding to the shifting aesthetics of the natural environment. Some animals once considered unsightly vermin are now cherished with full legal protection. The law has also maintained or tightened controls on the global trade in nature's endangered beauty, such as shells, horns, tusks, skins

---

[131] Animal Welfare Institute, *Label Confusion: How 'Humane' and 'Sustainable' Claims on Meat Packages Deceive Consumers* (Animal Welfare Institute, 2014) 1.

[132] Directive 2003/15/EC of the European Parliament and of the Council of 27 February 2003 amending Council Directive 76/768/EEC on the approximation of the laws of the Member States relating to cosmetic products, OJ L 66/26, 11.3.2003.

[133] California Civil Code (2002), s 1834.9.

[134] RK Wrock, 'Ignorance is Bliss: Self-regulation and Ag-Gag Laws in the American Meat Indus-try' (2016) 192 *Contemporary Justice Review* 237.

and flowers, though illegal practices have proved difficult to control. The history of acclimatisation societies shows a similar movement; their legacy brings shame today as citizens of the Antipodes take greater pride in their natural landscapes and native fauna as part of their redefined national identity, as evident in the motifs that appear on their nations' bank notes, coins, coats-of-arms and other stately symbols.

Yet, obstacles to change persist. In the food industry, political and business elites obstruct greater transparency of factory farm horrors for fear of how a shocked public would react. Indeed, in some jurisdictions they enlist the law to hide animal suffering from public observation. Public sentiment to animal welfare can also be highly contradictory: consider how many cultures view the dog as 'man's (sic) best friend', yet concomitantly persecute wild dogs (including wolves and dingoes). One chilling example I wish to mention is from the scene in the film *Ghost Dog* (1999) where the protagonist, an African-American hit man seeking to emulate the noble samurai warrior tradition, encounters two white hunters who have just illegally killed a black bear. After one of the poachers defends the killing because 'there are not too many of these big black fuckers left around here', the vigilante replies after shooting both dead that, 'in ancient cultures bears were considered equal with men'. Just as animals can conjure up mixed feelings, the same can be said for places; we may admire a beautiful forest in a national park but prefer to remove trees if they block scenic views, especially of water.[135] Aesthetic values thus often have highly situation-specific or place-based contexts.

And new threats loom, associated with the replacement of real nature with synthetic versions. At least public awareness of the menace of plastics has grown rapidly to the point that some businesses now voluntarily take symbolic measures, such as removing plastic bags, while the EU has adopted legislative controls, with agreement reached in May 2019 for a new directive to curb use of certain plastics.[136] The EU law seeks to ban a variety of single-use plastics (eg straws and cups) by 2021 and oblige Member States to recycle 90 per cent of all single-use bottles by 2025. A similar legal battle festers over GMOs. Aesthetics animate these struggles.

---

[135] This is more common than you might think: see eg, J Armstrong, 'Socialite in Scandal Over Chopped Trees' *Globe and Mail* 22 August 2000.

[136] Council of the European Union, Proposal for a Directive of the European Parliament and Council on the Reduction of Certain Plastic Products on the Environment, 5483/19, 18 January 2019; C Sanz, 'Single-use Plastics will be Banned in EU by 2021' *The Times* 22 May 2019.

5

Corporate Greenwashing

I. ORIENTATION

MANY OLDER PEOPLE remember the iconic 'Crying Indian' advert, televised by the Keep America Beautiful campaign on Earth Day on 22 April 1971.[1] Widely applauded as one of the cleverest marketing campaigns of the twentieth century, the 60-second clip features an actor in Native American attire paddling a canoe. Initially the canoeist moves through an unspoiled waterway that implies a pristine past, but as he travels further, the water becomes increasingly polluted and he eventually enters a bustling industrial port. Coming ashore, the 'Indian' strides towards a busy highway where a passing driver tosses a bag of trash that splatters on his moccasins. With a sonorous voice, the narrator exclaims: 'some people have a deep, abiding respect for the natural beauty that was once this country. And some people don't'. With only 27 words spoken, the message and strength of the advert rests on its aesthetic effects: the varied imagery and skilful photography set to a pulsating soundtrack of beating drums progressively overlaid with a chorus of trombones and trumpets. The advert generated huge public awareness and support for Keep America Beautiful.

The Crying Indian advert, however, was disingenuous. Apart from the deception of an Italian-American actor wearing a wig posing as an Indian, the anti-littering campaign was created with major beverage and packaging businesses wanting to obfuscate their responsibility. The advert was released when the US environmental movement was becoming more assertive against industry, which sought to shift the public perception away from themselves. The advert finishes with a close-up of the Indian's face shedding a single tear, with the narrator declaring, 'people start pollution, and people can stop it'. By focusing on uncouth litterbugs, the advert placed responsibility on the general public while deflecting attention from the corporate polluters. Indeed the businesses associated with the campaign kept a low profile, leaving the public to believe that corporate America was a non-complicit bystander. Unsurprisingly,

---

[1] See the advert at www.youtube.com/watch?v=j7OHG7tHrNM. This chapter draws partially on my article, 'Green Illusions: Governing CSR Aesthetics' (2019) 35 *Windsor Yearbook of Access to Justice*, in press.

contemporary Americans are far more wasteful than they were in the early 1970s, with the average citizen in 2012 generating 4.38 pounds of waste every day compared to 3.25 pounds in 1970.[2]

This deceptive environmental marketing persists, and it may relate to specific corporate merchandise, companies' general operations and policies or even to an entire industry sector. When businesses try to impress the public with their environmental performance, bragging about their low carbon footprint or other supposed green credentials, they frequently embellish their claims with aesthetic artefacts. Corporate sustainability reports bristling with technical data are seemingly not convincing enough. Instead, the public might see Renault's Twingo 'eco' car, in one advertisement pictured with leaves blowing from its exhaust, BP's stylised sunflower corporate logo, or the choir singing along to Fiji Water's commercial for the 'Earth's finest water'. Colloquially, we call this nonsense 'greenwashing'; but if done authentically, we might call it 'corporate social responsibility' (CSR).

Figure 5.1 BP logo at petrol station, Johannesburg; photograph by Benjamin J Richardson

---

[2] US Environmental Protection Agency, 'Municipal Solid Waste Generation, Recycling, and Disposal in the United States: Facts and Figures for 2012' (2015) 1, www.epa.gov/sites/production/files/2015-09/documents/2012_msw_fs.pdf.

The aesthetics of CSR matter to this book because the private sector is both an object and agent of environmental governance. From individual companies to collective industry associations, the private sector's environmental performance is shaped through codes of conduct, voluntary agreements, peer pressure and other means beyond official regulation. Contrary to the dominant narratives about the virtues of aesthetic appreciation for emotional gratification and moral improvement, this chapter highlights their negative connotations in the world of business. The beauty evoked by commercial marketing may induce consumers to act to their later regret on sober reflection, but more is at stake when these aesthetic charms camouflage environmental injury. Where regulation of corporate marketing and CSR practices fails, civil society activists and artists can become useful governance partners, a contribution that the final chapter explores.

The aesthetics of corporate marketing and CSR can penetrate further, into the very identity or personality of the business. Unlike a human being, the 'distinguishing feature of the body corporate is its invisibility', explains law professor Leslie Moran.[3] Generally lacking a discrete, singular presence, especially in the case of multinational corporations, business identity commonly manifests through its aural and visual logos, websites and the advertising and packaging of its products or services.[4] The corporation may seemingly be everywhere but also nowhere, without connection to any specific or tangible place, existing simply as symbols and signs.

The aesthetic artefacts of corporate identity feed off the broader aestheticisation of our post-modernising world. Sociologist Jean Baudrillard coined the term 'hyper-reality' to describe this milieu, habitually associated with shopping malls, amusement parks, television reality shows, tabloid celebrity gossip, social media and other realms that saturate consumers with spectacles and 'simulacra'. Philosopher Umberto Eco observes that the masses desire to consume or experience this hyper-reality as though it authentically expresses actual life. Like the advent of 'fake news' that has stained Donald Trump's presidency, this culture of illusion obfuscates understanding the external reality that lies behind such simulations.[5] As Baudrillard puts it, 'we live in a world where there is more and more information, and less and less meaning'.[6] Hyper-reality thus risks obfuscating our capacity to make critical judgements: 'aestheticization breaks into anaesthetization' remarks Wolfgang Welsch.[7] These trends can make it difficult

---

[3] L Moran, '"Skeleton Arguments": The Art of Corporate Criminal Capacity' in R Kevelson (ed), *Law and Aesthetics* (Peter Lang, 1992) 303, 307.

[4] P Hancock, 'Aesthetics and Aestheticization' in P Hancock and A Spicer (eds), *Understanding Corporate Life* (Sage, 2009) 46, 51–52.

[5] J Baudrillard, 'The Hyper-realism of Simulation' in C Harrison and P Wood (eds), *Art in Theory 1900–1990: An Anthology of Changing Ideas* (Blackwell, 1990) 1049.

[6] J Baudrillard, *Simulacra and Simulation*, translated SF Glaser (University of Michigan Press, 1994) 79.

[7] W Welsch, *Undoing Aesthetics* (Sage, 1997) 25.

to discern and control deceptive business aesthetics, as the problem goes beyond discrete misleading advertising to the corporations themselves and the marketplace at large embedded in this hyper-reality.

This aestheticisation of consumption should matter to environmental law because it fuels economic growth that over-burdens the planet. A report surveying changes in the US economy from 1901 to 2003 remarked that, 'mass consumption, spurred by advertising and consumer credit, has become a distinguishing characteristic of modern society'.[8] Worldwide consumer expenditure during the twentieth century soared from US$1.5 trillion in 1900 to $24 trillion in 1998 in real terms.[9] Consumer or household spending represents the largest share of gross domestic product (GDP) in the West, at about 60 per cent of British GDP[10] and 70 per cent of American GDP in recent years.[11] Such stupendous growth and consumer bingeing unsustainably enlarges the economy relative to the biosphere that could sustain it.[12]

While the law can discipline blatant deception, the larger aesthetic characteristics of the business world and their role in damaging consumption tend to defy effective legal scrutiny. Corporate logos, websites and other aesthetic expressions have subtle and nuanced connotations that regulators may not detect or act on. Counter-aesthetic strategies led by artists allied with environmental activists may help to unmask these unregulated green illusions, and thereby make consumers more discerning about corporate practices. Impersonating corporate personalities, reconfiguring logos, manipulating websites, defacing billboards and caricaturing advertisements to subvert their messages, are methods of aesthetic sabotage – also known as 'culture jamming' – that the final chapter examines. I will also argue there that the law cannot insouciantly watch these 'counter-aesthetic' strategies; rather, it must actively protect public spaces from business expropriation and uphold activists' freedom of expression.

Although this chapter critiques the corporate sector, we must recognise that governments themselves are no strangers to artful manipulation. Propaganda has long served totalitarian regimes to sway the *hoi polloi*,[13] and indeed all governments use aesthetic strategies in some ways to cultivate favourable impressions. Many also deploy greenwashed imagery in cultivating their national identity, as Chapter 2 acknowledged, such as the environmental motifs

---

[8] E Chao and K Utgoff, *100 Years of U.S. Consumer Spending, Data for the Nation, New York City, and Boston* (US Department of Labor, May 2006) 1.

[9] United Nations Development Programme (UNDP), *Human Development Report 1998* (UNDP, 1998) 1.

[10] Office for National Statistics, 'Consumer Trends, UK: July to September 2017', *Statistical Bulletin*.

[11] M Crutsinger, 'US Consumer Spending up 0.6 Percent, Best in 5 Months' *Associated Press* 31 March 2018, www.apnews.com/79a5d9b9d2a74f97b5819fd316b8d6c0/US-consumer-spending-up-0.6-percent,-best-in-5-months.

[12] See generally JR McNeill, *Something New Under the Sun: An Environmental History of the Twentieth-Century World* (WW Norton, 2001) passim.

[13] See generally J Auerbach and R Castronovo (eds), *The Oxford Handbook of Propaganda Studies* (Oxford University Press, 2013).

depicted in nation-states' currencies, flags, maps, coats-of-arms, monuments and national anthems, in addition to the hyped eco-tourism marketing they occasionally sponsor.[14] They not only describe but also guide attitudes, frame debates and shape policy. Although this chapter deals with the private sector, some of its critique applies equally to governments.

How should we conceptually frame and critique CSR aesthetics? The traditional modes of aesthetic enquiry offer little help. Although influential for understanding some forms of aesthetic appreciation, Kantian philosophy fails to aid our understanding of many everyday sensory experiences in the contemporary world including the marketplace.[15] 'Disinterested' aesthetic judgement might be credible for admiring a Rembrandt or Vermeer masterpiece at the Rijksmuseum, but becomes problematic once we acknowledge that aesthetic experiences infuse daily activities like shopping that lack 'disinterestedness'.[16] Apropos, the public reactions to CSR marketing can hardly be analysed through a Kantian framework. Also deficient is the literature on the *psychology* of aesthetic appreciation, as considered in Chapter 1, a research field that looks for correlations between mental or emotional reactions to sensory stimuli.[17] It may help to identify the aesthetic properties of corporate communications that influence business customers, perhaps owing to the symmetry of logos or colours of product packaging, yet does not assess whether corporate aesthetic practices are socially appropriate. The bespoke theories of environmental aesthetics, such as Carlson's 'cognitive model' and Berleant's 'aesthetics of engagement' are more relevant to our subject given that CSR encompasses environmental themes; yet these theories primarily serve aesthetic appreciation of the natural world, not corporate communications about it. The literature on 'everyday aesthetics', pioneered particularly by Yuriko Saito, is more helpful in characterising business and CSR aesthetics,[18] although this research is less helpful in framing the normative direction for its governance.

The most promising avenue of enquiry for this chapter is environmental art criticism, as I canvassed in Chapter 1. CSR communications are ubiquitously conveyed through film, photography, designs and music, with the aim to influence public opinion and consumer behaviour. The modernist trope of art as a medium of an autonomous and self-determined subject not only ignores the long history of art serving wider societal purposes, from government propaganda to religious dogma; it would not provide a framework for understanding CSR artefacts. The 'eco-critical' approach to art criticism can assist here, as it assesses art on criteria of 'environmental inter-connectedness, sustainability, and

---

[14] New Zealand offers a pertinent example: NJ Morgan, A Pritchard and R Piggott, 'New Zealand, 100% Pure: The Creation of a Powerful Niche Destination Brand' (2002) 9(4–5) *Journal of Brand Management* 335.

[15] I Kant, *Critique of Judgment*, translated JH Bernard (Cosimo, 2007; original 1790).

[16] A Light and J Smith (eds), *The Aesthetics of Everyday Life* (Columbia University Press, 2005).

[17] See PPL Tinio and JK Smith (eds), *The Cambridge Handbook of the Psychology of Aesthetics and the Arts* (Cambridge University Press, 2017).

[18] Y Saito, *Everyday Aesthetics* (Oxford University Press, 2017).

justice', and aims to unveil how art shapes the public's environmental attitudes and practices.[19] This methodology lends itself to scrutiny of CSR aesthetics, deconstructing its symbolism and revealing the missing narratives, such as about environmental pollution or social inequalities. Anti-capitalist commentators such as Naomi Klein's censure of corporate marketing and logos,[20] and Fredric Jameson's critique of capitalism's hyper-commodified character,[21] illustrate this mode of enquiry. These perspectives also provide a useful backdrop to understanding counter-aesthetic challenges to disingenuous marketing. Together, they suggest that the general public will lack a critical eye of CSR aesthetics without guidance from artists, activists and other dissenting stakeholders who can unmask green illusions and engage the public's imagination through humour, satire, irony and like tactics.

The next section examines the aesthetic dimensions of CSR discourse and practice, followed by a critique of corporate communications and marketing. The final section canvasses regulatory approaches to greenwashing, especially controls on misleading advertising and abuse of trademarks. As mentioned, I will discuss counter aesthetic strategies that challenge corporate deception in the last chapter.

II. FIGURATIVE CSR DISCOURSE

While the communication and marketing of CSR obviously dwells within an aesthetic realm, many wrongly perceive that the underlying CSR practices just reflect technical expertise and managerial prowess, involving cost-benefit calculation, technological innovation, executive leadership and skilful stakeholder negotiations. Only a handful of scholars have begun to scrutinise CSR practices through the lens of environmental aesthetics.[22] That said, the corporate management literature widely recognises that form and design are fundamental to organisations' identity and practice, and therefore that improvements in organisational effectiveness can come from greater sensitivity to aesthetic considerations, from the design of workplace offices to managers' relationships with employees.[23]

The field of CSR has several dimensions that an aesthetic lens can illuminate. At the outset, the very evolution of CSR responds partly to heightened sensory reactions to environmental and social adversity. Corporate hubris tends to be

---

[19] AC Braddock, 'Ecocritical Art History' (2009) 23(2) *American Art* 24, 26.

[20] N Klein, *No Logo: Taking Aim at the Brand Bullies* (Picador, 1998).

[21] F Jameson, *Postmodernism, or, the Cultural Logic of Late Capitalism* (Duke University Press, 1991).

[22] Eg J Waistell, 'Can Environmental Aesthetics Promote Corporate Sustainability?' (2016) 29(2) *Organization and Environment* 175.

[23] B Biehl-Missal, 'Business is Show Business: Management Presentations as Performance' (2010) 48 *Journal of Management Studies* 619; J Dobson, *The Art of Management and the Aesthetic Manager: The Coming Way of Business* (Quorum Books, 1999).

most damaging to a company's reputation when it results in visually dramatic impacts, such as a devastating oil spill (eg the 2010 Deepwater Horizon catastrophe) or a massive clear-felling forestry operation. Some companies' reluctance to disclose their environmental practices stems precisely from fear of arousing or amplifying awareness of such environmental trauma. The plethora of corporate environmental policies, plans and promises serves, at best, to prevent such unsightly impacts arising in the first place or, at worst, to deflect attention from those that inflict them.

Secondly, the making of CSR policies and plans can involve consultations with influential stakeholders, for example suppliers and local communities, and the negotiation of voluntary agreements. These processes can have aesthetic dimensions, such as the sensory atmosphere of consultation forums convened for liaising with local communities. When an Australian mining company negotiates an Indigenous Land Use Agreement with an Aboriginal community whose land it wishes to exploit, we could ask where and how is such an agreement negotiated? In the community itself, with company officials meeting local tribal elders in a setting and forum they find comforting, or in the company's austere headquarters in Sydney or Melbourne?[24] The concept of 'aesthetic atmospheres' introduced earlier in this book helps guide such enquiries by drawing attention to the spatial context and values that frame CSR activities. Corporate governance itself, from boardroom discussions to shareholder meetings, evokes aesthetic atmospheres where participants develop and review CSR policies and practices.

Thirdly, in actual business practices aesthetic factors can influence the design of products or delivery of services. A company might invest in green building standards for its headquarters in order to earn official certification of its CSR credentials – an overt and tangible aesthetic statement.[25] A socially responsible business might design products that are durable, reusable time and again and maintain consumers' interest as aesthetically appealing, and thus keep such products outside of 'ugly' waste streams longer.[26] Some business sectors directly engage in nature aesthetics, as in the eco-tourism sector where everything – from wildlife safaris to resort spas – is designed with strong sensory experiences in mind. This realm imparts the most obvious manifestation of CSR aesthetics to the general public.

Just as salient, in my opinion, is the aesthetic of CSR language. A distinctive vocabulary permeates CSR codes of conduct, reports, agreements, business conferences and media coverage, enriched by metaphors and other figurative language that help companies articulate a specific narrative for the public's assimilation.[27]

---

[24] M Langton and L Palmer, 'Modern Agreement Making and Indigenous People in Australia: Issues and Trends' (2003–04) 8 *Australian Indigenous Law Reporter* 1.

[25] International Living Future Institute, *Living Building Challenge 3.1 Standard*, https://livingfuture.org/product/lbc-3-1-standard.

[26] KH Harper, *Aesthetic Sustainability: Product Design and Sustainable Usage* (Earthscan, 2018).

[27] See H Kopnina, 'Metaphors of Nature and Development: Reflection on Critical Course of Sustainable Business' (2016) 22(4) *Environmental Education Research* 571.

Manipulative linguistic devices, however, aren't unique to CSR, pervading the business world at large. It includes seductive slogans such as the 'trickle-down effect' (alluding to how the disproportionate wealth of the rich should bring prosperity for society generally) and the market's 'invisible hand' (a metaphor about the supposed social benefits that flow from the efficiency of market forces in bringing supply and demand into equilibrium). This aestheticised language not only serves to render abstract economic ideas into simple formula that the mass public can comprehend, it also aims to influence mass opinion in politically significant ways, such as decisions about how to govern markets and business.

A sample of key CSR jargon illustrates their seductive power. The phrase 'triple bottom line' has become ubiquitous in CSR parlance, using the bottom-line metaphor from financial performance as a template for understanding the need for companies to perform along economic, social and environmental metrics. The metaphor appears to have been coined by John Elkington, a co-founder of SustainAbility, a CSR business consultancy.[28] By drawing on a concept founded in core business practice, the triple bottom line implies rigour and objectivity. In practice, its application has been flawed for several reasons: difficulties in quantifying social and environmental performance into neat metrics analogous to financial accounting; businesses' latitude as to how they seek to improve their sustainability performance; and thirdly, lack of transparency by businesses in communicating that performance.

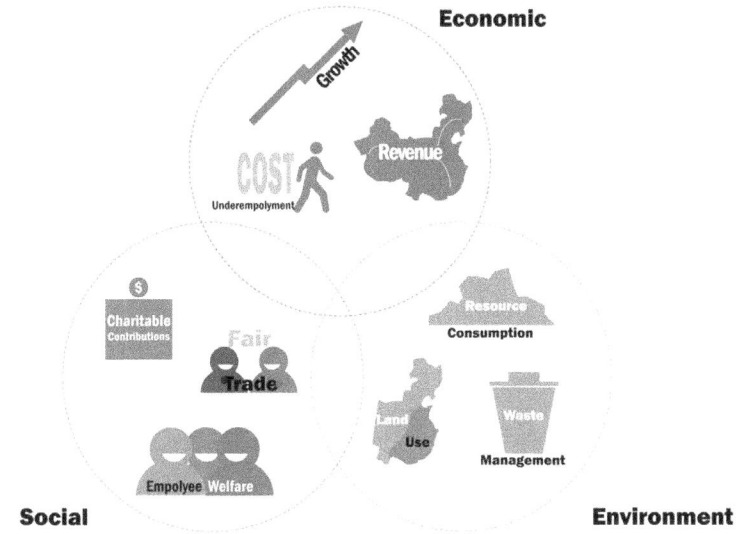

Figure 5.2 Triple Bottom Line pictogram, by Triplebotline; licensed under Creative Commons

---

[28] J Elkington, 'Enter the Triple Bottom Line' in A Henriques and J Richardson (eds), *The Triple Bottom Line: Does it All Add Up?* (Earthscan, 2004) 1.

Another seminal metaphor in CSR discourse is 'natural capital', depicting the natural world as performing functions similar to those of economic capital that require equal respect by business managers and policy makers. The metaphor appears to have been coined in the 1970s, and gained global currency with the publication of the book *Natural Capitalism* in 1999.[29] This terminology has become a framework for companies to report on their environmental performance, making visible the value of the natural world to corporate balance sheets and social welfare, and thereby creating incentives for business and governments to manage natural resources sustainably. The metaphor has also become formally incorporated into some CSR governance instruments, notably the Natural Capital Declaration adopted in June 2012, an initiative of the financial sector for promoting social investing.[30] As with triple bottom line, the concept of natural capital is open-ended and does not in itself present a standardised, rigorous methodology for managing or reporting on the value of natural resources and ecosystem services. It also has deeper implications for how we relate to the natural world; Brian Coffey suggests the metaphor provokes us to ask the wrong question, which should not be 'what's the value of nature' – a narrow, commodified view of the biosphere – but rather 'why is nature important' to our lives.[31]

Other influential terms in CSR discourse, and also government policy-making, are the inter-related 'circular economy' and 'cradle to grave'. They share the premise that the economy should function within a closed loop system without producing harmful waste and allowing goods to be recycled and reused indefinitely. These metaphors are sometimes linked to the umbrella goal of 'ecological modernisation', a prominent theme in some business and government policy circles that deftly reframes the ethical and political dilemmas of industrial capitalism as surmountable technical and managerial challenges.[32] By embracing it, CSR-conscious companies should benefit financially by gaining competitive advantages and improving production efficiency, all the while supposedly saving the planet without the need for systemic reform to market systems.[33] Like natural capital, the language of ecological modernisation assists the business world to maintain its preferred status quo.

In the realm of social investing, an important CSR niche, several bespoke literary devices have emerged. One is 'slow money', tied to a movement of

---

[29] P Hawken, AB Lovins and LH Lovins, *Natural Capitalism: Creating the Next Industrial Revolution* (Little Brown and Company, 1999).

[30] Natural Capital Finance Alliance, https://naturalcapital.finance.

[31] B Coffey, 'Cents and Sensibility: Why it's Unwise to Put Dollar Figures on Nature' *The Conversation* 27 November 2015, http://theconversation.com.

[32] See M Skou Andersen and I Massa, 'Ecological Modernisation – Origins, Dilemmas and Future Directions' (2000) 2 *Journal of Environmental Policy and Planning* 337; MA Hajer, *The Politics of Environmental Discourse: Ecological Modernisation and the Policy Process* (Oxford University Press, 1997).

[33] Eg World Business Council for Sustainable Development and United Nations Environment Programme, *Cleaner Production and Eco-Efficiency, Complementary Approaches to Sustainable Development* (World Business Council for Sustainable Development, 1998) 3.

this name that advocates patient, long-term investing to support social justice and ecological sustainability. The movement is most visibly associated with American social entrepreneur Woody Tasch, whose bestseller *Slow Money*[34] champions greater financial support for local food enterprises and organic farms. 'Patient capital' captures a similar idea, challenging the proverbial 'time is money' that permeates thinking in the roaring world of finance.[35] Another recent edition to the lexicon of social investing with significant traction in both the financial sector and mainstream media is 'stranded assets', a metaphor that climate change will cause some financial assets to lose value or become liabilities before the end of their economic life. It principally captures fossil fuel industries such as coal mining, powerfully invoking the prospect of being marooned and helpless.[36]

Clearly, CSR discourse and practice has a rich aesthetic fabric to influence how society should conceive of corporations and their environmental activities and impacts. The aestheticised terminology of CSR, leveraged through metaphors and catchy slogans, does not merely serve to explain complex environmental phenomena or business practice in everyday idiom, it surreptitiously reframes contexts or issues that politically and economically benefit business interests. In essence, this terminology has the power to prescribe behaviour and governance.

III. AESTHETICS AND CORPORATE COMMUNICATIONS

Business has had a long interest in environmental aesthetics for commercial reasons. From the late nineteenth century, Tasmanian nature photographer James Watt Beattie was recruited by the railway industry to photograph the island's spectacular scenery 'in order to cultivate a wilderness aesthetic and a market for a travelling public'.[37] Likewise, artists were recruited in North America to create scenic posters and postcards to entice tourists to patronise the railways and hotels created to service the new national parks, such as the example in Figure 5.3 created in 1925 for the Canadian Pacific Railway.[38] They and others to follow contributed to a crafted aesthetic of pristine wilderness untrammelled by human interference, ignoring such places' Aboriginal history or the more recent exploitation of their natural resources, including mining and logging.

---

[34] W Tasch, *Slow Money: Investing as If Food, Farms and Fertility Mattered* (Chelsea Green Publishing, 2008).

[35] V Ivashina and J Lerner, *Patient Capital: The Challenges and Promises of Long-term Investing* (Princeton University Press, 2019).

[36] D Shaw, 'Climate Change and Cost: What Are "Stranded Assets"?' *BBC News* 16 April 2015, www.bbc.com/news/av/business-32320825/climate-change-and-cost-what-are-stranded-assets.

[37] A Franklin, 'The Humanity of Wilderness Photography?' (2006) *Australian Humanities Review*, http://australianhumanitiesreview.org/2006/04/01/the-humanity-of-wilderness-photography.

[38] S O'Dowd, *Imagining Destinations: Art Posters and the Promotion of Tourism* (PhD thesis, Arizona State University, 2013) 2.

Figure 5.3 Canadian Pacific Railway travel poster, 1925; Library and Archives Canada, Acc No 1990-106-7

During this formative period, environmental hardship from droughts to fires could also provide opportunities for businesses to devise clever marketing campaigns to woo new customers. One that fascinates me is the song *The Breaking of the Drought* (see Figure 5.4), used as a marketing tool by the Canadian company Massey Harris following the end of Australia's infamous 'Federation Drought' in 1904. It was the equivalent to America's 'dust bowl' catastrophe, stretching over a decade and devastating farmers' livelihoods and the natural environment with brutal heat waves and dust storms. The drought also brought tough times for businesses selling farmers supplies, such as tractors and harvesters. The breaking of the drought thus inspired entrepreneurs to act quickly with catchy advertising to entice farmers to start spending again.

Business marketing has become even more pervasive today, not merely for selling wares but for expressing the essence of business identity. Put simply, the modern business corporation is an enlivened aesthetic phenomenon. You wouldn't think so by witnessing the generally austere rituals of shareholder meetings or boardroom deliberations. Their tedious formalities, from filing shareholder resolutions to listening to dull speeches, belie the enlivened corporate identity projected to the wider world. That external persona is also much

Figure 5.4 *The Breaking of the Drought*: song/words adopted from verses in 'The Argus' by Oriel; music by William Creser, 1904: Vincent Music Company for the Massey-Harris Company; Museums Victoria

more than stylish corporate offices or boardrooms adorned with fine art;[39] it transpires through corporate logos, websites, colourful publicity documents and ubiquitous product marketing. Philip Hancock, a leading researcher of business culture, finds that aesthetics permeates 'virtually every activity' of corporate life.[40] In their plea for *Beautiful Corporations*, Paul Dickinson and Neil Svenson claim successful companies must offer 'style, beauty, a positive attitude and pleasing experiences' for their staff and customers.[41] Corporate aesthetics has also penetrated a variety of cultural spheres beyond the marketplace, including sports, arts and leisure events, where business logos and marketing can sometimes have greater prominence than the activities being supported.[42]

[39] Although some edifices can be potent symbols of corporate values, notably the Chrysler building in New York and the Bank of China tower in Hong Kong.

[40] Hancock, 'Aesthetics' (above n 4) 52.

[41] P Dickinson and N Svensen, *Beautiful Corporations: Corporate Style in Action* (Prentice-Hall, 2000) 3.

[42] Klein, *No Logo* (above n 20).

Disciplining employees to boost their productivity is where the foregoing practices bring benefits to companies. In British call centres, Catrina Alferoff and David Knights found managers trying to mask the drudgery through colourful decorations, party games and dressing up themes.[43] Aesthetics also underpins a 'regime of surveillance', such as 'digital displays [...] reminiscent of seaside or Christmas illuminations' that monitor call handling and sales results.[44] The aestheticisation of the workspace strongly permeates the IT industry, where vibrant colour schemes and swish offices simulate a 'creative' atmosphere; Google's headquarters in Australia feature 'offices with picnic benches, fish tanks, local flora, the beach-themed Café Esky and a games room'.[45] Music sometimes adds to the aesthetic atmosphere, with some companies creating organisational theme songs to cultivate staff loyalty.[46] In *Sound Business*, Julian Treasure argues that a company's sound is becoming as important to its business success as its visual logo for enhancing worker productivity.[47]

Aesthetics has an even larger agenda in seducing consumers, with some firms' advertising expenditures outstripping the costs of producing their wares.[48] The aesthetic onslaught permeates television, the Internet, billboards, tabloids and increasingly even schools, museums and other realms once considered public spaces. Our postmodern culture has 'freed aesthetic experiences from the domain art, and made them more widely available to the masses' in which we now 'consume on the basis of style, symbolism and fashion', explains Hancock again.[49] In *The Substance of Style*, US cultural writer Virginia Postrel observes 'the look and feel of products will determine their success. Sensory, even subliminal, effects will be essential competitive tools'.[50] She cites Apple's brightly coloured computers and Visa's designer-look credit cards.[51] Even petrol stations, one of the most conceivably mundane businesses, can be spruced up with 'attention-getting aesthetic design'.[52] The aestheticisation of consumption

---

[43] C Alferoff and D Knights, 'We're All Partying Here: Target and Games, or Targets as Games in Call Centre Management' in A Carr and P Hancock (eds), *Art and Aesthetics at Work* (Palgrave Macmillan, 2003) 70.

[44] Ibid, 74–75, 87.

[45] UNSW Business School, 'Workspace Design: Will Aesthetics Give Your Business the Edge' 5 October 2010, reproduced at www.sapphirealuminium.com.au/index.php?task=news&num=12.

[46] N Nissley, S Taylor and O Butler, 'The Power of Organizational Song: An Organizational Discourse and Aesthetic Expression of Organizational Culture' in Carr and Hancock, *Art and Aesthetics* (above n 43) 93.

[47] J Treasure, *Sound Business* (Management Books, 2000).

[48] T Norris, *Consuming Schools: Commercialism and the End of Politics* (University of Toronto Press, 2011) 6.

[49] P Hancock, 'Aestheticizing the World of Organization – Creating Beautiful Unique Things' in Carr and Hancock, *Art and Aesthetics* (above n 43) 174, 174–75.

[50] V Postrel, *The Substance of Style: How the Rise of Aesthetic Value Is Remaking Commerce, Culture, and Consciousness* (Harper, 2003) 2.

[51] See further on product aesthetics: R Veryzer, 'The Place of Product Design and Aesthetics in Consumer Research' (1995) 22 *Advances in Consumer Research* 641.

[52] J Draeger and M Speltz, *Fill'er Up: The Glory Days of Wisconsin Gas Stations* (Wisconsin Historical Society Press, 2008) 18.

extends to individuals' own bodies: in 2017 the cosmetics market globally was worth US $532 billion.[53] Despite fiery feminist critiques such as Naomi Wolf's *The Beauty Myth*,[54] the industry flourishes thanks to ubiquitous fashion magazines, media advertising and celebrity endorsements.[55]

Shopping itself has become an aesthetic ritual. We live in an 'experience economy', write Joseph Pine II and James Gilmour, where the consumer 'buys an experience, [to] spend time enjoying a series of memorable events that a company stages – as in a theatrical play'.[56] Such 'memorable' experiences are not confined to amusement parks and glitzy casinos. 'Entertainment restaurants' led by Hard Rock Café and Planet Hollywood offer diners an orchestrated sensory milieu in which the décor, music, artwork and aromas coalesce to convey a well-defined aesthetic theme.[57] A coffee break at Starbucks might evoke a similar experience; according to its former CEO, Howard Schultz, 'every Starbucks store is carefully designed […] the artwork, the music, the aromas, the surfaces all have to send the same subliminal message as the flavor of the coffee'.[58] Shopping malls elevate these principles to a larger atmospheric scale with piped music, perfumed spaces and mood lighting to encourage shoppers to linger and spend.[59] Mall staff must also conform to fastidious aesthetic protocols, such as donning company uniforms and removing tattoos or body piercings. For consumers too lazy to leave home, continuous-streamed television stations devoted to shopping, such as the Shopping Channel and QVC, can keep the spending going.

These aesthetic attributes, especially for large multinational firms, coalesce into the *brand* that distils the company's values and promotes cultivated associations with certain lifestyles and status. The importance of brands to business success is often quantified by the value of its 'goodwill', which enables strong-brand firms to earn super profits beyond that which flow just from their tangible assets (eg property and machinery). According to *Forbes*, the value of the three most successful global business brands in 2018 were Apple (US$182 billion), Google (US$132 billion), and Microsoft (US$104 billion),[60] all companies active in media and communications where aesthetics matters the most. Although brand value is not generally itemised on a company's balance sheet, one study

[53] "Global Cosmetics Products Market Expected to Reach USD 805.61 Billion by 2023 – Industry Size and Share Analysis' *Reuters* 13 March 2018, www.reuters.com/brandfeatures/venture-capital/article?id=30351.

[54] N Wolf, *The Beauty Myth* (Chatto and Windus, 1990).

[55] G Jones, *Beauty Imagined: A History of the Global Beauty Industry* (Oxford University Press, 2010) 278–90.

[56] BJ Pine II and JH Gilmore, *The Experience Economy: Work is Theatre and Every Business a Stage* (Harvard Business School Press, 1999) 2.

[57] Ibid, 46.

[58] Postrel, *The Substance of Style* (above n 50) 20.

[59] M Brottman, 'The Last Stop of Desire: The Aesthetics of the Shopping Center' in A Berleant and A Carlson (eds), *The Aesthetics of Human Environments* (Broadview Press, 2007) 119.

[60] *Forbes*, 'The World's Most Valuable Brands', www.forbes.com/powerful-brands/list/3/#tab:rank.

estimated it to be worth 74 per cent of the market value of companies on the S&P500.[61] Strong brands benefit companies in two ways: consumers pay a premium for products that have brand recognition and secondly, investors prefer shares of companies they trust, resulting in a premium to purchase them. Individuals who patronise high-brand companies in turn can enhance their personal 'brand' in a culture where social status is often tied to conspicuous consumption. Lauren Greenfield has revealed a US youth culture bombarded with commercial advertising and showbiz images glamorising consumerism.[62] Flaunting a US$25,000 Birkin crocodile-skin bag can be the pinnacle statement of one's social standing in such circles.

Aesthetics not only promotes consumerism, thereby burdening the environment with exploitation and pollution; companies use aesthetic effects to 'reassure' consumers of their environmental responsibility in an effort to continue this bingeing. This strategy promotes business in overt environmental-themed sectors, such as eco-tourism.[63] The alluring music and imagery in corporate marketing can serve to bolster claims about a wide range of business practices masquerading as 'zero emissions', 'carbon neutral' or 'sustainable'. Disingenuous corporate communications can thereby make the public complacent, especially in the absence of regulatory oversight to curb such drivel.

Here are a few telling examples of corporate greenwashing.[64] The Fiji bottled water commercials, typically filmed in some ravishingly beautiful nature backdrop, clash with the reality of the plastic packaging, the carbon emissions from transporting the bottles internationally, and the landfill waste after their fleeting consumption. The Nissan LEAF advert shows a polar bear ambling through the countryside until it meets a motorist about to get into his Nissan electric car, whereon it receives a comforting hug: the inference that the car can help motorists do their bit to curb fossil-fuels omits the cognate environmental impacts (from car manufacture to road construction).[65] The labels on Dawn's antibacterial soap depict cute ducklings and seal pups with the assurance that 'Dawn helps save wildlife', as it donates soap to wash animals after oil spills and funds rescue volunteers; but the product contains a toxic chemical that environmentalists want banned. In 1990 DuPont – a large US industrial and chemical company – unveiled its safer, double-hulled oil tankers with advertisements featuring seals and other marine life approvingly clapping their flippers or wings to

[61] J Knowles, 'How of Enterprise Value is Intangible?' 8 March 2017, www.linkedin.com/pulse/how-much-enterprise-value-intangible-jonathan-knowles.

[62] L Greenfield, R Rodriguez and C Fisher, *Fast Forward: Growing Up in the Shadow of Hollywood* (Chronicle Books, 2004).

[63] See A Campelo, R Aitken and J Gnoth, 'Visual Rhetoric and Ethics in Marketing of Destinations' (2011) 50(1) *Journal of Travel Research* 3.

[64] See the Greenwashing Index, from which some examples are drawn: www.greenwashingindex.com.

[65] See the film clip at www.youtube.com/watch?v=P5IJcysD18s.

Beethoven's *Ode to Joy*.[66] As several of these unbelievable examples show, CSR garners its deceptive power by taking images or sounds out of their original context to spin a seductive narrative.

Consumer aesthetics also levies a high burden on the armies of workers who slave to produce all this stuff. Sweatshops in the Global South, notably in the textile and garments sector, are synonymous with human rights and labour standard violations relating to inhumane working conditions, child labour, occupational hazards, exploitative wages and intimidation of union representatives.[67] Workers crammed into squalid and unsafe factories labour under gruelling hours without legal recourse. The pressure comes from fast fashion retailers in the developed world; one *Guardian* report on the industry observed, 'a few years ago, a factory supplying a major retailer would have expected to manufacture 40,000 garments across four styles for 20 weeks. Today it will be lucky to get commitment from the retailer to manufacture four styles at 500 garments per week for just five weeks'.[68] Not surprisingly, many deaths or injuries ensue; an unsafe Bangladeshi sweatshop building that collapsed in 2013 killed 1,134 workers and seriously maimed another 2,500.[69]

Logos can provide a potent symbol of corporate eco-friendly pretences. In response to criticism of its environmental practices, BP (formerly British Petroleum and BP Amoco) in 2000 launched a massive re-branding effort that included a new logo of a green-and-yellow sunflower, official symbolising the sun god of ancient Greece, and the firm adopted the name BP with the tagline 'Beyond Petroleum'.[70] This is the same company later responsible for the 2010 Deepwater Horizon oil spill and for whom fossil-fuel sales still account for the bulk of its revenue. In 2009, the fast-food chain McDonalds experimented with literally greenwashing its logo, by swapping the red backdrop of its famed golden arches for a comforting green shade.[71] Sometimes the mischief arises from a company exploiting the logo or label associated with an environmental certification system; class action lawsuits were taken against SC Johnson over its misleading Greenlist logo put on some of its products that didn't adhere to the standards implied by the logo.[72] Companies invest heavily in their logos because they know consumers are more likely to recall a visual symbol than a written description; respected US entrepreneur Paul Hawken remarks that the average American can recognise 1,000 corporate logos but fewer than 10 native plants in their locality.[73]

---

[66] Advertisement available at www.youtube.com/watch?v=zJZFfeLRCJs.

[67] E Cline, *Overdressed: The Shockingly High Cost of Cheap Fashion* (Penguin, 2012).

[68] L Siegle, 'Why Fast Fashion is Slow Death for the Planet' *The Guardian* 8 May 2011.

[69] T Hoskins, 'Reliving the Rana Plaza Factory Collapse: A History of Cities in 50 Buildings, Day 22' *The Guardian* 23 April 2015.

[70] D Pittis, 'Remembering Back When BP was Green, Like its Ads Said' *CBC News* 3 June 2010, www.cbc.ca/news/canada/remembering-back-when-bp-was-green-like-its-ads-said-1.919998.

[71] 'McDonalds's Rolling Out Green Logo in Europe' *NBC News* 23 November 2009, www.nbcnews.com/id/34111784/ns/business-us_business/t/mcdonalds-rolling-out-green-logo-europe.

[72] J Bardelline, 'SC Johnson Settles Lawsuit Over Greenlist Logo' *GreenBiz* 8 July 2011, www.greenbiz.com/news/2011/07/08/sc-johnson-settles-lawsuits-over-greenwashing-greenlist-logo.

[73] P Hawken, *The Ecology of Commerce* (HarperBusiness, 1993) 214.

Corporate websites have become just as crucial platforms for similar messaging, offering space for disseminating misinformation and obfuscation. The homepage of Monsanto, the global agricultural chemicals supplier, is dominated by a photograph of a verdant field of crops illuminated by a brilliant sunrise.[74] The homepage of Adani Australia, a major coal miner, features assorted benign images that include sunlit wind turbines and coastal scenery.[75] The Ford car manufacturer's website displays revolving images of its vehicles, mostly in scenic backdrops like rugged countryside, and certainly without traffic jams or pollution.[76] Kentucky Fried Chicken's homepage centres on a short video clip of happy families being delivered the finger-lickin' chicken wings by Colonel Sanders himself, but no sight of the horrendous factory farms that supplied them.[77] The website of British American Tobacco, the world's largest such business, also has a pop-up video, telling 'touching' stories of the farmers and others who serve 'a progressive company that's proud of its heritage and excited about the future'.[78] Researchers who have studied corporate websites closely observe that any detailed information about CSR, such as the firm's sustainability reports, 'can often be found only by burrowing through the obscure recesses of corporate websites – available to the literati'.[79] It would appear that businesses sweat over the presentation of their CSR messaging more than giving their stakeholders meaningful, tangible information on which to scrutinise their efforts.

The foregoing discussion should be enough to convey the picture: aesthetics matters greatly to corporate identity and communication of business practices and products to influence investors and consumers in an information-saturated world. Workers also toil under its spell. This does not mean that companies fail to provide other sources of information about their environmental policies or impacts, but technical reports require considerably more attention from consumers to notice and comprehend. The enquiry that follows from this analysis relates to the efficacy of the law to discipline deceptive CSR claims.

IV. REGULATING GREEN ILLUSIONS

A. Fair Trading and Advertising Controls

Government regulation has not responded comprehensively to the foregoing issues. Indeed, in the name of intellectual property (IP) protection, some states have been more preoccupied with safeguarding corporate creations than curbing

---

[74] Monsanto, https://monsanto.com.
[75] Adani Australia, www.adaniaustralia.com.
[76] Ford, www.ford.com.
[77] Kentucky Fried Chicken, www.kfc.com/videos/oB5GrmaxH8k.
[78] British American Tobacco, www.bat.com.
[79] S Garnett, K Zander and M Lawes, 'A Simple Greenwash Detection Tip: Check What the Firm Puts on its Homepage' *The Conversation* 11 November 2015, http://theconversation.com.

their misleading connotations. Copyright law in the United States, a leading shaper of global IP standards, has several times extended the duration of legal protection to authors' creations to protect corporate interests, such as the Walt Disney Company who aggressively lobbied for such extensions it ultimately secured in 1998.[80] Trademarks also receive generous legal protection to safeguard corporate brands.

Concomitantly, authorities have ceded more responsibility to businesses to manage their own environmental performance, through codes of conduct, advisory guidance and contracts, thereby augmenting opportunities for unscrupulous behaviour given the mixed record of business self-regulation.[81] Indeed, many companies actively lobby against stricter environmental regulation, such as GE, whose 'Ecomagination' campaign was run whilst the company fought the US Environmental Protection Agency against pollution regulation and liability.[82] Many of these voluntary CSR codes and standards contain expectations that participant companies will publicly disclose their environmental and social performance, but such expectations either relate to narrow technical data, such as reporting greenhouse gas (GHG) emissions, or are cast too broadly, and without the means to hold companies measurably accountable.[83] A 2010 international study conducted by TerraChoice, an environmental marketing firm, found that about 95 per cent of the seemingly pro-environmental products that it reviewed were tainted by some greenwashing.[84] Studies commissioned in 2009 by the US Federal Trade Commission showed that a product's environmental reputation influences the purchasing decisions of many consumers.[85]

Regulations governing fair-trading, investor protection and trademarks are the legal bulwark against greenwashing. Common law remedies in contract and tort are also available in some jurisdictions for aggrieved consumers or investors, but because of limitations in their scope and the costly burden placed on litigants, government regulators now assume primary responsibility for supervising corporate communications. A few examples to follow will illustrate the most prevalent governance regimes around the world. None will assist business employees, for whom the protections offered by labour law focus on negotiation of fair contracts, salaries and other conditions rather than shielding employees from aesthetically overbearing workplaces.

Fair trading regulation aims to help consumers make informed purchasing decisions, and assist businesses by promoting a level playing field in the market.

[80] S Schlackman, 'How Mickey Mouse Keeps Changing Copyright Law' *Art Law Journal* 15 February 2014, https://alj.orangenius.com/mickey-mouse-keeps-changing-copyright-law.

[81] V Haufler, *A Public Role for the Private Sector: Industry Self-regulation in a Global Economy* (Carnegie Endowment for International Peace, 2001) 31–52; R Gibson (ed), *Voluntary Initiatives: The New Politics of Corporate Greening* (Broadview Press, 1999).

[82] N Sullivan and R Schiafo, 'Talking Green, Acting Dirty' *New York Times* 12 June 2005.

[83] See eg, the Global Reporting Initiative, www.globalreporting.org.

[84] TerraChoice, *The Sins of Greenwashing: Home and Family Edition* (2010) 6.

[85] Federal Trade Commission (FTC), *Environmental Marketing Consumer Perception Study* (FTC, 2009).

Regulations target false or misleading advertising likely to influence consumers' decisions, covering all forms of business communications including product packaging, websites, television, radio and other mediums. Both active statements and omissions can amount to deceptive communications. For instance, Australia's Competition and Consumer Act 2010 (Cth) forbids 'a business to make statements that are incorrect or likely to create a false impression', and 'when assessing whether conduct is likely to mislead or deceive' the regulator considers 'the *overall* impression' created by the impugned conduct.[86] As these controls apply regardless of the medium of communication, they could capture some of the modes of marketing canvassed in the previous section. The EU's relevant directive defines 'misleading advertising' as 'a representation in any form' that 'deceives or is likely to deceive' and 'is likely to affect [consumers'] economic behaviour or which, for those reasons, injures or is likely to injure a competitor'.[87] The US Federal Trade Commission works within a comparable regulatory framework under the Federal Trade Commission Act,[88] and has advised that it 'looks especially closely at advertising claims that can affect consumers' health or their pocketbooks' (which it goes on to specify as including claims about food, drugs, dietary supplements, alcohol and the Internet).[89] Additional standards are sometimes imposed on product packaging. Canada's Consumer Packaging and Labelling Act 'prohibits the sale, importation or advertisement of a pre-packaged product that has a label applied to it that contains false or misleading representations'.[90] Advertising controls in some countries are formalised into codes prepared jointly by government and industry, such as Great Britain's Committee of Advertising Practices Codes and Canada's Code of Advertising Standards, which restrict certain advertising conduct and provide a process for receiving complaints from the public.[91]

Fair trading regulation has limitations. Absent *positive* disclosure obligations, such as to divulge on packaging the ingredients in cosmetics or foodstuffs, or to report on GHG emissions, such regulations serve only to control false or misleading communications. In most jurisdictions, companies are not generally obliged to report on their overall sustainability performance. Secondly, although controls on deceptive advertising extend to implied representations, such as images of beautiful scenery in product marketing, seasoned experts

---

[86] Australian Competition and Consumer Commission, 'False or Misleading Statements', www.accc.gov.au/business/advertising-promoting-your-business/false-or-misleading-statements. See also Competition and Consumer Law 2010 (Cth), s 18.

[87] Directive 2006/114/EC of the European Parliament and of the Council of 12 December 2006 Concerning Misleading and Comparative Advertising and Repealing Council Directive 84/450/EEC, 2006 OJ (L 376) 23, art 2(a)(b).

[88] 15 USC ss 41–58, as amended.

[89] Federal Trade Commission, 'Truth in Advertising', www.ftc.gov/news-events/media-resources/truth-advertising.

[90] Consumer Packaging and Labelling Act, RSC 1985, c C-38, s 7(1).

[91] D Harker, 'Achieving Acceptable Advertising: An Analysis of Advertising Regulation in Five Countries' (1998) 15(2) *International Marketing Review* 101.

have observed that: 'implied claims are more difficult to challenge because their meaning is not always apparent or indisputable'.[92] Courts and regulators in major jurisdictions have struggled to account for the impact of the changing aesthetics of business advertising; as Linda Demaine explains in the relation to gaps in US law, 'the printed and spoken word, through which advertisers once urged consumers to purchase goods and services […] has yielded almost entirely to the photograph, video sequence, and computer-generated image'.[93] Misleading advertising law applies a 'word-centric' model that privileges written text over the audio-visual dimensions of marketing and branding.[94] Thirdly, regulation lacks uniform or clear definitions for many common terms associated with corporate brands and products such as 'cruelty-free', 'natural' or 'climate friendly', and thus their aesthetic representation by companies is even harder to control. Lastly, consumer protection generally only applies where consumers are reasonable in their interpretation of corporate marketing. Case law from the United States suggests that authorities do not generally treat adults as vulnerable consumers when evaluating deception in advertising imagery.[95]

Deceptive disclosures may incur civil and criminal sanctions, as levied for instance by Canada's Competition Act 2002 on companies that 'knowingly or recklessly make a representation to the public that is false or misleading in a material respect',[96] and without the necessity to prove that consumers relied on such statements or personally suffered damage. Misleading environmental claims occasionally result in such sanctions. The Australian power retailer Momentum Energy was fined AU$50,000 by the Australian Competition and Consumer Commission because the firm's electricity supplied to customers was not entirely generated renewably from 'thin air and fresh water', as it had boasted.[97] In 2013, two New Zealand plastic bag manufacturers were fined NZ$30,000 and NZ$60,000 respectively for misleading the public with their marketing about the biodegradability and eco-friendliness of their disposal plastic rubbish bags; investigations by the Commerce Commission found that the bags would not in fact biodegrade in typical landfill conditions.[98] British authorities banned BMW from falsely advertising its i3 model as a zero-emission

---

[92] JP Nehf, 'Misleading and Unfair Advertising' in G Howells, I Ramsay and T Wilhelmsson (eds), *Handbook of Research on International Consumer Law* (Edward Elgar Publishing, 2018) 90, 92.

[93] LJ Demaine, 'Seeing is Deceiving: The Tacit Regulation of Deceptive Advertising' (2012) 54 *Arizona Law Review* 719, 722.

[94] R Tushnet, 'Looking at the Lanham Act: Images in Trademark and Advertising Law' (2011) 48(4) *Houston Law Review* 861, 862.

[95] Discussed in Demaine, 'Seeing is Deceiving' (above n 93) 751.

[96] RSC 1985, c C-34, s 52(1).

[97] R Baines, 'Momentum Energy Ads Falsely Claimed Power Generated 'From Thin Air and Fresh Water', ACCC Rules' *ABC News* 21 April 2016, www.abc.net.au/news/2016-04-21/hydro-tasmania-fined-over-misleading-ads-by-momentum-energy/7345290.

[98] 'Rubbish Bag Maker Fined $60k Over Environmental Claims' *New Zealand Herald* 19 November 2013.

'clean car'.[99] Although occasionally severe penalties are imposed for deceit, such as against VW for falsifying claims about low emission cars and manipulating the emission test results,[100] in most cases regulators take a conciliatory approach to merely stop the offending behaviour and educate businesses to do better.[101] Newspapers often report of companies receiving a mere 'slap on the wrists', which typically involves a regulator's direction to cease offending.[102] Although the foregoing literature focuses on fair trading law in Western countries, some research on practices in developing countries such as China suggests they have even greater difficulties in controlling deceptive marketing.[103]

In limited contexts, governments have harnessed the same persuasive aesthetic techniques to influence consumer behaviour. In some jurisdictions such as Australia, lawmakers oblige tobacco companies to place visually graphic warnings on cigarette packages about their horrible consequences, such as images of a person's diseased lungs or a tracheotomy hole.[104] Counter-advertising is also deployed by some authorities against alcohol beverages to highlight their damaging health effects, combined with restrictions on advertising of alcohol beverages such as during children's television viewing times.[105] Yet governments also raise considerable revenue from taxes on tobacco and alcohol purchases, so they have an incentive to keep the businesses going.

B. Certifications and Trademarks

While fair trading regulation focuses on the overall impression of business conduct in determining whether it is misleading, such regulation primarily assists with sanctioning misleading advertisements about products or services rather than tackling the brand identity of a company that may itself contribute to the greenwashing. The aesthetic character of a company's logo, website or other expressive elements of its brand tend to be difficult to judge as deceptive, as their connotations about environmental quality or other claims are more

---

[99] J Clark, 'BMW Electric Car Advert Banned for "Misleading" Zero-emissions Environmental Claims' *The Independent* 6 December 2017.

[100] 'Diesel Emissions Scandal: VW fined €1bn by German Prosecutors' *BBC News* 13 June 2018, www.bbc.com/news/business-44474781.

[101] JP Nehf, 'Misleading and Unfair Advertising' in Howells, Ramsay and Wilhelmsson, *Handbook of Research on International Consumer Law* (above n 92) 90, 107–109.

[102] Eg C Page, 'Talktalk Gets its Wrists Slapped by the ASA for "Misleading" Broadband Ads' *The Inquirer* 9 July 2014; M Russell, 'Slap on Wrist for Power Balance' *Sydney Morning Herald* 21 November 2010.

[103] Eg Z Gao, 'Controlling Deceptive Advertising in China: An Overview' (2008) 27(2) *Journal of Public Policy and Marketing* 165.

[104] Eg The US's Family Smoking Prevention and Tobacco Control Act, Public Law 111–31, 123 Stat 1776 (2009).

[105] Eg Australia's Children's Television Standards 2009, enacted under the Broadcasting Services Act 1992 (Cth).

subtle and open to interpretation. Trademark law, however, can help discipline some aspects of corporate brand identity.

Trademark law protects corporate brands while ensuring that there is legal accountability through the nexus between products or services and their providers. Trademarks are a form of symbolic capital, which provide an 'aesthetic monopoly' for their holders in the market.[106] A trademark can take a variety of forms, including a sign (eg logo), a stylised mark or a non-stylised mark (ie text), or a phrase, such as 'Blue Mountain View', for my own eco-sanctuary in Tasmania that I have trademarked.[107] Many businesses rely on distinctive logos or other trademarks to attract consumers, as they 'reduce transaction costs by giving consumers concise and reliable ways to identify goods and services in the marketplace'.[108] Trademarks are intimately tied up with corporate brands, and may even serve to represent the distinctive environmental characteristics and qualities of businesses and their products. In order to attain these economic advantages, trademarks need legal protection, especially to prevent consumers from being misled by rival businesses passing off similar logos.

Analogous to bans on misleading advertising, trademark registration procedures bar registration of deceptive marks. In recent years trademark regulators have received many applications for registrations with environmental connotations, notably marks that include words such as 'green', 'eco-', 'clean' 'sustainable', 'natural' and other environmental buzzwords.[109] Between 2004 and 2012, 2,267 trademark applications in Australia alone used such language.[110] Aesthetic symbols that may also be part of such a trademark application include a leaf, tree, animal or planet Earth. Some trademark offices are becoming more vigilant with such applications. In 2013, the US Patent and Trademark Office (empowered under Lanham (Trademark) Act 1946 to bar registration of deceptive trademarks)[111] did so in relation to an application to register the trademark 'Green Seal' for adhesive tape because it was considered to falsely and materially indicate that the applicant's goods are eco-friendly.[112] Trademarks may also factor into misleading advertising controls: the US Federal Trade Commission has also warned that use of corporate logos by affiliates of a company could result in unlawful deceptive conduct if they mislead consumers about whether

---

[106] FW Haug, *Critique of Commodity Aesthetics: Appearance, Sexuality, and Advertising in Capitalist Society* (University of Minnesota Press, 1982) 41.

[107] See www.bluemountainview.com.au.

[108] A Perzanowski, 'Unbranding, Confusion and Deception' (2010) 24(1) *Harvard Journal of Law and Technology* 1, 18.

[109] 'Eco Trademarks Made Big Gains in 2007' *Greenbiz.com* 28 April 2008, www.greenbiz.com/news/2008/04/28/eco-trademarks-made-big-gains-2007.

[110] Data cited in R Ryan, 'Academic Sets Sights on Eco-label Loopholes' *ABC News* 9 February 2012, www.abc.net.au/news/2012-02-08/academic-sets-sights-on-eco-label-loopholes/3818746.

[111] Public Law 79-489, 60 Stat 427, s 2(a).

[112] Interestingly, but immaterial to the ruling, the applicant had not claimed that its products are eco-friendly but rather that the 'Green Seal' mark was merely one of several colour-coded adhesive tapes it sold.

an affiliated business in a corporate group in fact adheres to the same policies and practices of the principal company.[113]

The law can also re-use corporate trademarks to 'name and shame' businesses who violate environmental regulations. This can be done when authorities oblige companies to place public notices in the media disclosing their violations, with the notices including the offender's logo prominently displayed to ensure audiences will readily identity the culprit. This sanction has been applied in some Australian prosecutions of corporate polluters.[114]

A related legal mechanism for protecting business goods is the geographical indication, taking the form of a name or sign, sometimes displayed as a visual logo, to attach to certain products that correspond to a particular place of origin, such as a town or region. The geographical indication (also known as 'appellations of origin') serves to designate product quality and highlight brand identity, and is often associated with food, such as French champagne, and specialist manufactured wares, for instance Swiss watches. They benefit producers by increasing their market recognition and ability to command premium prices. They may also have non-commercial applications to protect traditional knowledge and community rights. In trying to harmonise countries' practices, the Lisbon Agreement for the Protection of Appellations of Origin and their International Registration (1958) stipulates criteria for geographical indicators and establishes a register of such indicators,[115] while the Agreement on Trade-Related Aspects of Intellectual Property Rights (1994) obliges state parties to prevent the public being misled as to the geographical origin of goods.[116] Whereas a trademark informs consumers about a good's commercial source, a geographical indication distinguishes the good itself, and in particular highlights its environmental qualities such as food grown organically in a specific region. The UN Food and Agriculture Organization (FAO) has thus promoted geographical indications as a pathway for sustainable development in rural communities.[117]

Another tool for corralling environmental marketing is official guidelines to encourage clear, accurate and substantiated claims. The International Chamber of Commerce and the International Organization for Standardization have issued environmental marketing codes, which have influenced guidelines adopted in many countries.[118] The US Federal Trade Commission's

---

[113] Federal Trade Commission, *Competition and Consumer Protection Perspectives on Electric Power Regulatory Reform* (FTC, 2000) s VIII.

[114] H Jackson, 'Victorian Environment Protection Authority Prosecution Update July 2002–April 2003' (2003) 2 *National Environmental Law Review* 27.

[115] As revised in 1967, 923 UNTS 205.

[116] (1994) 33 ILM 81, art 22.

[117] E Vandecandelaere et al, *Strengthening Sustainable Food Systems Through Geographical Indications* (UN FAO and European Bank for Reconstruction and Development, 2018).

[118] WY Ongkrutraksa, 'Green Marketing and Advertising' in SK May, G Cheney and J Roper (eds), *The Debate Over Corporate Social Responsibility* (Oxford University Press, 2007) 365, 368–69.

'Green Guides' published in 1992 and 2012 assist businesses to avoid misleading advertising accusations or lawsuits.[119] The governing principles of the Green Guides, which are stated to apply not merely to explicit statements but also claims 'by implication, through [...] symbols, logos',[120] are that businesses should: (1) make 'clear, prominent, and understandable' statements; (2) identify what products or services the claims apply to; (3) do not 'overstate [...] an environmental attribute or benefit'; and (4) substantiate the basis to any comparative claim.[121] The combination of text and images in marketing can amount to an asserted environmental benefit, as illustrated by the following example in the Green Guides: '[a] marketer's advertisement features a picture of a laser printer in a bird's nest balancing on a tree branch, surrounded by a dense forest. In green type, the marketer states, "Buy our printer. Make a change"'.[122] The Guides explain: 'although this advertisement does not expressly claim that the product has environmental benefits, the featured images, in combination with "buy our printer, make a change", likely convey that the product has far-reaching environmental benefits', which the Guides explain is probably deceptive in the absence of collateral evidence.

Authorities have also issued specialist guidance on marketing that relates to climate change. New Zealand's Commerce Commission has done so, cautioning businesses against making 'carbon-neutral' or 'low-carbon' claims 'indiscriminately', and suggesting that they ought to provide 'a clear statement about which elements of the product lifecycle or your business activities have been offset'.[123] Such guidance may help to control formal statements from companies about their climate-related performance but it says nothing about how visual, symbolic or acoustic representation of such issues should be portrayed.

Recognising the power of aesthetics, some governments have turned to the same strategy to control ambiguous advertising by introducing their own symbols certifying pro-environmental practices. The oldest example is Germany's Blue Angel program, created in 1977 on the initiative of the German government to allow for eco-friendly products and services to be labelled and marketed with an easily identifiable label.[124] Certified products and services, of which there are now some 12,000, can display the logo of the Blue Angel. Other examples of government-sponsored eco-labels include the Canadian Environmental Choice Program, Nordic Swan and the EU's Flower eco-label. The US Department of

---

[119] Federal Trade Commission, 'Green Guides', www.ftc.gov/news-events/media-resources/truth-advertising/green-guides.

[120] Code of Federal Regulations, *Part 260 – Guides for the Use of Environmental Marketing Claims*, s 260.1(c).

[121] Ibid, s 260.3.

[122] Ibid, s 260.4.

[123] Commerce Commission, *Guidelines for Carbon Claims: Fair Trading Act 1986* (Commerce Commission, 2009) 5.

[124] See www.blauer-engel.de/en.

Agriculture (USDA) also certifies organic food producers, which can market using its organic logo.[125]

Some certification schemes are now administered by independent organisations in the private sector. The LEED® tmark is one, and a highly esteemed certification trademark, signifying buildings of high energy-efficiency and other sustainability criteria. The Forest Stewardship Council's eco-label, featuring a symbol of a checkmark and a tree above the initials 'FSC', is found on many paper and wood products. Other prominent private sector eco-certifications include Carbonfree and Fair Trade.[126] The financial sector also uses eco-certifications embellished with logos, such as for designating companies as socially responsible options for investors; the Dow Jones Sustainability Indices is a notable such mechanism, with only firms meeting prescribed environmental and social standards being eligible for inclusion in the stock market indices.[127]

Some researchers, however, doubt the impact of these aesthetic symbols on consumer behaviour, as the labels do not in themselves question the very necessity of investment or consumption, as 'in some circumstances the most environmentally sustainable option is no purchase at all'.[128] This suggests that if aesthetics is to have a wider role in tackling consumerism, it needs to go further in promoting anti-consumer behaviours, an issue considered in Chapter 8.

The proliferation of aesthetic eco-labels has also created legal problems. One is the potential for consumers' confusion – in 2014 it was estimated that there were 455 label schemes across 25 industry categories worldwide.[129] Unverified claims and minimal regulatory oversight add to such confusion or scepticism. Another serious problem is that eco-labels may be challenged by companies or foreign governments as unfair trade restrictions. This happened with regard to the sale of canned tuna labelled as 'dolphin-friendly' in American supermarkets, which were successfully challenged in 2012 in an international trade court as unfair to Mexican fishers. The label scheme, which the US government supported, was introduced to promote safer tuna fishing that reduced lethal dolphin by-catches, and enabled consumers to easily differentiate canned tuna because of the prominent label of a jumping dolphin.[130] But the scheme in practice tended to exclude more foreign fishing industries than their US counterparts.

In securities regulation, another relevant legal tool, sanctioning misleading communications generally hinges on whether the information is 'financially

---

[125] US Department of Agriculture, 'Organic Seal', www.ams.usda.gov/rules-regulations/organic/organic-seal.

[126] See https://carbonfund.org/product-certification, and http://fairtrade.com.au.

[127] See www.sustainability-indices.com.

[128] RE Horne, 'Limits to Labels: The Role of Eco-labels in the Assessment of Product Sustainability and Routes to Sustainable Consumption' (2009) 33 *International Journal of Consumer Studies* 175, 181.

[129] L Atkinson, '"Wild West" of Eco-labels: Sustainability Claims are Confusing' *The Guardian* 4 July 2014.

[130] T Carman, 'WTO: "Dolphin-safe" Label Discriminates Against Mexico' *Washington Post* 16 May 2012.

materially' and would probably influence an investor's dealings with the company such as to buy its stock. A finding of misleading information rests heavily on the substantive content of the verbal or written communications made by the company's managers. Under Australia's Corporations Act 2001 (Cth), reflective of a common legal approach, the disclosure standards target financial information given to shareholders,[131] and a company's environmental performance is reported only with regard to the effects of 'any particular and significant environmental regulation'.[132] More expansive is the EU's non-financial reporting directive that requires large firms to publish reports periodically on the environmental and social impacts of their activities.[133] Yet neither of these approaches is likely to have any direct relevance to the aesthetic attributes of corporate communications: their focus is the formal written reporting of financial and non-financial data.

Governance gaps in disciplining corporate communications are not substantively filled by private law rights and remedies. Common law rules that respond to misleading corporate communications are available under tort and contract law, and their remedies may assist aggrieved consumers or investors where regulators fail to intervene.[134] Yet, they have drawbacks. Consumers cannot easily succeed with the tort of injurious falsehood, as they must demonstrate that companies acted maliciously when making a deceptive advertisement. And because of the doctrine of privity of contract, consumers have difficulty benefiting from contractual remedies against retailers where products do not match the quality promised in advertisements made by the manufacturers.[135] Also, in misrepresentation cases, individual consumers typically only suffer minor economic losses from purchasing a product, unless they suffer physical injuries (eg from a cosmetic containing carcinogenic ingredients). Litigation itself is an expensive and risky proposition, although consumers might cooperate through class actions, which can also overcome the burden of proving sufficient personal losses. In sum, the legal system offers an incomplete framework for acknowledging and regulating the aesthetic qualities of the corporate persona and its communications.

V. CONCLUSIONS

Corporate identity and CSR practice is intimately bound up in aesthetics, and consequently in disciplining unscrupulous corporate activities the law has had to become more sensitive to these aesthetic characteristics. Fraudulent or deceptive

---

[131] Part 2M.3 Financial Reporting.

[132] Section 299(1)(f).

[133] Directive 2014/95/EU of the European Parliament and of the Council of 22 October 2014 amending Directive 2013/34/EU as regards disclosure of non-financial and diversity information by certain large undertakings and groups, OJ L 330, 15.11.2014.

[134] J Goldring et al, *Consumer Protection Law* (Federation Press, 1998) 96–99 (discussing Australian common law).

[135] See *Singer v Schering-Plough Canada Inc,* 2010 ONSC 1737, where a company made misleading statements in its advertisements and product labelling about the protection its sunscreens offered against UV light.

environmental claims are amplified by corporate trademarks, websites, product packaging and general marketing. Current laws regulating advertisements, trademarks and investor protection provide the principal means of governing their aesthetic properties and content. They tend to capture only the most serious or overt abuses, require considerable resources to prosecute, and generally fail to recognise the ubiquitous and subtle permeations of corporate aesthetics that contribute to ecologically damaging consumerism. The green illusions of business communications create difficulties for regulation, which is better suited to disciplining discrete misleading statements about retailed products or trademarks rather than tackling the broader aesthetic character of business and the marketplace. Consumption itself is completely outside the scope of these legal controls, but may be regulated through other means, such as via waste control or recycling standards.

Without adequate legal controls in this domain, businesses that actually adhere to high environmental standards may not benefit from their efforts, as consumers or investors struggle to differentiate the impostors from genuinely eco-friendly firms. The advent of environmental certification schemes can help genuinely pro-environmental businesses through visual symbols that give consumers an easy way to identify best practice. Nongovernmental watchdogs can assist in educating consumers to be more discerning, such as through publicly available databases like Greener Choices[136] and the Greenwashing Index,[137] which provide independent analysis of environmental logos and labels. Such initiatives, however, do not in themselves take any stance against pervasive consumerism, and ironically may even encourage it. Chapter 8 closes this book with analysis of another NGO strategy known as 'culture jamming', aiming through artistic activism to forge a counter aesthetic to greenwashed corporate malfeasance. These culture-jamming strategies also face legal impediments of their own, however, including diminishing access to public spaces, restrictions on freedom of speech, defamation law, and companies' stentorian enforcement of their intellectual property rights.

While this chapter might appear to readers to offer reasons why we should not expect environmental aesthetics to play a major role in the transformation of environmental practices and governance, it ultimately speaks to the importance of taking aesthetics seriously in law, because unscrupulous uses of corporate marketing and discourse can undermine it. We need to conceive of the corporation and its environmental practices as having aesthetic characteristics in order to properly understand their societal impact and the appropriate governance response. The aestheticised realm of CSR, from catchy slogans to captivating logos, surreptitiously reframes issues that politically and economically benefit business interests. Taking aesthetics seriously will help governance become more attentive to devising or enabling corrective responses, sometimes through aesthetic techniques.

---

[136] See www.greenerchoices.org.
[137] See www.sustainable.org/economy/economics-a-finance/140-greenwashing-index.

6

Ecological Restoration

I. AESTHETICS OF NATURE'S DAMAGE AND RECOVERY

Environmental aesthetics inhabits a dynamic world. Not only does human culture change, and thus potentially aesthetic preferences, the biosphere does too. It's in constant flux as biological systems and elements evolve through their internal mechanisms and in response to anthropogenic influences. Many of these permutations are too subtle for us to perceive during our daily lives, be it the trees nudging taller, the climate gradually warming or the plastic debris littering the seas. The tempo of species evolution and geological change defy human observation even more, even over a person's entire lifespan. In urban neighbourhoods, where anthropogenic influence and cultural change reverberate most strongly, we are much more likely to discern shifting aesthetics, from the din of congesting traffic to the sight of elevating skylines.

While humanity's eco-footprint accumulates over time, often leaving a legacy of environmental degradation, sometimes communities resolve, or are legally obliged, to reverse the damage.[1] Growing efforts to repair it have led in recent years to observable changes, at least to the scientists, as forests regrow, wetlands replenish and threatened animals rebound. These projects, commonly known as environmental restoration, remediation or rehabilitation (hereafter generically called 'eco-restoration' except where more precise terminology is necessary) also alter nature's aesthetic properties.

Eco-restoration projects may address aesthetic factors explicitly. Old mining pits and quarries can be filled and re-vegetated. Coastlines and sea life smothered in the ugly grime from an oil spill can attract teams of workers to remove the contaminants. The blackened scars of a forest fire may also heal as saplings are replanted to hasten the rejuvenation with more pleasing greenery. Eco-restoration certainly involves other goals, aimed at rebuilding ecological integrity and biodiversity, but appearances matter and indeed degradation obvious to the eye may trigger a quicker response than hidden or obscured deprivation such as the invisible soil contaminants or the missing invertebrates. Where damage is visible from where people inhabit, eco-restoration is even more likely to emphasise visual considerations.

---

[1] See generally A Akhtar-Khavari and BJ Richardson (eds), *Ecological Restoration Law: Concepts and Case Studies* (Routledge, 2019).

Eco-restoration may also seek to recover acoustic ambience. This matters particularly in nature conservation areas given that unnatural noises, even modest ones, can disturb biodiversity and diminish tourists' experiences. The US National Park Service's management policies address soundscapes, and specify its commitment to 'restore to the natural condition wherever possible those park soundscapes that have become degraded by unnatural sounds (noise)'.[2] The abatement measures taken include designating quiet zones, managing visitor facilities and road traffic to reduce noise, and educational campaigns. Noise levels in urban areas also matter to human well-being, and authorities may restore soundscapes by the installation of traffic noise barriers along highways, and the repaving of roads with noise-dampening asphalt.

Eco-restoration offers an invaluable case study for the *Art of Environmental Law* because it foregrounds fundamental narratives about what is 'natural' from which we may derive aesthetic pleasure. Our cultural conceptions of landscape, such as evoked by the aesthetic 'picturesque', become tested when decisions rendered about how to reconstitute the biological and ecological elements of damaged environments. At this juncture, we must confront our assumptions and biases about whether holding to a cherished landscape aesthetic is aligned with, or should prevail over, scientific norms about ecological integrity, resilience and sustainability that also inform restoration practice. In choosing an historic reference point for returning nature to its former condition, we must also confront the critical question of whether it even makes sense to conceive of a 'nature' separate from or coming before human settlement. Rather than understanding the natural world as comprising a biosphere subject to human disturbances, it might be more authentic to view landscapes as 'anthropogenic biomes' because, as geographers Erle Ellis and Navin Ramankutty sum up, 'most of the world's "natural" ecosystems are embedded within lands altered by land use and human populations'.[3]

The oldest such anthropogenically altered ecosystems in the world are arguably in Australia, as settled by Aboriginal peoples for 60,000 years, perhaps longer. Bruce Pascoe's ground-breaking account of their agricultural practices debunks the 'accepted view of Indigenous Australians simply wandering from plant to plant, kangaroo to kangaroo, in hapless opportunism'.[4] Similarly, Bill Gammage's *The Biggest Estate on Earth: How Aborigines Made Australia* reveals that 'there was no wilderness' but rather a landscape domesticated by fire to maximise its productivity for its Aboriginal stewards, as John Lycett's painting (see Figure 6.1) vividly depicts.[5] Other regions of the world have experienced

---

[2] US National Park Service, *Management Policies 2006* (US Government Printing Office, 2006) 56.
[3] EC Ellis and N Ramankutty, 'Putting People in the Map: Anthropogenic Biomes of the World' (2008) 6(8) *Frontiers in Ecology and the Environment* 439, 445.
[4] B Pascoe, *Dark Emu* (Magabala Books, 2018) 2.
[5] B Gammage, *The Biggest Estate on Earth: How Aborigines Made Australia* (Allen and Unwin, 2011) 2.

their own anthropogenic transformations over millennia: Tim Flannery's recent synthesis of European natural history reveals *Homo sapiens'* hand in mega fauna extinctions starting some 37,000 years ago, well before the better known transformations from agriculture and animal husbandry commencing 11,500 years ago.[6] Equally momentous upheavals loom in the twenty-first century as climate change intensifies.

Figure 6.1 *Aborigines Using Fire to Hunt Kangaroos*, 1817 Joseph Lycett (1774–1828), watercolour; National Library of Australia

Eco-restoration projects must thus reckon with a complex and contested conceptualisation of landscape (and seascape) involving scenic beauty, cultural history and ecological values. Some may cling to a nostalgic memory of landscape as pristine, unpeopled wilderness, which eco-restoration should aim to reinstate, while others prefer retention of heritage landscapes and rural vistas compatible with a domesticated environs that accommodates some level of anthropogenic change and the novel ecosystems humankind has created. These tensions may not be acute in the projects cleaning up former mines or industrial operations, but they can easily interpolate ambitious landscape- or ecosystem-scale restorations.

The latter projects are sometimes called 'rewilding', and are commonly led by environmental non-governmental organisations (NGOs) without government succour because of the financial costs and political sensitivities. Australia hosts several examples, such as the Newhaven Restoration Project restoring

---

[6] T Flannery, *Europe: A Natural History* (Text Publishing, 2018) 225–38.

65,000 hectares of outback by erecting a giant fenced reserve to exclude feral pests and weeds that compete with recovering native species.[7] Also led by grass-roots initiative, Western Australia's Gondwana Link is reconnecting fragmented, remnant wildlife habitat across a 1,000 km stretch of the state's southwest blighted by irresponsible land clearing and farming.[8] In North America, the Y2Y project – denoting Yellowstone to Yukon – uses a similar approach over a bigger scale along the Rockies.[9] Even densely populated Europe is hosting rewilding projects, some under the auspices of the organisation Rewilding Europe that has targeted ten core areas cumulatively totaling at least a million hectares.[10] Some European projects implemented on a smaller scale include the Oostvaarder-splassen, covering about 56 km^2 in the Netherlands, which I will comment on shortly. The rewilding agenda is also starting to touch marine environments, such as the interest in re-establishing seagrass meadows and kelp forests to enable fisheries and other aquatic biodiversity to regenerate.[11]

Apart from the debatable prospects of such projects re-establishing ecological and biodiversity values, the authenticity of their restored aesthetic qualities is contentious. Of relevance here are philosophical debates about whether perceptually similar places have different aesthetic values where one is an original, wild nature and the other a reconstructed version. Wading into this debate, Allen Carlson has queried the difference between a natural coastline and a hypothetical one that's 'perceptually indistinguishable' but created by human landscaping.[12] He argued that the two coastlines should be evaluated differently because they belong to different *categories*, one being an artefact and the other resulting from natural processes. Although they may have similar perceptual qualities in their shapes and colours, the natural coastline reflects the power of the sea eroding the shoreline whereas the engineered coastline reflects human ingenuity. These different, second-order properties matter because aesthetic appreciation is not simply about sensory stimulation, in what one sees or hears, but is embedded in one's emotional and cognitive state. And these different properties have consequences for how we may use and manage such places; the artificial coastline might thus be judged differently if it has lower ecological value (eg for biodiversity habitat) than a natural shore. Thus, it is tempting to concur with Carlson's conclusion that: 'if our aesthetic appreciation of nature helps to determine our ethical views concerning nature, then our aesthetic appreciation of nature should be of nature as it in fact is rather than as what it may appear to be'.[13]

[7] Australian Wildlife Conservancy, *Newhaven Endangered Wildlife Restoration Project* (2017).
[8] See www.gondwanalink.org.
[9] See https://y2y.net.
[10] See https://rewildingeurope.com.
[11] RKF Unsworth and R Callaway, 'How Underwater Gardening Can Rewild the Atlantic Ocean' *The Conservation* 6 November 2017, http://theconversation.com/how-underwater-gardening-can-rewild-the-atlantic-ocean-85794.
[12] A Carlson, 'Nature, Aesthetic Judgment and Objectivity' (1981) 40(1) *Journal of Aesthetics and Art Criticism* 15, 22.
[13] Ibid, 24.

Yet, given a natural world imprinted with pervasive anthropogenic change, where would this 'natural' coastline that Carlson conjures up exist? In fact, coastlines, like other dimensions of land- and seascapes, exist in various states along a spectrum of human impact: there is rarely a pure dichotomy between the natural and artificial. Likewise, decisions to restore degraded coastlines, as with other environments such as wetlands and forests, will be situated along this spectrum. Restoration is a facsimile of a desired nature, resulting in an environment that certainly is 'authentic' in that it contains real sand and soil, animals and plants, and so on, rather than synthetic, engineered properties. But nonetheless it will be an environment that reflects a degree of human judgment and ingenuity, such as about the species chosen for recovery or how the terrain is landscaped. The important takeaway here for eco-restoration governance is that we should not disavow restored environments simply because they fail to embody an unadulterated, unspoiled nature.

Just as challenging for eco-restoration are host communities' disapproval of the aesthetic changes despite environmental gains. A healthier, recovering nature is not always admired because restoration can unleash a wilder nature – unkempt, dangerous and more unpredictable than its predecessor. We may be more enamoured by the aesthetics of placid, bucolic landscapes than the dishevelled forest harbouring fierce creatures, and the fallen trees and animal carcasses left to perform their regenerative roles. Encouraging the reintroduction of wolves in Western Europe or dingoes in Australia to their former ranges in order to allow them to perform their ecosystem-stabilising role is welcomed by many conservationists but equally abhorred by many landholders, who fear these creatures' predatory instincts.[14]

British academics Jonathan Prior and Emily Brady identify two instances of these challenges in Western Europe.[15] One is the Oostvaardersplassen reserve in the Netherlands, contributing to the 'de-domestication' of introduced species such as Heck cattle and Konik ponies homed on the 56 km^2 of polder reclaimed in 1968.[16] In the name of rewilding, its wildlife have been left to the vagaries of nature, which in some instances has led to mass die-offs during winter food shortages – a negative aesthetic for animal welfarists who tried unsuccessfully in court to challenge the reserve's management. The other example they cite is Scotland's Carrifran Wildwood. This project, led by an environmental NGO, to revegetate a denuded valley to its condition 6,000 years ago has been controversial for some in the local community. They evidently prefer the area's existing aesthetic and recreational values associated with open, pastoral countryside to

---

[14] A Vaughan. 'Rewilding Britain: Bringing Wolves, Bears and Beavers to the Land' *The Guardian* 19 September 2014.

[15] J Prior and E Brady, 'Environmental Aesthetics and Rewilding' (2017) 26(1) *Environmental Values* 31.

[16] See further J Lorimer and C Driessen, 'Wild Experiments at the Oostvaardersplassen: Rethinking Environmentalism in the Anthropocene' (2014) 39(2) *Transactions* 169.

the uncertain, future aesthetics of a forest that will take a few centuries to fully mature.[17] This controversy has played out more extensively across the UK with debates over whether to re-vegetate the highland moors of Wales and Scotland beloved by the National Trust; George Monbiot has waded into the controversy, pointing out that these revered uplands were once verdant forests until logged or grazed over the centuries to become biological barrens.[18]

To add to the controversy, some artists provoke us to re-think the aesthetics of environmental degradation. In his seminal works *Manufactured Landscapes* (2006) and *Oil* (2009), Edward Burtynsky's photography unveiled how industrialisation has transformed the planet, from Chinese industrial blight to Canadian oil sands. The images, however, can confuse viewers with their terrifying beauty. Using large format aerial images, Burtynsky's works at first glance might seem rather appealing with their hues and shapes reminding viewers of pretty fabric designs. Closer examination of their textures however, shows shocking disfigurement from shipbreaking yards to industrial refineries. Other artists also play with the ambiguous aesthetics of anthropogenic change, such as American photographer J Henry Fair who reveals industrial sites as legacies of rampant human consumerism.[19] One reviewer of Fair's work summed up their ambiguity, '[t]he vivid color photographs of J Henry Fair lead an uneasy double life as potent records of environmental pollution and as ersatz evocations of abstract painting'.[20] Scientific knowledge matters here, Carlson would assert;[21] the educated viewers' knowledge that the pollution in these images is unnatural and harmful should ultimately tilt their judgement away from any aesthetic gratification.

The public perception of eco-restoration projects that respond to such disfigurement matters: environmental governance is legitimated by community participation, and in some cases it may decisively influence outcomes. During the 1970s, when eco-restoration began to be more commonly practised to address the legacies of mining and industry as a result of tightening regulations, it was conceived as a technical, specialist endeavour shaped by experts. Eco-restoration governance has since evolved to incorporate an additional social component, in which public participation informs the process alongside scientific knowledge, from the selection of areas to restore to their implementation through tree planting, clean-ups and other labour-intensive activities.[22] In landscape-scale restorations, the community's interests may prevail because such projects are

---

[17] See www.carrifran.org.uk.

[18] G Monbiot, 'Why are Britain's Conservation Groups so Lacking in Ambition?' *The Guardian* 18 October 2013.

[19] As reproduced in JH Fair, *Industrial Scars: The Hidden Costs of Consumption* (Papadakis, 2017).

[20] R Smith, 'J Henry Fair: "Abstraction of Destruction"' *New York Times* 13 January 2011.

[21] A Carlson, 'Nature, Aesthetic Appreciation, and Knowledge' (1995) 53(4) *Journal of Aesthetics and Art Criticism* 393.

[22] D Martin, 'Ecological Restoration Should be Redefined for the Twenty-first Century' (2017) 25(5) *Restoration Ecology* 668.

typically initiated voluntarily by environmental NGOs needing the cooperation of local landholders.

Some eco-restoration projects require going beyond community partici-pation to restoration of communities themselves, where ecological recovery is intertwined with cultural recovery. This cultural dimension may be tied to healing historic grievances, such as those associated with the dispossession of Indigenous peoples from their ancestral territories. Alternatively or as well, cultural recovery may be a practical consideration where such peoples offer environmental husbandry skills and wisdom to aid restoration. Relevantly, the Convention on Biological Diversity 1992,[23] ratified by some 190 nations, obliges its parties to 'respect, preserve and maintain knowledge, innovations and prac-tices of indigenous and local communities embodying traditional lifestyles relevant for the conservation and sustainable use of biological diversity'.[24] Today, some 370 million Indigenous peoples live across 90 countries,[25] many owning or managing large areas. About 22 per cent of Australia is under Aboriginal control and a further 9 per cent subject to some level of Aboriginal tenure.[26] In New Zealand, Māori groups hold 6 per cent of the country,[27] while Native Americans own about 4.5 per cent of the United States, including a particu-larly large share of Alaska.[28] Given such numbers, it isn't surprisingly that the international Society for Ecological Restoration (SER) in 1995 launched an Indigenous Peoples Restoration Network to support 'eco-cultural restoration' by working closely with grassroots communities and promoting use of tradi-tional ecological knowledge.[29]

The restoration of Indigenous culture may also introduce distinctive envi-ronmental aesthetic values. Aboriginal Australians prefer to speak of 'country' than 'landscape', implying a sentient environment 'in which the ancestral and living beings have a spiritual and physical presence and they have obligations to look after the landscape, its resources and sacred sites'.[30] This active, lived aesthetic experience, a desire to belong to the land, departs radically from the Western trope of detached, scenic admiration. An 'intercultural' approach to eco-restoration, explains Catherine O'Neill, a US academic specialising in

---

[23] (1992) 31 ILM 818.

[24] Ibid, art 8(j).

[25] UN Permanent Forum on Indigenous Issues, 'Who are Indigenous Peoples?' Factsheet (2015).

[26] J Altman and F Markham, 'Values Mapping Indigenous Lands: An Exploration of Develop-ment Possibilities' (Native Title Research Unit, Australian Institute of Aboriginal and Torres Strait Islander Studies, 1 May 2013) 6.

[27] Controller and Auditor-General, *Maori Land Administration: Client Service Performance of the Maori Land Court Unit and the Maori Trustee* (Audit Office, 2004) 8.

[28] National Congress of American Indians Policy Research Center, *Geographic and Demographic Profile of Indian Country* (NCAI, 2012).

[29] See www.ser.org/iprn.

[30] JL Lennon, 'Caring for Country: A New Landscape Paradigm in Australia' in G Fairclough, IS Herlin and C Swanick (eds), *Routledge Handbook of Landscape Character Assessment* (Routledge, 2018) 203.

this subject, validates Indigenous environmental knowledge in restoration and involves its holders as equal partners in project design and execution.[31] Tensions may arise, however, in implementing intercultural approaches because of divergent aesthetic, spiritual and ecological values. One example from New Zealand is where conservation authorities' efforts to eradicate the exotic, egg-eating kiore rat (*Rattus exulans*) from areas set aside for the recovery of endangered birds have clashed with the desires of some Māori to protect this culturally significant species which arrived in New Zealand with their Polynesian ancestors.[32]

These issues will be revisited and explored further over the rest of this chapter in its following three major sections. The next evaluates how the law currently considers aesthetic criteria in rehabilitation of post-mining sites, a case study selected because eco-restoration regulation is more highly developed in the mining sector than any other realm. Aesthetics feature in a variety of eco-restoration responses,[33] but have had the greatest salience in the mining context because mining, especially the open-cast variety, can ruin the appearance of landscapes. Section III examines aesthetics in eco-restoration law in other contexts, notably forestry and biodiversity conservation. The final substantive section reviews the art of eco-restoration, looking at how artists have interpreted and participated in restoration projects. The chapter concludes with an anecdote relating to nuclear waste repositories to highlight the centrality of aesthetics and the arts in eco-restoration governance.

II. POST-MINING REHABILITATION

Mining is an ugly business. Its environmental impacts are often visually arresting: cavernous craters, eroded voids, rock waste mounds, tailing ponds and barren surroundings corroded by acid and metalliferous drainage. While active surface mines harbour many of these eyesores, as well as noise and vibrations from blasting and drilling, most operate for only a few decades relative to the potentially long-lasting aesthetic and ecological legacies of closed mines. Mining legacies have ostensibly become a major focus of environmental regulation since the 1970s, in contrast to the tradition of 'just boarding up shafts and fencing open cuts'[34] once the minerals ran out. Laws can require that former mining sites not only be rendered safe but returned to a reasonably acceptable aesthetic and ecologically functional condition.

---

[31] C O'Neill, 'Restoration Affecting Native Resources: The Place of Native Ecological Science' (2000) 42 *Arizona Law Review* 343.

[32] K Chanwai and BJ Richardson, 'Re-working Indigenous Customary Rights? The Case of Introduced Species' (1998) 2 *New Zealand Journal of Environmental Law* 157.

[33] M Golivets, *Aesthetic Values of Forest Landscapes* (Master thesis, Swedish University of Agricultural Sciences, 2011).

[34] M Pepper, CP Roche and GM Mudd, 'Australia's Mining Legacy Challenge' (Life-of-Mine Conference, 2014) 6.

Aesthetic considerations have become routine for numerous mine-closure rehabilitations.[35] Their goal is generally to return the site to a condition resembling its pre-mining environmental condition. The term 'rehabilitation' is commonly used in this sector, and is defined by the SER, the peak global body devoted to restoration, as the 'reparation of ecosystem processes, productivity and services'.[36] The terms 'remediation' and 'reclamation' are sometimes also used interchangeably with rehabilitation to denote similar goals for mining closures. They all differ, however, from 'ecological restoration' or 'rewilding' that involves large, landscape-scale interventions with more complex goals. Methods to improve the aesthetic character of post-mining sites, especially open-cast mines, include backfill, vegetation screening, re-vegetation of barren surroundings and creation of wetlands.[37] The methods adopted are influenced by the proximity of the mine to a local community, with aesthetic considerations having more priority in 'areas that face townships, residences, or the highway'.[38]

The market economy shows little capacity to respond to the costly legacies of mining and allocate resources between different generations to pay for rehabilitation. In Queensland, Australia, approximately 12,000 out of 15,000 abandoned mines sit on private land and thus are deemed not to be the government's responsibility.[39] The cost of rehabilitating open-cast coal mines in Queensland in 2002 was estimated at A$26,000 per hectare while the price of surrounding (not mined) land was less than A$1,000 per hectare.[40] The overall cost of rehabilitating some super mines in Australia tops about A$500 million (2015 figures).[41] However, in urban landscapes where land values are generally much higher, the economic benefits of rehabilitation may be sufficient for the market to stimulate such action. Restoration can sometimes result in an environment having greater economic and aesthetic appeal than the site's predecessor; the famous Butchart Gardens on Vancouver Island, Canada, were formerly a limestone quarry until the early twentieth century. They have been open to the public since the 1920s and now receive one million visitors annually for their beautiful flowers and landscaping. In most cases, unlike this example, legal regulation is necessary to ensure restoration of post-mining sites.

---

[35] G McKenna, *Techniques for Creating Mining Landforms with Natural Appearance* (Proceedings of Tailings and Mine Waste, Banff, Alberta, 1–4 November 2009).

[36] Society for Ecological Restoration (SER) International Science and Policy Working Group, *The SER International Primer on Ecological Restoration* (SER, 2004) 12.

[37] Australian Government, *Mine Closure. Leading Practice Sustainable Development Program for the Mining Industry* (Commonwealth of Australia, 2016) 102.

[38] NSW Mining Council, *Improving Mine Rehabilitation: Discussion Paper* (NSW Mining Council, February 2018) 13.

[39] C Unger, 'What Should We do with Australia's 50,000 Abandoned Mines?" *The Conversation* 23 July 2014, http://theconversation.com.au.

[40] B Golding, *Cost-effective Rehabilitation of Mined Land in the Strip Coalmines of Queensland* (Master thesis, University of Queensland, 2002) abstract.

[41] M Stevens, 'Rio Tinto Signs Ranger Uranium Mine Death Warrant' *Australian Financial Review* 12 June 2015.

Regulation of post-mine rehabilitation typically begins with the initial licensing of the mine and the environmental impact assessment studies undertaken in that licensing process. Such studies should identify how to remedy mining impacts once the mining ends. Mining legislation does not refer to aesthetic values, nor generally to the criteria for assessing the adequacy of restoration. South Africa, with one of the world's largest mining industries, has extensive rules governing closure and environmental rehabilitation under the National Environmental Management Act 1998 and the Minerals and Petroleum Resources Development Act 2002, and these regimes can encompass protection and restoration of aesthetic values.[42] In Australia, the New South Wales (NSW) Mining Act 1992 makes no mention of aesthetics in its official definition of 'rehabilitation', defined as 'the treatment or management of disturbed land or water for the purpose of establishing a safe and stable environment'.[43] Offering a little more detail, South Australia's Mining Act 1971 defines the 'environment', to which its rehabilitation obligations apply,[44] as including 'the aesthetic or cultural values of an area'.[45] In practice the scope of rehabilitation will usually be a matter for the discretionary judgement of environmental regulators. Aesthetic effects are not necessarily the primary consideration in post-mining rehabilitation. The Queensland government's guidance on rehabilitation, pursuant to the Environmental Protection Act 1994 (Qld), specifies four core goals of safety, stability, removal of pollution and to sustain post-mining land use, while restoration of aesthetic values is listed among possible secondary considerations that may apply on a site-by-site basis.[46]

Rehabilitation of closed mines typically encounters a number of governance challenges that may hamper reinstatement or improvement of aesthetic values. Firstly, in an era of industrial-scale mines, their closure has become more financially onerous and the financial securities provided by mine operators often prove to be insufficient to meet the agreed restoration plan.[47] Secondly, environmental restoration involves multi-disciplinary skills and expertise, including that from landscape architects, cultural heritage experts, restoration ecologists and civil engineers, thus creating risks that rehabilitation may emphasise one set of values (eg safety) over another (eg landscape aesthetics). Researchers have found that the aesthetics function of post-mining landscapes is 'much more difficult to define, evaluate and protect than its ecological function' because

---

[42] E Swart, *The South African Legislative Framework for Mine Closure* (South African Institute of Mining and Metallurgy, 2003).

[43] Section 4.

[44] Eg, s 70F(1).

[45] Section 6(4)(f).

[46] Queensland Department of Environment and Heritage, *Guideline: Rehabilitation Requirements for Mining Resource Activities* (Queensland Government, 2014) 8.

[47] P Keneall, 'Mine Rehabilitation Security Bonds Inadequate, NSW Auditor General Finds' *The Guardian* 11 May 2017.

of the nature of aesthetic values and the expertise of restoration managers.[48] Thirdly, because of the scale and complexity of many restoration projects, uncertainty arises about the future appearance and function of the reclaimed landscape, and this may prevent the miners and their regulators signing off on the restoration as complete.[49] Fourthly, the desire to retain some of the mining landscape as part of a community's historical heritage may clash with other goals of restoration relating to mimicking natural appearance or achieving ecological objectives such as re-creation of wildlife habitat. The aesthetic values to be restored may also depend on the type of land use envisioned for the former mine, such as agriculture, forestry or a nature reserve. Finally, industry practitioners note that 'one of the greatest impediments is the lack of knowledge of successes (and failures) at other mine sites and the techniques employed', which requires development of case histories and tools for measuring the degree of success of restoration.[50] Indeed, sometimes it may take several decades before one can verify the results of a rehabilitation project. I will explore a few of these issues in more detail.

Restoration of the aesthetic qualities of the pre-mine landscape may not be possible if the responsible company is insolvent or inadequate financial security was provisioned for the mine closure. While contemporary mining regulation contains a variety of fiscal mechanisms to provide resources to restore closed mining sites, such as cash bonds, non-refundable levies and compulsory insurance, they invariably contain loopholes. Methods to shirk such responsibilities include 'putting a mine to "care and maintenance", using up cash reserves, selling mines cheaply to smaller companies, and expanding a mine instead of closing it'.[51] One possible solution, as devised in Tasmania under its Mineral Resources Development Act 1995, empowers the regulator to recalculate the security deposit over the life of the mine to ensure adequate security is available to meet mine closure and rehabilitation costs.

A larger problem is the thousands of legacy or orphan mines from historical mining where no responsible operator remains to pay for rehabilitation. About 60,000 legacy sites have been identified in Australia, many from its mid-nineteenth century gold rush, and they remain without rehabilitation (and some sites may never be because they contain features such as old mine shafts that authorities have now designated as cultural heritage.[52] Even in recent years some

---

[48] P Sklenička and I Kašparová, 'Restoration of Visual Values in a Post-mining Landscape' (2008) 1 *Journal of Landscape Studies* 1, 1.

[49] McKenna, *Techniques for Creating Mining Landforms* (above n 35) 603.

[50] Ibid, 611.

[51] J Lodge, 'Queensland Mining Companies Avoid Clean-up Costs with Government Consent, Lawyers Say' *ABC News* 15 April 2016, www.abc.net.au/news/2016-04-15/mining-companies-avoiding-cleanup-costs-say-lawyers/7329716.

[52] Lateline, 'Mining Report Finds 60,000 Abandoned Sites, Lack of Rehabilitation and Unreliable Data' *ABC News* 16 February 2017, www.abc.net.au/news/2017-02-15/australia-institute-report-raises-concerns-on-mine-rehab/8270558.

mines have been closed without any requirement to fully rehabilitate the sites: in NSW, authorities have given permission for 45 massive coal pits to remain unfilled after the mining ceases.[53] The United States has about half a million abandoned mines, many leaving an unremediated environmental legacy.[54] The Brazilian Amazon is dotted with numerous abandoned artisanal gold mines leaching mercury and other pollutants.[55] Deserted mines have also been identified as a huge problem across in Canada, which the National Orphaned/Abandoned Mines Initiative is attempting to identify through a national inventory.[56]

Where sufficient private or public funds exist for rehabilitation, authorities must choose which aesthetic values to prioritise and their relationship to other goals such as renewal of ecological processes. Rehabilitation, like other domains of eco-restoration practice, starts with intertwined assumptions about the possibility and desirability of re-establishing the original ecological conditions of a site. Disagreements rage among scholars and practitioners over whether and how to restore ecosystems to their historic condition, which may be unrealistic given the complexity of natural, background change over time and the impossibility of ever returning to a 'pristine' baseline.[57] In post-mining rehabilitation, the question of what former time period to use as a benchmark is less contentious than in other types of eco-restoration because it will ordinarily be when the mine began.

The history of the mine, particularly if it has a long history, may itself become a legacy that some people desire to preserve, in part. A report by Australia's Mining Policy Institute observed that 'some may see mining and remnant waste dumps as a sign of progress, others may see them as aesthetically offensive'.[58] A report prepared by Canadian mining engineers on the Lake Louise mine closure observed that 'while some argue that aesthetic reclamation should be done for purely aesthetic purposes [...] others argue that preserving some of the historic/industrial features of a mining landscape is an important way of connecting humans to the land and its history'.[59] In a 2017 Australian parliamentary inquiry into rehabilitation of mining, a submission from the International Council on Monuments and Sites (Australian chapter) advised that 'mining sites

---

[53] Ibid.

[54] Data from Abandoned Mines, www.abandonedmines.gov//ep.html.

[55] MM Veiga and JJ Hinton, 'Abandoned Artisanal Gold Mines in the Brazilian Amazon: A Legacy of Mercury Pollution' (2002) 26 *Natural Resources Forum* 13.

[56] See.www.abandoned-mines.org.

[57] See the views of P Alagona, J Sandlos and Y Wiersma, 'Past Imperfect: Using Historical Ecology and Baseline Data for Conservation and Restoration Projects in North America' (2012) 9(1) *Environmental Philosophy* 4; E Marris, *Rambunctious Garden: Saving Nature in a Post-Wild World* (Bloomsbury, 2013).

[58] C Roche and S Judd, *Ground Truths: Taking Responsibility for Australia's Mining Legacies* (Mineral Policy Institute, 2017) 11.

[59] G McKenna et al, 'Aesthetics for Mine Closure' in AB Fourie, M Tibbett and A Beersing (eds), *Mine Closure 2011, Volume 1: Lake Louise, Canada* (Australian Centre for Geomechanics, 2011) 603, 603.

have important cultural heritage values' and 'may also have potential [for] tourism', and thus it recommended that 'rehabilitation of mining sites, should adopt practices that ensure their cultural values are assessed and conserved, consistent with other rehabilitation objectives'.[60] The historic Wieliczka Salt Mines in Poland, begun in the thirteenth century, now enjoy legal protection as a World Heritage-listed site owing to their cultural heritage significance, including extensive artworks housed in the former mining tunnels.[61]

The tensions in these different aesthetic considerations also have ramifications for the ecological goals of rehabilitation. Considerable research suggests 'a direct association between the visual quality of a reclaimed landscape (ie aesthetics) and its ecological sustainability'.[62] The picture is more complicated, however, as surveys of people's visual preferences of different restored habitats reveal some differences between the preferences of local residents and the general public living outside the former mining area.[63] Aesthetic preferences can also be quite divergent in urban landscapes with significant historic and cultural values, where policy makers must consult the public to decide on the future appearance and uses of derelict industrial areas and contaminated brownfields.

Public consultation increasingly informs post-mine restoration governance. Creation of visual diagrams and 3D visualisation presentations are practical ways to allow the public to perceive changes in the appearance of restored landscapes.[64] Portuguese researchers of the aesthetic rehabilitation of quarry found that 'computer simulations such as photomontages and digital fly-over videos helped in three-dimensional imaging and characterisation of the landscape'.[65] Equally important, affected communities will wish to express their views and be heard rather than merely be offered opportunities to visualise how their local environs will be restored. While such consultation frequently is required by mining or environmental legislation, mining companies may consult affected stakeholders in order to maintain their social licence to operate. 'Social licence' means the tacit permission that communities may give a company to engage in an activity, such as mining, in light of how it mitigates its environmental impacts and provides social and economic benefits.[66] A company's social endorsement can motivate it to improve its environmental governance even though its legal licence remains unchanged. The need to have a social licence

---

[60] Australia ICOMOS, *Senate Inquiry into: Rehabilitation of Mining and Resources Projects as it Relates to Commonwealth Responsibilities, Submission by Australia ICOMOS* (International Council on Monuments and Sites) (April 2017) 1–2.

[61] UNESCO, 'Wieliczka and Bochina Royal Salt Mines', https://whc.unesco.org/en/list/32.

[62] SA Roberts, *Landscape Aesthetics and Surface Mine Reclamation* (Master thesis, Faculty of Agricultural Sciences, University of British Columbia, 1999) 3.

[63] P Sklenicka and K Molnarova, 'Visual Perception of Habitats Adopted for Post-Mining Landscape Rehabilitation' (2010) 46(3) *Environmental Management* 424.

[64] Ibid.

[65] B Ramos and T Panagopoulos, *Aesthetic And Visual Impact Assessment of a Quarry Expansion* (Proceedings of the 2006 IASME/WSEAS, 11–13 July 2006) 378, 379.

[66] L Black, *The Social Licence to Operate* (Routledge, 2017).

thus makes meaningful and transparent consultation with local communities particularly important for mining companies, and indeed for many other types of businesses.

Such public consultation may be canvassed before a mine commences operations, as part of the initial regulatory approval process. In a decision of the NSW Land and Environment Court in early 2019 to reject a proposed open-cast mine partly because of its visual and amenity impacts on the local community, Chief Justice (CJ) Preston found that the mitigation and restoration measures proposed by the mining company would not be sufficient to ameliorate the lasting impacts, and they could actually worsen them. In his words:

> the proposed mine will have a high visual contrast with the surrounding landscape, which will not be ameliorated by the amenity barriers or the revegetation of the amenity barriers, permanent overburden emplacements or rehabilitated post mining landforms.[67]

The proximity of the mine to a township contributed to CJ Preston's determination that the project would have a 'high visual impact' observable from 'multiple viewpoints' that will 'significantly affect' the 'amenity, use and enjoyment of residential and rural residential properties'.[68] This case illustrates the weight that authorities can attach to public opinion on the aesthetics of mining operations and subsequent remediation, and addressing public concerns at the start of the regulatory process rather than as an ex post facto consideration.

III. ECOSYSTEM RESTORATION

Unlike regulation of post-mining rehabilitation, nation states have struggled to develop commensurate governance regimes for large-scale restoration of ecosystems. Mining-context rehabilitation typically targets discrete, small sites unlike the temporal and spatial scope of eco-restoration across landscapes over thousands of hectares and long timeframes. Non-state actors such as environmental NGOs and community groups often take the initiative here, where the role of the state is limited to facilitating action through seed funding and furnishing legal tools such as conservation covenants. Aesthetics are just as relevant to eco-restoration as post-mining rehabilitation, although with some different considerations and contexts. Nature conservation legislation in many jurisdictions provides for the recovery of endangered or threatened species, which may encompass restoring their habitat as well. Aesthetic biases can influence which species receive priority, with charismatic fauna more likely to benefit than the ugly or mundane. Forestry management may also include eco-restoration, in which logging is followed by replanting and measures to tidy up logged coupes,

---

[67] *Gloucester Resources Ltd v Minister for Planning* [2019] NSWLEC 7, para 160.
[68] Ibid, para 218.

along with retention of trees along visually accessible areas such as hill tops and roads passing through forestry zones. Eco-restoration measures in the law, however, do not generally refer explicitly to aesthetic criteria, leaving matters to authorities' discretionary judgement.

Existing legal standards for eco-restoration are brief, broad and aspirational. At an international level, the EU's Habitats Directive[69] obliges its Member States 'to maintain or restore, at favourable conservation status, natural habitats and species of wild fauna and flora of Community interest'.[70] The European Biodiversity Strategy supports the Directive, seeking by 2020 to restore 'at least 15% of degraded ecosystems'.[71] The Convention on Biological Diversity of 1992 obliges its parties, as far as possible, to 'rehabilitate and restore degraded ecosystems and promote the recovery of threatened species',[72] with the enabling Aichi Biodiversity Targets setting the goal of restoring at least 15 per cent of degraded ecosystems.[73] The Convention on International Trade in Endangered Species of Wild Fauna and Flora,[74] which aims to restrict trade in wildlife, rather than restore biodiversity, observes in its preamble 'the ever-growing value of wild fauna and flora from aesthetic [...] points of view'. Other examples of international legal standards for eco-restoration surveyed by Telesetsky, Cliquet and Akhtar-Khavari suggest gaps between official edicts and state practices.[75] These largely hortatory norms have limited traction in shaping eco-restoration within nation-states for reasons that include economic costs, community opposition, existing land use entitlements and the lack of meaningful legal accountability.

Of specific examples, the US National Forest Management Act's standards for forest management require that logging and the regeneration of timber resources make provision for protection of aesthetic values.[76] Furthermore, the Act's 'Statement of Policy' stipulates that 'the Nation's forested land [...] should be managed at levels that realize its capabilities to satisfy the Nation's need for [...] esthetic values'.[77] Yet, in the most ambitious forests restoration project in the United States, known as the Collaborative Forest Landscape Restoration Program, as enacted in 2009 under Title IV of the Omnibus Public Land Management Act,[78] one can find no mention of aesthetic values. The restoration goals of this program serve the forestry economy and control of destructive wildfires.[79] In Canada, Ontario's then visionary Crown Forest Sustainability

---

[69] Council Directive 92/43/EEC of 21 May 1992.
[70] Ibid, art 2(2).
[71] See http://ec.europa.eu/environment/nature/biodiversity/strategy.
[72] (1992) 1760 UNTS 79; arts 8(f) and 9(c).
[73] Target 15.
[74] (1973) 12 ILM 1085.
[75] A Telesetsky, A Cliquet and A Akhtar-Khavari, *Ecological Restoration in International Environmental Law* (Routledge, 2017).
[76] (1976) Public Law 94-588 s 1604(g)(3)(F)(ii) and (v).
[77] Ibid, s 1606(f)(2).
[78] Omnibus Public Land Management Act 2009, Public Law 111-11, 123 Stat 991.
[79] Ibid, ss 4001, 4003.

Act 1994 omits any reference to aesthetic values or related terms,[80] although its sister Forestry Act specifies consideration of aesthetics as among the criteria of 'good forestry practices'.[81] British Columbia, another Canadian province with a huge forestry industry, specifies 'visual qualities' as a matter that can be the subject of subsidiary regulations, including for designation of 'scenic areas' under its Forest and Forest Practices Act 2002.[82] The enacting regulations specify visual quality objectives for protection in designated scenic forests, although the law focuses on retention of scenic qualities rather than their restoration after logging.[83] In Australia, the NSW forestry authorities recommend retention of a 'roadside visual aesthetic zone', and 'visual aesthetics' are among the 12 specified 'special values' to manage sensitively in forestry operations on public lands.[84] Zambia's Forest Act 2015 identifies promotion of aesthetic values as one of its governing principles.[85] China's Forestry Law 1998 classifies forests into five categories, one of which includes 'scenic forests' and 'forest trees at scenic spots', and the legislation emphasises afforestation and community participation.[86]

Species recovery programs for threatened biodiversity are articulated under the auspices of general nature conservation legislation or occasionally under statutes dedicated to threatened species protection. Such laws draw on a science-based framework, where zoology, botany, conservation biology and other natural sciences inform determinations about the classification of species and design of recovery programs. For instance, the NSW Biodiversity Conservation Act 2015 declares its core purposes as including 'to assess the extinction risk of species and ecological communities, and identify key threatening processes, through an independent and rigorous scientific process'.[87] Special scientific committees are often established under such legislation to make determinations or provide advice. Such legislation typically acknowledges aesthetic values just sporadically, mainly as one of the guiding rationales for nature conservation rather than as a methodology of decision-making. Illustratively, the US Endangered Species Act 1973 declares that America's wildlife has 'esthetic value [...] to the Nation and its people'.[88]

Sometimes authorities orchestrate eco-restoration over an entire bio-region to achieve effective recovery of threatened species. Islands can provide ideal opportunities for such projects because of their relative isolation from threatening incursions after removal of endemic threats. Consider the example of

---

[80] SO 1994, c 25.
[81] RSO 1990, ch F 26, s 1(1).
[82] SBC 2002, C 69, ss 149(1)(b), 150.3.
[83] Government Actions Regulation, BC Reg 582/2004, cl 7.
[84] Forestry Corporation of NSW, *Managing Our Forests Sustainably: Forest Management Zoning in NSW State Forests* (Forestry Corporation of NSW, 1999) 24–26.
[85] Section 8(j).
[86] Forestry Law of the People's Republic of China, 1998, arts 4(5), 11 and 12.
[87] Section 1.3.
[88] Public Law 93-205; 87 Stat 884, s 2(a)(3).

Macquarie Island, a subantarctic outpost of 12,800 hectares controlled by the Tasmanian government. It had suffered from ravenous feral mammals such as rats and cats, which since the mid-nineteenth century had devastated the island's flora and seabirds, resulting in ugly, eroded hillsides stripped of vegetation. Over several decades of intensive restoration that concluded in 2013, the Tasmanian Parks and Wildlife Service eradicated all the vermin.[89] Its efforts in restoring the World Heritage-listed island were enabled by it having legal control of the entire area, pursuant to Tasmania's National Parks and Reserves Management Act 2002 (Tas). While the legislation does not refer to aesthetic values, the World Heritage Convention does, as do the management plans for Macquarie Island's restoration. The government's rabbit eradication plan for the island acknowledged that the place was inscribed on the World Heritage list because, inter alia, it contains 'superlative natural phenomena or areas of exceptional natural beauty and aesthetic importance'.[90] New Zealand has pioneered similar eco-restoration of many of its offshore islands, driven by biodiversity conservation considerations and 'the scenic quality of the islands and their aesthetic appeal' which 'have an emotional impact on all who visit them'.[91]

Biodiversity management on scientific grounds and criteria increasingly challenges the bias towards recovery of beautiful species and places. Environmental NGOs, long guilty of glorifying charismatic fauna, now more commonly embrace the importance of 'ordinary' species. The Wilderness Society, one of Australia's major such NGOs, in 2018 launched its 'Save Ugly?' campaign that uses a four-minute musical comedy video and social media, starring Hollywood actress and activist Rosario Dawson, to raise public awareness of the lesser known, 'ugly' creatures like 'grubby mangroves, flaky lichen [and] squirmy worms' in maintaining healthy ecosystems on which humankind depends.[92] The Save Ugly campaign itself uses visual and acoustic effects to present unsightly creatures more attractively. Others have spread a similar message. The British-based Ugly Animal Preservation Society describes its mission as 'raising the profile of some of Mother Nature's more aesthetically challenged children',[93] and its leader Simon Watt has even published a book, *The Ugly Animals: We Can't All be Pandas*,[94] aimed at enlivening young readers.

---

[89] J Scott, 'Macquarie Island – Exciting Changes in Vegetation after Eradication of Rabbits and Rodents' (2014–15) 27 *Australian Plants* 351.

[90] Department of Primary Industries and Water, Tasmania, *Plan for the Eradication of Rabbits and Rodents on Subantarctic Macquarie Islan*d (Government of Tasmania, 2007) 26.

[91] LF Molley and PR Dingwall, 'World Heritage Values of New Zealand Islands' in DR Towns, CH and IAE Atkinson (eds), *Ecological Restoration of New Zealand Islands* (Department of Conservation, 1999) 194, 203.

[92] Wilderness Society, 'Save Ugly', www.wilderness.org.au/work/ugly.

[93] Ugly Animal Preservation Society, 'About', http://uglyanimalsoc.com.

[94] S Watt, *The Ugly Animals: We Can't All be Pandas* (History Press, 2014).

Among individual landholders, aesthetic preferences also matter in land use practices. Their desire for views of wildlife and forests can contribute to nature conservation practices,[95] yet other preferences for neat and tidy countryside, such as by removal of dead trees and rocks, can be counterproductive by removing micro-habitats for wildlife.[96] Legal regulation has limited options to directly influence the aesthetic preferences of landholders to encourage practices that help restore degraded landscapes because of the difficulty of defining specific aesthetic features that should be retained and ensuring compliance in areas where the authorities have limited oversight. Conservation covenants can help landowners to ensure long-term environmental stewardship of their properties and tie the hands of future property owners, but they are usually a voluntary, altruistic undertaking in the first place rather than prescribed by regulation.[97] I placed a conservation covenant on 66 acres of forest that I purchased in Tasmania in 2015, a decision taken voluntarily without legal obligation or financial reward.[98] I do not regard my property an aesthetic gem but nor is it devoid of sensory pleasure. Because conservation covenants tend to be available only for places of existing high conservation value, landholders who wish to environmentally restore their properties cannot benefit from ensuring preservation of the fruits of their labour by future landowners.

To recap, environmental regulation supports eco-restoration in a variety of contexts to aid the recovery of endangered wildlife and their ecosystems. These laws do not exclude aesthetic considerations, but neither do they embrace them in any systematic or comprehensive fashion. This case study illustrates tangibly the wider problem of not taking aesthetics seriously. But when we look at eco-restoration governance beyond the state, as the following section does, the picture shifts radically.

IV. RESTORATIVE ART

In a field once dominated by scientists and land use planners, artists are becoming an indispensable stakeholder in eco-restoration, including to assist local communities interpret recovering environments, and sometimes interceding to help with the actual recovery process. This contribution is not entirely unprecedented, as artists have a history of collaboration with natural scientists in documenting and communicating their work, as during the European 'Age of Discovery' expeditions noted earlier in this book. Redolent of this tradition, in 2013 the SER sponsored the 'Print Project' that paired up 11 artists and

---

[95] D Erickson and R De Young, 'Management of Farm Woodlots and Windbreaks: Some Psychological and Landscape Patterns' (1993) 22 *Journal of Environmental Systems* 233.
[96] D Lindenmayer et al, *Wildlife Conservation in Farm Landscapes* (CSIRO Publishing, 2016).
[97] T Kabii and P Horwitz, 'A Review of Landholder Motivations and Determinants for Participation in Conservation Covenanting Programmes' (2006) 33(1) *Environmental Conservation* 11.
[98] See www.bluemountainview.com.au.

restoration ecologists to create a pictorial story of the ecologist's work, for later exhibition at an SER conference to facilitate a new visual explanation of restoration practice. Governments too have used art to help communicate policies and advice about nature conservation and eco-restoration, such as government-commissioned posters on land care distributed to farmers, as in the example depicted in Figure 6.2. The poster 'Plains Farms Need Trees' was created in 1940 by for US federal government as part of its Prairie States Forestry Project to improve retention and establishment of trees to halt soil erosion.

Figure 6.2 *Plains Farms Need Trees*, poster, 1940; US Work Projects Administration Poster Collection; US Library of Congress

Some artists desire more ambitious and critical roles that go beyond being transmission belts for the interpretation of scientific knowledge and practice. They seek more socially and politically salient opportunities for questioning scientific practice and offering new pathways of nature aesthetics experiencing and learning, often through site-based installations and performance works. Some are also doing the restoration: 'art that cleans water, creates habitat, controls erosion. The art itself has an ecological and restorative function', explains

Sarah DeWeerdt.[99] The notion that art can have non-aesthetic functions or benefits should come as no surprise when one considers how commonly artistic design contributes to the making of practical objects, such as ceramics or furniture and as well as landscape architecture.[100]

This artistic contribution features most in eco-restoration projects driven by non-state actors, including environmental NGOs, Indigenous peoples and private landholders. Government supervision of eco-restoration, as we learned earlier in this chapter, predominantly targets former mines and industrial brownfields while downplaying large-scale, landscape or ecosystem-wide restorations. This latter realm has become the focus of non-governmental efforts, voluntarily filling the governance void. In some of these efforts, artists' creative ardour assists with restoring and healing communities that have suffered from environmental damage or who have an important stake in ecological recovery.[101]

A variety of restoration projects around the globe illustrate the growing presence of artists. At one end of the spectrum of approaches, artists intervene to increase publicity about environmental disasters or degradation needing remediation. Of this genre, Edward Burtynsky's dramatic photographs of mines, quarries and dams reveal a litany of devastation levied on the planet. Some artists go further in empowering affected communities to respond, as with the Rio de La Plata oil spill. When an oil tanker spill struck in Argentina's Rio de La Plata in January 1999, it caught the attention of the eco-arts fraternity Al Plastica, who sought to publicise the devastation through a photographic montage to go with the riverside survey it conducted.[102] Al Plastica engaged reed harvesters, fishermen, scientists and a fauna rescue group in successfully broadcasting the local impacts of the disaster and persuading the responsible company, Shell, to clean up the polluted riverfronts that stretched over 16 kms, some in a UNESCO Biosphere Reserve.

Some artists go even further, interceding in actual recovery work. The difference, as commentator Eric Nay explains, centres on the 'remarkable gap' between art that 'celebrates, waxes poetic and speaks in metaphors that can then be sold in galleries [...] and the art that does remain and can "fix" parts of the earth that have been broken'.[103] The partnership between US artists Helen Mayer Harrison and Newton Harrison represents one of the earliest forays into this genre. Since the 1970s they have investigated environmental problems around

[99] S DeWeerdt, 'Restorative Art' *The Conservation* 8 March 2013, www.conservationmagazine.org/2013/03/restorative-art.

[100] R van Etteger, 'Aesthetic Creation Theory and Landscape Architecture' (2016) 11(1) *Journal of Landscape Architecture* 80.

[101] D Blandy, K Congdon and D Krug, 'Art, Ecological Restoration, and Art Education' (1998) 39(3) *Studies in Art Education: A Journal of Issues and Research* 230.

[102] L Ball, 'Called to Action: Environmental Restoration by Artists' (2008) 26(1) *Ecological Restoration* 27, 27–28.

[103] EM Nay, 'Contextualizing Ecological Restoration through Art' (2011) 1(21) *International Journal of Humanities and Social Science* 31, 33.

the globe and devised artistic solutions. Their work creates practical solutions for environmental regeneration, and extensively documenting it work through maps, photographs and texts enables a wider audience to learn from their interventions. The Spoils Pile project, begun in 1976, exemplifies the Harrisons' oeuvre.[104] They regenerated a quarry filled with debris from the construction of the Niagara Power Plant in order to create a lush meadow for community recreational use. This project involved depositing hundreds of truckloads of earth and mulch on 8 hectares of degraded land to enable the meadow and trees to regenerate. This organic artwork illustrates how the Harrisons' do not see their art as a 'product' but rather an ongoing engagement with ecological places to improve their vitality. And they create their work through an 'extensive consultation process [...] confer[ring] with a variety of people including journalists, mayors, public officials, artists and farmers'.[105]

Another pioneer in this realm is Patricia Johanson. Her creations can be seen at the California's Ellis Creek Water Recycling Facility, where one can observe from an aerial vantage an image of the salt marsh harvest mouse (*Reithrodontomys raviventris*), one of the area's smallest mammals. Designed by Johanson, the 'mouse' comprises several water-treatment ponds over 14 hectares, with two islands for eyes and rounded earth banks that resemble its ears.[106] For the past 35 years, Johanson has designed impressive civic works incorporating impressions of species resident in each site. Her designs go beyond renditions of animals to develop viable habitat for them and recreational opportunities for local people. Several kilometers of public trails and interpretive signage at Ellis Creek inform visitors of the life patterns of the mouse, along with the wastewater treatment process, the tidal cycle, and the delicate relationships between microhabitats and ecosystems. Habitat islands in each sewage treatment pod offer nesting and refuge for birds, which birding enthusiasts come to observe. As Johanson explains of the significance of her Ellis Creek project, 'one of my missions as a designer is to create inclusive, life-supporting landscapes that broaden human understanding. Artists have always changed the way we see. Now we need to change the way we act'.[107]

Rehabilitating urban and industrial environments has preoccupied New Yorker Alan Sonfist, creating natural monuments that restore ecologies and commemorate their geography and natural history. From 1965 to 1978, he created, in conjunction with the Metropolitan Museum of Art, city planners, and community boards, *Time Landscape* in Greenwich Village, Manhattan. It re-creates the original indigenous vegetation of New York, and Sonfist selected the species after conducting research at New York Public Library and consulting

---

[104] See http://theharrisonstudio.net/art-park-spoils-pile-reclamation-1976-1978-ongoing.

[105] J Wildy, 'A Sculpted Land: Ecological Landscape Art of the Harrisons, Patricia Johanson and Agnes Denes', *EarthZine* 5 January 2013, https://earthzine.org/2013/01/05.

[106] See http://patriciajohanson.com/.

[107] See http://patriciajohanson.com/timeline/ellis_creek_petaluma.html.

with experts from the City Botanical Gardens. The project represents the processes of nature rebuilding itself and reclaiming its space and evoking the memory of the re-vegetated site. Through *Time Landscape*, Sonfist sought to demonstrate that the survival of people depends on our understanding of the interdependence of culture with natural systems. Sonfist has since repeated this intervention in many other cities, creating narrative landscapes to show how the given area looked in different epochs. His work has resonated with some municipal planners, such as the New York City's Parks Department, which has sought to emulate Sonfist's example by restoring small green spaces in other parts of Manhattan.[108]

In other countries, German artist Joseph Beuys was a pioneer in this field; his *7000 Oaks* was a massive tree-planting action begun in June 1982 at the Documenta 7 exhibition in the city of Kassel, as an intended 'ecological sign'. Each tree was paired with a basalt stone, all deposited on the entrance lawn of the Museum Fridericianum with the plan that the pile would shrink with each tree planting. It took Beuys five years to complete, and inspired other artistic urban regenerations around the world. New Zealander Chris Booth's art helps to revegetate degraded sites while creating new sculptural forms in living nature. His *Celebration of a Tor* (1993) sculpture was a contribution to the Grizedale project in England. The Grizedale forest, managed by the English Forestry Commission, was partially dedicated as a public sculpture park, using the natural materials at hand. While the sculptures were not felled, it was recognised that they will erode under natural processes of decay. Also working in this genre, artist Harriet Feigenbaum's project *Erosion and Sedimentation Plan for Red Ash and Coal Silt Area – Willow Rings* (1985) converted a six-hectare site, damaged from strip mining, into a wetland reserve for wildlife with meticulously planted willow trees in three perfect circles around the pond.[109]

Another innovator in this field is Hungarian Agnes Denes, whose art strives both to critique commodification of nature and promote its recovery. In *Wheatfield – A Confrontation: Battery Park Landfill* (1982), her 'canvas' was a two-acre landfill created with debris from the construction of the World Trade Centre. Denes planted and harvested 2,200 kilograms of wheat, then worth US$93, on a site valued at US$4.5 billion. For Denes, the wheatfield confronted misplaced priorities and social values: world hunger and waste juxtaposed to a global financial citadel.[110] Other examples of Denes' work, such as *Tree Mountain – A Living Time Capsule – 11,000 Trees, 11,000 People, 400 Years* (1992–96),[111] which involved planting 11,000 trees on a Finnish hilltop, make a more traditional eco-restoration contribution without acknowledging the cultural context even though the project required hundreds of volunteers.

[108] N Blanc and BL Benish, *Form, Art and the Environment* (Earthscan, 2016) 84.
[109] J Kastner (ed), *Land and Environmental Art* (Phaidon Press, 1998) 149.
[110] J Clark, 'Fields of Thought: The Art of Agnes Denes' (1997) 16 *Public Art Review* 9.
[111] See www.agnesdenesstudio.com/works4.html.

Collaboration between environmental organisations and artists is also the goal of the 2015 Memorandum of Understanding between Rewilding Europe and the Artists for Nature Foundation, with the partnership centring on projects working with school children taken to landscapes restored by Rewilding Europe.[112] Another collaboration of this genre is between the US Nature Conservancy and the Nevada Museum of Art's Center for Art + Environment for restoring the Eastern Sierra's rivers; the project, called 'the Nature of Art', began in 2014, and aims to create living sculptures from the native willow trees planted along the river's edge. As the Nature Conservancy explains, the 'sculptures – up to 350 feet long – are designed to sprout and grow, creating important habitat for willow flycatchers, monarch butterflies and other wildlife. They also improve water quality by reducing erosion and filtering pollutants'.[113]

We should not expect ecological recovery to endure over the long term if the underlying anthropogenic drivers of degradation remain unchecked. Given the high cost of eco-restoration projects, it's usually cheaper to take preventative measures and thereby avoid creating harm at the outset. Addressing harmful behaviour, and encouraging positive practices, requires linking eco-restoration to wider strategies of social and institutional change. Models of eco-restoration that conceive of nature as separate from – or even devoid of – human beings risk failure, because of a misguided assumption that such places never had and never will have a human presence.

Eco-restoration theory no longer sits within a purely natural science framework, as it was in the 1970s, but contemporary policies and regulations often lack acknowledgement of the vital social dimension.[114] By conceiving of restoration as combining ecological and cultural elements, we can more easily align restoration with an understanding of environmental aesthetics as about living relationships rather than observed objects, as scholars such as Yuriko Saito and Arnold Berleant advocate.[115] I don't wish to discuss the ways by which the law has or should facilitate community participation in eco-restoration, as I have done so extensively in my other writings.[116] Rather, in the following pages that conclude this chapter I wish to consider how the arts can facilitate community engagement in eco-restoration.[117]

---

[112] Rewilding Europe, 'What do Rewilding and Art have in Common?' 1 October 2015, https://rewildingeurope.com/tag/artists-for-nature-foundation.

[113] Nature Conservancy, 'The Nature of Art: Watershed Sculpture on the Truckee and Carson Rivers', www.nature.org/ourinitiatives/regions/northamerica/unitedstates/nevada/placesweprotect/the-nature-of-art.xml.

[114] D Martin, 'Ecological Restoration Should be Redefined for the Twenty-first Century' (2017) 25(5) *Restoration Ecology* 668.

[115] Y Saito, *Aesthetics of the Familiar: Everyday Life and World-Making* (Oxford University Press, 2017).

[116] A Berleant, *Living in the Landscape: Toward an Aesthetics of Environment* (University Press of Kansas, 1997).

[117] L Ball et al, 'Environmental Art as Eco-cultural Restoration' in D Egan, EE Hjerpe and J Abrams (eds), *Human Dimensions of Ecological Restoration: Integrating Science, Nature and Culture* (Island Press 2011) 299.

Art practices and outputs can help arouse community interest in eco-restoration projects and have 'the potential to reconfigure the community's aesthetic perception and valuation' of landscapes as well as 'propose new sustainable ways of using them for recreation'.[118] In turn, artists can become more 'open to challenges to their own artistic approaches and perspectives'.[119] Davd Curtis and others highlight the value of 'participatory art forms' that can 'foster an improved social climate from which community-based environmental work may more readily emerge',[120] and suggest that art can have practical environmental benefits when integrated in 'farm forestry, rural regeneration, and land rehabilitation initiatives, or where farmers incorporate principles of landscape design into farm planning'.[121] Let us look at some examples of using art to help integrate social and ecological dimensions in restoration projects.

British artist Ian Hunter has promoted the revitalisation of traditional trades such as willow craft to revive both the ecology and economy of areas damaged by industrial pollution. His *Willow Tree* (1988) is an 80-foot tunnel-maze woven of living willow, planned and built over three years with a class of primary schoolchildren. This 'growing' sculpture functions as an environmental interpretation centre hosting children to play games.[122] Hunter also played a key role in setting up Projects Environment, a UK trust founded in 1989 to promote new art and craft practices in the context of social and economic change. Since 1991, Projects Environment has hosted a series of residencies for fibre artists and has now established the first British Fellowship in Basket Making at Manchester Metropolitan University. Such projects challenge commodity capitalism and point to new postcolonial forms of art practice synthesising ecological ethics with social and economic justice.

Another example closer to my home is the Island Ark project in Tasmania's Midlands, a region with a long history of agriculture yet one of Australia's biodiversity hotspots.[123] Here farmers have partnered with Greening Australia (an NGO) and artists to undertake the largest habitat restoration ever in Tasmania.[124] The project seeks to recover 6,000 hectares of new habitat on privately held properties to protect endangered wildlife,[125] and includes collaboration with the

[118] Ibid.

[119] M Murzyn-Kupisz and J Dzialek, 'Theorising Artists as Actors of Urban Change' in M Murzyn-Kupisz and J Dzialek (eds), *The Impact of Artists on Contemporary Urban Development in Europe* (Springer, 2017) 1, 33.

[120] I Reeve, D Curtis and N Reid, *Arts and Environmental Behaviour: Policy Recommendations, Report to Land and Water Australia* (University of New England, 2005) 13.

[121] Ibid, 17.

[122] See www.irwellsculpturetrail.co.uk/sculpture.html?name=Willow%20Tree.

[123] Bush Heritage Australia, 'A Biodiversity Hotspot' 12 June 2017, www.bushheritage.org.au/newsletters/2017/winter/biodiversity-hotspot.

[124] N Morris, 'Greening Australia and Midlands Farmers Unite to Restore Habitat' *ABC Rural* 4 September 2014, www.abc.net.au/news/rural/2014-08-22/greening-midlands/5686216.

[125] Greening Australia, 'Tasmania Island Ark', www.greeningaustralia.org.au/programs/tasmania-island-ark.

University of Tasmania's School of Creative Arts to implement a landscape arts project. Artists have engaged with local schools and communities in creating sculptures to place in the countryside that not only support the community's interpretation of the restoration of natural biodiversity but also directly aid their conservation (the sculptures serve as 'species hotels' for birds, bats and other small mammals, as depicted in Figure 6.3).[126] One notable art installation called *Hearth*, was placed on Julian and Annabel Von Bibra's farm. *Hearth* evokes the idea of temporal and spatial connections in the Tasmanian landscape, the connections between the past, present and future, and the spatial connections between ecological and human cultural elements in the landscape.

Figure 6.3 *A Species Hotel*, 2016, Tasmanian Island Ark project; photograph by Nina Hamilton

Another multi-disciplinary project is 'Operation Crayweed Art-Work-Site', in Sydney, where in 2016 artists teamed up with scientists and local school children to create an art installation that helps to engage the public in replanting forests

---

[126] Greening Australia, 'Building Hotels for Tasmania's Unique Species', www.greeningaustralia. org.au/news/building-hotels-for-tasmanias-unique-species.

of seaweed that had died out along the Sydney coastline since the 1980s.[127] Such projects shift artistic expression from the gallery or museum to the outdoors in a manner that enriches the aesthetic appeal of a relatively barren expanse that lacks the stereotypical scenic splendour that has worked against aesthetically mundane environments.

Some of these artistic and community contributions to eco-restoration can also apply to post-mining and industrial rehabilitation. In East Germany's Lustia region, a polluted wasteland of former coal mines and derelict industry has been transformed since 2000 into a scenic environment of 'soaring pine forests, glistening lakes and immaculate asphalt cycle paths' that now attract tourists.[128] Another success story is the Heartlands project in Cornwall, England, where a 20 acre decaying industrial eyesore was transformed into a thriving precinct with recreational parks, artists' studios, cafes, housing, along with retaining some of the industrial architecture as a tourist attraction.[129] The project was funded by a £22.3 million grant from the Big Lottery Fund's Living Landmarks program.

Detroit is the epitome of social and environmental decay, a city blighted by massive deindustrialisation since the 1960s with consequential enormous depopulation and financial distress. Many city precincts are littered with dilapidated buildings and empty lots, a source of aesthetic pollution to some (see Figure 6.4). Yet such degeneration also attracts some tourists intrigued by the phenomenon known as 'ruin porn'. Despite the blight, community generation projects abound, with artists heavily involved in helping to ease the 'anxiety of decline', as Dora Aopel describes the condition afflicting many Detroiters.[130] One urban regeneration project is the Squash House, a community space designed around a renovated old house that provides a space for community gardening, workshops and sports.[131] Another restorative effort is the Ride it Sculpture Park, where artists and designers turned a run-down lot into a public park offering a skateboarding facility and art works.[132] These projects lack the publicity of the Heidelberg Project, a vast outdoor art installation spanning two city blocks that began in 1986 with the stated mission 'to improve the lives of people and neighborhoods through art'.[133] As a consequence, 'vacant lots literally became "lots of art" and abandoned houses became "gigantic art sculptures"'.[134] The project has created an aesthetically vibrant social space that helps the community to overcome its anxieties.

---

[127] For further details, see www.operationcrayweed.com/artwork-site.

[128] P Sullivan, 'East Germany's Old Mines Transformed into New Lake District', *The Guardian* 17 September 2016.

[129] See www.heartlandscornwall.com.

[130] D Apel, *Beautiful Terrible Ruins: Detroit and the Anxiety of Decline* (Rutgers University Press, 2015).

[131] See www.powerhouseproductions.org/projects/squash-house.

[132] See www.powerhouseproductions.org/projects/ride-it-sculpture-park.

[133] Heidelberg Project, 'Mission', www.heidelberg.org/mission-vision.

[134] Heidelberg Project, 'History', www.heidelberg.org/history.

Another artistic practice that brings the social dimension into eco-restoration is the recycling of urban and industrial waste into art works.[135] Some artists refashion recycled wrappers, tyres, bottles, cigarette boxes, plastic toys, auto and electronic parts, cereal boxes, and aluminum cans, and some of their creations acquire functional uses such as children's toys, utensils or furniture. The recycled object carries a 'memory' of its prior existence, referring to technologies, uses and histories, but also a future 'aspiration', signalling how some can remake rubbish into items of enduring practical use. One practitioner is Michelle Reader, who has spent 20 years in the UK making recycled materials into eye-catching sculptures that can function as children's toys. Belgian artist Wim Delvoye tackles one of the most difficult items of trash to repurpose into art – used tires. His delightful creations out of black synthetic rubber depict comforting flowers and vines. South African Ryan Frank designs practical and funky furniture from recycled materials, as does American Nick Marco. A different approach is that of the UK-based Hacking Plastic group, which has sought to improve community literacy about plastics by offering opportunities for people to work with artists to make collaborative artworks from different kinds of waste plastic, with the art-making educating participants about the composition and degree of recyclability of different plastics.[136]

Figure 6.4 Detroit abandoned building, 2018; photograph by Tobias Richardson

[135] C Cerny and S Seriff (eds), *Recycled Re-Seen: Folk Art from the Global Scrap Heap* (Museum of International Folk Art, 1996).
[136] D McKay and E Giraud, 'Five Ways the Arts Could Help Solve the Plastics Crisis' *The Conversation* 23 February 2018, https://theconversation.com.

V. CONCLUSION

If humankind survives the Anthropocene, our descendants might encounter one of our most toxic environmental legacies that so far cannot be remediated – the radioactive waste repositories holding thousands of tonnes of discarded materials from the nuclear energy and weapons industries, which will remain hazardous for millennia. The daunting problem facing regulators today has been not just to find suitable deep underground voids to store the waste indefinitely, but also to communicate the dangers of entering these sites far into the future, as people 10,000 years from now will probably not understand today's written languages. (The English of the twenty-first century bears little resemblance to its antecedent of the eleventh century.) To this end, authorities have turned to art, trying to create a radiation warning pictogram, whose images would hopefully be intelligible to audiences of any culture in the remote future.

It has proved a challenge nearly as difficult as engineering the deep geological repositories.[137] The triangular international warning symbol for radiation created in 1946 – the three-bladed black trefoil on a yellow background – remains poorly understood. In 2007, after a major cross-cultural study, the International Atomic Energy Agency found that the symbol 'has no intuitive meaning and little recognition beyond those educated in its significance'.[138] As a result, the Agency released a new symbol, of radiating waves, a skull and crossbones and a running person against a red background, which its research suggests will be more widely understood (see Figure 6.5). Still, this effort has not settled the worries of some authorities, such as in Finland where at Onkalo authorities have created a giant geological repository for the country's radioactive waste to last for 100,000 years. No international consensus in the nuclear industry has emerged yet on how to design pictograms that will be intelligible for posterity over such time spans. Yet stakeholders widely concur that that artists can help resolve this conundrum; for instance, in 2015 France's nuclear agency Andra commissioned a competition for artists to suggest designs to overcome this problem.

Figure 6.5 Nuclear radiation warning symbols, 1946 and 2007; International Atomic Energy Agency

---

[137] M Stothard, 'Nuclear Waste: Keep Out for 100,000 Years' *Financial Times* 14 July 2016.

[138] International Atomic Energy Agency, 'New Symbol Launched to Warn Public About Radiation Disasters', press release, 15 February 2007, www.iaea.org/newscenter/pressreleases/new-symbol-launched-warn-public-about-radiation-dangers.

This anecdote fittingly concludes this chapter by reminding us that its subject deals with a profound aesthetics challenge for policy makers, a challenge that requires artists as much as ecologists or planners. While the problem posed by nuclear waste cannot be effectively remediated with current knowhow, the alternative policy goal to minimise risks of contamination requires the involvement of artists just as much as for other issues considered in this chapter, Recovery of degraded environments requires decisions that touch on aesthetics in many contexts, including the desired future appearance of restored places, and the artistic practices that can help communicate or undertake ecological recovery. Ultimately, eco-restoration is a powerful means of putting into practice some of the major ideas in the field of environmental aesthetics: participatory engagement of affected communities and improving their scientific knowledge together can guide appreciation and stewardship of nature aesthetics.

7

Climate Change

I. THE ISSUES

CLIMATE CHANGE SHOULD be so familiar to students and scholars of environmental law that its importance needs no introduction here. This chapter evaluates the connections between climate change governance and aesthetics and the arts, a subject few have yet explored.[1] The climate at large defies easy aesthetic evaluation when quantified as 'meteorological parameters such as temperature, air pressure, humidity, wind force, etc'.[2] Yet a *changing* climate induces a variety of sensory effects of aesthetic significance. They stem from ecological impacts that alter the appearance of environments, as well as human responses to those impacts. Mitigation measures, especially wind and solar farms, introduce new infrastructure with aesthetic consequences that host communities may oppose. Measures for adaptation to climate change, such as coastal sea defences, can alter the aesthetic properties of the recipient places. The prospects of geo-engineering to stave off disastrous global warming also have potent aesthetic implications, potentially literally changing the colour of skies and oceans. Public discourse about the foregoing, from eco-artists clamouring for climate action to corporate public relations, also contributes to the aesthetics of this field of governance. Dissemination of climate science itself has aesthetic qualities, beginning with the visual graphics for representing climate drivers and impacts. Literary metaphors in climate science, as in the 'hole in the ozone layer', 'carbon sink' and 'carbon budget', also influentially engage the public and policy makers by 'anchoring novel phenomena in familiar and shared ideas'.[3]

Distilling such issues, this chapter spans three broad themes. Firstly, I argue that policy makers should account for the aesthetics of climate change, alongside its more familiar impacts relating to biodiversity and human livelihoods. Secondly, I assess how activists use art to influence climate governance, via

---

[1] This chapter draws partially on my article, 'Climate Change Law: Encounters with Aesthetics and Art' (2018) 8 *Climate Law* 279.

[2] J Knebusch, 'The Perception of Climate Change' (2017) 40(2) *Leonardo* 113, 113.

[3] SV Grevsmuhl, 'The Creation of Global Imaginaries: The Antarctic Ozone Hole and the Isoline Tradition in the Atmospheric Sciences' in B Schneider and T Nocke (eds), *Image Politics of Climate Change: Visualization, Imaginations, Documentations* (Verlag, 2014) 29; C Shaw and B Nerlich, 'Metaphor as a Mechanism of Global Climate Change Governance: A Study of International Policies, 1992–2012' (2015) 109 *Ecological Economics* 34, 37.

photography, music and other artistic media to shape public opinion for stronger climate laws. Artists also challenge corporate greenwashed claims about low carbon footprints. Finally, I consider how aesthetic issues arise in climate mitigation and adaptation laws, as well as proposals for climate engineering. In canvassing trends and seminal precedents, we must appreciate that climate change has diverse environmental, economic and aesthetic implications for different societies; affluent countries may be more startled by images of starving polar bears and melting icebergs than impoverished people facing life-threatening water shortages or crop failures.

The inclusion of aesthetic considerations in climate governance debates should not lessen the vital importance of understanding the science of global warming, or downplay the power of economics to incentivise better behaviour. Aesthetic values, including their artistic expression, can help to emotionally engage people in climate action as well as ensure that adaptation and mitigation measures garner community support. As Liselotte Roosen and others explain in a recent paper:

> art can provide people with visualisations of the problem and give them a personal experience with the subject-matter, which is especially important regarding climate change as many people still see it as an abstract issue that poses no direct threat.[4]

This hypothesis was explored in Chapter 1's analysis of the social influence of environmental art and aesthetics. Recognition of climate aesthetics can dovetail with efforts to cultivate stronger ethical positions for climate action, in which aesthetics not only gratifies our senses but also leverages attitudinal and behavioural changes.

The remainder of this chapter unfolds over five substantive sections. Section II identifies and assesses the aesthetics of climate change. Section III examines artists as agents of climate governance in shaping public opinion and collaborating with environmental NGOs. I explore in section IV how aesthetic values inform the law on climate mitigation, such as in regulation of wind farms, and do likewise for climate adaptation in section V. Concluding this chapter, section VI considers the aesthetic implications of climate geo-engineering. My reflections on how to bring aesthetic considerations more productively into climate change governance are incorporated in the final chapter.

II. AESTHETICS AND CLIMATE CHANGE

By altering the natural environment, climate change alters our aesthetic appreciation of it.[5] While nature never stands still, global warming accelerates its

---

[4] LJ Roosen, CA Klockner and JK Swim, 'Visual Art as a Way to Communicate Climate Change: A Psychological Perspective on Climate Change-Related Art' (2018) 8(1) *World Art* 85.

[5] See especially E Brady, 'Climate Change and Future Aesthetics' in A Elliott, J Cullis and V Damodaran (eds), *Climate Change and the Humanities* (Palgrave Macmillan, 2017) 201.

tempo and precipitates upheavals beyond what we habitually experience. Melting glaciers, rising seas, droughts, forest fires, and species migrations or extinctions are among these upheavals that will distort how we aesthetically experience our surroundings. People themselves will also suffer, by displacement or destitution of the most vulnerable, and creating distressing imagery for observers. However, some climatic impacts such as ocean acidification will simmer unobserved except to astute scientific researchers. Climate change thus opens new aesthetic outlooks while foreclosing others.[6]

As I wrote in Chapter 1, the study of environmental aesthetics has created several competing ideas about nature-based sensory experiences. To briefly recap, these comprise the cognitive model, tied to knowledge of the natural sciences, secondly, participatory engagement and immersion in the natural world, and lastly, everyday aesthetics. The relationships between these approaches are not necessarily antagonistic, however, and all can have some applicability to climate change, albeit sometimes in different contexts.

We can facilitate action on climate change by linking aesthetic judgements to scientific knowledge, even when presented in lay terms (eg causes, trajectories and impacts). The cognitive model of aesthetics can thus reinforce governance based on climate science to justify reducing greenhouse gas (GHG) emissions. In other words, we can highlight the scientific case to address climate change while using aesthetic experiences to strengthen people's willingness to act. Art itself can help illuminate scientific concepts in more familiar language. The cognitive model might also facilitate understanding the aesthetics of climate impacts that unfold temporally and spatially remote from our daily lives, without direct sensory experience.

Concomitantly, Berleant's participatory model of aesthetic valuation matters where impacts of or responses to climate change directly enter people's lives, such as coping with droughts, wildfires or rising seas. The concept of 'sense of place', as developed in the cultural geography literature, is pertinent here to understanding our spiritual and aesthetic attachment to specific localities that we inhabit.[7] Thus, responding to climate change can often hinge on having direct sensory engagement with its effects. I find Berleant's model less compelling in validating climate-related aesthetic experiences that arise outside one's direct experience.

Climate change is only just beginning to inhabit our 'everyday aesthetics'. Farmers struggling in parched, drought-afflicted landscapes will already sense it, as do property owners near increasingly fire-prone forests (my own patch of Tasmanian forest came within a few kilometres of the front of some horrific fires that scorched 200,000 hectares over the recent summer). These negative aesthetics contrast with the sensory enrichment one enjoys from encountering new

---

[6] Ibid.
[7] See S Bott, J Cantrill and OE Myers Jr, 'Place and the Promise of Conservation Psychology' (2003) 10(2) *Human Ecology Review* 100.

types of birds, butterflies or flowers that have migrated into one's environs with the shifting climate. Yuriko Saito's advocacy of the value of 'everyday aesthetics' helps us to understand climate change as impacting our daily lives rather than just transforming that of places or times outside of ours.[8]

Nonetheless, climate change remains largely an *anticipated* rather than experienced aesthetic realm. One consequence is to decide how we should predict and experience the *future* aesthetics of altered environments, explains philosopher Emily Brady.[9] Should we consider landscapes transformed by global warming as beautiful, even when we know that their condition is a tainted legacy of fossil fuel profligacy?[10] Glenn Parsons and Allen Carlson once postulated that positive aesthetic values inhere best in unadulterated nature, unscarred and orderly, a position that might imply rejection of aesthetic values associated with a climate-altered future.[11] Yet, that conclusion would be unrealistic in the Anthropocene, as virtually the entire planet bears the imprint of some human activity. Furthermore, however climate change alters environmental aesthetics, societies similarly evolve their aesthetic preferences, as history shows: European settlers to Australia in the early nineteenth century waged war on an 'alien landscape' but belatedly came to appreciate and conserve many of its aesthetic and ecological values.[12] Brady recommends we take climate change aesthetics seriously, and accept that the aesthetic gains or losses can have educative value, adding to the emotional depth of our consideration of climate change, and thereby inspiring ethical stances such as to improve respect for the needs of future generations.[13]

For now, the aesthetics of climate change reach most people indirectly or vicariously, such as via documentary films, news coverage and social media, and even then, these mostly touch affluent societies with the greatest access to such media. Persistent imagery of environmental upheaval shocks some viewers, including calamitous weather, searing droughts and disintegrating icebergs.[14] Some may even feel 'solastalgia' at the prospect of an increasingly impoverished biosphere.[15] Some of this discomfort no doubt comes from awareness of the scientific explanations for the environmental mayhem, an association that Carlson postulates is relevant to guiding viewers to make valid aesthetic judgments.[16] Let's now canvass in more detail the variety of aesthetic themes

[8] Y Saito, *Aesthetics of the Familiar: Everyday Life and World-Making* (Oxford University Press, 2017).

[9] Brady, 'Climate Change' (above n 5).

[10] Ibid.

[11] G Parsons and A Carlson, *Functional Beauty* (Oxford University Press, 2008) 123.

[12] See D Watson, *The Bush: Travels in the Heart of Australia* (Penguin, 2017).

[13] E Brady, 'Aesthetic Value, Ethics, and Climate Change' *International Society for the Philosophy of Architecture*, 1 December 2012.

[14] J Knebusch, 'The Perception of Climate Change' (2007) 40(2) *Leonardo* 113.

[15] G Albrecht et al, 'Solastalgia: The Distress Caused by Environmental Change' (2007) 15 Supp 1(1) *Australasian Psychiatry* S95.

[16] A Carlson, *Aesthetics and the Environment: The Appreciation of Nature, Art and Architecture* (Routledge, 2000).

associated with climate change, as they may produce different reactions from the affected public and thereby may influence divergently the legal responses to such impacts.

For some viewers, imperilled biodiversity stirs the strongest emotions. Some species will become extinct or suffer reduced populations, thereby removing objects of aesthetic pleasure from nature. Conversely, some adroit species thrive as the climate warms. In Australia, cane toads and European wasps, both considered 'ugly' pests that decimate native invertebrates, colonise more areas as the climate shifts favourably for them.[17] Charismatic, large fauna particularly enamour the public. Heart-wrenching images of emaciated polar bears staggering through iceless terrain circulate the Web as powerful symbols of the canary in the coalmine. The *New York Times* reported one example in December 2017, remarking that 'when the world saw, millions recoiled in heartbroken horror'.[18] Al Gore's film *An Inconvenient Truth* also featured a polar bear – albeit computer-animated – swimming forlornly in a vast iceless ocean.[19] Using polar bears to rouse the public dovetails with the tradition of environmentalists capitalising on sentimental imagery of charismatic animals to rally support,[20] although such imagery might just as easily encourage viewers to feel despair and hopelessness.

Entire ecosystems will also be jolted, with aesthetic reverberations. Already, unprecedented heat stress in Australia's famed Great Barrier Reef has precipitated mass bleaching and death of corals, thus threatening lucrative reef tourism.[21] Interestingly, marine scientists have begun tracking changes in coral reef aesthetics as a proxy for their ecological health. Californian scientists scrutinised photographic records of corals worldwide to compile 109 key visual features (eg size, form and colour) to assess the reefs' aesthetic appeal. From their novel findings, the researchers concluded that 'human perception of aesthetics is not purely subjective but influenced by inherent reactions towards measurable visual cues' that indicate healthy or degraded conditions.[22] Scientists have identified other relationships between environmental degradation and negative aesthetics, such as algal blooms in waterways, and tree mortality from diseases, insects and heat stress – all associated with a changing climate.[23]

[17] W Steffen et al, *Australia's Biodiversity and Climate Change* (Commonwealth of Australia, 2009).

[18] M Stevens, 'Video of Starving Polar Bear "Rips Your Heart Out of Your Chest"' *New York Times* 11 December 2017.

[19] A Gore et al, *An Inconvenient Truth* (Paramount, 2006).

[20] B Clucas, K McHugh and T Caro, 'Flagship Species on Covers of US Conservation and Nature Magazines' (2008) 17 *Biodiversity Conservation* 1517.

[21] M Slezak, 'More Coral Bleaching Feared for Great Barrier Reef in Coming Months' *The Guardian* 3 November 2017.

[22] AF Haas et al, 'Can We Measure Beauty? Computational Evaluation of Coral Reef Aesthetics' (2015) 3(e) *PeerJ* 1390.

[23] WRL Anderegg, JM Kane and LDL Anderegg, 'Consequences of Widespread Tree Mortality Triggered by Drought and Temperature Stress' (2013) 3(1) *Nature Climate Change* 30; and N Arnell, 'Climate Change and Water Resources in Britain' (1998) 39 *Climatic Change* 83, 104.

Glaciers too face growing risks, and their melting has become a potent visualisation of runaway planetary warming. According to the US National Snow and Ice Data Center, 'since the early twentieth century, with few exceptions, glaciers around the world have been retreating at unprecedented rates. [...] [and] many are retreating so rapidly that they may vanish within a matter of decades'.[24] Many of these shrinking ice fields are 'protected' within national parks that attract visitors for their splendid scenery. Montana's Glacier National Park had about 150 glaciers when established in 1910, but only about 30 remain today.[25] New Zealand's famous Fox and Franz Josef glaciers are melting so rapidly that authorities have banned tourists from hiking on them for safety fears.[26] Alaska's Pederson Glacier, also 'protected' in a national park, has contracted significantly over the past century as shown in Figure 7.1. These and other permutations in environmental aesthetics have ramifications for people's emotional and cultural affinity to nature.[27]

Figure 7.1 Pedersen Glacier, Alaska in 2005 (top) and 1917 (below), photographs by Louis H Pedersen (1917) and Bruce F Molina (2005); Glacier Photograph Collection, National Snow and Ice Data Center/World Data Center for Glaciology

[24] National Snow and Ice Data Center, 'Glaciers and Climate Change', https://nsidc.org/cryosphere/glaciers/questions/climate.html.
[25] D Glick, 'The Big Thaw' *National Geographic* September 2004, 13.
[26] N Perry, 'Two Stunning New Zealand Glaciers are Beginning to Melt Away' *Washington Post* 17 March 2016.
[27] On 'sense of place', see YF Tuan, *Space and Place: The Perspective of Experience* (Edward Arnold, 1977).

Polar bears and glaciers, however, do not convey the full story because they fail to put a human 'face' on global warming. Images of famine, flight and other human trauma have become central motifs for the consequences of climate change in many poorer nations in South Asia and sub-Saharan Africa. A 2018 report from the World Bank predicts that about 140 million people fleeing climate change impacts in the latter region may become involuntary 'internal migrants' by 2050.[28] These implications of climate change are now entering the mass media. A leading British newspaper in 2017 reported on these issues with the headline of 'Looming "Catastrophe" in East Africa', with a photograph of two Somalia pastoralists struggling to erect a shelter.[29] A major US media outlet recently carried the storyline 'Climate Change-driven Famine Poses Global Security Threat', with an accompanying slideshow featuring grim images of impoverished Yemeni, entitled 'The face of famine'.[30] Some of the 'image politics' of the climate change discourse combine human rights and ecological themes, such as imagery of native Arctic communities at risk from an ice-free pole that will undermine their traditional livelihoods.[31]

Rising sea levels provide another lens for depicting human ruin; Australia's national broadcaster carried such a story in 2018 headlined 'Rising Seas Will Displace Millions of People', supplemented by an image of people mired in a water-logged village.[32] While this widening of the aperture for perceiving climate change appropriately draws the public's attention to the human rights and social justice dimensions of our severest environmental threat, the sensational headlines and disturbing imagery can oversimplify the issues, as environmental adversity will likely transpire over many decades and involve many intersecting drivers. The aesthetics of climate change are more insidious than those of the explosive 'disaster imagery' associated with acts of God, such as the 2004 Indian Ocean tsunami that claimed the lives of 230,000 people and displaced many more.

Climate change may also bring positive aesthetic experiences for some. As wildlife shifts to more hospitable locations, its human denizens may encounter previously unseen creatures that bring pleasure. Warmer winters are already luring newcomers, as detected in eastern North America where warm-adapted avifauna have begun to linger further north during the colder months, to the delight of bird watchers.[33] Greater butterfly diversity and abundance in Finland

[28] KK Riguard et al, *Groundswell: Preparing for Internal Climate Migration* (World Bank, 2018) 181.

[29] I Johnston, 'Looming "Catastrophe" in East Africa Proves Why World Must Tackle Climate Change, Says Oxfam' *The Independent* 27 April 2017.

[30] P Park, 'Climate Change-driven Famine Poses Global Security Threat' *CBS News* 22 June 2017, www.cbsnews.com/news/climate-change-famine-poses-global-security-threat-un-warns.

[31] V Herrmann, 'Climate Change, Arctic Aesthetics, and Indigenous Agency in the Age of the Anthropocene' (2015) 7(1) *Yearbook of Polar Law* 375.

[32] J McAdam and J Church, 'Rising Seas Will Displace Millions of People – and Australia Must be Ready' *ABC News* 23 August 2018, www.abc.net.au/news/2018-08-23/rising-seas-displace-millions-people-australia-must-be-ready/10155636.

[33] K Prince and B Zuckerberg, 'Climate Change in Our Backyards: The Reshuffling of North America's Winter Bird Communities' (2015) 21(2) *Global Change Biology* 572.

have been recorded as some species benefit from the warming climate.[34] Parallel changes unfold in the plant kingdom, which may bring aesthetic pleasure for those able to observe longer flowering seasons or new species in their midst. Climate change is also generating new hybrids from the interbreeding of species thrown together.[35] Most research and media coverage, however, reflects on adverse aesthetic consequences.

Some researchers have attempted to gauge the impact of these shifting aesthetics on the public, whether experienced directly or vicariously via the media. A few studies conclude that these 'fear-inducing images [can] distance or disengage individuals, rendering them feeling helpless, overwhelmed and not empowered to act'.[36] A study of farmers in Western Australia's 'wheatbelt' – already showing discernable impacts from a changing climate, such as lower rainfall – found that their sense of place in the landscape was eroding, to the detriment of their mental health.[37] Other research that sampled the public's perception of climate change imagery in newspapers in Australia, the United Kingdom, and the United States concluded that the 'imagery can play a role in either increasing the sense of importance of the issue of climate change (saliency) or in promoting feelings of being able to do something about climate change (efficacy)'.[38] A survey on Spanish television news noted that the limited media coverage of climate issues was related to the paucity of visually interesting images available to the broadcasters.[39]

Societal responses to climate change themselves have aesthetic consequences.[40] The erection of wind farms, solar facilities, hydro-dams, public-transport infrastructure and dykes can reshape our visual and acoustic perception of environments. As our landscapes, even in rural areas, are already heavily modified by centuries of human settlement (buildings, roads, electricity pylons, etc), the placement of additional infrastructure to mitigate or adapt to climate change rarely violates an unadulterated 'wilderness'. Still, introduction of any infrastructure, even for environmental purposes, can disturb the aesthetic status quo, altering environments that people are accustomed to and

---

[34] J Pöyry et al, 'Species Traits Explain Recent Range Shifts of Finnish Butterflies' (2009) 15(3) *Global Change Biology* 732.

[35] C Welch, 'Half of All Species Are on the Move – and We're Feeling It' *National Geographic* 27 April 2017, https://news.nationalgeographic.com/2017/04/climate-change-species-migration-disease.

[36] SJ O'Neill et al, 'On the Use of Imagery for Climate Change Engagement' (2013) 23(2) *Global Environmental Change* 413, 414 (referring to the research findings of SJ O'Neill and S Nicholson-Cole, 'Fear Won't do it: Promoting Positive Engagement with Climate Change Through Imagery and Icons' (2009) 30(3) *Science Communication* 355).

[37] N Ellis and GA Albrecht, 'Climate Change Threats to Family Farmers' Sense of Place and Mental Wellbeing: A Case Study from the Western Australian Wheatbelt' (2017) 175 *Social Science and Medicine* 161.

[38] O'Neill, 'On the Use of Imagery' (above n 36) 420.

[39] B León and MC Erviti, 'Science in Pictures: Visual Representation of Climate Change in Spain's Television News' (2015) 24(2) *Public Understanding of Science* 183.

[40] Brady, 'Climate Change' (above n 5).

treat as 'natural'. Societies differ in their tolerance of wind farms, with people in the United States reportedly having less favourable opinions compared to those in the Czech Republic and India.[41] But with time, wind farms and other new facilities might also become perceived as 'normal' features of the landscape, gaining host communities' tolerance, as other long-standing infrastructure has done.[42]

Geo-engineering technologies, presently a largely speculative venture, loom on the horizon as a major dimension of future climate policy unless efforts to curb GHG emissions accelerate rapidly. Geo-engineering has weighty aesthetic implications. Solar radiation management projects, which seed the atmosphere with sulphur particulates or aluminium oxides in order to reflect sunlight, and thus reduce global warming, could turn blue skies redder. Furthermore, reducing incoming solar radiation would have knock-on effects that destabilise the weather, such as altering monsoonal patterns or promoting drought, which bring additional aesthetic changes. Carbon dioxide (CO_2) sequestration projects, which would 'capture' carbon from the atmosphere and put it out of harm's way, could in some forms have unwelcome aesthetic impacts, such as that associated with mechanical, artificial trees. The numbers needed to decarbonise the planet would be huge, and thus visually noticeable; engineers have proposed a forest of 100,000 artificial trees.[43] The aesthetics of marine environments may also change; ocean fertilisation projects that release iron sulphates can spawn huge algae blooms, changing the water to a greener hue. Urban landscapes could also be affected; scientists have proposed putting reflective white surfaces on the roofs and walls of buildings to reduce incoming solar radiation. Our cities could thereby resemble Greek towns, where this practice makes homes cooler and more energy efficient.[44] While tourists find these Greek white-washed villages pretty, we may not think the same about New York or Jakarta blanketed permanently in white. Similarly, the creation of green roofs in urban areas, for climate and biodiversity benefits, has both positive and negative aesthetic connotations for the public.[45]

The future aesthetics of climate change also resonates through the work of scientific and policymaking communities, whose reports and website are frequently embellished with 'colored global maps, barren graphs and curves'

---

[41] B Frantal and J Kunc, 'Wind Turbines in Tourism Landscapes Czech Experience' (2011) 38(2) *Annals of Tourism Research* 499; AM Dinnell and AJ Russ, 'The Legal Hurdles to Developing Wind Power as an Alternative Energy Source in the United States: Creative and Comparative Solutions' (2007) 27 *Northwestern Journal of International Law and Business* 535, 575.

[42] T Wizelius, *Wind Power Projects: Theory and Practice* (Routledge, 2015).

[43] J Burns, '"Artificial Trees" to Cut Carbon' *BBC News* 27 August 2009, http://news.bbc.co.uk/2/hi/science/nature/8223528.stm.

[44] D Lewis, 'Cool Roofs: Beating the Midday Sun With a Slap of White Paint' *The Guardian* 13 April 2017.

[45] J Jungels et al, 'Attitudes and Aesthetic Reactions Toward Green Roofs in the Northeastern United States' (2013) 117 *Landscape and Urban Planning* 13.

that provide simplified condensates for visually communicating the findings of the highly complex research field of climate change'.[46] The Intergovernmental Panel on Climate Change (IPCC) reports contain extensive visual representations of its scientific data and commentaries. The cover of the 2007 IPCC report on adaptation and vulnerability shows a child carrying buckets of water – evoking the human dependency on natural resources at risk to a changing climate, and thus the vulnerability of some people too to climatic change.[47] Like most of its reports, the IPCC's 2014 synthesis report contains extensive pictorial representations of trends associated with global warming, such as escalating GHG emissions, temperature and precipitation changes and sea-level rises.[48] These visual representations make the large data sets and complex climate models accessible to a general public lacking specialist expertise. The images may even become more important than the text; as Schneider and Nocke explain, 'when the figures are communicated and distributed beyond the field of science, the accompanying texts might be cut out in the process and the images might start to travel independently, detached from their original background'.[49]

The knock-on public reaction to IPCC aesthetics also matters. Brigitte Nerlich and Rusi Jaspal examined 'images of extreme weather used to illustrate articles and blogs written after the release of the draft [IPPC] special report'.[50] Many showed human suffering, including people deluged by heavy precipitation, but also sometimes human resilience to adversity.[51] Ashley Cooper's website, Global Warming Images, hosts a library of thousands of photographs complied over a decade about climate change-related impacts around the world, capturing visually the impacts on people, animals and landscapes.[52] Conversely, the climate sceptic media and think-tanks can fabricate their own images to push a counter-narrative that casts doubt on mainstream climate research.[53]

The imagery associated with climate science communications is thus politically salient, and contributes to the political and legal decisions on climate change. While public awareness of the aesthetics of climate change will become highly important for generating attitudinal and behavioural changes, the acknowledged aesthetic impacts can be quite diverse. After seeing heart-wrenching images of polar bears, the distressed populace might believe that

[46] B Schneider and T Nocke, 'Image Politics of Climate Change: Introduction' in Schneider and Nocke, *Image Politics* (above n 3) 9.
[47] IPCC, *Climate Change 2007: Impacts, Adaptation and Vulnerability*. Contribution of Working Group II (Cambridge University Press, 2007).
[48] IPPC, *Climate Change 2014: Synthesis Report*. Contribution of Working Groups I, II and III to the Fifth Assessment Report of the IPPC (IPPC, 2015).
[49] Schneider and Nocke, 'Image Politics' (above n 46) 17.
[50] B Nerlich and R Jaspal, 'Images of Extreme Weather: Symbolising Human Responses to Climate Change' (2014) 23(2) *Science as Culture* 253, 254.
[51] Ibid, 270.
[52] See www.globalwarmingimages.net.
[53] B Schneider, T Nocke and G Feulner, 'Twist and Shout: Images and Graphics in Skeptical Climate Media' in Schneider and Nocke, *Image Politics* (above n 3) 153.

policymakers should prioritise saving an iconic endangered species, but other responses might make a larger difference. The Climate Visuals project, which researches the effect of climate change imagery in engaging audiences, has found that images containing people are more effective than images without, such as pictures of victims of catastrophic droughts or floods.[54] Nerlich and Jaspal observe that dissemination of images showing 'fear, guilt, helplessness and defencelessness and other negative emotional experiences are unlikely to have favourable outcomes',[55] as despondent individuals might shun positive counter-measures in the belief that they will not make any difference. I have also earlier noted possible differences in how people in the Global North and South might regard environmental aesthetics and thus priorities in climate policy. In other words, aesthetics is vital for eliciting social engagement, but it may lead to responses to climate change that on scientific or economic grounds are not the most helpful, and might even engender despondency and apathy.

These potential deficits or limitations of aesthetics bring us to the role of artists in mediating awareness of climate change and helping to channel the public's concern into positive action.

III. CLIMATE ART AND ACTIVISM

Climate change evokes environmental upheaval on the largest conceivable scale, yet much of it defies immediate sensory appreciation. Timothy Morton calls it a 'hyperobject', operating over temporal and spatial dimensions that dwarf human lives.[56] Without direct experience, which helps to validate aesthetic judgements according to Berleant's theory, we face difficulties discerning how climate change will shape our sensory perception of future surroundings, or the aesthetics of places geographically remote from our lives. Yet, access to these aesthetic experiences matters if we are to be emotionally provoked by global warming, so as to put pressure on policymakers to act, as well as to curb our own carbon-profligate lifestyles.

The arts are stepping up to this challenge, assisting people to imagine climate aesthetics beyond their lived experience, and building solidarity for urgent legal reform. Artists do not generally create solutions to climate change, but their work can provoke deeper reflection about the problems and thereby hopefully inspire action. Susanne Moser explores the power of the arts in climate change communications, arguing that the arts can foster changes in social norms, convey the urgency of the challenges and motivate the public to act.[57] Rob Rosenthal

---

[54] Climate Visuals, www.climatevisuals.org.

[55] Nerlich and Jaspal, 'Images of Extreme Weather' (above n 50) 272.

[56] T Morton, *Hyperobjects: Philosophy and Ecology After the End of the World* (University of Minnesota Press, 2013).

[57] SC Moser, 'Communicating Climate Change: History, Challenges, Process and Future Directions' (2010) 1(1) *Wiley Interdisciplinary Reviews: Climate Change* 31.

and Richard Flacks suggest that activist art can help in 'framing' ideas for the public that may reinforce or challenge prevailing assumptions.[58] Popular music about climate change, concurs Josh Woda, 'engages audiences more emotionally than intellectually'.[59] Other researchers reflecting on Australia's largest ever climate art exhibition, held in Melbourne in 2015, suggest that art has long 'been a powerful portal to understanding how we feel about our world'.[60] Yet, this research tends to rest on anecdotal evidence rather than formal cause-and-effect experiments, which would be difficult to measure as I explained in Chapter 1. Although artists can make visible the invisible and the unimaginable real, artists are no less neutral or objective than any other stakeholder, and may even assert positions not always aligned with climate change action.[61] The arts community has been scrutinised for its own carbon footprint, though this concern relates more to major museums and galleries rather than individual activists.[62]

Climate change art spans diverse themes: depicting rising seas, coral bleaching, polar melting, climate refugees and wildlife extinctions, as well as the politics of climate governance and inaction.[63] Helen and Newton Harrison created an installation map called *Greenhouse Britain* (2007) depicting how the country may look under rising seas, with areas of inundation highlighted.[64] Another installation called *Exceeding 2 Degrees* (2007), by Tue Greenfort, involved the artist persuading the host gallery, the Sharjah Art Museum, to adjust its air conditioning by two degrees, which is also the temperature tipping point that scientists believe will trigger run-away warming.[65] After the exhibition, Greenfort had the estimated savings from the reduced air conditioning donated to an environmental organisation to purchase a carbon-offsetting piece of Ecuadorian rainforest, a gesture itself intended by the artist to problematise the offset market given its embeddedness in the very economic system that degradingly commodifies nature. Carbon offsetting also motivated German artist-entrepreneur Dirk Fleischmann's project *My Forest Farm* (2008–), using proceeds from his art sales to support a reforestation scheme in the Philippines. Although his project results in carbon offsetting, none of the carbon credits are for sale. Instead, Fleischmann offers art; each of the planted, carbon-sequestering trees is photographed and

[58] R Rosenthal and R Flacks, *Playing for Change: Music and Musicians in the Service of Social Movements* (Routledge, 2010).

[59] J Wodak, 'Shifting Baselines: Conveying Climate Change in Popular Music' (2018) 12(1) *Environmental Communication* 58, 65.

[60] J Gergis and P Whatton, 'Can Art Put Us in Touch with Our Feelings About Climate Change?' *The Conservation* 4 May 2017, http://theconversation.com.

[61] Schneider and Nocke, 'Image Politics' (above n 46).

[62] M Bunting, 'The Rise of Climate-Change Art' *The Guardian* 3 December 2009.

[63] See www.climart.info; R Taplin, 'Contemporary Climate Change Art as the Abstract Machine: Ethico-Aesthetics and Futures Orientation' (2014) 47(5) *Leonardo* 509.

[64] The Harrison Studio, 'Greenhouse Britain 2007–2009', http://theharrisonstudio.net/greenhouse-britain-2007-2009.

[65] L Skrebowski, 'Tue Greenfort, Exceeding 2 Degrees (2007)' in EE Scott and K Swenson (eds), *Critical Landscapes: Art, Space, Politics* (University of California Press, 2015) 193.

its GPS location recorded, and then sold to the public via his project website for €10 each, with the earnings recycled to support his project. Climate geo-engineering also has attracted artists' attention. Mexican performance-artist Pedro Reyes in 2017 staged in New York a 193-participant mock UN General Assembly meeting that debated geo-engineering (the building itself was the forum for such UN meetings from 1946 to 1950).[66]

Artists also use imagery of the sources of climate change – the oil fields, mines and fossil-fuel industries – to dramatise their environmental devastation locally. Canadian photographer Edward Burtynsky has garnered global attention with his massively enlarged photographs of blistering steel furnaces, ravenous oil sands, and other 'manufactured landscapes', as he calls them.[67] While Burtynsky's early work showed ambivalence about his stance towards environmental transformation, many now regard him as 'the aesthetic standard-bearer of global environmentalism'.[68]

Music has yet to be as widely availed for these purposes. The Climate Music Project unites scientists and musicians to create and stage 'science-guided music and visual experiences to inspire people to engage actively on the issue of climate change'.[69] Its outputs include new musical compositions in which pitch and tempo are used as analogies of global warming processes. Visual animations and post-concert public forums enable audiences to engage with the project's members to help interpret the music. A few independent music groups have created songs that engage with climate change, such as the US punk-rock group Bad Religion's song *Kyoto Now*, released in 2002, which became an anthem for some activists seeking to uphold the Kyoto Protocol. Yet as a BBC report in 2015 on the lack of hit songs in this field observed, 'no-one's managed a popular song about what's meant to be the most important issue of our time'.[70]

Climate change science-fiction novels, with plots about apocalyptic upheaval and dystopian futures, are also starting to stir the public's imagination, such as James Bradley's *Clade* (2015), Paolo Bacigalupi's *The Windup Girl* (2009) and Kim Stanley Robinson's *New York 2140* (2017), as have sci-fi films (some originating in novels) such as *The Day After Tomorrow* (2004) and *Snowpiercer* (2013), the latter depicting a failed climate geo-engineering experiment that unintentionally created a freezing planet. Futuristic dystopias about the climate crisis, however, often get the science wrong and can be so unreal as to shift audiences' understanding that global warming is a looming reality for themselves.

[66] K Brooks, 'Pedro Reyes is Solving The World's Problems, One Art Performance at a Time' *Huffington Post* 7 December 2017.

[67] See www.edwardburtynsky.com/projects/films/manufactured-landscapes.

[68] M Ziser and J Sze, 'Climate Change, Environmental Aesthetics and Global Environmental Justice Cultural Studies' (2007) 29(2) *Discourse* 384, 398.

[69] Climate Music Project, 'What We Do', www.theclimatemusicproject.org/what-we-do.

[70] A Marshall, 'Where are All the Climate Change Songs?' *BBC News* 18 November 2015, www.bbc.com/news/magazine-34844244.

Climate change art has acquired an institutional presence through organisations and networks dedicated to engaging the public for policy and legal action. One trailblazer is the Australian-based CLIMARTE, with the mission of 'harnessing the creative power of the arts to inform, engage and inspire action on climate change'.[71] Co-founded by lawyer Guy Abrahams, CLIMARTE plays a synergistic role fostering collaboration among artists, arts-sector bodies, patrons, and scholars for the exchange of ideas and public engagement for action on climate change.[72] A book sponsored by CLIMARTE featuring creations from its 2015 climate art festival in Melbourne aims to demonstrate the 'creative capacity of art to raise awareness and engage people in both local and global efforts to tackle climate change'.[73] Also from Australia, Carbon Arts' mandate seeks to combine arts with technology, science and other fields to promote public dialogue and innovation in responding to global warming.[74] A similar synergistic role is played by Cape Farewell, launched in England in 2001 with the mission to 'engage artists for their ability to evolve and amplify a creative language, communicating on a human scale the urgency of the global climate challenge'.[75] Cape Farewell has global reach through its website, YouTube clips and blogs, and it facilitates collaborative expeditions of artists and scientists to hotspots, such as the melting ice sheets of Greenland. The climate-arts collective Arctic Cycle uses theatre to stimulate public dialogue about the climate crisis, as supplemented by editorials and blogs to enrich global dialogue.[76] In the United States, the Canary Project is a leading hub for sponsorship of climate art for a broader social and political agenda.[77]

To maximise their impact, some of these groups stage strategic interventions at key global policy meetings, notably the UNFCCC's Conference of the Parties (COPs). The 2009 Copenhagen COP was a milestone: the official program included an art exhibition, *RETHINK, Contemporary Art and Climate Change*, featuring 26 works of international contemporary artists in four precincts of the Danish capital.[78] Also coinciding with the lead-up to the Copenhagen COP, the international photo agency NOOR launched an ongoing project to document climate change in images, providing 'an eyewitness record of the devastating humanitarian effects of climate change around the globe' and capture 'solutions to climate change and the individual stories of those trying to live a more sustainable existence'.[79] At the Cancun COP in 2010 the creative dimension achieved greater visibility through street art, murals, and other participatory

---

[71] See https://climarte.org.
[72] Ibid, https://climarte.org/more-about-climarte.
[73] G Abrahams, 'Foreword' in G Abrahams, K Gellatly and B Johnson (eds), *ART+CLIMATE= CHANGE THE BOOK* (Melbourne University Press, 2016) foreword.
[74] Carbon Arts, www.carbonarts.org.
[75] See www.capefarewell.com/about.html.
[76] See www.thearcticcycle.org/initiatives.
[77] See www.carbonarts.org/the-canary-project.
[78] See www.rethinkclimate.org.
[79] See http://noorimages.com/project/climate-change-by-noor.

interventions facilitated by the 350.org movement, whose leader Bill McKibben declared that 'art can help us understand differently than science, the threat that global warming poses to our planet'.[80] 'Earth Art' by 350.org was held in 20 locations around the world, shortly before the Cancun COP.[81] A recent example is ARTCOP21, a global festival of climate art staged to coincide with the 2015 Paris COP.[82] It assembled artists from some 50 countries contributing to events staged not only in Paris but in other global cities from Jakarta to Rio de Janeiro.

The release of major IPCC reports has also been a cue for arts events. The Live Earth music concerts of 2007 sought to raise awareness about climate change to coincide with the release of the IPCC's *Fourth Assessment Report*.[83] Live Earth featured some 150 music acts in a dozen locations around the world, streaming 22 hours of entertainment to a global audience. Coinciding with the release of the IPCC's *Fifth Assessment Report* in October 2014, artists Olafur Eliasson and Minik Rosing unveiled *Ice Watch* at Copenhagen City Hall Square (see Figure 7.2).[84] Their work comprised many tons of ice from Greenland arranged in a clock formation to enable the public to observe the physicality of the ice melting, as a statement to world leaders for urgent action.

Figure 7.2 *Ice Watch*, Copenhagen 2014, Olafur Eliasson and Minik Rosing; photograph by Jorge Lascar; licensed under Creative Commons

Climate-concerned artists are also collaborating with activist groups to target corporate polluters. One sensational effort was called 'Flood Wall St', employing

---

[80] Quoted from A Audouin, 'Art and COP History', www.aliceaudouin.com/art-of-change-21-2/art-and-cop-history.

[81] 'Giant Earth Art Displays Dramatize Climate Urgency' *Environment News Service* 26 November 2010, www.ens-newswire.com/ens/nov2010/2010-11-26-02.html.

[82] See www.artcop21.com.

[83] 'Live Earth Concerts Will Strengthen Awareness' *New York Times* 6 July 2007.

[84] See https://olafureliasson.net/archive/artwork/WEK109190/ice-watch.

music, colourful banners, costumes and theatre to enliven a protest against the complicity of Wall Street financiers in the climate crisis, and timed to coincide with a UN summit for business leaders and heads of state held in September 2014. It was highly successful in garnering publicity. The *New York Times* reported,

> many of the demonstrators dressed in blue to symbolize a wave of water – water that could engulf the low-lying streets near the New York Stock Exchange, as the storm surge from the East River and New York Harbor did during Hurricane Sandy.[85]

The protestors also inflated a 'carbon bubble' balloon, which with poignant irony the police deflated on the horns of the Wall St bull sculpture. Though scores of protesters were arrested, the charges against them were thrown out by the Manhattan court because their constitutional First Amendment civil liberties were deemed to have been violated.[86]

Figure 7.3 Flood Wall St protest, New York, 2014; photograph by Resa Sunshine; licensed under Creative Commons

Subversive art also targets corporate greenwashing, as I will discuss further in the following chapter. At the 2015 Paris COP, the irreverent Brandalism placed 600 posters around the city mocking climate-polluting big businesses, such as Exxon and Air France, for supporting the conference.[87] The activist

---

[85] C Moynihan, 'Climate Change Protesters Tangle With Police at Wall St' *New York Times*, 22 September 2014.

[86] S Lazare, 'Not Guilty: Flood Wall Street Protestors Vindicated by Manhattan Court' *Commons Dreams*, 6 March 2015, www.commondreams.org/news/2015/03/06.

[87] 'COP21: Eco Activists Brandalism Launch Paris Ad Takeover' *BBC News* 29 November 2015, www.bbc.com/news/world-europe-34958282.

Greenwash Guerillas, whose speciality is street theatre and performance art,[88] has targeted climate polluters such as at its 2010 protests outside London's National Portrait Gallery and Tate Gallery to highlight public opposition to BP's sponsorship of the arts.[89] That campaign eventually had some success when BP ended some of this sponsorship in 2017.[90]

The impact of climate change art on public opinion, and ultimately environmental law, remains hard to fathom. That the arts have long been deployed in government propaganda, business advertising, and religious iconography suggests they have some proselytising influence.[91] In the realm of climate change specifically, the available evidence is anecdotal or ad hoc. The clearest effect of the arts shows on public education and dialogue. That influence may lead to knock-on effects, such as to help erode the social licence of the fossil-fuel industry, in the same manner currently sought by the fossil-fuel divestment campaign.[92] Damaging companies' social licence to operate represents governance-like discipline to the extent that hurt businesses are compelled by the social opprobrium to genuinely improve their environmental performance.[93] Tim Hollo, director of the Green Institute, examined the role of the creative industries in Australia in leveraging social change in regard to climate change, interviewing a variety of artists and arts-industry personalities. His 2014 report discerned that 'art can both trigger and create space for new discussions and, perhaps more easily, galvanise and support pre-existing campaigns [and help keep] discussion of ideas going in new and innovative ways'.[94]

Of specific empirical studies, a Yale University study sought to measure the effect of the Live Earth 2007 concert in Washington DC on US public opinion through telephone interviews conducted shortly before and after the event. The researchers concluded that: 'Live Earth did reinforce and amplify attitudes about global warming among those watchers who were already concerned, while having a smaller impact on other watchers'.[95] Such research does not in itself tell us whether people and institutions ultimately improve their behaviour. A rare study into this question was undertaken by Julia Blasch and Robert Turner in 2016 to assess 'the influence of environmental art on individual willingness to purchase

---

[88] Greenwash Guerrillas, https://greenwashguerrillas.wordpress.com/about.

[89] J Vidal and O Bowcott, 'Galleries and Museums Face Summer of Protest Over BP Arts Sponsorship' *The Guardian* 25 June 2010.

[90] N Khomami, 'BP to End Tate Sponsorship After 26 Years' *The Guardian* 11 March 2016.

[91] T Clark, *Art and Propaganda in the Twenty-first Century* (Harry N Abrams, 1997) 47–102; T Miller, *Greenwashing Culture* (Routledge, 2013).

[92] BJ Richardson, 'Divesting from Climate Change: The Road to Influence' (2017) 39(4) *Law and Policy* 325.

[93] N Hall et al, 'Social Licence to Operate: Understanding how a Concept has been Translated into Practice in Energy Industries' (2015) 86 *Journal of Cleaner Production* 301.

[94] T Hollo, *The Role of the Creative Industries in Climate Change Action* (Music Australia, 2014) s 2.1.

[95] Yale University, Gallup and Clear Vision Institute, *Surveying the Impact of Live Earth on American Public Opinion* (Yale Project on Climate Change Communication, 2007) 5.

voluntary carbon offsets'.[96] They found that the 'respondents who were shown photographs [from an arts group] that illustrate the impacts of climate change were more likely to purchase carbon offsets than were respondents in a control group'.[97] Another study probed the influence of climate disaster science-fiction on readers, a genre which it found appeals to a 'younger, more liberal' audience already concerned about climate change. In acknowledging that we need more empirical research, the study author concluded:

> While it may not play a significant role in convincing skeptics and deniers to recon- sider their positions (partially because they are less likely to read these works of fiction), it might effectively nudge moderates and remind concerned liberals and left- ists of the severity and urgency of anthropogenic climate change.[98]

Rather than trying to decipher the precise cause-and-effect relationships, which remain the subject of long-term empirical research, a more productive way to summarise the role of the arts in climate governance is to identify the specific and material patterns of interaction. The foregoing discussion suggests four patterns, as follows.

The influence of climate art is linked to the capacity of artists to engage with stakeholders beyond mainstream galleries and museums, such as by collab- orating with activist NGOs who can help publicise their art and combine it with their political lobbying and community engagements. The collaboration between 350.org and climate artists, and protest art expressed during inter- national COPs, demonstrate this collaboration. Secondly, climate art is often conveyed through global forums, such as multinational music concerts and arts festivals, and thus caters to a culturally diverse audience in a manner consistent with the goals of global climate law to forge a shared agenda for collectively pursued targets. In other words, the arts are reaching out to a wide range of constituents to give their efforts social legitimacy and impact. Thirdly, the timing of the release of climate art matters, as its dissemination is often staged to coincide with important meetings and events associated with climate govern- ance, such as a COP or the release of an IPPC report, or a government decision on a proposed coal mine. The right timing helps to maximise the impact of the art on both the general public and policymakers. Lastly, the arts cannot 'solve' any specific climate-governance challenges, such as justice for climate refugees or sanctioning fossil-fuel polluters. Rather, art has value in fostering public enquiry and dialogue about the context of such issues, by highlighting inequities or articulating aspirations. In this role, art can help render visible the spatial and temporal dimensions of climate change that transcend the sensory perception of individuals' daily lives.

---

[96] J Blasch and RW Turner, 'Environmental Art, Prior Knowledge about Climate Change, and Carbon Offsets' (2016) 6(4) *Journal of Environmental Studies and Sciences* 691, 691.

[97] Ibid, 702.

[98] M Schneider-Mayerson, 'The Influence of Climate Fiction: An Empirical Survey of Readers' (2018) 10(2) *Environmental Humanities* 473, 493.

Thus, while art has aesthetic significance that we can evaluate using the philosophical and psychological frameworks for the study of aesthetics, it is preferable for our purposes in this chapter to link such research to the arts' cultural and governance effects. We may appreciate the aesthetic qualities of an artwork, but what matters here is how those qualities can arouse viewers and engender behavioural changes. The foregoing examples of climate art also highlight the negative aesthetics of climate change, which may counter-productively encourage despair and the motivation to act. We need more art that also considers the aesthetic gains from responding to climate change, such as reforestation schemes and clean-energy technologies, as illustrated by some photographers trying to present wind turbines as beautiful.[99]

IV. CLIMATE CHANGE MITIGATION

Legal responses to climate change also have aesthetic consequences. Aesthetic values may be relevant considerations within public education and engagement strategies mandated by international climate agreements and legislation. Secondly, climate change mitigation measures, such as green-energy projects, can have aesthetic impacts subject to regulation or they may be resolved through private law (eg the tort of private nuisance). Thirdly, climate-adaptation measures can introduce aesthetic changes to local environments that require management through land-use planning, development-control laws or other mechanisms.

Before looking at these three patterns, we must acknowledge that some realms of climate governance lack overt sensory qualities. Notably, the economic policy instruments such as carbon taxes, emissions trading schemes and offset markets enable transactions between climate polluters through an empty, invisible space. There is no physical market with traders haggling over prices, like the market places we visit where antiques or groceries are sold, but rather transactions occur through computerised trading platforms remote from public observation. The global financial economy itself, which facilitates the pricing of CO_2 emissions, operates through this opaque realm that has no obvious aesthetic reference point except the buildings housing the financial organisations or the projects they finance. The global fossil fuel divestment movement, which challenges the complicity of the financial backers of the coal, oil and gas industries, seeks to challenge this aesthetic anonymity through protest actions like placarding outside bank offices and staging music festivals to raise public awareness.

International climate law largely ignores aesthetics. The United Nations Framework Convention on Climate Change 1992 (UNFCCC) contains some provisions that oblige parties to promote education and awareness about climate change as well as citizen participation in such processes.[100] To illustrate, article 6

---

[99] See eg 'The Beauty of Windfarms in Pictures' *The Guardian* 2 May 2014.
[100] (1992) 31 ILM 849.

specifies that state parties shall cooperate 'in the development and exchange of educational and public awareness material on climate change and its effects', a requirement that could encompass aesthetics and the arts. The Kyoto Protocol 1997 is even more parsimonious in its acknowledgement of such issues.[101] The preamble of the Paris Agreement 'affirm[s] the importance of education, training, public awareness, public participation, public access to information and cooperation at all levels on the matters addressed in this Agreement'.[102] Articles 11 and 12 of the Agreement similarly refer to such aspirations, and thus they could be interpreted to encourage state parties to use the arts to help engage and educate people about global warming. Though not creating binding obligations, these articles do signal the increasing importance of this issue. Such frugal recognition of aesthetic values is perhaps understandable given that these international instruments can do little themselves to shape the actual governance of aesthetic issues and impacts when they manifest primarily within specific localities.

National climate legislation has few explicit provisions on climate-related aesthetics, although governments' land-use planning, environmental impact assessments (EIAs), and nature conservation laws typically contain sufficiently broad, omnibus provisions to take aesthetic matters into account, as was considered in Chapter 2. The same could be said for dedicated climate legislation. The Australian state of Victoria's Climate Change Act of 2017 specifies that the relevant considerations that government authorities must have regard to include 'potential long and short term [...] social impacts', a term that conceptually could encompass this agenda.[103] Furthermore, the Act's guiding principle of 'community engagement' conceivably provides a pathway for authorities to consider local aesthetic issues in climate mitigation and adaptation measures.[104] Kenya's Climate Change Act 2016 also omits explicit reference to aesthetics, but several statutory provisions could assist, such as the obligation on authorities to consider 'social circumstances' in formulating the National Climate Action Plan.[105] Statutory references to adaptation measures may also be construed as encompassing aesthetic criteria, as in Mexico's General Law on Climate Change 2012, which defines 'adaptation' broadly enough for this purpose.[106] The same analysis would apply to government climate action plans and policies: Germany's Climate Action Plan 2050, adopted in 2016, seemingly ignores aesthetics but is replete with references to the need to address 'social concerns'.[107]

---

[101] Kyoto Protocol to the United Nations Framework Convention on Climate Change, (1998) 37 ILM 22, art 10(e).

[102] Paris Agreement, 13 December 2015, in UNFCCC, COP Report No 21, Addendum, at 21, UN Doc FCCC/CP/2015/10/Add, 1, 29 January 2016.

[103] Section 17(3)(b).

[104] Section 27.

[105] Section 13(5)(e).

[106] Ley general De Cambio Climatico, Última Reforma DOF 01-06-2016, art 3.I.

[107] German Federal Government, *Climate Action Plan 2050* (November 2016) 10.

Turning to climate change mitigation, aesthetic values may arise in legal governance in various guises. The failure to regulate GHG emissions may also be legally challenged by affected persons on the basis that uncontrolled climate change may lead to adverse aesthetic effects such as impairment of scenic landscapes. In one US case taken by environmentalists against authorities in the state of Washington over their failures to regulate carbon emissions from the state's five oil refineries under the Clean Air Act, the court accepted that the plaintiff could meet the injury requirement for *locus standi* by alleging that the imputed activity 'impairs his or her economic interests or *aesthetic* and environmental well-being'.[108] Aesthetic injuries were also recognised by a California court as legitimate grounds to sue in a 2002 case concerning enforcement of the Energy Policy Act's provisions for promotion of alternative fuel vehicles.[109]

Additional to the aesthetic legacies of global warming, the fossil fuel projects themselves can have legally salient aesthetic repercussions locally. A notable example is the decision of the New South Wales (NSW) Land and Environment Court in February 2019 to reject an open-cast coal mine proposed near the town of Gloucester because of its visual and amenity impacts, along with sizeable GHG emissions. The case deserves comment because of the Court's unusually detailed scrutiny of the aesthetic impacts and its efforts to delineate a systematic method for their analysis. Chief Justice (CJ) Brian Preston adopted the following criteria for assessing the visual sequalae of the Rocky Hill Coal Project:

(a) an analysis of the existing visual environment to determine the baseline against which the visual impacts of the proposed mine are to be assessed;

(b) a viewpoint analysis to identify sites likely to be affected by the proposed mine;

(c) an assessment of the extent of the visual impacts of the proposed mine on the viewpoints, including the visual impacts during the life of the mine and, after completion of mining, the cumulative visual impacts; and

(d) an assessment of the extent to which the visual impacts are mitigated by the proposed mitigation measures.[110]

Applying these tests, CJ Preston considered numerous submissions from the affected community of Gloucester, the vast majority of which opposed the eyesore, along with concerns about noise and dust intrusions that he assessed under the rubric of 'amenity' issues. The views of denizens were corroborated by the preponderance of visual impact experts who gave evidence. Finally, CJ Preston respected the aims of the governing land use planning schemes, acknowledging that the historic and cultural heritage values associated with the affected landscape that the plans sought to protect were relevant to the visual impact assessment. In ruling that the aesthetic and amenity fallout would be

---

[108] *Washington Environmental Council v Bellon*, 732 F 3d 1131, 1140 (9th Cir 2013) (emphasis added).

[109] *Center for Biological Diversity v Abraham*, 218 F Supp 2d 1143 (ND Cal July 30, 2002).

[110] *Gloucester Resources Limited v Minister for Planning* [2019] NSWLEC 7, para 90.

'significant' and couldn't be satisfactorily mitigated by the proponent, whose project would not deliver outweighing economic benefits, CJ Preston summed up:

> an open cut coal mine in this part of the Gloucester valley would be in the wrong place at the wrong time. Wrong place because an open cut coal mine in this scenic and cultural landscape, proximate to many people's homes and farms, will cause significant planning, amenity, visual and social impacts. Wrong time because the GHG emissions of the coal mine and its coal product will increase global total concentrations of GHGs at a time when what is now urgently needed, in order to meet generally agreed climate targets, is a rapid and deep decrease in GHG emissions. These dire consequences should be avoided. The Project should be refused.[111]

While this NSW court's decision makes clear that aesthetic issues are legitimate governance criteria, in this case the visual and acoustic effects were assessed as matters of land use planning, like any major economic development, rather than as having an innate connection to climate change itself. Still, this precedent has relevance to many fossil fuel projects such as oil refineries, pipelines, as well as mines, that tend to be very visually intrusive.

Aesthetic issues in climate change law have most commonly been considered in proposals for green infrastructure such as wind farms and solar-energy facilities.[112] In these contexts, aesthetic injuries tend to be asserted by plaintiffs as reasons for *stopping* climate mitigation actions. From an economics perspective, the essential problem is that such infrastructure 'suffer[s] from an imbalanced allocation of costs and benefits: their costs (aesthetic and cultural) are concentrated among residents of their host communities, whereas their benefits (cleaner air, energy) are diffused over large geographic regions'.[113] Modern wind turbines, the source of most aesthetic concerns, 'do not evoke the quaint images of yesterday's windmills slowly turning amidst a bucolic backdrop', explain Adam Dinnell and Adam Russ.[114] In *Brander v Town of Warren Town Board*, the presiding New York court explained:

> the introduction of the sleek ultra-modern four hundred foot tall kinetic wind turbines [...] throughout this landscape forever alters and changes the rural setting, which itself [...] serves as the backdrop of the architectural and cultural heritage of these communities.[115]

American litigants opposed to wind turbines have also objected to their noise and the 'flicker' or 'strobe' effect from light reflecting off the turbine blades.[116]

---

[111] Ibid, para 699.

[112] J Good, 'The Aesthetics of Wind Energy' (2006) 13(1) *Human Ecology Forum* 76.

[113] M Vaccaro, 'The Role of Community Values in Wind Energy Development: Exploring the Benefits and Applications of Community Wind for Reducing Local Opposition to Wind Energy Systems' (Georgetown Law Student Paper Series, 2008) 4.

[114] AM Dinnell and AJ Russ, 'The Legal Hurdles to Developing Wind Power as an Alternative Energy Source in the United States: Creative and Comparative Solutions' (2007) 27 *Northwestern Journal of International Law and Business* 535, 537.

[115] *Brander v Town of Warren Town Board*, 847 NYS 2d 450, 2007 NY Slip Op 27498 (NY Sup. 2007) 456.

[116] SH Butler, 'Headwinds to a Clean Energy Future: Nuisance Suits Against Wind Energy Projects in the United States' (2009) 97(5) *California Law Review* 1337, 1337.

Yet, these effects have tended to be assessed by courts largely on aesthetic grounds, as in *Burch v Nedpower Mount Storm* decided by the Supreme Court of Appeals in West Virginia.[117] In Massachusetts, the proposed Cape Wind offshore project was ultimately scuttled after a dozen lawsuits over 16 years led by the affected coastal denizens who had considerable economic and political clout to fend off the development.[118] Climate change sceptics cite the aesthetics of renewable-energy projects as a rationale to stick with fossil fuels: Australia's former Prime Minister Tony Abbot, who infamously orchestrated the repeal of the country's carbon tax, once described wind farms as 'visually ugly'.[119] These sentiments have resonated with some land-use regulators, as in Victoria, which amended its planning legislation in 2011 to give greater weight to the aesthetic preferences of impacted local communities and to ban wind turbines in certain localities.[120] But some jurisdictions have gone the other way to stack the law in favour of green-energy projects through 'fast-track' project approval procedures, as done in Ontario through the Green Energy Act 2009.[121]

The difficulties of weighing aesthetic values against other policy criteria of environmental governance, such as biodiversity conservation or climate integrity, in addition to problems reconciling different aesthetic preferences, stem from the lack of a common metric allowing straightforward comparisons or trade-offs. These tensions arise in both common law suits, where the courts consider competing considerations under generic rubrics of 'social utility' and 'reasonableness', and municipal planning regulations that involve consideration of public submissions, EIA reports and the appropriateness of the locality in light of land use zoning. Both the common law and the planning process seek to balance conflicts over land uses by enabling neighbours and other stakeholders to express their views.

The difficulties of reconciling these competing considerations are illustrated by the dispute over the Taralga wind-farm development in NSW, Australia. The litigation coalesced around the social benefits of renewable energy pitted against the aesthetic impacts on the Taralga township, located near the proposed 62 wind turbines.[122] In approving the controversial development, the NSW Land and Environment Court invoked the principle of intergenerational equity to justify a project that would help mitigate climate change. The court received considerable evidence of the aesthetic impacts, including testimony from 'visual impact assessment experts' and photomontages that depicted the turbines

---

[117] *Burch v Nedpower Mount Storm*, LLC 647 S E2d 879, 891 (WV, 2007).

[118] KQ Seelye, 'After 16 Years, Hopes for Cape Cod Wind Farm Float Away' *New York Times* 19 December 2017. For analysis of the aesthetic issues, see A Briggle, 'Visions of Nantucket: The Aesthetics and Policy of Wind Power' (2005) 2(1) *Environmental Philosophy* 54.

[119] Quoted in K Joshi, 'Think Windfarms are Ugly? It's Not Only a Matter of Perception, But Policy Too' *The Guardian* 12 May 2017.

[120] E de Wit and A Guild, 'Winds of Change: Wind Farm Amendments to Victorian Planning Schemes' (Norton Rose Fulbright, 17 March 2011).

[121] SO 2009, c 12, Sch A.

[122] *Taralga Landscape Guardians Inc v Minister for Planning and RES Southern Cross Pty Ltd* [2007] NSWLEC 59 (12 February 2007).

from different vantages. The presiding judge conceded that 'insertion of wind farms into a rural landscape involves interrupting the rural and natural cohesion of that landscape',[123] yet he found the evidence of the expert testimony to be 'of little assistance as there was no agreement between [them]'.[124] Only in regard to the potential noise impacts did the court find its analysis straightforward because technology allows for precise quantification of noise levels. The Taralga wind-farm case shows how the judicial processes to evaluate aesthetic values – through site visits, commissioning expert evidence, and receiving public submissions – do not easily generate clear solutions for reconciliation of such values with competing policy considerations.

Solar-power projects also sometimes incur community opposition for their unsightly appearance. Residents of Boston successfully persuaded local authorities to reject a proposed 3.3 megawatt solar installation on 20 hectares of farmland which they viewed as 'ugly' and thought would 'devalue their properties'.[125] In Australia, a solar farm with 26,000 panels, proposed for near the village of Uriarra, was also successfully opposed by its residents, with the development relocated to a site away from any human settlement.[126] As with wind farms, these aesthetic impacts can sometimes be resolved through timely community consultations that enable identification of alternate, less sensitive sites to host such developments.

The common law lacks the consultation processes of administrative regulation but offers remedies for landholders who suffer unreasonable impacts, including some aesthetic impacts from neighbours' activities even where they are licensed. The tort of private nuisance encompasses interference with a neighbour's comfort and convenient enjoyment of his or her property, and has been used in some litigation against wind-energy projects. Issuance of an official licence for a wind farm or other development does not in itself satisfy the well-recognised defence of 'statutory authorisation' for private nuisance.[127] Nonetheless, any such licence would probably be taken into account by the courts in assessing what is an unreasonable nuisance for the given location based on its existing character and planning zones. In the 2009 English case of *Munday v Vale of the White Horse District Council*, the magistrate upheld a statutory nuisance claim from a noisy wind turbine even though the operator had complied with all the relevant licence conditions.[128]

The visual and acoustic impacts of wind turbines can have different legal consequences. The law of private nuisance does not generally give redress for

---

[123] Ibid, para 116.
[124] Ibid, para 123.
[125] K Conti, 'Solar Projects Increasingly Meeting Local Resistance' *Boston Globe* 5 May 2013.
[126] K Lawson, 'Uriarra Solar Farm Relocated to Williamsdale' *Canberra Times* 24 March 2015.
[127] *Allen v Gulf Oil Refinery Limited* [1980] QB 156, 174.
[128] Cited in P Crossley, 'Private Nuisance: An Ill Wind for Wind Energy Projects?' (2011) 19(2) *Torts Law Journal* 135, 147.

visual impacts,[129] perhaps on the rationale that visual judgements supposedly reflect subjective taste. Yet the law more readily accommodates noise complaints, which have furnished the primary grounds against wind turbines.[130] For one such development in Maine, the 'industrial whoosh-and-whoop of the 123-foot blades is making life in this otherwise tranquil corner of the island unbearable', according to the affected residents interviewed by the *New York Times*.[131] In a dispute in New Jersey where an injunction was granted against a noisy turbine, the court explained:

> its intrusive quality is heightened because of the locality. The neighborhood is quiet and residential [...] Sounds which are natural to this area – the sea, the shore birds, the ocean breeze – are soothing and welcome. The noise of the windmill [...] is particularly alien here.[132]

Nonetheless, even in such circumstances the courts will always consider the 'social utility and the public interest [...] to determine whether an interference [is] unreasonable'.[133] Given the steady growth of other visually intrusive infrastructure in the countryside, such as cell phone towers and electricity pylons, which residents routinely demand for their convenience, it is improbable that aesthetic concerns will hold back the spread of renewable-energy projects, except in limited cases of particularly onerous impacts in landscapes or seascapes of high scenic value. Big renewable-energy projects are becoming an increasing presence worldwide as states seek alternatives to fossil fuels. According to the International Energy Agency, in 2016 an additional 165 gigawatts of renewable power were added worldwide, mainly from solar and wind projects, with considerably more in the pipeline over the next decade.[134] Aesthetics will probably only factor into *where* such projects are located, rather than whether they will go ahead, with community concerns managed primarily through planning law consultation processes rather than private law mechanisms.[135]

Finally, climate change governance itself evokes its own aesthetic atmosphere, from the theatre of international climate negotiations to the performance antics of fossil fuels divestment activism. The latter campaign combines savvy financial tactics with artistic stunts to grab media attention.[136] In September 2014 divestment activists in London gathered outside the Houses of Parliament,

---

[129] Eg *Rankin v FPL Energy*, LLC 266 SW 3d 506 (2008).

[130] See cases citied in Crossley, 'Private Nuisance' (above n 128) fn 48.

[131] T Zeller Jr, 'For Those Near, the Miserable Harm of Clean Energy' *New York Times* 6 October 2010, A1.

[132] *Joel Rose et ux v Joseph Chaikin et ux*, 187 NJ Superior 210, 215 (1982).

[133] Crossley, 'Private Nuisance' (above n 128) 147.

[134] International Energy Agency, 'Renewables 2017', www.iea.org/publications/renewables2017.

[135] J Firestone, B Hoen and J Rand, 'Are Public Objections to Wind Farms Overblown?' *The Conversation*, 2 May 2018, http://theconversation.com.

[136] E Howard and E Hilaire, 'The Fossil Fuel Divestment Movement: Top 10 Campaign Stunts' *The Guardian* 12 June 2015.

holding giant black balloons that symbolised the 'carbon bubble' economy that will eventually burst. In November 2017 in San Francisco, activists painted a large mural on the street pavement fronting the Wells Fargo headquarters to stigmatise its financial sponsorship of fossil fuel industries.[137] Within companies, where these issues are sometimes taken up by concerned shareholders in more orderly settings, such as at shareholder meetings where participants can file resolutions calling for specified environmental performance acts, the decorum is quite muted and cold owing to the governing procedures. Unless, of course, climate change activists gatecrash the meeting, as has happened, notably in June 2018 when 250 Greenpeace activists gatecrashed Total's annual shareholders' meeting in Paris to protest the oil company's environmental performance.[138] We return to the 'counter aesthetics' of such activism in the following chapter.

V. CLIMATE CHANGE ADAPTATION

Aesthetics also enters climate adaptation law through measures intended to protect the existing aesthetic character of environments, as well as adaptation interventions that introduce novel aesthetic features. Measures to protect prevailing aesthetic traits might include tree planting and species relocations in order to maintain the preferred characteristics of a landscape that might alter if left unmanaged. In places of high economic value, such intervention is more likely. Some climate adaptation proposals are bizarre, like the plan to save some of Queensland's coral reefs being bleached by warming oceans. The tourism industry and the Reef and Rainforest Centre proposed that they could protect six reefs of high tourist value by pumping in cold water to counteract the summer heat stress. The idea was dismissed as 'ridiculous' by the former head of the Great Barrier Reef Management Park Authority.[139]

Climate adaptation measures can trigger legal approval requirements through processes similar to those for climate mitigation projects, including activation of EIA and public consultation procedures. Most commonly, aesthetic issues in the adaptation sphere become legally salient when they might alter the appearance of a site. Because of their typically bespoke locations, climate adaptation measures can directly touch people's attachment to places.[140] In Cornwell, southwest England, Vera Köpsel's study of local communities' responses to climate change, particularly about erosion of the region's

---

[137] N Sawyer, 'Activists Paint Anti-DAPL Mural Outside Wells Fargo' *SF Weekly* 6 November 2017.
[138] M Sweney, 'Greenpeace Protesters Abseil into Oil Firm Total's AGM' *The Guardian* 1 June 2018.
[139] C Knaus, 'Plan to Pump Cold Water on to Barrier Reef to Stop Bleaching Labelled "Band-aid"' *The Guardian* 7 April 2017.
[140] SC Moser, 'Communicating Climate Change: History, Challenges, Process and Future Directions' (2010) 1(1) *Wiley Interdisciplinary Reviews: Climate Change* 31.

scenic coastlines, valuably aids our understanding of the centrality of place-based values and local actors' involvement in decision making on landscapes and seascapes undergoing profound change.[141] Thus, public consultation in environmental decision-making has particular salience in gauging the affected community's views.

Even more invasive, we face inundation of low-lying areas from rising seas and storm surges. Since 1880, sea level has risen worldwide on average by about 20 cm according to a recent study,[142] and the IPCC forecasts a further 98 cm increase by 2100 if GHG emissions fail to drop (but as low as 26 cm under best-case scenarios).[143] Installation of seawalls, dykes, floodgates and other defensive infrastructure can dramatically reshape coastlines, as acknowledged by the IPCC.[144] Buildings and other structures are also vulnerable to more extreme weather events, which may require aesthetically problematic retrofit-ting to improve their structural durability.[145] On the other hand, doing nothing might bring just as unwelcome aesthetic effects: the City of Sydney's 2017 report on planning for climate change adaptation observed that 'rising sea levels and coastal inundation could have the potential to reduce accessibility to and the aesthetic qualities of the City's iconic cultural and tourism precinct'.[146] Already, in South Carolina, a legal dispute recently arose after environmentalists opposed the aesthetic and ecological impacts of a gated community's plans to erect a seawall to protect its valuable real estate.[147]

Another context where aesthetic values enter is bushfire risk-mitigation measures adopted in fire-prone areas, as in parts of California and Australia. Such measures can include enlarged vegetation-clearance zones around at-risk houses,[148] resulting in unsightly, pockmarked landscapes. Conversely, large-scale reforestation projects in the name of carbon sequestration and climate adaptation can disrupt the bucolic aesthetic of agricultural landscapes. Susan Goodall's research on commercial tree farms in Tasmania, often planted over agricultural land, found that they have problematic aesthetic effects that she describes as follows: 'tree plantations stand tall and silent; they are a dense, dark

---

[141] V Köpsel, *New Spaces for Climate Change: The Societal Construction of Landscapes in Times of a Changing Climate* (Springer, 2018).

[142] RD Hardy and BL Nuse, 'Global Sea-level Rise: Weighing Country Responsibility and Risk' (2016) 137(3–4) *Climate Change* 333.

[143] JA Church et al, 'Sea Level Change' in TF Stocker et al (eds), *Climate Change 2013: The Physical Science Basis. Contribution of Working Group I to the Fifth Assessment Report of the Intergovernmental Panel on Climate Change* (Cambridge University Press, 2013) 1138, 1140.

[144] RT Watson, MC Zinyowera and RH Moss (eds), *The Regional Impacts of Climate Change* (IPPC and Cambridge University Press, 1997) 8.3.7.2.1.

[145] M Dave, A Varshney and P Graham, *Assessing the Climate Change Adaptability of Buildings* (Faculty of Built Environment, University of New South Wales, 2012) 17.

[146] City of Sydney, *Adapting for Climate Change* (City of Sydney, 2017) 42.

[147] S Fretwell, 'With Seas Rising, Georgetown Coastal Resort Abandons Plan for Controversial Seawall' *Grenville News* 11 July 2018.

[148] See, for instance, the findings of the Victorian Bushfires Royal Commission, *Final Report* (Government Printer for the State of Victoria, 2010) passim.

crop, engulfing the topography, dramatically and semi-permanently altering the visual landscape'.[149]

Some climate adaptation and mitigation measures may bring aesthetic benefits. Reforestation in cities can reduce urban-heat-island effects, while the added greenery can enliven the appearance of neighbourhoods.[150] Similarly, some cities are encouraging green roofs, with collateral aesthetic benefits.[151] Such benefits can also flow from ecological restoration of degraded lands, offering associated improvements 'to the land's former beauty and integrity'.[152] Ecological restoration is not generally undertaken in response to climate change thus far, but its practitioners will increasingly make the connection as the benefits of restoring healthy ecosystems become apparent for boosting social and ecological resilience.

What do the foregoing examples reveal about the overall role of aesthetics in current climate law interventions? They suggest that aesthetics matter, and indeed can fuel major legal controversies, but primarily in national legal systems rather than international law because the aesthetic issues tend to have cultural salience in specific localities and communities governed by domestic environmental laws. Secondly, legal systems have yet to develop *ex ante* criteria for evaluating or adjudicating aesthetic issues that arise in climate adaptation decisions; there is considerable ad hocery in climate governance thus far. Thirdly, reconciling aesthetic values with other policy considerations relating to climate change science or economic impacts remains fraught with difficulty. The seeming absence of a common metric in such legal decisions contributes to its apparently ad hoc nature.

Beyond these issues of legal instrumentalism, climate change adaptation raises a deeper governance challenge that relates to the aesthetics of vulnerability. Our sensory perception of vulnerability rests primarily on threats that we readily sense, and that are usually imminent. We have an intensely evolved fear of spiders, snakes and large carnivores, as well as of heights and darkness, but seemingly lack a similar instinctive wariness about temporally- and spatially-displaced environmental adversities posed by modern life, such as climate change. As Rolf Lidskog puts it, 'these threats are becoming more remote from our perceptual apparatus and acquiring form as abstract prognoses that are

---

[149] S Goodall, *Trees as Farms: Painting the New Landscape* (Master thesis, University of Tasmania, 2012) 9.

[150] For an Australian example, see City of Stirling, *Climate Change Adaptation Plan* (Stirling, June 2013) 27.

[151] US Environmental Protection Agency (EPA), *Reducing Urban Heat Islands: Compendium of Strategies* (EPA, 2008); J Jungels et al, 'Attitudes and Aesthetic Reactions Toward Green Roofs in the Northeastern United States' (2013) 117 *Landscape and Urban Planning* 13.

[152] M Hall, *Earth Repair: A Transatlantic History of Environmental Restoration* (University of Virginia Press, 2005) 133.

beyond lay people's knowledge and experience'.[153] Most societies worldwide have shown themselves to be not particularly proactive in dealing with environmental problems of a long-term nature. Instead, the gravity of the threats is struthiously denied or trivialised until they materialise to the point of demonstrably interfering with our self-interest, such as menacing forest fires, floods or droughts. Not only do we lack fear of these new threats, we are inclined to hubris, to believe we can master nature: we boldly dam majors rivers, like China's behemoth Three Gorges Dam, and chisel huge canals, as in Panama, to literally reconfigure nature to our economic convenience.

Some scientists explain that irrational behaviour, like burning fossil fuels in the face of catastrophic climate change, reflects a universal human tendency to denial or self-deception.[154] These attitudes are related to a cognate tendency of having an overly confident view of human progress. Psychologists suggest that individuals (with exceptions, of course) tend to be overly optimistic, be it from inflated positive images of themselves (the so-called 'better than average' attitude) to their insouciance towards harmful risks.[155] Being insufficiently risk-averse has a deeply evolved purpose, not easily displaced. Robert Trivers, an American evolutionary biologist, suggests 'that there are intrinsic benefits to having [...] a more optimistic view of the future than the facts would seem to justify'.[156] Edward O Wilson adds that this is probably because '[w]ithout it the mind, imprisoned by fatalism, would slow and deteriorate'.[157] In other words, being pessimistic might in evolutionary terms cause individuals to forgo opportunities because of a fear of failure. Taking risks, in other words, can be biologically adaptive.

Regrettably, while some illusions about future prospects might have once been an evolutionary advantage, they have become problematic in a planet under siege from over seven billion *Homo sapiens* wielding dangerous technologies. A fear of snakes or spiders does not inculcate in our minds an appropriate sensory vulnerability to the upheavals of the Anthropocene. Stephen Boyden, an Australian biohistorian, concludes that our evolved propensities to fear ancestral dangers but not modern perils reflect the widening dissonance between human beings' slow biological evolution and rapid cultural advance.[158]

---

[153] R Lidskog, 'Scientific Evidence or Lay People's Experience: On Risk and Trust with Regard to Modern Environmental Threats' in MJ Cohen (ed), *Risk in the Modern Age: Social Theory, Science, and Environmental Decision-Making* (Palgrave, 2000) 202.

[154] D Goleman, *Vital Lies, Simple Truths: The Psychology of Self-deception* (Simon and Schuster, 1996); RL Trivers, 'The Elements of a Scientific Theory of Self-deception' (2000) 908 *Annals New York Academy of Sciences* 114.

[155] JR Chambers, PD Windschitl and J Suls, 'Egocentrism, Event Frequency and Comparative Optimism: When What Happens Frequently is "More Likely to Happen to Me"' (2003) 29(11) *Journal of Personality and Social Psychology Bulletin* 113.

[156] Trivers, 'The Elements of a Scientific Theory' (above n 154) 125.

[157] EO Wilson, *Consilience: The Unity of Knowledge* (Alfred A Knopf, 1998) 120.

[158] S Boyden, Western Civilization in Biological Perspective: Patterns in Biohistory (Oxford University Press, 1987) 264–65.

This 'eco-deviation', as Boyden labels it, can, however, be counteracted through well-designed policies and laws that encourage more prescient and risk-averse behaviours.

Returning to climate change adaptation, the governance difficulty is that to invest in appropriate defensive measures to minimise our (and other species') exposure to the sequalae of global warming (in addition to mitigating GHG emissions) requires an updated aesthetics of vulnerability. So far, an aesthetics of vulnerability has its strongest cultural traction around themes of poverty and displacement, such as climate refugees, which increasingly feature in graphic imagery found in international climate science and policy reports.[159] In developed nations, the onset of more frequent and intense 'natural' disasters including forest fires and drought, as experienced in California and eastern Australia lately, are beginning to stir a greater sense of vulnerability for these impacted peoples to climate change. In turn, these societies may start to invest more seriously in climate adaptation measures, such as designing buildings that are less vulnerable to flammable vegetation. But equally, we should consider accepting that the goal should not always be to make ourselves more resilient to nature, to defeat its adversities, and instead tolerate co-existence with it. Some degree of sensory vulnerability to nature will remind us that we cannot vanquish nature but must make peace with it and respect it because we are embedded and dependent on the health and sustainability of the biosphere. In some cases this will mean conceding to the rising waters or relinquishing the farming of increasingly drought-afflicted lands.

In sum, the aesthetics of climate adaptation law demands more than just thinking about designing seawalls or planting trees in visually acceptable ways. Our underlying sensory perception of vulnerability to environmental adversity on which we can build support for adaptive measures or even accept that nature will gain the upper hand, matters too. This book's concluding chapter returns to the aesthetics of vulnerability and its consequences for environmental law.

VI. CLIMATE ENGINEERING

The aesthetic impacts of climate engineering were introduced earlier in this chapter, being potentially momentous, from green algae blooms triggered by ocean fertilisation to skies tinged red from dispersion of sunlight-reflecting sulphur particulates. With an explicit legal framework for climate engineering still emerging and little experimentation thus far, such aesthetic impacts are hardly discernable to regulators. International law anticipates the need for climate engineering to achieve global emission reduction targets.[160] The UNFCCC 1992

---

[159] Eg UN High Commissioner for Refugees (UNHCR), *Climate Change and Disaster Displacement: An Overview of UNHCR's Role* (UNHCR, 2017).

[160] MB Gerrard and T Hester (eds), *Climate Engineering and the Law: Regulation and Liability for Solar Radiation Management and Carbon Dioxide Removal* (Cambridge University Press, 2018).

stipulates that its state parties will mitigate climate change by both limiting GHG emissions and by protecting and enhancing GHG sinks.[161] Likewise, the Paris Agreement 2015 envisions that its parties will achieve their climate mitigation targets through both reduction in emissions and removal of gases by sinks and reservoirs.[162] The UNFCCC definition of 'sinks' broadly encompasses 'any process, activity or mechanism which removes a greenhouse gas, an aerosol or a precursor of a greenhouse gas from the atmosphere'.[163] Similarly, the UNFCCC definition of 'reservoir' relates to storage of GHGs, which would encompass some forms of geo-engineering.[164] As these definitions are not restricted to naturally occurring processes, they presumably can encompass geo-engineering interventions. Article 5 of the Paris Agreement addresses sinks specifically, with the direction that parties should 'conserve and enhance' them.

Other international environmental law has tentatively acknowledged geo-engineering as an emerging regulatory issue. The recommendation of the Conference of the Parties to the Biodiversity Convention (CBD) in October 2010 to put a moratorium on climate-related geo-engineering that might adversely affect biodiversity until adequate scientific knowledge can resolve the risks, was the first regulatory measure at the international level to address geo-engineering in general, and it followed a call from the CBD parties in 2008 to restrict ocean fertilisation experiments.[165] The Convention on the Prevention of Marine Pollution by Dumping of Wastes and Other Matter (London Convention)[166] and the 1996 Protocol to the Convention[167] effectively restrict ocean fertilisation activities because of their prohibitions on uncontrolled waste dumping in the oceans.[168] Overall, international law leaves unresolved who should decide whether to approve a geo-engineering project, what criteria would be taken into account, including aesthetic impacts, and who would be responsible if something went awry.

Apart from a few rogue experiments, climate geo-engineering has not yet been deployed, although scientists are modelling a variety of methods and debating their likely efficacy, safety and cost. Solar radiation techniques involve reflecting some of the sun's energy back into space, thereby counteracting the temperature rise caused by increases in GHGs in the atmosphere. One such

---

[161] UNFCCC, art 4.

[162] Paris Agreement, art 4.

[163] UNFCCC, art 1.

[164] Ibid.

[165] Decision Adopted by the Conference of the Parties to the Convention on Biological Diversity at Its Tenth Meeting, UNEP/CBD/COP/DEC/X/33, 29 October 2010; Conference of the Parties, Convention on Biological Diversity, *Report of the Conference of the Parties to the Convention on Biological Diversity on the Work of its Ninth Meeting*, Held in Bonn from 19 to 30 May 2008, UNEP/CBD/COP/9/29, 9 October 2008, decision IX/16, section C.

[166] (1972) 1046 UNTS 120.

[167] Protocol to the Convention on the Prevention of Marine Pollution by Dumping of Wastes and Other Matter (1996) 36 ILM 1.

[168] L Kovac, 'Ocean Fertilisation – What Next?' (2013) 9(2) *Macquarie Journal of International and Comparative Environmental Law* 39, 50–53.

technique is marine cloud brightening, implemented by generating a sea-salt mist sprayed from ships (the exhaust from ships already causes some brightening of clouds over the oceans). Removal of CO_2 from the atmosphere can take many forms, including afforestation and reforestation, and ocean fertilisation that stimulates carbon-absorbing phytoplankton. Mimicking the effect of large volcanic eruptions, sulphur injection involves adding fine particles into the stratosphere to increase the sunlight reflected back into space. The eruption of Mount Pinatubo, Philippines in 1991 cooled global average temperatures by 0.5°C. While the feasibility of climate engineering remains speculative for now, it will surely garner policy makers' increased attention in the absence of rapid reduction of GHG emissions.

Geo-engineering's aesthetic effects may sit only within our imagination, but climate control technologies have already entered our visual culture through imagery contained in media news, scientific reports and art works. Computer-generated schematic representations of geo-engineering proposals, as from the Oxford University Geo-engineering Programme and the Kiel Earth Institute,[169] simulate the impression of objectivity and neutrality. We should doubt that. Isabell Schrickel's analysis of images accompanying the climate engineering discourse cautions that they 'show very simple cycles [and] cause-effect chains' while 'ethical considerations and critical evaluation of potential side-effects are completely omitted from the images'.[170] They reinforce the risky narrative that climate engineering is solvable by technological prowess where 'the natural environment serves as the milieu and the input for eco-technological control'.[171]

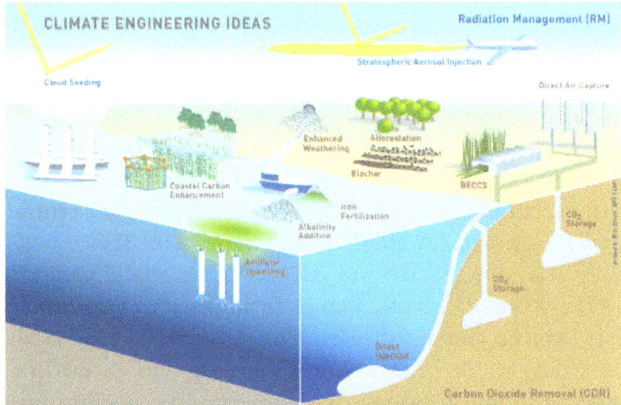

Figure 7.4 Geo-engineering technologies pictogram, German Research Foundation; licensed under Creative Commons

[169] See www.geoengineering.ox.ac.uk/what-is-geoengineering/what-is-geoengineering; and www.kiel-earth-institute.de/scoping-report-climate-engineering.html.

[170] I Schrickel, 'Images of Feasibility: On the Viscourse of Climate Engineering' in Schneider and Nocke, *Image Politics* (above n 3) 363, 374.

[171] Ibid, 378.

Some artists have rendered alternative visualisations of climate engineering that disturb the foregoing narrative. A cartoon published in the *New York Times* on 24 October 2007 with the caption 'Screwing (with) the Planet' showed a pair of overheated polar bears anxiously trying to pump sulphur onto the air but apparently in trouble with their iceberg upturning.[172] Alternatively Emily Parsons-Lord has created art that aims to help us visualise a climate-engineered atmosphere. Her installation *Then Let Us Run (The Sky is Falling)* (2018), erected in South Australia's Vitalstatistix Waterside Workers Hall, comprises an inflated parachute filled with artificial smoke and lit by coloured spotlights tuned to illuminate how the sky might look as a result of some geo-engineering experiments. Arts commentator Lucien Alperstein concludes that this work ultimately 'asks what is most important: the blue sky or a cooler planet?'.[173]

Initiating any climate engineering will first need the imprimatur of some public consultative processes, to enable deliberation of such concerns. Rob Bellamy and others argue that the public's principal concerns with geo-engineering experiments are uncertainty about outcomes, containing an experiment, the reversibility of any impacts and the goals sought.[174] While meaningful public consultation may transpire at a national level through the sponsoring state's environmental law procedures, large-scale experiments with transboundary dimensions necessitate an international consultative process that would be far more difficult to orchestrate. These challenges would dwarf those of adjudicating wind farm projects, even without adding the drastic aesthetic impacts of climate engineering.

To recap and close this chapter, climate change has emerged as an aesthetic phenomenon of growing legal significance. The aesthetic injuries or permutations that global warming will create remain, at this stage, largely as forecasts, with legal frameworks yet to be established to provide explicit or comprehensive governance of these issues. Climate mitigation, adaptation and geo-engineering governance can address distinctive clusters of aesthetic issues. So far, unsightly wind farms have generated the most legal disputes, an issue that the following chapter will return to in considering directions for future governance of environmental aesthetics. Public consultation or negotiation will be a central element in creating socially legitimate governance of climate aesthetics.

Also highly relevant, the arts are educating the public about the impacts, aesthetic or otherwise, of climate change. In addition to the creation of formal artworks that explore climate themes, climate change activists routinely use aestheticised strategies in their political campaigning as evident in protest posters, banners and music. So too, intergovernmental institutions such as the

---

[172] Discussed in JR Fleming, 'Picturing Climate Control: Visualizing the Unimaginable' in Schneider and Nocke, *Image Politics* (above n 3) 345, 356.

[173] L Alperstein, 'Utilitarian Environmentalism in Art' *Fine Print* 2018 www.fineprintmagazine.com/utilitarian-environmentalism-in-art.

[174] R Bellamy, J Lazaun and J Palmer, 'Public Perceptions of Geoengineering Research Governance: An Experimental Deliberative Approach' (2017) 45 (July) *Global Environmental Change* 194.

IPCC rely heavily on visual representations of climate science to engage public audiences. Some scholars identify a further role for the arts in actually helping to adjudicate disputes, such as over the perceived aesthetic impacts of wind farms.[175] As a catalyst for the cultural transformation that we need in order to create stronger laws to protect the global climate, the arts can help convey and interpret the gravity of climate change and enliven scientific information in more engaging and interesting ways for public discourse.

[175] MK Layne, 'What Environmental Art Can Teach Us About Wind Farms: Exploring the Boundaries of Cultural Aesthetics in Scottish Landscapes' (2018) 43(2) *Landscape Research* 248.

Part III

Aspirations

8

Critical Aesthetics

I. LAW AND CURATING AESTHETICS

A. Developing a Critical Aesthetics

OUR ENVIRONMENTAL AESTHETICS need renewal so we can better sense and respond to the upheavals of the Anthropocene. This begins by understanding 'aesthetics' in its broadest and original meaning, as relating to sensory perception rather than just artistic quality or beauty. The iconography of the sublime and the picturesque that enamoured the West in the nineteenth century, in a world far less crowded and degraded, has become an even more unfit aesthetics for the planet's contemporary mayhem. The associated trope about the autonomy of the aesthetic, as though when listening to Mozart or admiring a Van Gogh masterpiece 'the only genuinely aesthetic experiences are those solely or exclusively directed at intrinsic features without any distracting intrusions',[1] ignores the pervasive 'everyday aesthetics' and their power to leverage social change. That visceral power resonates in the enduring adages 'seeing is believing', 'a picture tells a thousand words' and 'where words fail, music speaks'. In other words, we are moved to act more often and profoundly by aesthetic experiences 'than by intellectual arguments, abstract appeals to duty or even fear'.[2] Equally germane, aesthetic experiences offer more than trivial pleasure: they inform the basic human needs that some believe matter more – from the therapeutic benefits that come with sensory access to nature, to the influence of colour and smell in choosing healthful food.

The renewal of environmental aesthetics requires not only greater aesthetic literacy but also, as Marcia Eaton puts it, 'an aesthetic "language" that will communicate ethical ecological health'.[3] It must illuminate insights and feelings on conservation of biodiversity, the renewal of urban ecologies, adaptation to global warming and numerous other challenges. Thereby, explains Joan Nassauer, 'landscapes that are ecologically sound, and that also evoke enjoyment and approval, are more likely to be sustained by appropriate human care

---

[1] M Eaton, *Merit, Aesthetic and Ethical* (Oxford University Press, 2001) 63–64.

[2] D Orr, *The Nature of Design: Ecology, Culture and Human Intention* (Oxford University Press, 2002) 178–99.

[3] Eaton, *Merit, Aesthetic and Ethical* (above n 1) 193.

over the long term'.[4] Equally, we must open our senses to the aesthetic deprivation of the Anthropocene, be it plastic pollution or animal extinctions. Otherwise, an uncritical outlook might cause us to miss how environmental beauty may deceive, like the iridescent colours of a smog-induced scarlet sunset, or what Cheryl Foster calls 'aesthetic disillusionment'.[5] We must also ward against unscrupulous aesthetic practices associated with corporate greenwashing or government propaganda that lead us astray.

At stake then, we need a *critical* aesthetics that not only enriches our sensory engagement with nature but also guides it productively. It will ensue from adopting a number of principles and strategies to inform legal governance. It begins by broadening our interest from aesthetic judgements to aesthetic *experiences*. Bence Nanay's advice that 'the obsessive focus on aesthetic judgment has done more harm than good in aesthetics'[6] recognises that aesthetic experiences usually enliven people more than their judgements: the hours spent hiking through the woods bring pleasure and interest rather than any ultimate verdict about the forest's beauty. The same could be said for many other aesthetic experiences, from listening to a music concert or exploring an art gallery. Indeed, we may decline to make any definitive judgment at all, and the absence of one does not preclude sharing and discussing aesthetic experiences with others. This orientation may seem at odds with some Western aesthetics theorising, but it dovetails with that in many cultures including Islamic and Chinese aesthetics that emphasise experiences over judgements.[7]

This stance also takes us away from being fixated on objects, as though endowed with precise and stable aesthetic characteristics, to their wider context and our relationship with it. By broadening our vista beyond the individual animal, plant or artwork, we should more critically understand the environmental issues involved. Consider the aesthetics of fruit; whereas food retailers prefer consumers to dwell on their colour, size and taste, a contextual perspective extends one's perceptual depth to consider how the fruit was produced, including any land clearance, chemical additions or other problematic environmental transformations and, indeed, its transportation to point of sale. Politically engaged artists, whose role I examine in more detail below, embrace this challenge by aesthetically unveiling the social or environmental negatives of consumerism that corporate marketing seeks to obscure, such as the sweatshops making our clothes or the fossil fuels exploited for growing our food.

---

[4] JI Nassauer, 'Cultural Sustainability: Aligning Aesthetics with Ecology' in JI Nassauer (ed), *Placing Nature: Culture and Landscape Ecology* (Island Press, 1997) 65, 69.
[5] C Foster, 'Aesthetic Disillusionment: Environment, Ethics and Art' (1992) 1(3) *Environmental Values* 205, 212–13.
[6] B Nanay, 'Against Aesthetic Judgements' in JA McMahon (ed), *Social Aesthetics and Moral Judgement* (Routledge, 2018) 52, 62.
[7] Ibid.

A second contour of critical aesthetics shifts the experiencing agent from being a detached spectator to an *active participant*, a posture that helps overcome the 'otherness' of nature. As Yuriko Saito explains, 'the typical focus is on how a spectator "receives" and "responds" to an aesthetic object, such as a work of art or a natural object', but this overlooks the aesthetic richness and value that comes from 'doing' things such as planting flowers or painting a picture.[8] Likewise, Berleant's theory of aesthetics applauds active engagement over detached viewing or listening.[9] Nature thereby becomes no longer something just to 'look at', but a multi-sensory experience – the aroma of flowers, the melody of the dawn chorus or the gush of wind, along with sometimes unappealing encounters with ugly or odorous degradation.

One does not have to inhabit a wilderness to experience some of the foregoing. In cities and towns, where most of the world's population now congregates, already one finds numerous accounts of people bringing nature into their lives. Community gardens, explains Laura Lawson in *City Beautiful*, have adorned many US urban neighbourhoods for over a century, beautifying vacant lots, schoolyards and community spaces, as well as feeding a growing urban populace.[10] One million garden allotments now adorn German cities, supporting a surging interest in urban agriculture.[11] Community gardening also brings an aesthetic experience that enriches participants' ecological literacy and strengthens neighbourliness by promoting social cooperation and conversation. The Incredible Edible Project, began in Yorkshire, England, in 2008 as an urban gardening initiative, has since spread to over 700 groups worldwide following strategies of self-sustained, local food production.[12] The spread of green roofs and walls to abate the effects of global warming will add another appealing aesthetic layer to our urban environs.

Art can both mediate and facilitate some of this aesthetic engagement. Through their works, artists can powerfully shape and compel their audiences intellectually and aesthetically. Artists can use their aesthetic literacy to curate a sensory experience to elicit an affective response, especially of any natural phenomena obscured from our sensory realm.[13] Consider artists Giles Revell and Dorothy Cross: their subjects are common garden insects and jellyfish respectively, rendering them into larger forms and working with scientists

[8] Y Saito, *Aesthetics of the Familiar: Everyday Life and World-Making* (Oxford University Press, 2017) 53–54.

[9] A Berleant, *Living in the Landscape: Toward an Aesthetics of Environment* (University of Kansas Press, 1997).

[10] L Lawson, *City Beautiful: A Century of Community Gardening in America* (University of California Press, 2005).

[11] S Gallup, 'Living the Good Life in Berlin's Allotments – But for How Long?' *BBC News*, 9 January 2016, www.bbc.com/news/world-europe-35008648.

[12] Incredible Edible, www.incredible-edible-todmorden.co.uk.

[13] D Tracey and A MacDonald, 'Sanitising Landscapes: Implications for Meaning Making' (2018) 12(1) *Journal of Artistic and Creative Education* 6.

to intrigue audiences about these creatures' delicate biological and aesthetic qualities. While we commonly think of art as just the resulting works, such as paintings or music, art *practice* itself constitutes aesthetic engagement. It takes participants from being passive observers to being actively present in nature. Art practice involves not just professionals who specialise in recording nature soundscapes or plein air painting; it could be the amateur nature photographer or hobby painter, or even a recreationist perambulating through the woods, as 'walking artists' Richard Long and Hamish Fulton demonstrate.

Thirdly, we need an aesthetic of *vulnerability* that lifts us beyond our own active engagement with the natural world to respect the agency and engagement of nature in ours. It's a reciprocal relationship. 'Vulnerability' means jettisoning the arrogance that humankind exists autonomously from or without dependence on nature. In its place we make space for natural forces, be they wildlife, weather or various ecological processes and cycles which may sometimes make our lives discomforting, and even occasionally dangerous, but they vitally maintain ecological integrity and sustainability. We will thereby come to appreciate Ronald Hepburn's wisdom that 'we are in nature and a part of nature; we do not stand over against it as over against a painting on a wall'.

By making our lives more vulnerable to the agency of nature, we become better sensitised to its behaviours and well-being. We will be more attuned to its cues and better able to adjust our behaviour. An aesthetics of vulnerability to nature necessitates letting go of the obsessive drive to domesticate and subjugate natural forces, be they floods, fires or dangerous creatures. I am not suggesting insouciance about exposure to hostile natural elements such as going without water or shelter, but rather to agree that governments should not be expected to pacify nature into an aesthetically and ecologically impoverished condition that would also ultimately jeopardise our own long-term well-being.

Fourthly, a critical perspective requires a *social* aesthetics. Philosopher Jennifer McMahan explains, 'instead of conceiving aesthetic engagement in terms of an individual's isolated experience, [...] [it] is more accurately conceived [as] the network of minds that create the conditions for communicating and hence cultivating sociable feelings'.[14] Social aesthetics emphasises shared aesthetic experiences and ensuing dialogue including over any aesthetic judgements. The spaces for people to meet enliven such communal experiences, contributing to the aesthetic 'atmosphere', as Gernot Böhme and others have shown in arguing for recognition of the 'atmosphere' as an aesthetic realm.[15] It could be forums for public participation in environmental decision-making, such as a public inquiry or courtroom, or just a natural setting such as a forest visited by walkers. The type of atmosphere affects these aesthetic experiences; the encroachment of consumerism and corporate advertising into public spaces

---

[14] J McMahon, 'New Prospects for Aesthetic Hedonism' in J McMahon (ed), *Social Aesthetics and Moral Judgment* (Routledge, 2018) 1, 1.
[15] G Böhme, *The Aesthetics of Atmospheres* (Routledge, 2017); B Anderson, 'Affective Atmosphere' (2009) 2 *Emotion, Space and Society* 77; S Grant, 'Performing on Aesthetics of Atmosphere' (2013) 23(1) *Aesthetics* 12.

has adverse consequences, as Chapter 6 showed. Challenges to corporate greenwashing by culture jamming activists, as discussed below, offer means of positively reshaping social aesthetics.

A fifth pillar of critical aesthetics is sensitivity to the intertwined aesthetic and ecological deprivation of the world beyond our immediate sensory perception – making absent aesthetics *present*. We need to feel the manifold environmental changes and impacts distanced by time or space from our lived experiences, be they future climate change or distant marine plastic debris. We also must recognise the aesthetic deprivation caused by our exploitation of nature at a distance in the name of aesthetics – the ugly mining or ravenous forestry that furnishes the raw materials to decorate our lives with beautiful homes, cars, jewellery and so forth. These new directions were introduced in Chapter 3 in my discussion of the 'proximity' principle as a necessary underpinning of overcoming absent aesthetics. Jonathan Maski calls this challenge one of being aware of 'the aesthetics of elsewhere'.[16] It also necessitates 'designing with nature', says David Orr, to avoid creating 'ugliness, human or ecological, somewhere else or at some later time'.[17] Sensitivity to these temporally or spatially displaced aesthetic impacts, to overcome the 'out of sight, out of mind' insouciance, requires the aid of mediating institutions in capturing the aesthetic deprivation elsewhere. Museums and art galleries can play such a mediating role, as Jennifer Newell and others explore in relation to arousing the public to the dangers of climate change.[18] They can also, no doubt, be limiting where they offer only didactic presentation of objects behind glass cabinets, as Chapter 4 touched on.[19]

Finally, we need *multi-disciplinary integration* of aesthetic and non-aesthetic factors to facilitate holistic environmental governance. These factors cannot remain in separate decision-making silos. The concepts of cultural landscapes and cultural heritage illustrate some approaches to bringing aesthetic values into wider governance frameworks for managing places. They capture the interrelated aesthetic, historic, social and scientific values of a place.[20] A critical aesthetics requires that we do not quarantine aesthetics from other realms of knowledge and human experience but rather explore how to productively integrate them. This should include collaborations between scientists and artists in understanding and communicating insights into human beings' environmental activities and impacts.

---

[16] J Maskit, 'The Aesthetics of Elsewhere: An Environmentalist Everyday Aesthetics' (2011) 1(2) *Aesthetic Pathways* 92.

[17] D Orr, *The Nature of Design: Ecology, Nature and Human Intention* (Oxford University Press, 2002) 4.

[18] J Newell, L Robin and K Wehner (eds), *Curating the Future: Museums, Communities and Climate Change* (Routledge, 2017).

[19] There are some promising innovations, however, such as the Melbourne Museum, which includes a living forest complete with various birds and wildlife that visitors can walk through, to complement the indoor taxidermy collection.

[20] For instance, as recognised in the Australia ICOMOS Charter for Places of Cultural Significance, The Burra Charter, 2013, art 1.2.

Science and the arts have a long history of collaboration. Artists regularly joined scientists in the 'Age of Discovery' of European overseas exploration and colonisation, with artistic renderings of newly-discovered plants and animals being instrumental in the dissemination of scientific knowledge. One famous effort was the Baudin Expedition, a voyage of scientific discovery to 'New Holland' (as Australia was known in the early nineteenth century) sponsored by the French government, involving 24 scientists and artists led by naval officer Nicolas Baudin.[21] Their collections, many beautifully depicted in drawings and paintings, as in the example in Figure 8.1, contributed to the emerging European understanding of the biodiversity of the continent.

Figure 8.1 *Long-spine Porcupine Fish*. *Diodon holocanthus (Linnaeus, 1758)*, Charles-Alexandre Lesueur, Nicolas Baudin expedition, 1801–04; Muséum d'histoire naturelle, Le Havre

Today, artists no longer meekly serve as the secondary partner – as a transmission belt for documenting and communicating the sciences – but rather critically challenge the nature of knowledge itself. In *Art and Science*, Siân Ede reveals the rich varieties of contemporary science-art collaborations invigorating one another. In a world where science has lost much of its esteem – think of GMOs, cloning, climate change and nuclear weapons – the arts help to link its endeavour to spiritual and ethical concerns, while conversely the crass commercialisation of the arts industry is moderated by those engaging with tangible and pressing social and environmental problems that preoccupy some scientists.[22]

B. Implications for Law

The law cannot remain a laissez-faire bystander to the advancement of a critical environmental aesthetics, as though judgements about natural beauty or ugly

---

[21] J Fornasiero, L Lawton and J West-Sooby (eds), *Nicolas Baudin's Voyagers 1800–1804* (Wakefield Press, 2016).
[22] E Ede, *Art and Science* (IB Taurus, 2005).

pollution lack consequences for our environmental attitudes and behaviours. Already, the law's insouciance has allowed the unleashing of the destructive commodity aesthetics of the business world. Unfortunately, we still encounter new environmental laws or policies ignorant of aesthetics. Notably, the proposal for a Global Pact on the Environment, launched in 2017 to integrate and update the preeminent principles of environmental law for the international community, fails at the time of writing to refer to aesthetics.[23] Equally problematic, however, would be to expect that the law could didactically prescribe our aesthetic judgements or codify natural beauty into timeless formulae. The disciplines of landscape assessment and cultural heritage assessment, both encompassing aesthetic values, have supported environmental law thus far in this endeavour,[24] but they capture only a segment of the multifarious dimensions of aesthetics governance.

Under a critical aesthetics, the law will expand and shift into a curatorial role anchored in the following elements that flow from the preceding discussion. Firstly, it must provide communal spaces for aesthetic experiences and artistic expression to flourish. This should include access to national parks, a right to roam the countryside, even on private property, and bringing nature into our cities through smarter land use planning. Secondly, the law must encourage an aesthetics of vulnerability to nature's agency, allowing nature to engage with us. This requirement has implications for the management of natural hazards including floods, fires and droughts, as well as adaptation to climate change. Rather than obsessive domestication of nature, the law should allow for greater co-existence with the natural world, such as letting rivers run wild rather than be impounded, and giving carnivores from sharks to wolves space to thrive. Thirdly, the law must curb inappropriate aesthetic elements that foment environmental harm, as associated notably with corporate greenwashing. Sometimes advertising controls and consumer law protections may need to be supplemented by giving space for counter-aesthetic activism to sensitise the public to the deceptive messages and practices masquerading as corporate social responsibility (CSR). Fourthly, we need multi-stakeholder forums and processes that foster interdisciplinary thinking and decision-making, especially for the mixing of scientific and artistic knowledge. A variety of institutions from public museums to environmental impact assessment (EIA) procedures can further such interactions to nurture more informed aesthetic experiences and judgements. Finally, as disputes are inevitable over competing aesthetics values, and between aesthetic and non-aesthetic considerations, the law must enable adjudication

---

[23] The initiative has UN backing: UN General Assembly, 'Toward a Global Pact for the Environment', A/RES/72/277, 14 May 2018; for the preliminary draft text of the Pact, see www.iucn.org/sites/dev/files/content/documents/draft-project-of-the-global-pact-for-the-environment.pdf.

[24] C Swanwick, *Landscape Character Assessment, Guidance for England and Scotland* (Countryside Agency and Scottish Natural Heritage, 2002); Australian Heritage Commission, *Protecting Local Heritage Places: A Guide for Communities* (Australian Heritage Commission, 1998).

and implementation of the resulting preferred aesthetic values. I will elaborate on these elements below.

A central underpinning of this agenda is the quality of the processes and spaces by which people share and debate aesthetic experiences. These institutions may range from public environmental inquiries and courts and, outside the law, cultural bodies such as museums, as well as spaces for non-state actors to self-organise and communicate. Jurgen Habermas defended the public sphere as a crucial site for public deliberation and rational discourse for the pursuit of shared ethical and social concerns.[25] Its erosion by market forces and intrusive government oversight was observed by Hannah Arendt in the 1950s,[26] but its more recent decline is inflamed by rampant consumerism and corporate inroads into the public realm.[27] Stjepan Mestrovic's prescient book on the *Postemotional Society* warns of the risks posed by our incessant exposure to a hyper-aestheticised consumer culture.[28] Similarly, Wolfgang Welsch recognises that commercialisation of aesthetic stimuli becomes counterproductive, as 'total aestheticization results in its own opposite. [...] continued excitement leads to indifference'.[29] In other words, a degraded public sphere robs civil society of space for creative and critical dialogue, ethical development and remedial action.

Curating critical aesthetics must thus protect realms for environmental non-governmental organisations (NGOs) and artists to play their creative role. Some already do this, through dissident activism that challenges deceptive corporate marketing or government propaganda. These 'counter aesthetic' strategies artfully subvert corporate communications – slogans, songs, logos, billboards or other elements of the business brand. With humour and hoaxing, counter aesthetics can expose deceptive corporate practices that degrade the environment. These 'culture-jamming' strategies, as they are more commonly known, face legal impediments, however, including diminishing access to public spaces, restrictions on freedom of speech, defamation law, and companies' stentorian enforcement of their intellectual property rights. If the law is to curate a critical social aesthetics, it must attenuate these restrictions on creative and dissident expression.

The foregoing agenda makes two important assumptions: the instrumental function of critical aesthetics and its capacity to promote social change. The former offends those who value aesthetic experiences as an end in themselves, believing that their harnessing for other purposes diminishes such experiences and distorts aesthetic judgements. This is untenable. To maintain this hands-off stance would leave untouched the problem of negative aesthetics associated

---

[25] J Habermas, *The Structural Transformation of the Public Sphere*, translated T Burger (MIT Press, 1991).

[26] H Arendt, *The Human Condition* (University of Chicago Press 1958).

[27] G Ritzer, *McDonaldization of Society* (Pine Forge Press, 2001); A Bryman, *The Disneyifiication of Society* (Sage, 2004).

[28] S Mestrovic, *Postemotional Society* (Sage, 1997).

[29] W Welsch, *Undoing Aesthetics* (Sage, 1997) 25.

with commerce and politics that fuels environmental degradation. Visual and acoustic pollution pervades our lives, like ugly power lines, billboards and noisy shopping centres, as matched equally by the oppressive aesthetic blandness of industrialised farmscapes and strip-mined lands. Equally, protecting the less damaged parts of the natural world often requires us to highlight their positive aesthetic values. This instrumental turn also dovetails with the aesthetic traditions of some cultures. As Saito explains on Japanese culture, 'there is no indication that this understanding of aesthetics as having an instrumental value compromises the aesthetic value of art, our experience of it, or our engagement with everyday practice'.[30] In sum, an environmental aesthetics disconnected from the rest of life would impair nature and our place in it. Taking this stance will not deprive individuals of the freedom to personally enjoy natural beauty or whatever aesthetic virtues they find in their midst.

Similarly important, a paradigm shift in aesthetics must help change our values and behaviours. This book has already shown how nature aesthetics evolved over the centuries and its influence in the history of environmental law. Shifts in Western landscape aesthetics through the arts have altered perceptions of nature, especially wilderness, from a hostile or alien realm to the benign or beautiful worthy of conservation in national parks. Likewise, the graphic, ugly aesthetics of environmental damage, from whaling to oil spills, has helped strengthen marine conservation and pollution control laws respectively. We have also learned, in Chapter 1, about the burgeoning research on the psychological and cultural influence of aesthetics, and the arts specifically, in shaping environmental attitudes and behaviours. I do not suggest that aesthetics always will or should prevail over other non-aesthetic values or concerns, such as economic pressures, but through the law aesthetics can be taken more seriously. I will now look more closely at the specific elements of the agenda of critical aesthetics.

II. COUNTER AESTHETICS

A. Challenging the State: Counter Monuments and Maps

Art has an esteemed history of expressing political dissent. Vince Carducci cites examples during China's Han Dynasty and the European Renaissance where songs, theatre and cartoons deployed parody and satire against authoritarian regimes.[31] The Dada movement in early twentieth century Europe harnessed art to challenge bourgeois nationalist and colonialist ideologies.[32] The arts were

---

[30] Saito, *Aesthetics of the Familiar* (above n 8) 214.
[31] V Carducci, "Culture Jamming: A Sociological Perspective' (2006) 6(1) *Journal of Consumer Culture* 116, 130.
[32] T Papanikolas, *Anarchism and the Advent of Paris Dada* (Ashgate, 2010).

also crucial for insinuating criticism of totalitarian communist regimes where overt freedom of expression was denied. In liberal democratic societies, with ostensibly more tolerance of public dissent, the arts also can adroitly insinuate challenges to political and business elites.

In recent decades the arts have been mobilised, often by environmental NGOs, to contest government policies. Eco-activists bring a distinctive aesthetic to their work through their campaign banners, murals and even colourfully painted ships (eg the Rainbow Warrior and Sea Shepherd's flotilla). Renowned for its publicity stunts and brazen tactics, Greenpeace has been described as a 'theatre company'.[33] Such aesthetic campaigning often combines with clever word plays – posters and stickers that proclaim 'think globally, act locally', 'small is beautiful' and 'feed the planet and it will nourish you'. Sometimes professional artists collaborate in these struggles or assert their own stance. Joseph Beuys's provocative sculptures and theatrics broadened the traditional boundaries of art and the role of the artist into overt political struggles (Beuys was even a candidate for the German Green Party in the 1976 German Bundestag and the 1979 European Parliament elections). This book has already canvassed arts activism in the making of environmental law (Chapter 2) and climate change policy (Chapter 7), so I do not need to offer further illustrations here.

Figure 8.2 Environmental protesters – 'Think Globally Act Locally', photograph by Jeremy Buckingham; licensed under Creative Commons

Sometimes the very aesthetic persona of a nation-state is challenged by those desecrating its symbols of national identity or sovereign power. This may involve

---

[33] S Durland, 'Witness The Guerrilla Theater of Greenpeace' (1987) 40 *High Performance* 31.

flag burning, disrespectful postures during recitations of the national anthem or defacing political landmarks and monuments. These subversive gestures can generate considerable publicity for the protagonists' causes, but may not in themselves create any alternate aesthetic that redefines nationalism or governance.

One approach that does is the 'counter monument', a form of counter aesthetics. Monuments influence how we interpret spaces by literally inscribing official histories or narratives onto the landscape. Counter monuments, a phrase apparently coined by US academic James Young, defy the conventional subject matters and techniques of traditional memorials in speaking for the marginalised or oppressed. Young observes in this genre a rejection of the heroic, figurative monument in favour of humble installations that not only memorialise alternative histories or issues, but by their very form and position challenge hegemonic narratives. He evaluates Holocaust memorialisation in Germany, whose citizens over recent decades have agonised over how to come to terms with their nation's shameful past. One effort is the *Monument Against Fascism*, erected in Hamburg in 1986 by Jochen Gerz and Esther Shalev-Gerz.[34] The column, initially 12 metres high and then gradually lowered into the ground and no longer visible since 1993, allowed viewers to inscribe their names onto its surface as a pledge of support for the monument's stance against fascism.

Such gestures come from the belief the traditional elements of monumentality sponsored by governments – associated with large scale, prominence and separation from viewers – would in this context have problematically evoked the very values of fascism, with its connotations of strength and bravery. Counter monuments thus tend to avoid grandiose monumental forms (eg sculptures that sink beneath the ground) and invite viewers to embrace a more intimate, multisensory engagement (eg by touching or even altering the monument).[35] These techniques, besides the very subject matter represented by counter monuments, can help recover marginalised histories or narratives. By contrast, traditional public monuments serve social memory poorly, burying them beneath layers of national myths and symbols.

Some counter monuments also champion issues closer to this book's subject. Aboriginal Australian culture, and the landscapes they stewarded, were devastated by British colonisation, whose laws treated the continent as *terra nullius*. The Aboriginal Tent Embassy (ATE) is the most famous counter monument to this still unresolved history.[36] Erected on Australia Day (also derided as 'Invasion Day'), 26 January 1972, on the lawns of the then Parliament House in Canberra, and since periodically dismantled and re-established, the ATE symbolises

---

[34] JE Young, 'The Counter Monument: Memory Against Itself in Germany Today' (1992) 18 *Critical Inquiry* 267.

[35] Q Stevens, KA Franck and R Fazakerley, 'Counter-monuments: The Anti-Monumental and the Dialogic' (2012) 17(6) *Journal of Architecture* 951.

[36] G Foley, A Schaap and E Howell (eds), *The Aboriginal Tent Embassy: Sovereignty, Black Power, Land Rights and the State* (Routledge, 2014).

Aboriginal resistance to the Australian nation-state and the dominant white culture. It isn't the work of a professional architect or sculptor, having begun when Indigenous activists erected tents and sheds. The ATE stands against theft of Aboriginal land, as well as standing for self-determination and sovereignty for Aboriginal peoples. Since they had been reduced to the status of 'aliens' in their own land, as 'aliens' they felt they should have their own 'embassy'.[37] The ATE challenges the conventional aesthetic criteria for monuments in a city brimming with nation-building edifices: a small, dishevelled and flimsy structure in contrast to the elegance, grandeur, and 'planned geometry' of Canberra's monuments.[38] Indeed, the assemblage's dilapidated aura reflects the living conditions of many Aboriginal communities. Many now recognise the success of the ATE in helping activists 'gain direct access to senior government figures'.[39]

Figure 8.3 Demonstration, Aboriginal Tent Embassy, Parliament House, Canberra, 1972; National Archives of Australia

Staying with the Aboriginal context, cartography has offered another aesthetic realm for challenging nation-state authority, and specifically about how nature

---

[37] Ibid, xxv.

[38] P Walker, 'Tents and Monuments' (2015) 25(3) *Fabrications: Journal of the Society of Architectural Historians, Australia and New Zealand* 304, 307.

[39] D Browning, 'Chicka Dixon and the Tent Embassy' *ABC Radio National (Awaye)* 18 October 2008, www.abc.net.au/radionational/programs/awaye/chicka-dixon-and-the-tent-embassy/3669418.

and culture are spatially represented and governed. In the arts world, some have deconstructed or reinvented maps as a tool for revealing obscured ecological and cultural issues: Ruth Watson identified 24 major art exhibitions from 1977 to 2009 devoted to cartography.[40] Community groups and Indigenous peoples seeking public acknowledgement of their traditional territories and resource claims have challenged state-imposed maps that erased their history. The term 'counter mapping' was coined in 1995 by academic Nancy Peluso to describe how forest users in Kalimantan, Indonesia, commissioned their own maps to contest official forestry plans that had ignored their long-standing rights to forest lands and produce.[41]

Aboriginal Australians have also designed counter maps to document their asserted cultural and legal interests. Australia's huge Murray-Darling river basin, occupied by their ancestors for millennia, became highly degraded during the twentieth century owing to state-imposed governance attuned to the myopic water needs of riparian settlements and farmers, along with the political rivalries of the state governments sharing the river catchment.[42] In 2018 the Aboriginal traditional owners mapped the cultural landscapes of the northern reaches of the river to 'record their locations for hunting, fishing, ceremonies, harvesting plants and herbs, as well as burial mounds, campsites and sacred areas of deep spiritual significance'.[43] They identified some 25,000 places of significance, thereby contributing to their claims for sharing in the governance of the Murray-Darling today.[44] Another example, also from Australia, is the cultural landscape mapping of the massive Lake Eyre basin: after 12 years of preparation, in 2018 the first map was published showing cultural 'songlines', historical trade routes and other cultural information, and as a 'living record' the map will be updated.[45]

Counter monuments and maps thus provide aesthetic tools for marginalised groups and their histories to assert against official narratives, and help their protagonists articulate their future ambitions and gain public recognition. These counter aesthetic strategies inject new voices and issues into the public sphere, and thereby should help make the political milieu more receptive to legal reform. This has already been demonstrated in Australia with the advancement

---

[40] R Watson, 'Mapping and Contemporary Art' (2009) 46(4) *The Cartographic Journal* 293.

[41] NL Peluso, 'Whose Woods are these? Counter-mapping Forests Territories in Kalimantan, Indonesia' (1995) 27(4) *Antipode* 383.

[42] D Connell, *Water Politics in the Murray Darling Basin* (Federation Press, 2007).

[43] Murray-Darling Basin Authority, 'Traditional Owners Map Land and Water Use in Northern Murray-Darling', media release 31 July 2018, www.mdba.gov.au/media/mr/traditional-owners-map-land-water-use-northern-murray-darling.

[44] P Timms, 'Murray-Darling: Indigenous Leaders Call for "Meaningful" Consultation Over Basin Plan' *ABC News* 27 June 2017, www.abc.net.au/news/2017-06-27/aboriginal-people-are-the-ones-who-speak-for-the-river/8653808.

[45] K Beavan, 'Aboriginal Map of Lake Eyre Basin, an Area Twice the Size of France, Released After 12 Years in the Making' *ABC News (Rural)* 2 August 2018, www.abc.net.au/news/rural/2018-08-02/lake-eyre-basin-aboriginal-map-released/10061664.

of some Aboriginal rights across several domains especially management of natural resources.[46]

B. Unmasking Corporate Greenwashing

Reclaiming the public sphere also involves challenging the corporate usurpation of public discourse. Ubiquitous business marketing and the culture of consumerism, as discussed in Chapter 5, are targets for counter aesthetics, along with increasing corporate sponsorship of cultural institutions and the concentration of the media industry in the hands of business moguls.[47] Led by critical artists partnering with activist NGOs, this counter aesthetics supplements official regulation as a governing mechanism, though by influencing public opinion it may also eventually promote stronger legislation.

Such anti-corporate strategies are often known as 'culture jamming'.[48] Drawing on the traditions of guerrilla street art and media pranks,[49] and the growing appeal of taking politically-oriented art beyond galleries into public spaces,[50] culture jamming commonly involves hijacking billboards, reconfiguring logos and parodying advertisements to radically subvert their messages. Such antics may feature colourful, figurative, sculptural or performative elements, often rendered anonymously. This cultural sabotage is striking because it 'makes use of a corporation's own method of communication to send a message starkly at odds with the intended one'.[51] And, crucially, it does so by reclaiming public spaces, including town squares, pavements, bus stops and civic buildings, where ubiquitous corporate marketing has often encroached.

Such creative activism, suggest commentators such as Eleftheria Lekakis, reflects a 'political consumerism' in which political values and acts are transferred to the marketplace 'to resist and reuse the logic of appropriation'.[52] As many public issues and social voices are marginalised by the dominance of market values and commercial communication, activists have had to turn to the market itself to express their grievances. Political consumerism has particular relevance to environmental activism that seeks to destabilise market forces that

---

[46] JC Altman, *People on Country: Vital Landscapes, Indigenous Futures* (Federation Press, 2012).

[47] HI Schiller, *Culture Inc: The Corporate Takeover of Public Expression* (Oxford University Press, 1989) 32.

[48] N Klein, *No Logo: Taking Aim at the Brand Bullies* (Picador, 1999) 279–330; M DeLaure and M Fink (eds), *Culture Jamming: Activism and the Art of Cultural Resistance* (New York University Press, 2017).

[49] See N Ganz, *Graffiti World: Street Art from Five Continents* (Harry N Abrahams, 2004).

[50] J Lossau and Q Stevens (eds), *The Uses of Art in Public Space* (Routledge, 2015).

[51] M Kohn, *Brave New Neighborhoods: The Privatization of Public Space* (Routledge, 2004) 167.

[52] EJ Lekakis, 'Culture Jamming and Brandalism for the Environment: The Logic of Appropriation' (2017) 15(4) *Popular Communication: The International Journal of Media and Culture* 311, 312.

drive ecologically degrading consumption.[53] Unlike other forms of political consumerism such as consumer and investor boycotts (eg the fossil fuels divestment campaign), culture jamming uses artistic creativity to make transparent the environmental damages or the social suffering associated with a product or its company.

Culture jamming was pioneered by the Australian BUGA UP activists (short for Billboard Utilising Graffitists Against Unhealthy Promotions), who in the late 1970s began ingeniously defacing billboards touting tobacco and alcohol.[54] A variety of groups dedicated to culture jamming have since sprung up, such as the Canadian-based Adbusters Media Foundation that challenges corporate propaganda by defacement of logos, satirical street performances, fake advertisements, and as well producing a magazine and website to publicise its antics.[55] Most environmental groups, however, engage in jamming as just one of a variety of activist tactics rather than an exclusive strategy.

Environmental culture jamming has had memorable moments. Following the shocking 1989 Valdez oil spill, the Billboard Liberation Front re-messaged two towering billboards in San Francisco to proclaim 'Shit Happens. New Exxon'.[56] Thousands of commuters saw them. The US-based Earth First, renowned for particularly radical stunts, also has decapitated unsightly billboards or defaced them by inscribing pro-environmental messages. The culture-jamming duo Yes Men specialise in impersonating business and government leaders, creating attention-grabbing humour from these hoaxes.[57] One was staged on the twentieth anniversary of the Bhopal pollution disaster in December 2004, when the Yes Men impersonated a Dow Jones executive interviewed on the BBC to announce that it fully accepted responsibility and would pay for the cleanup of the contaminated site and provide health care for the thousands of victims.[58] At the 2015 Paris Summit on Climate Change, the irreverent Brandalism placed 600 posters on city bus stops mocking some big businesses, including Air France as depicted in Figure 8.4, for sponsoring the conference.[59] Brandalism 'directly links the advertising industry to climate change and it calls for a debate on the ethics of advertising as a key battlefield over cultural meaning and environmental sustainability'.[60]

---

[53] JB Schor, 'Towards a New Politics of Consumption' in JB Schor and DB Holt (eds), *The Consumer Society Reader* (New Press, 2000) 446.

[54] M Deitz, 'Cut and Paste: Australia's Original Culture Jammers, BUGA UP' (2017) 11(2) *Global Media Journal*, www.hca.westernsydney.edu.au/gmjau/?p=816.

[55] Adbusters, www.adbusters.org.

[56] Billboard Liberation Front, 'Shit Happens', August 1989, http://billboardliberation.com/shit.html.

[57] J Servin, 'The Yes Men' in R Martin (ed), *The Routledge Companion to Art and Politics* (Routledge, 2015) 194, 197.

[58] The BBC interview is available at www.youtube.com/watch?v=LiWlvBro9eI.

[59] 'COP21: Eco Activists Brandalism Launch Paris Ad Takeover' *BBC News* 29 November 2015, www.bbc.com/news/world-europe-34958282.

[60] Lekakis, 'Culture Jamming' (above n 53) 312.

Figure 8.4 *Air France: Part of the Problem*, 2015, poster; Brandalism and Revolt Design

Corporate logos also incur criticism; in 2002 Greenpeace launched a campaign against dirty oil, mocking images of the Esso company logo and then US President George W Bush.[61] Another Greenpeace action, involving a clean-up of a Philippines beach, named the responsible businesses with a banner inscribed with 'polluted by ....', and showed the logos of the companies identified in the clean-up audit.[62]

With the growing corporate presence in cyberspace, anti-business activism has had to update its tactics. Some believe that digital spaces have revolutionised such activism by enabling collaboration from local to global scales cheaply and effectively through email, social media and webpages.[63] The Occupy Movement exemplifies this success. Cyberspace also has limitations for such campaigns,

---

[61] J Doyle, 'Picturing the Clima(c)tic: Greenpeace and the Representation Politics of Climate Change Communication' in B Schneider and T Nocke (eds), *Image Politics of Climate Change* (Transcript Verlag, 2014) 225, 239.

[62] S King, 'My Week on a Plastic Beach Helping to Name and Shame its Polluters' Greenpeace Canada 4 October 2017, www.greenpeace.org/canada/en/story/405/my-week-on-a-plastic-beach-helping-to-name-and-shame-its-polluters.

[63] M McCaughey (ed), *Cyberactivism on the Participatory Web* (Routledge, 2014).

as it just as strongly empowers listeners to tune out by choosing their own web browsing and social media networks.[64] Whereas street protests and culture jamming in sidewalks, plazas and other public spaces enable activists to directly confront the passing public, in cyberspace people have greater control over where they wish to roam or what they wish to see. The Internet also gives corporations greater means of surveillance to identify and prosecute infringers of their copyright or trademarks.[65] And in some countries, notably China, extensive Internet censorship severely limits dissenting voices altogether.

Despite these obstacles, the Internet has become a major resource for digital activism, especially through social networking facilities such as Facebook and Twitter that help mobilise supporters and publicising actions. Some efforts go further: 'hactivism' has been coined to describe online culture jamming that includes 'web site defacements, redirects, denial-of-service attacks, information theft, website parodies, virtual sit-ins, [and] virtual sabotage'.[66] Where they cannot breach website security, hactivists may create website clones. One imitated Dow's, with messages for reparation for the victims of the 1984 Bhopal disaster and other allegations against Dow.[67] Efforts by companies to rebuff culture jamming can also backfire. Multinational coal miner Xstrata sought to remove from YouTube a parodied mining commercial, created as part of an Australian trade union campaign against environmentally destructive mining, but Xstrata's demands simply reignited public interest, and other YouTube users promptly reloaded the video.[68]

Some counter-aesthetic activism targets the actual damaging or unethical practices of industry, a phenomenon that Kevin DeLuca calls 'image politics'.[69] Anti-whaling campaigners in Greenpeace and Sea Shepherd get close to the action to photograph bloody whale carcasses being dismembered by behemoth Japanese whaling ships.[70] The Oscar and Academy award-winning film *The Cove* (2009) exposed dolphin hunting in Japan. Without official permissions, the filmmakers used covert operations like those used to unmask factory farms. *The Cove* includes commentary on the International Whaling Commission's obsequious stance to Japan in declining to protect small cetaceans. Another eye-opening film is *Leviathan* (2014), which takes viewers into the apocalyptic world of the North American fishing industry. One reviewer praised how the film 'plunges us into the sights and sounds of this visceral business [...] from the

---

[64] Kohn, *Brave New Neighborhoods* (above n 52) 210 (referring to Andrew Shapiro's opinion).

[65] Ibid, 215.

[66] A Samuel, *Hactivism and the Future of Political Participation* (PhD thesis, Harvard University, 2004) iii.

[67] The website was originally www.dow-chemical.com, and later shut down.

[68] R Butler, 'Xstrata Parody Leaves Mining Giant Fuming Yet Again' *Sydney Morning Herald* 24 April 2012.

[69] K DeLuca, *Image Politics: The New Rhetoric of Environmental Activism* (Routledge, 2005).

[70] P Heller, *The Whale Warriors: The Battle at the Bottom of the World to Save the Planet's Largest Mammals* (Free Press, 2007).

slashing and ripping of blades upon silver flesh to the piercing cries of greedy gulls overhead'.[71] *Leviathan* was created by the Harvard Sensory Ethnography Lab, which describes its mission as to give 'attention to the many dimensions of the world, both animate and inanimate, that may only with difficulty, if it all, be rendered with words'.[72]

Figure 8.5 Sea Shepherd crew hurls a bottle of rotten butter at Japanese ship, 2009, photograph by Guano; licensed under Creative Commons

Where footage cannot be obtained, activists may stage publicity stunts that resemble performance art. To dramatise the violence of cosmetic testing on animals, artist Jacqueline Traide collaborated with the retailer Lush Cosmetics in April 2012 to allow herself to be a 'tortured' test subject, force-fed and chemically stained.[73] The realistic theatrics were staged in a Lush shop window in London's Regent Street and live-steamed to an online audience. The US-based Earth First has done many performance stunts, notably its 1981 'cracking' of the Glen Canyon Dam in Arizona.[74] Its activists tossed something over the edge of the dam that created what appeared to be 'tiny black gash'; it was, however, just a roll of black plastic. The so-called crack 'was a wisecrack, a daring bit of humour in an environmental movement that had become glum and solemn'.[75] Earth First's pranks, some playful, some illegal, offer particularly memorable aesthetics of environmental protest.

[71] P Howell, 'Leviathan: a Fish-eye View Aboard a Commercial Trawler: Review' *Toronto Star* 14 March 2013.

[72] Harvard Sensory Ethnography Lab, http://sel.fas.harvard.edu.

[73] T Omond, 'Lush's Human Performance Art was about Animal Cruelty Not Titillation' *The Guardian* 27 April 2012.

[74] SA Standing, 'Earth First's "Crack the Dam" and the Aesthetics of Ecoactivist Performance' in W Arons and TJ May (eds), *Readings in Performance and Ecology. What is Theatre?* (Palgrave Macmillan, 2012) 147.

[75] R Scarce, *Eco-Warriors: Understanding the Radical Environmental Movement* (Noble Press, 1990) 57.

C. Impact and Influence

We know much more about the goings-on of counter-aesthetic activism than its efficacy. The impact and influence of such work cannot be stated definitely here, as it requires major, long-term empirical studies; but some pertinent anecdotal evidence corroborates its avowed importance.

Certainly, some antics attract much publicity; Brandalism's stunt at the 2015 Paris Summit enthralled mainstream media, some with sympathetic reporting in the Huffington Post and the BBC.[76] Such publicity may smear the targeted companies' social licence, and thereby exert governance-like discipline to the extent that hurt businesses must genuinely raise their game.[77] Adverse economic repercussions from consumers or investors may also ensue. One closely studied example is the Yes Men's impersonation of Dow Jones on BBC television (discussed earlier), which gave the story direct media access and extensive secondary publicity, resulting in the company's share price temporarily plunging 4 per cent. But the long-term effect of this hoax may have been minimal; researchers found that ironically the hoax appeared to reduce media coverage of the underlying environmental and health consequences of the Bhopal disaster because attention shifted to the Yes Men themselves.[78] Culture jamming may even help the targeted businesses through free advertising, as the irreverent and rebellious qualities of culture jamming may be confused with the marketing style that some companies borrow to engage certain consumer subcultures.[79]

Other evidence suggests that culture jamming sometimes can publicly shame the targeted businesses to induce improvements. Consider Greenpeace's video parodying a Kit Kat commercial. The 2010 clip features a tired office worker who, upon hearing the brand's famous slogan 'Have a break?', opens a Kit Kat wrapper to find not fingers of chocolate but the bloodied finger of an orangutan. The 'advert' closes with viewers urged to 'give the orangutan a break'.[80] The prank was intended by Greenpeace to expose Nestlé's buying of palm oil (a key ingredient in Kit Kats and other products it makes) from destroyed rainforests once home to these apes and many other creatures. Nestlé's was put on the back foot by Greenpeace's stunt, which quickly went viral across the Internet.

---

[76] Cited in Lekakis, 'Culture Jamming' (above n 53) 318.

[77] N Hall et al, 'Social Licence to Operate: Understanding How a Concept has been Translated into Practice in Energy Industries' (2015) 86 *Journal of Cleaner Production* 301.

[78] The researchers found that 'only 2 of the 17 articles discussing the Yes Men's hoax actually explored the health care situation in Bhopal, which was the entire point of the hoax': N Robinson and G Castle Bell, 'Effectiveness of Culture Jamming in Agenda Building: An Analysis of the Yes Men's Bhopal Disaster Prank' (2013) 78(4) *Southern Communication Journal* 352, 363.

[79] C Harold, 'Pranking Rhetoric: "Culture Jamming" as Media Activism' (2004) 21 *Critical Studies in Media Communication* 189.

[80] P Armstrong, 'Greenpeace, Nestlé in Battle Over Kit Kat Viral' *CNN* 20 March 2010, http://edition.cnn.com/2010/WORLD/asiapcf/03/19/indonesia.rainforests.orangutan.nestle/index.html.

Within eight weeks the company agreed to Greenpeace's demands to change suppliers of palm oil.[81]

Another arguable success story comes from anti-coal campaigner Jonathan Moylan, who in 2014 distributed a fake ANZ bank media release causing a AUD $300 million slump in the sharemarket value of Whitehaven, a coal mining company in Australia.[82] Moylan's goal was to publicise the ANZ's support for an environmentally controversial mining project proposed by Whitehaven. Although the company's stock price recovered and the mine went ahead, the publicity damaged the ANZ, which has since tightened its lending criteria for coal mining projects. And although Moyan was successfully prosecuted by authorities for disseminating false information to the market, this sanction also gave his cause more publicity.[83]

Highly skilled in counter aesthetics, animal liberationists seek to shock the public consciousness with often gruesome images and sounds of farm cruelty. Advocates for animal welfare, such as People for the Ethical Treatment of Animals (PETA), use visual and acoustic effects to sensitise us to animal suffering, as though one is literally inside the slaughterhouse. Others take aim at the plight of animals in zoos, aquariums and circuses, although these differ from factory farms and medical labs because they are far more open to public access and observation.[84] Documentary films assembled from covert footage have become a powerful tool for conveying the aesthetics of animal cruelty. The director of the film *Dominion*, which unveiled the horrors of Australia factory farms, explained the goal:

> Industries that profit from the exploitation and abuse of animals hide behind a wall of secrecy – they know that if consumers were to see for themselves what actually occurs in the production of meat, dairy, eggs, leather, etc, they'd stop being consumers and those industries would quickly cease to exist.[85]

Anecdotal evidence suggests such strategies garner publicity that puts pressure on the farming industry. The documentary film *Lucent* (2014), exposing savagery in the pig industry, led the industry to make 'significant changes in its practices in response to community concern', according to one academic assessment.[86]

---

[81] Y Sheffi, 'Profits v Planet: Can Big Business and the Environment Get Along?' *The Guardian* 7 September 2018.

[82] S McVeigh, 'I Wanted to Stop the Mine': Jonathan Moylan and the $300 Million Hoax' *ABC (Triple J)* 3 October 2017, www.abc.net.au/triplej/programs/hack/jono-moylan/9010874.

[83] L Hall, 'Jonathan Moylan Avoids Jail Term for Fake ANZ Media Release About Whitehaven Coal' *Sydney Morning Herald* 25 July 2014.

[84] See eg C van Tuyl, *Zoos and Animal Welfare (Issues That Concern You)* (Greenhaven Press, 2007); M Kiley-Worthington, *Animals in Circuses and Zoos: Chiron's World* (Aardvark Publishing, 1990).

[85] C Delforce, quoted on the Dominion website, www.dominionmovement.com/about.

[86] J Mitchell, 'Dominion "Animal Cruelty" Documentary Angers Farmers' *Farm Online National* 1 April 2018, www.farmonline.com.au/story/5324513/industry-braces-for-documentary-backlash-video/ (interviewing Paul Hemsworth).

We should also assess the impact of counter-aesthetic strategies against changes in government policy and law. Culture jamming aims not only to expose corporate malfeasance and enable consumers to make informed decisions; it also serves to reduce the legitimacy of business in order to achieve better regulation. One notable success is from the Australian pioneer of culture jamming, the BUGA UP group, which from the late 1970s was defacing tobacco and alcohol billboards to thwart their marketing. Its efforts were instrumental not only in achieving advertising bans in Australia, the first major country to prohibit tobacco advertising, it 'helped reframe the global debate about tobacco control'.[87] The hoax Jonathan Moylan perpetrated against the ANZ bank and Whitehaven did not in itself alter the law, but it stimulated scholarly and public debate about the value of civil disobedience as legitimate means of political expression and it pressured the market regulator, the Australian Securities and Investment Corporation, and the major banks, to improve their assessment and disclosure of climate change-related risks, as has since occurred.[88]

The courts have also occasionally been successfully used to defend culture jamming, which thus has ramifications for upholding freedom of speech on social and environmental issues. In the South African case of *Laugh It Off Promotions v South African Breweries International*, the courts considered a claim of trademark infringement from a caricature of the Carling Black Label trademark, with the words 'Black Labour, White Guilt' inserted over Black Label and Carling respectively, and imprinted by the defendant on t-shirts sold for modest commercial gain. Laugh It Off defended its actions, inter alia, as an exercise on constitutionally protected freedom of expression. In weighing up the rights of the trademark proprietor against freedom of expression, the Constitutional Court concluded that the culture jamming prank had no effect on the beer brewer's market dominance or sales, while the 'valuable expressive rights' exercised by Laugh it Off 'ought not to be lightly trampled upon by marginal detriment [...] to the commercial value that vests in the mark itself'.[89]

III. SOCIAL AESTHETICS

A. Protecting the Public Sphere

Enabling a critical social aesthetics requires the law to defend opportunities for non-violent, artistic dissent and dialogue while curbing the intrusive

---

[87] L Partridge and A Chesterfield-Evans, 'BUGA UP Founder Made Unique Push to Ban Tobacco Advertising' *Sydney Morning Herald* 20 March 2018.

[88] M Rimmer, 'Stand with Jono: Culture-jamming, Civil Disobedience, and Corporate Regulation in an Age of Climate Change' in M Maloney and N Rogers (eds), *Law as if Earth Really Mattered: Wild Law Judgments* (Routledge, 2017) 293, 314–20; C Yeates, 'ASIC Warns on Climate Risk as Heat Turns on Directors' *Sydney Morning Herald* 19 June 2018.

[89] *Laugh It Off Promotions CC v South African Breweries International (Finance) BV t/a Sabmark International and Another* [2005] ZACC 7, para 56.

commercial and political aesthetics that undermines them. Corporate marketing and government propaganda, explains James Boy White in his plea to revive
a vibrant public discourse, 'is largely built upon a diminished and diminishing
image of the human being as merely a cluster of wants and desires and upon a
conception of speech as the manipulation of those desires'.[90] The reduction of
the public sphere to an impoverished realm of personal consumption, entertainment and cheap political slogans weakens our capacity to generate a deeper
ethical understanding and commitment to live within the planetary boundaries.
White explains that 'propaganda and advertising [...] are not simply noise we
must put up with, but deeply affect the character of the culture and our minds.
They constitute a kind of speech that destroys real speech'.[91] The aesthetic
blight of advertising and its cousin propaganda ubiquitously invades our urban
and rural landscapes, evident in billboards, neon signs, junk mail, posters, as
well as the parallel realm of cyberspace, in incessant competition for the public's
attention. Not only do they spawn visual and acoustic clutter, their messages
peddle crap and simplify the human experience to consumerist and prejudicial
thinking.

For the law, the challenge begins with defending basic civil liberties for freedom of association and expression; in many jurisdictions, such as China, these
cannot be taken for granted. Even in Western, liberal-democratic regimes, civil
liberties are under threat from regulations in the name of blunting terrorist
threats or protecting business interests. So-called 'anti-protest' legislation has
been fervently adopted in several Australian states recently to curb social activism, under the guise of 'protecting the rights of workers' to labour free from
harassment.[92] These laws not only criminalise a variety of ordinary protest
actions, they can give bureaucrats broad powers to ban or control rallies and
demonstrations on public lands.[93] In 2019, the South Dakota legislature adopted
another type of anti-protest law, which penalises so-called 'riot boosting' with
fines by allowing the state government and third parties to sue anyone that offered
support (eg financial or organisational) for a protest that was later declared by
the state to have fomented a 'riot'.[94] The law, since challenged in court, aims to
deter the state's anti-pipeline protesters. Ag-gag laws, as discussed in Chapter 4,
can exert a similarly chilling effect on activists, specifically in the animal rights
field. The extension of defamation law protections to corporations can likewise

---

[90] JB White, *Living Speech* (Princeton University Press, 2006) 27.
[91] Ibid.
[92] L White and B MacKenzie, 'New Protest Regulations Labelled "A Fundamental Attack
on Democracy" Will Start in NSW from July 1' *ABC News*, 26 June 2018, www.abc.net.au/
news/2018-06-26/new-protest-regulations-labelled-attack-on-democracy/9905676.
[93] Eg Workplaces (Protection from Protesters) Act 2014 (Tas); Crown Land Management Regulation 2018 (NSW). The Tasmanian law was successfully challenged by environmentalists in the
High Court as an infringement of the constitutional right of political communication, but as I write
authorities are redrafting the legislation to get around this setback: *Brown v Tasmania* [2017]
HCA 43.
[94] South Dakota Senate Bill 189, 2019.

embolden the business sector to silence culture-jamming critics. Consumer and investor protection law also serve this purpose (as against the greenwashing companies); for instance Jonathan Moylan was charged (and convicted) under Australia's Corporations Act 2001 (Cth)[95] for making false and misleading statements associated with his prank against the ANZ bank and Whitehaven.[96] Governments also undermine public dialogue by reducing funding for public broadcasters while allowing more concentrated private ownership of media industries, as with Murdoch's omnipresent News Corp.

Public spaces such as town squares, plazas, parks, pavements and other areas open for people to mingle and converse are also threatened by commerce and consumerism. Shopping malls, which have become a major 'public' gathering place in modern society, with over 45,000 established in the United States in the last half of the twentieth century,[97] in fact are commonly managed by their proprietors as private spaces with restrictions on what patrons can wear, say or do, as policed by private security forces. American courts have deemed the constitutional rights of freedom of expression do not extend to shopping malls, defined to be unlike the traditional public town square.[98] Through these and other legally sanctioned stances, 'the opportunities for political conversation are diminished' explains political scientist Margaret Kohn.[99] Public speaking, demonstrations, leafleting and petitioning, which allow for direct engagements and live debates, thereby get pushed further aside.

Corporate encroachment into the public arena has extended to schools, which in North America are being 'transformed into a commercial enterprise, and reoriented towards a more integrated relationship with commercial interests', explains Trevor Norris who has studied the surge in corporate sponsorships of and marketing in public (and private) schools.[100] School classrooms, gymnasiums and other facilities display brandings of their corporate sponsors, while unsolicited marketing pervades school buses, textbooks and drink-vending machines.[101] Business target schools because they offer formative milieux for instilling ideological messages in vulnerable, receptive audiences.

While the Internet has created a new type of public space, it has potential limitations as a substitute for intimate and direct encounters. As Kohn succinctly explains, 'face-to-face political debate allows for citizens to ask questions and challenge answers. Furthermore, the politics of public space requires few resources and therefore allows marginal viewpoints to be expressed

---

[95] Section 1041E.

[96] Australian Securities and Investment Commission, '14-179MR Jonathan Moylan Convicted' media release, 25 July 2014.

[97] WS Kowinski, *The Malling of America: Travels in the United States of Shopping* (Xlibris, 2002).

[98] Kohn, *Brave New Neighborhoods* (above n 52) 70–74.

[99] Ibid, 2.

[100] T Norris, *Consuming Schools: Commercialism and the End of Politics* (University of Toronto Press, 2011) 43.

[101] Ibid, 44–49.

[and] debated'.[102] Twitter 'debates', blogs or email exchanges do not allow for participants to come together with the same intimacy. The private nature of website site hosting and browsing also makes it difficult for third parties to hijack advertisements to propagate their political discourse.

Encouragingly, some interesting legal precedents putting the brakes on corporate aesthetics have emerged in a few localities. Some municipalities restrict intrusive advertising. The Brazilian city of São Paulo, home to 12 million, has since 2007 banned billboards and posters in public areas including buses and trains to rid the city of 'visual pollution'.[103] Canberra, Australia, has likewise maintained a long-standing ban on roadside billboards, except on bus shelters, with the overwhelming approval of its residents.[104] Indeed, a global movement to restrict the proliferation of outdoor advertising is intensifying, with the law rolling back aesthetic pollution in Chennai (India), Tehran and Paris, among many cities.[105] And in 2014 Farida Shaheed, the UN Special Rapporteur in the field of cultural rights, called on governments to protect their societies 'from undue levels of commercial advertising and marketing while increasing the space for not-for-profit expressions'.[106] Much more of course must be done beyond banning unsightly billboards.

A bit of headway is also being made in some jurisdictions with intellectual property law, which should be reconciled with the need to protect freedoms of expression and protest in an open democracy. Culture jamming actions can amount to infringement of trademarks or copyright protected works, as well as violations of the creator's moral rights of attribution of authorship. Researchers have recommended that legislators create more generous 'fair use' exceptions for defined spheres of activity such as culture jamming.[107] Australia's Copyright Act 1968 (Cth) was amended in 2006 to protect those manipulating copyright material for the fair use purpose of parody and satire, although with amendments that also made it easier to sustain criminal prosecution against unlawful infringements.[108] As earlier noted, already the South African courts in the *Laugh it Off* case sided with the culture jammer's rights of expression.[109]

---

[102] Kohn, *Brave New Neighborhoods* (above n 52) 4.

[103] A Downie, 'São Paulo Sells Itself' *Time* 8 February 2008, http://content.time.com/time/specials/2007/article/0,28804,1709961_1711305_1860002,00.html.

[104] An Ordinance Relating to Roads and Other Public Spaces, No 24, 1937, s 12; E Baker, 'Canberra Billboard Ban: New Polling Shows Disapproval for Relaxing of Laws' *Canberra Times* 18 February 2018.

[105] A Mahdawi, 'Can Cities Kick Ads? Inside the Global Movement to Ban Urban Billboards' *The Guardian* 13 August 2015.

[106] United Nations Human Rights, 'UN Expert in Cultural Rights Calls for Greater Scrutiny and Control of Commercial Advertising', media release 28 October 2014, www.ohchr.org/EN/News Events/Pages/DisplayNews.aspx?NewsID=15229&LangID=E.

[107] B Fitzgerald and D O'Brien, 'Digital Sampling and Culture Jamming in a Remix World: What Does the Law Allow?' in B Fitzgerald, J Coates and S Lewis (eds), *Open Content Licensing: Cultivating the Creative Commons* (Sydney University Press, 2007) 156.

[108] Sections 103AA, and132AA-AT.

[109] *Laugh It Off Promotions CC* (above, n 90).

Several US cases have also condoned parodying of business trademarks as protected non-commercial free speech, so long as parodying does not devalue the mark by affecting consumer preferences – an outcome of course that culture jammers often wish to achieve.[110]

B. Enhancing Social Aesthetics

Governments must not only protect the integrity of the public sphere, they must enable social aesthetics to flourish. I will comment here on two strategies of particular importance, one being interdisciplinary, multi-stakeholder collaborations, especially between the arts and natural sciences. The other is civic environmentalism, through a variety means from public participation in environmental governance to opening public museums to more engaging modes of aesthetic appreciation. These strategies are closely intertwined.

Civic environmentalism, meaning the involvement of grassroots communities in environmental practices and decisions, matters because it dovetails with the goals of increasing the opportunities for people to experience nature aesthetics, as well as improving the legitimacy of their aesthetic judgements. This impetus benefits from trends in many jurisdictions to offer a variety of opportunities for public involvement in environmental policy making and regulation, including in EIAs, development licensing, public inquiries and access to the courts. Such participatory governance ostensibly treats all members of society as competent to contribute because of the axiological character of many environmental decisions. Public participation may thus influence decisions of aesthetic significance, such as protection of scenic landscapes. Yet, environmental law also draws heavily on the expertise of specific stakeholders, such as scientific professionals, and its governing norms, for example the precautionary principle and polluter pays principle, are premised on the application of specialist knowledge.

This tension in the law between lay and expert knowledge mirrors a similar tension in aesthetics theory. Allen Carlson expresses scepticism that uneducated lay people's preferences will correlate with aesthetic quality because of their supposed lack of experience and knowledge about aesthetic judgement.[111] Instead, like the connoisseur of fine art, Carlson recommends that expert environmental critics provide objective assessments of nature aesthetics. As we also already know, Carlson has opponents. Robert Ribe for one directly challenged him in their exchange in the journal *Landscape and Planning*, arguing that

---

[110] See eg *Mattel Inc v Walking Mountain Prods*, 353 F3d 792 (9th Cir 2003). See also E McDonnell, 'Never Mind the Bullocks: Shepard Fairey's Fight for Appropriation, Fair Use, and Free Culture' in M DeLaure, M Fink and M Dery (eds), *Culture Jamming: Activism and the Art of Cultural Resistance* (New York University Press, 2017) 179, 188–89.

[111] A Carlson, 'On the Possibility of Quantifying Scenic Beauty' (1977) 4 *Landscape and Planning* 131, 145.

'[u]nlike art objects, natural scenery is all about us every day and becomes integrated with our recreational values and our understanding of the world. Consequently, many people gain valuable experience at appreciating landscapes'.[112]

Emphasising public participation should not necessarily mean succumbing to a 'free for all' in aesthetic judgements, because opportunities for voice do not mean the views of each are equally valid. We sense aesthetic properties subjectively, such as the sound of a bird or view of a mountain, but the significance and value of these properties are open to debate. Informed aesthetic judgements that prevail in such debates, and thereby influence environmental governance, might ensue from scientific knowledge or a personal understanding of the history and culture of a place. Aesthetic judgements, in other words, hinge on giving persuasive reasons to make them socially relevant. The final section of this chapter examines this issue further under the rubric of adjudicating aesthetics where the law must reckon with competing aesthetic preferences. Aesthetic *experiences*, of more relevance to a critical aesthetics, may help reduce differences in how we judge nature aesthetics when supported by governance systems tied to interdisciplinary collaboration and civic environmentalism.

Enhancing the public's aesthetic experiences in nature can be curated through opportunities for hands-on activities that integrate environmental science into aesthetic appreciation. The arts and natural sciences are being wedded through new mediums such as documentary films. Examples such as *Plastic Ocean* (2013) (exposing marine plastic pollution), *The End of the Line* (2019) (challenging global overfishing), and Al Gore's *Inconvenient Truth* (2006) (climate change), have become a popular strategy for eco-artists and scientists to collaboratively shape public discourse.[113] These partnerships, no doubt, may also foster narratives that marginalise certain perspectives and issues, but they at least generate critical public debate that helps justify them.

A more grassroots mode of interdisciplinary collaboration is 'citizen science', a global phenomenon that provides direct community participation in nature aesthetics. Citizen science projects involve lay people participating in environmental monitoring to help researchers understand environmental baselines and changes that can then feed into management actions. Citizens' science taps into a valuable community resource while enhancing participants' ecological knowledge and ethical commitment. Citizen science projects include tracking marine plastic debris,[114] counting birds[115] and monitoring butterflies.[116] Advances in

---

[112] RG Ribe, 'On the Possibility of Quantifying Scenic Beauty – A Response' (1982) 9 *Landscape and Planning* 61, 64.

[113] L Henderson, 'Q&A: A Plastic Ocean – Can a Movie Help Us See this Invisible Crisis?' *The Conversation* 7 June 2016, https://theconversation.com.

[114] PE Duckett and V Repaci, 'Marine Plastic Pollution: Using Community Science to Address a Global Problem' (2015) 66(8) *Marine and Freshwater Research* 665.

[115] J Greenwood, 'Citizens, Science and Bird Conservation' (2007) 148 *Journal of Ornithology* 77.

[116] E Howard and AK Davis, 'Documenting the Spring Movements of Monarch Butterflies with Journey North, a Citizen Science Program' in KS Oberhauser and MJ Solensky (eds), *The Monarch Butterfly: Biology and Conservation* (Cornell University Press, 2004) 105.

information technology, both in recording and sharing the data such as the Global Positioning System and remote camera 'trapping', have greatly expanded opportunities for citizen science to recruit larger audiences of volunteers. Citizen science projects may also involve curated explorations of specific environments, such as South Africa's 'Journey of Water' in which groups are taken on guided walks to trace the source of their water. The project, coordinated by World Wide Fund for Nature, helps communities to understand the importance of protecting water catchments and saving water, an increasingly scarce resource as climate change makes South Africa's rainfall less reliable.[117] The treks can last several days, allowing participants to encounter and learn about 'abandoned mines that pollute [their] water sources, irresponsible land use that accelerate creeping erosion and collapsed sewage infrastructure that pour human waste into rivers'.[118] The aesthetic dimensions of such citizen science accrue in the time spent outdoors, collecting environmental data or reflecting on the results such as wildlife imagery or guided talks.

Eco-restoration offers another realm for participatory social aesthetics. In Chapter 6 we considered examples of community participation in restoration projects, such as the Tasmanian Island Ark project. Here artists were engaged with regional schools and local communities in designing sculptures to place in the rehabilitating countryside, not only to support the community's interpretation of the recovering natural biodiversity but also to directly aid its conservation by serving as 'species hotels' for birds, bats and other small mammals.[119] Even without such artistic embellishments, numerous eco-restoration projects worldwide tap into grassroots community support and thereby enrich participants' opportunities for nature aesthetic appreciation while improving their ecological literacy. They include restoration of Mexico's Tehuacán-Cuicatlán biosphere reserve, Scotland's Trees for Life project, Africa's Great Green Wall program, the Misiones reforestation project in Argentina and coral reef restoration in Bali, Indonesia, among probably thousands of examples globally.[120]

Urban environments matter equally for social aesthetics. A limitation of some thinking about environmental aesthetics is to conceive of the natural world as "out there" in remote mountain ranges, in rainforests, in the depths of the oceans', a dichotomy that Sim van der Ryn and Stuart Cowan explain 'has allowed us to conveniently believe that our activities can be carried out without consideration of their wider consequences'.[121] Concomitantly, the infrastructure and services that draw on nature for our sustenance or to remove

[117] Journey of Water, www.journeyofwater.co.za.

[118] WWF, 'It's Time to Take the Journey of Our Water', *Our News*, 11 May 2017, www.wwf.org. za/?20861/Its-time-to-take-the-journey-of-our-water.

[119] Greening Australia, 'Building Hotels for Tasmania's Unique Species', www.greeningaustralia. org.au/news/building-hotels-for-tasmanias-unique-species.

[120] See further ME Krasny and KG Tidball, *Civic Ecology: Adaptation and Transformation from the Ground Up* (MIT Press, 2015).

[121] S van der Ryn and S Cowan, *Ecological Design* (Island Press, 2007) 188.

our waste are hidden away.[122] These may be the landfills, water pipes, or abattoirs that we wish to keep out of sight, and even the wind turbines that some consider eyesores. Yet we need to connect nature intimately to our senses if we are to make more environmentally responsible decisions. Responding to this challenge, landscape architect Robert Thayer advocates an aesthetic of 'visual ecology', in which we design built environments to make visible the underlying natural processes and resources on which society depends.[123]

The concept of 'reconciliation ecology' provides a useful focus for the aesthetics of environmental recovery around human settlements. Best theorised by Michael Rosenzweig,[124] reconciliation ecology describes restoration projects that benefit people by drawing them closer to their natural environs, including aesthetic and recreational benefits. Such reconciliation often takes place in urban areas to bring nature back into human lives, such as expanded city parks, restored waterways, green roofs and other ways to embed nature in our surroundings. One outstanding example is 'Zealandia', a restored bird-rich sanctuary located near the heart of Wellington, the capital city of New Zealand.[125] Another, acclaimed by Rosenzweig himself, is the creation of crocodile-attracting habitat in the cooling canals of the Turkey Point power station near Miami, Florida.[126] This agenda requires land use planning to protect and restore urban parks and greenbelts, plus measures to boost the creation of green roofs and green walls.

Natural history museums are another vital public realm where governments can promote science-informed aesthetic experiences for everyone. While museums have shared complicity in the aesthetics of vanquished nature, as Chapter 4 showed, in recent years many have redesigned their displays with different narratives and aesthetic tools better aligned to contemporary environmental challenges. I will give one concrete example.

The Tasmanian Museum and Art Gallery (TMAG) curated a special exhibition in 2017–18 called *The Remarkable Tasmanian Devil*,[127] which helped to engage and educate the public about a marsupial carnivore once persecuted with official bounties, but which in recent years has become a treasured tourist ambassador and Tasmania's official animal emblem with full legal protection. The exhibition featured a variety of artworks, taxidermy specimens and historical memorabilia that trace the shifting public perceptions of the species over

---

[122] Ibid.

[123] R Thayer Jr, *Gray World, Green Heart: Technology, Nature and the Sustainable Landscape* (John Wiley and Sons, 1994) passim.

[124] M Rosenzweig, *Win-Win Ecology* (Oxford University Press, 2003).

[125] Zealandlia, www.visitzealandia.com.

[126] Johns Hopkins Bloomberg School of Public Health, 'Ecologist Urges Sharing Land with Other Species to Foster Biodiversity', 22 March 2004, www.jhsph.edu/news/stories/2004/reconciliation. html.

[127] This discussion draws partially on my co-authored publication: BJ Richardson and J Hogan, 'The Remarkable Tasmanian Devil: The Aesthetics of Persecution and Protection' (2018) 43(4) *Alternative Law Journal* 269.

two centuries since Europeans colonised Tasmania.[128] The TMAG exhibition not only successfully conveyed how aesthetics has powerfully mediated the devil's legal and cultural status, it deepened visitors' understanding of the scientific value and conservation significance of the species. The opening display delved into the origins of its common name, given by early European settlers encountering its nocturnal growls. By 1830, just 27 years after the founding of the Tasmanian penal colony, bounties were offered for dead devils; its negative aesthetics and outlawed status went hand-in-hand. The other galleries in the TMAG exhibition traced how public affection for the devil later blossomed, such as with memorabilia about its status as a mascot for an army battalion in the First World War and its depiction as a Warner Brothers' cartoon character in the 1950s.

One of the most poignant displays was the contrasting, real road signage to warn motorists of crossing devils. The TMAG caption of the pre-2010 sign explained, 'road signs depicted the Tasmanian devil as an evil creature with large teeth and an angry expression'. The relevant image (below, to the left) shows gunshot damage, which the caption notes was once a 'not uncommon' public reaction. In contrast, the post-2010 signage (below, to the right) depicts a devil with the faint suggestion of a smile or 'almost panda-like appearance', notes the caption.

Figure 8.6 Tasmanian devil road signage, 2018; photograph by Benjamin J Richardson; Tasmanian Museum and Art Gallery

Greater scientific knowledge of the devil, along with public awareness of its ecological value, has helped lift the creature's aesthetic appeal. One exhibit at the TMAG deals with the official proclamation on 25 May 2015 of the devil

---

[128] Threatened Species Act 1995 (Tas); Environment Protection and Biodiversity Conservation Act 1999 (Cth).

as Tasmania's official animal emblem, a concrete example of how aesthetics can symbolically inform expressions of governmental authority. The same endorsement is found at Tasmania's international airport at Hobart, where photographs and sculptures of devils adorn the arrival hall.

The TMAG exhibition dovetails with the agenda of social aesthetics. Specifically, it exemplifies Jane Bennett's argument about the importance of public spaces of 'vital materiality' that can help society cultivate more environmentally sensitive discourse.[129] Natural history museums can assimilate art, science and even law for enabling visitors to re-imagine the plight of wildlife to support their protection rather than persecution. While the law does not usually regulate the content or curating of museum exhibitions, government authorities can use soft governance mechanisms such as museum funding, community education, road signage and symbolic gestures including official animal emblems to facilitate aesthetic appreciation of imperilled wildlife or other environmental issues.[130] Natural history museums provide unique forums for public education and dialogue about environmental aesthetics, and their pedagogical benefits are vital collateral elements for cultivating critical aesthetics. Their public salience has also made them an enticing target for activists looking for novel ways to propagate their message; London's Natural History Museum was inundated by climate change protesters in April 2019 staging their 'Extinction Rebellion' to raise awareness of the 'sixth mass extinction' that looms.[131]

IV. AESTHETICS OF ENGAGEMENT AND VULNERABILITY

A. Right to Roam

Facilitating social aesthetics must extend to reclaiming physical spaces for the community to experience nature's aesthetic complexity. People need opportunities to connect closely with a lived nature, as opposed to just one in a museum – a nature they can see, hear, feel and smell. While the arts can sensitise the public to the aesthetics of environmental change on temporal and spatial scales beyond what we can personally sense, challenging 'out of sight, out of mind', we must still promote the direct and intimate sensory engagement with the natural world.

As we should all know, modern life has progressively distanced humanity from nature, resulting for many not only in impoverished sensory engagement but accompanying low ecological literacy including limited knowledge of how our food is produced, where our energy comes from or where our waste goes. Research surveys reveal just how rare it is for many people to spend time in

---

[129] J Bennett, *Vibrant Matter: A Political Ecology of Things* (Duke University Press, 2010).

[130] E Archer, Minister for Environment and Parks, 'Our Remarkable Devil', press release, 7 December 2017.

[131] T Whipple, 'Climate Group Stages "Die-in" at Natural History Museum' *The Times* 23 April 2019.

nature, for example by hiking and camping. An Australian Bureau of Statistics study in 2000 revealed that just 3.2 per cent of Australians had gone bushwalking in the previous year, a paltry figure for a country renowned for its extensive outdoor opportunities.[132] Far more Australians played tennis or went jogging than nature hiking for their outdoor experience. Studies of North Americans and Europeans have found that about 90 per cent of people spend close to 22 hours indoors every day.[133] A 2016 British study of declining time spent outdoors in our digitised world carried the headline 'three-quarters of UK children spend less time outside than prison inmates'.[134] Having personally visited Chinese cities, I fear that in the world's most populous country even fewer of its citizens get to experience nature than these numbers from Western countries.

We should not underestimate the importance of getting into nature, not just for invigorating one's personal health but also to shape environmental attitudes. Australian bush walking clubs, established from the late nineteenth century for amateur naturalists, were pioneers for engaging people with both the aesthetics and science of nature conservation, and from this interest they became pioneers in lobbying for legal protection for nature.[135] While these clubs were somewhat socially elitist and wedded to a wilderness aesthetic that excluded Australia's Aboriginal history, they did foster a less exploitative view based on the aesthetic and recreational values of nature.

The law can facilitate public access to nature not only in the conventionally understood way of setting aside national parks for aesthetic and recreational pleasure, but also by legislating rights of access to private lands. I wish to comment on the latter, because the so-called 'right to roam' has stirred controversy in some countries. In Canada, Australia, Ireland and the United States, among examples, the public cannot roam on private property, even in uncultivated and unsettled areas.[136] In its 1979 ruling in *Kaiser Aetna v United States*, the US Supreme Court affirmed the landowner's right to exclude others as 'one of the most essential sticks in the bundle of rights that are commonly characterized as property'.[137] The United States, along with Canada and Australia, have quite substantial national park systems, but many reserves are remote from major population clusters (Toronto and New York for instance), and some parks do not allow camping or foraging for wild produce.

By contrast, many European countries affirm a public right of access to nature that overrides landowners' right to exclude. Their right to roam laws open up private and public lands to all for hiking, picnicking, camping, collecting plants and other activities that can enrich people's appreciation of nature

---

[132] Australian Bureau of Statistics (ABS), *Participation in Sport and Physical Activities* (ABS, 2002).

[133] Cited in S Walden, 'The "Indoor Generation" and the Health Risks of Spending More Time Inside' *USA Today* 15 May 2018.

[134] Reported in D Carrington, 'Three-quarters of UK Children Spend Less Time Outdoors Than Prison Inmates – Survey' *The Guardian* 25 March 2016.

[135] M Harper, *The Ways of the Bushwalker: On Foot in Australia* (UNSW Press, 2007).

[136] K Ilgunas, *This is Our Land: How We lost the Right to Roam and How to Take it Back* (Penguin, 2018).

[137] *Kaiser Aetna v United States*, 444 US 164, 176 (1979).

aesthetics while improving their ecological literacy. The exercise of these rights sometimes alienates some landowners, such as disputes over lack of upkeep of trails, and civil liability claims from injured walkers, but the social positives outweigh these objections.[138]

Great Britain has some 225,000 km of paths and rights of way through government and private lands, which the public may roam through under legislated rights.[139] The Countryside and Rights of Way Act 2000 affirms a public right to roam on certain upland and uncultivated lands, as well as registered common lands, across England and Wales. More generous, the Land Reform (Scotland) Act 2003 codifies a customary norm of public access to open countryside so long as roamers do not damage or interfere with agricultural activities. The Scottish Outdoor Access Code guides the exercise of these rights, including specifying permissible activities that comprise horse riding, swimming, canoeing, nature photography and dog walking.[140] Campers may stay up to three nights in the same place, and leave 'no trace' under the duty to avoid littering or create other environmental desecrations.

In Scandinavia, the law offers copious rights for roamers. In Norway, the ancient *'allemannsrett'* (the 'everyman's rights') is formally codified under the Outdoor Recreation Act 1957, which defines its purpose as 'to safeguard the public right of access to and passage through the countryside' for 'leisure activity that is healthy, environmentally sound and gives a sense of well-being'.[141] The Norwegian Government's 'Visit Norway' website explains 'you can walk nearly anywhere you want', excluding cultivated fields, military sites or near dwellings, so long as one causes no damage and asks the landowner's permission if one wishes to camp more than two nights in the same place.[142] The Norwegian right to roam extends, in forests, to picking flowers, berries and mushrooms. Unlike the wilderness philosophy that decrees exclusion of human beings, the Norwegian ethos embraces people's active presence in the landscape. Also, many Norwegians maintain their own log cabins and huts in these areas, or utilise shared facilities maintained by clubs such as the Norwegian Trekking Association.

Among its peers, Iceland's Nature Conservation Act 1999 contains 15 articles that extensively delineate the public's right to roam, including for camping, picking berries and mushrooms, along with a duty to respect the natural environment with 'the utmost care'.[143] The Swedish right to roam is similar to

---

[138] See eg K Højring, 'The Right to Roam the Countryside – Law and Reality Concerning Public Access to the Landscape in Denmark' (2002) 59(1) *Landscape and Urban Planning* 29.

[139] JL Anderson, 'Britain's Right to Roam: Redefining the Landowner's Bundle of Sticks' (2006–07) 19 *Georgetown International Environmental Law Review* 375.

[140] See www.outdooraccess-scotland.scot.

[141] Act of 28 June 1957 No 16, s 1.

[142] 'The Right to Roam: Joys and Responsibilities', www.visitnorway.com/plan-your-trip/travel-tips-a-z/right-of-access.

[143] Act No 44, 1999, art 12; and also arts 13–27.

Norway's and affirmed in the national constitution.[144] Swedish roamers enjoy few limitations, among them the standard prohibition on causing environmental damage or intruding on homeowners' privacy.[145]

Importantly, rights to roam on private property or access to national parks centre on *walking*. Some philosophers construe walking as an aesthetic experience, enabling far greater sensory immersion in nature than from inside a motor vehicle.[146] In addition, vehicles can cause roadkill, soil disturbance and noise. Sometimes vehicles are essential where one might encounter dangerous animals, such as on African safaris, but mostly this isn't so. Not surprisingly then, environmental lawyers have occasionally had to fight against the encroachment of roads and SUV motorists into natural areas. One such conflict in Tasmania resulted in litigation challenging the government's decision in 2014 to open tracks in an area of Aboriginal heritage significance to four-wheel vehicles.[147] Walking through nature, by contrast, enables one to hear, smell and see a much greater variety of natural elements, and for artists such as Hamish Fulton constitutes an art practice in its own right.[148]

The right to roam concretely can give legal effect to the aesthetics of engagement advocated by Berleant and Saito. The law can curate such aesthetic experiences in a low level way, by upholding access rights, delineating permissible activities such as picking berries and camping, and affirming roamers' responsibilities to tread carefully. Where roaming occurs on private lands, one is unlikely to find any interpretative signage, such as that used in national parks, which educates ramblers about the ecology or history of the place. Such curatorial guidance might instead be found in travel books and wildlife field guides. If the right to roam extends our opportunities to enter nature, how can the law allow nature to enter our lives? The next section turns to this other side of the relationship.

B. The Aesthetics of Vulnerability

The concept of vulnerability, or more specifically the vulnerable human subject, is no stranger to aesthetics theory and art practice.[149] It matters especially for

---

[144] Constitution of Sweden (Instrument of Government), c 12, art 15.

[145] Visit Sweden, 'About the Right to Access Swedish Nature', https://visitsweden.com/about-the-right-of-public-access.

[146] C Tilley, 'Walking: The Past in the Present' in A Arnason et al (eds), *Landscapes Beyond Land: Routes, Aesthetics and Narratives* (Berghahn Books, 2012) 15.

[147] The Federal Court of Australia found that the government's decision-making was contrary to the Environmental Protection and Biodiversity Conservation Act 1999 (Cth): *Secretary, Department of Primary Industries, Parks, Water and Environment v Tasmanian Aboriginal Centre Incorporated* [2016] FCAFC 129.

[148] See his website, www.hamish-fulton.com.

[149] M Coeckelbergh, *Human Being @ Risk: Enhancement, Technology, and the Evaluation of Vulnerability Transformations* (Springer, 2013); JM Ganteau, *The Ethics and Aesthetics of Vulnerability in Contemporary British Fiction* (Routledge, 2015).

conceiving our frail dependencies on the natural world, as introduced in the previous chapter on climate change. Unlike the aesthetics of engagement, which emphasise our sensory immersion in nature, the aesthetics of vulnerability embrace the engagement of nature in our world including even the risks of encountering environmental adversity. Tolerating such vulnerability matters, as it underpins an ethic of respect for other creatures and the ecological processes on which they and we depend. Vulnerability isn't just about intellectualising our dependence on the life-sustaining biosphere, be it for water or soil, but extends to more intimate sensory engagement with nature's forces by allowing them to enter our lives tangibly and directly. Nature cannot be desensitised as a realm 'out there', quarantined in a few national parks, but should envelop our daily lives in material and sensory dimensions. This agenda overlaps with the principle of proximity, as introduced in Chapter 3, which behoves environmental decision-making to reduce the sensory gap between our activities and their impacts so that we become more sensitive to the otherwise 'absent' aesthetics of environmental degradation.

Our aesthetics of vulnerability have changed over the centuries. Earlier this book revealed how in the West the arts helped shift unfavourable perceptions of nature, once stigmatised for harbouring supernatural forces or dangerous beasts, to a more comforting reputation associated with the 'picturesque' and 'bucolic'. Even nature's most unruly elements, as in violent storms associated with the 'sublime', were capable of being aesthetically admired through 'disinterested' observation. Yet fear of nature's darker side has never been entirely purged from our psyche; it lingers in popular films set in gloomy woods or disaster movies featuring earthquakes or other acts of God. Pacification of such unruly natural forces occupies many countries. Government policies for draining wetlands, impounding rivers and clearing forests in the name of 'progress', serve to domesticate or simplify nature to suit our convenience and comfort. Such policies imply that an untamed nature not only wastes economic potential but also threatens our well-being because of the personal dangers of floods, fires, pestilence or other menaces.

With an intensifying Anthropocene that engenders species extinctions and even loss of entire ecosystems, a new uneasiness about nature has emerged, combining a fear of calamitous change with the mournful loss of some of our once familiar surroundings.[150] One increasingly publicised anxiety is the decline in the abundance and diversity of pollinating insects, especially bees, which threatens the collapse of our food systems – the ultimate vulnerability.[151] Climate change, associated with intensifying natural calamities, is inspiring searches for new ways of dominating nature through so-called climate geo-engineering,

---

[150] A Consolo and KR Landman (eds), *Mourning Nature: Hope at the Heart of Ecological Loss and Grief* (McGill-Queen's University Press, 2017).
[151] M Schacker, *A Spring Without Bees* (Lyons Press, 2008).

which offers the prospect of the most comprehensive suppression conceivable of our vulnerabilities to nature.

Responding to the foregoing issues, vulnerability as an element of critical aesthetics hinges on two key dimensions. Firstly, we must be sensitive to the living needs of plants, animals, ecological cycles and other natural elements because humanity's long-term survival depends on their flourishing. In calling for greater acceptance of vulnerability, Katie Woolaston argues that the Western ideology of personal autonomy and individualism has engendered an ideological unwillingness in government policies to adequately recognise the realities of humanity's symbiosis with the biosphere.[152] Secondly, the aesthetics of vulnerability requires co-existence with rather than suppression of natural forces, from forest fires to floods. Making ourselves less vulnerable to nature's agency not only changes the environmental aesthetics, by removing or insulating us from some of the sensory dimensions of encounters with nature, it also ultimately damages nature by diminishing its life-sustaining processes. The following examples elaborate these ideas further.

One illustration is the legalised control of floodplains, serving to reduce or prevent calamitous inundation of low-lying riparian lands. Dams, diversion canals, river defences and levees designed by civil engineers serve to reduce our vulnerability. Such measures initially allow for more housing, farming and other 'productive' uses to take over nature's space. It's not always successful however, as occasionally monster deluges overwhelm even the most ambitious flood defences (which in turn sometimes trigger more concerted defensive efforts). The loss of floodplains, a wetland, removes a vital ecological process that spreads nutrients and other organic materials to enrich lowland soils, and replenishes water resources necessary for a variety of biodiversity. Diminution of floodplains also removes from our sensory realm one of nature's most dramatic ephemeral environments, still evident in a few places such as Botswana's Okavango Delta and Brazil's Pantanal.

As I finish this book, a dispute is brewing in NSW over the government's plan to enlarge the Warragamba Dam that supplies the city of Sydney with drinking water, aiming to reduce the risk of flooding downstream on the Hawkesbury-Nepean floodplain that currently accommodates 130,000 people. Raising the height of the dam by 14 metres would supposedly increase its capacity to hold back a deluge, but at the expense of up to 4,700 hectares of World Heritage-listed national park that would be inundated.[153] The NSW government's scheme, legislated via the Water NSW Amendment (Warragamba Dam) Act 2018, is predicated on allowing more people to move into the floodplain; but no amount

---

[152] K Woolaston, 'Ecological Vulnerability and the Devolution of Individual Autonomy' Griffith Law School Research Paper No 18-24 (SSRN, 2019), drawing on M Fineman, *The Autonomy Myth: A Theory of Dependency* (New Press, 2004).
[153] M McGowan, 'Warragamba Dam Wall Plan Could Cause "Irreversible" Damage, NSW Premier Told' *The Guardian* 2 October 2018.

of human ingenuity can rule out exposure to a super flood, as global warming exacerbates the risks of extreme events, while an important slice of the Blue Mountains National Park would disappear.

An aesthetic of vulnerability would move us to accept that floodplains should usually be tolerated rather than subdued, and in turn we might even suffer less loss of life or infrastructure by avoiding settlement in their path. For those wishing to remain, we could adopt less intrusive, non-flood control alternatives that might include 'improvements to flood evacuation routes [and] increased flood forecasting capacity', according to one expert.[154] We could also build houses on stilts. Allowing lowlands to periodically flood would respect and restore the agency of nature, to which we make ourselves sensorily and materially vulnerable but without forgoing the taking of circumscribed defensive measures that minimise loss of life and property.

Wildlife is also subject to officialdom's control, by limitations on interactions with people considered too risky or unnatural. Katie Woolaston has researched wildlife-human interactions and our penchant for controlling ensuing conflicts, be it insects that devour our crops or unwanted rodents in our houses. She has looked closely at the management of wild dingoes on Fraser Island, Queensland, where conservation authorities have implemented policies to separate tourists from the canines to minimise 'unnatural' exchanges such as feeding, despite the fact that Aborigines introduced dingoes to Australia 3,500 years ago as a companion and hunting aid.[155] Instances of dingo attacks, which rarely happen but generate frenzied media coverage, are cited by authorities as justifications for such policies.[156]

More familiar examples of wildlife-people conflicts for international media readers include the occasional lethal encounters with sharks, crocodiles or tigers, which typically spark calls for extermination of the 'man-eater'. In 2018, newspapers reported on the success of hunters finally dispatching an elusive Indian tiger allegedly responsible for killing 13 villagers.[157] A similar fate awaits predatory sharks, as in Queensland waters where those believed to have mauled two swimmers in 2018 were quickly hunted down. The manager of the government's shark control program defended the culling, explaining:

> the Queensland Government believes that human life must come first, so I know people have different views on the shark control program, but we've had two severe shark attacks within 24 hours and we've got to try and make the waters in that area safer for people to swim in.[158]

---

[154] Quoted in ibid.

[155] K Woolaston, 'Wildlife and the Anthropocene: What is Vulnerability Really?' Frontiers Environmental Law Colloquium, 14–15 February 2019, Queensland University of Technology.

[156] B Smee, 'Fraser Island Dingo Attack: Boy in Hospital After Running into Pack of Wild Dogs' *The Guardian* 20 January 2019.

[157] H Kumar and J Gettleman, 'Man-Eating Tiger is Shot in India' *New York Times* 3 November 2018.

[158] Jeff Krause, quoted in 'Tiger Sharks Shot and Killed Where Two People Were Attacked in Queensland's Whitsundays' *ABC News* 22 September 2018, www.abc.net.au/news/2018-09-22/tiger-sharks-shot-killed-where-two-people-attacked-in-north-qld/10289928.

A law that respects vulnerability would take a different approach, such as designating waters where people can safely swim behind protective netting while warning that swimming elsewhere is at one's peril without resorting to punitive expeditions. Creative, locally adapted interventions can also greatly help mitigate conflicts with wildlife without loss of life. In Botswana and Uganda, where hungry elephants regularly invade farmlands bordering national parks, farmers have ingeniously turned to growing the cash crop chilli, which the pachyderms won't eat, as well as burning chilli-dung mixes for the same repelling effect.[159]

The aesthetics of vulnerability also pertains to how we perceive and respond to the injurious environmental transformations we engender. This requires, suggests Afshin Akhtar-Khavari, a more broadly conceived 'fear' that will engender deeper respect for nature. He explains: 'we are accustomed to thinking about fear simply in terms of immediate or significant sensorial experiences – like coming face to face with a snake'.[160] This understanding of fear, argues Akhtar-Khavari, is too narrow for the necessary broader emotional and cognitive reorientation that sensitises us to the ecological-scale changes and impacts of the Anthropocene.

Climate change looms as our ultimate source of fear associated with nature, including precipitating more forest fires and droughts, as well as exposure to new threats from rising sea levels. So far, officialdom has sought ever-greater means to hazard-proof our vulnerability to these adversities. The parlance of 'climate change adaptation' and 'resilience' that has entered the lexicon of environmental law in recent years speaks directly to this agenda. The notion of 'resilience', introduced in the 1970s by Crawford Holling to aid our understanding of the behaviour of ecological systems to absorb change,[161] has under the aegis of contemporary policy-makers shifted its meaning to focus on making societies more hardy in overcoming environmental adversity. I believe that our response to any global warming that we fail to mitigate should not necessarily aim to make societies more 'resilient' to 'adapt' to the ensuing upheavals. Instead, we may need to tolerate the agency of nature by changing our underlying activities. Take droughts, which will become more frequent and enduring in years to come; rather than try to drought-proof farming in marginal rangelands through sinking more bore wells or investing in expensive irrigation systems, we may need to radically change farming practices or abandon farming altogether in some areas.[162] With sea level rises, we may similarly need to accept our vulnerability to the changes by not trying to hold back the ocean at huge expense through dykes and walls, but to begin retreating.

---

[159] S Dasgupta, 'How to Scare Off the Biggest Pest in the World' *BBC News* 7 December 2014, www.bbc.com/earth/story/20141204-five-ways-to-scare-off-elephants.

[160] A Akhtar-Khavari, 'Fear and Ecological (in)Justice in Edvard Munch's *The Scream of Nature*' (2015) 2(6) *Naveiñ Reet: Nordic Journal of Law* 93, abstract.

[161] CS Holling, "Resilience and Stability of Ecological Systems' (1973) 4 *Annual Review of Ecology and Systematics* 1.

[162] A Vidot and L Barbour, 'Dry Argument: Australia's Drought Policy Dilemma' *ABC News* 24 February 2014, www.abc.net.au/news/rural/2014-02-21/drought-assistance-in-australia/5269062.

Increasing forest fires, already evident in California, southern Europe and parts of Australia, and bearing the fingerprints of climate change, also necessitate that authorities embrace new approaches. Rather than waging costly, military-style campaigns against infernos, which have largely failed,[163] fire ecologists argue we must learn to live with fires, for instance by reducing human settlement near flammable vegetation and adopting better land management practices, as practised by some Indigenous peoples, to reduce the build-up of dangerous fuel loads.[164] In turn, such policies can allow for less intense wild fires to play their generally benign role as a mechanism of ecological regeneration.

An aesthetics of vulnerability thus is premised on affirming that we are not autonomous from nature but rather dependent on it in myriad ways for our daily survival. Vulnerability begins by allowing nature to enter our lives and our sensory realm. We shouldn't, however, assume that mere increased familiarity with nature would always inspire greater respect and pro-environmental behaviours.[165] A farmer living off the land has a more intimate engagement with nature than any white-collar worker, and awareness of the vulnerability of her livelihood to the climate, insects and nature's other vicissitudes; but the economic use value she draws from the land can interfere with her aesthetic judgements and environmental values.[166] Without legal controls and effective curating of aesthetic values, many farmers seek to subdue nature – think of their penchant for spraying pesticides, shooting pests or draining wetlands – rather than aspire to co-exist. For the white collar workers and other urban denizens, an aesthetics of vulnerability may require bringing nature more into their lives. Robert Thayer recommends sustainable design practice that makes visible the environmental conditions on which we depend, such as bringing wind turbines, solar panels and natural storm drainage into our cities.[167] The theory of reconciliation ecology, discussed earlier, provides guidance on further such directions.

The law must accept and respond to environmental vulnerability, rather than try to supress or ignore it on the assumption that we can create and subsist from a synthetic world or overcome any degradation. This does not mean disregarding nature's dangers and exposing ourselves carelessly or haplessly to death or destruction. Rather, it entails learning to co-exist with the natural world, and therefore redesigning where and how we live in fire-prone or flood-prone

---

[163] DE Calkin, MP Thomson and MA Finney, 'Negative Consequences of Positive Feedbacks in US Wildfire Management' (2015) 2 *Forest Ecosystems* 9.

[164] AMS Smith et al, 'The Science of Firescapes: Achieving Fire-Resilient Communities' (2016) 66(2) *Bioscience* 130.

[165] I Brook, 'Aesthetic Appreciation of Landscape' in P Howard, I Thompson and E Watson (eds), *The Routledge Companion Studies to Landscape* (Routledge, 2013) 108, 115.

[166] Many farmers oppose laws that give greater protection to wildlife or trees at the expense of their economic livelihoods: A McCosker and M Hendry, 'Grazier Says Queensland Land Clearing Laws Will Cost Family Millions' *ABC News* 27 March 2018, www.abc.net.au/news/2018-03-27/farmers-protest-new-queensland-land-clearing-laws/9592738.

[167] Thayer, *Gray World, Green Heart* (above n 124).

landscapes, and restructuring our relationships with wildlife to tolerate their presence in our midst. It's a managed vulnerability to nature that enriches our sensory appreciation and respect for it, whilst ensuring that our safety does not come at the expense of degrading the very things on which we depend.

V. ADJUDICATING AESTHETICS

We often disagree in our aesthetic judgements, as well as dispute how to reconcile aesthetic and non-aesthetic considerations. Wind farm projects, as considered in Chapter 7, are a well-publicised example of these tensions, but many others simmer, including conflicts over public rights to roam, rehabilitation of post-mining lands and the aesthetics of vulnerability to nature's agency. How might we recalibrate environmental governance to adjudicate such conflicts?

One option is the better integration of aesthetics and scientific knowledge in environmental decision-making, including in EIAs, land use planning and environmental standard setting. Carlson's cognitive theory of environmental aesthetics stresses the enlightenment that the natural sciences bring to aesthetic appreciation.[168] With knowledge of the environmental effects of harmful activities such as open-cast mining or clearfell forestry, our sensory perception can shift negatively. It should thereby become difficult for educated observers to separate aesthetic appreciation from awareness of these adverse activities. However, as examples from Chapter 4 on 'vanquished nature' show, many people may still find beauty in a domesticated nature of less biodiversity or ecological complexity.

Moreover, with wind farms, the evidence suggests that this hypothesis does not apply so easily in the reverse context, namely knowledge of the positive environmental benefits of clean, renewable energy does not seem to temper opponents' aesthetic concerns. It suggests, according to Saito, a 'kind of asymmetry, in that environmental values are aesthetically relevant only when they are negative but not when they are positive, so that they can uglify but not beautify'.[169] Saito suggests a few strategies to mitigate this apparent limit to aesthetic discourse. They can apply not just to her case study, wind farms, but others such as eco-restoration projects that bring ecological benefits yet alter a place's aesthetic qualities in ways that may displease some. In forestry management, tensions have been identified between the public's desire for neat and tidy tree canopies versus the benefits of maintaining a 'dishevelled' forest with decaying logs and tree stags that can enrich biodiversity.[170]

---

[168] A Carlson, *Aesthetics and the Environment: The Appreciation of Nature, Art and Architecture* (Routledge, 2000).

[169] Saito, *Aesthetics of the Familiar* (above n 8) 103.

[170] PH Gobster, *Forest Aesthetics, Biodiversity, and the Perceived Appropriateness of Ecosystem Management Practice*, Technical report (US Forest Service, 1996).

Environmental education and citizen science projects may help overcome aesthetic prejudices, as the cognitive model of aesthetic appreciation predicts. Take bats, a family of species often perceived negatively, along with spiders and snakes.[171] Sheila Lintott cites an example from Austin, Texas, where local opposition to a bat colony that established under a reconstructed bridge that was designed to provide roosting space was substantially reduced when Bat Conservation International intervened to educate the public about the bats' ecological value, and eventually the nocturnal creatures became an object of aesthetic appreciation for many visitors.[172] I have similarly observed such a shift through my coordination of a citizen science bat monitoring project in southern Tasmania, in which talks by chiropterologists and community participation in bat monitoring has stimulated appreciation of these traditionally uncharismatic species.

Another strategy for adjudicating aesthetics, and which also responds to the conundrum identified with wind farms, is to enliven the imagination of opponents to compare the offending development to others at the same site but with adverse environmental sequalae. With an offshore wind farm, Saito suggests that local opposition might lessen if the community can imagine the site hypothetically occupied by dirty, fossil fuel-based activities, such as an oil rig, which will more likely be viewed by all as 'both environmentally and aesthetically unacceptable'.[173] Asking opponents to imagine an oil spill, like the Deepwater Horizon disaster, could embellish the comparison. This contrast, in the realm of opponents' imagination, might be nurtured by collaborations between artists and technical experts, such as engineers and ecologists, to depict how an alternate use of the contested site might look. It might induce opponents to 'unsightly' developments of environmental benefit to transform their aesthetic judgement into a positive one.

A related strategy invokes actual examples of changed aesthetic reactions to altered landscapes where a community's judgement shifted over time from negative to positive. Cultural geography research demonstrates that given time, aesthetic tastes can change, indeed quite dramatically.[174] Consider, for instance, the historic windmills of the Netherlands, which now attract tourists in droves. The Kinderdijk windmill complex, comprising 19 windmills some 250 years old, has been listed under the World Heritage Convention since 1997, and is so popular that the local community has asked authorities to place restrictions on

---

[171] A J Knight, '"Bats, Snakes and Spiders, Oh My!" How Aesthetic and Negativistic Attitudes, and Other Concepts Predict Support for Species Protection' (2008) 28(1) *Journal of Environmental Psychology* 94.

[172] S Lintott, 'Toward Eco-friendly Aesthetics' in A Carlson and S Lintott (eds), *Nature, Aesthetics and Environmentalism: From Beauty to Duty* (Columbia University Press, 2008) 380, 393.

[173] Saito, *Aesthetics of the Familiar* (above n 8) 95.

[174] Eg A McCumber, 'Building "Natural" Beauty: Drought and the Shifting Aesthetics of Nature in Santa Barbara, California' (2017) 12(3) *Nature and Culture* 246.

the number of tourists visiting.[175] Equally demonstrative, the Eiffel Tower was initially derided by Parisians when erected for the World Fair in 1889; a petition from artists was sent to the government, denouncing the structure as tall as an 80-storey building, as a 'useless and monstrous' blight on the 'hitherto untouched beauty of Paris'.[176] But today Parisians generally adore the city's most iconic edifice.

Aesthetic preferences about natural phenomenon also change. The Tasmanian devil, discussed earlier in this chapter, was severely persecuted under government and private bounty schemes during the nineteenth century, being loathed as 'ugly' and causing 'great ravages among the sheep' according to one 1864 newspaper.[177] Yet, the marsupial carnivore was in 2015 proclaimed as Tasmania's official animal emblem, dovetailing with its heightened aesthetic appeal with both locals and tourists. Aesthetic preferences, however, may also change the other way; take Tasmania's massive Lake Pedder hydro-dam, which when erected in 1972 drowned an aesthetically stunning and ecologically unique remnant glacial lake to the uproar of nature conservationists, but in recent years has brought pleasure to many as a mecca for fishing and sailing, along with views of the now much enlarged lake.[178]

Legal governance may facilitate appropriate imaginative thinking by mandating that development approval procedures include engaging the affected community through information and consultation processes that utilise collaborations between artists, historians and scientists. Use of visual diagrams, including 3D models, in public consultations can help people to participate intelligently in decision-making about aesthetic issues. Artists can also play a useful role in designing projects to improve their aesthetic effects, a role that can be incorporated through EIA procedures and development licensing that identify design issues and prescribe solutions. Renewable energy expert Paul Gipe has produced aesthetic guidelines for wind power projects, with recommendations on how to minimise visual clutter by spacing turbines further apart, using consistent height and colour schemes, and synchronising the direction of the movement of turbine blades.[179] These and other aesthetic qualities can contribute to integrating wind farms more harmoniously into landscapes. Likewise, for post-mining rehabilitation, the site's resulting appearance may be improved by retaining mining relics of cultural heritage significance and blending the restored

---

[175] D Boffey, '"We've been Here Since 1747 – Dutch Windmill Villagers Take on Tourist Hordes' *The Guardian* 13 November 2018.

[176] Quoted in W Frost and J Laing, *Commemorative Events: Memory, Identities, Conflict* (Routledge, 2013) 141.

[177] 'The Mammals of Tasmania' *Mercury* 27 April 1864, 3.

[178] Eg, see the eco-tourist operator Wild Pedder: www.wildpedder.com.au.

[179] P Gipe, 'Design as if People Matter: Aesthetic Guidelines for a Wind Power Future' in MJ Pasqualetti, P Gipe and RW Righter (eds), *Wind Power in View: Energy Landscapes in a Crowded World* (Academic Press, 2002) 173.

site with the surrounding area in regard to tree plantings, terrain contouring and other features.[180]

Community participation in environmental decision-making introduces another strategy in many contexts for adjudicating disputes over aesthetic values. Aesthetic taste is embedded in people's cultural, economic and political context, and thus an environment such as an industrial landscape that to one observer (such as painter John Kane, represented on the cover of this book) represents beautiful progress to another represents grimy and odorous blight. While we would be naïve to expect that any governance regime can achieve a consensus among protagonists, we have options to attenuate their differences.

One common driver of disagreement stems from the perception that authorities have imposed development projects on a community without consultation. Opposition to the creation of national parks (to protect scenic beauty but at the expense of economic activities like mining or forestry) or erection of cable cars (to promote tourism but intruding on the landscape) are linked to feelings of lack of input into decisions. Saito believes that governance should enfranchise grassroots community participation in key decisions that have aesthetic ramifications, such as the location and design of projects. Drawing on the 'sense of place' theory from cultural geography, she explains, 'very often our direct involvement in altering a landscape seems to generate our affection and attachment toward the landscape that results, which then leads to positive aesthetic appreciation'.[181]

Aesthetic experiences are clearly enhanced when we can relate to objects or places that hold wider significance in our lives and culture. Consider the differences between the appreciation of historic Dutch windmills and the modern industrial version: the former are nearly universally admired, unlike the latter. The difference has to do with how these objects connect with their surroundings. The old Dutch windmills are embedded in a local farm landscape, where farmers once (and occasionally still) took their grain for grinding, which thus gave the windmills ties to a social practice, interacting with their surroundings. By contrast, industrial wind turbines, usually of much larger scale, represent an impost, both physically and culturally, in the landscape. The turning blades provide green electricity but otherwise lack cultural connection to the host community. Having deeper interactions with things such as windmills or wind turbines helps to soften their 'otherness'.

While such strategies may lessen conflict over the aesthetics of environmental decisions at local scales, they become more difficult to apply in global or transborder contexts, such as those involving climate change or marine plastic pollution. Though the slogan 'think globally, act locally' suggests

---

[180] P Skleni~čka and I Kašparová, 'Restoration of Visual Values in a Post-mining Landscape' (2008) 1 *Journal of Landscape Studies* 1.
[181] Saito, *Aesthetics of the Familiar* (above n 8).

Figure 8.7 *A Windmill Against a Cloudy Sky*, 1845, Constant Troyon (1810–65), oil and chalk; The National Gallery, London

interrelationships between environmental responsibility at different governance scales, localism also spawned a countervailing negative aspect known as 'nimbyism' (from the acronym NIMBY, meaning 'not in my back yard'). It may result in proponents shifting aesthetically undesirable projects to less politically effective communities.

International environmental law has surely only a limited contribution to make here. A few international treaties acknowledge aesthetic values but very rarely take aesthetics seriously, as the World Heritage Convention 1972 does to some extent. Place-based treaties such as this, as well as the European Landscape Convention 2000 and the Madrid Protocol 1991, have a clear mandate for identifying and protecting nature aesthetics, but their implementation still depends substantially on action at the national level. The nomination of properties for inclusion in the World Heritage List illustrates a rare instance where an international body, in this case UNESCO's World Heritage Committee, can actually adjudicate over aesthetic values as relevant criteria for a site's nomination. Non place-based instruments, such as the UNFCCC and the Paris Agreement 2015, only touch on aesthetics indirectly, for example by encouraging parties to promote the arts within public education and to stipulate criteria for local decision-making, such as climate adaptation measures. Aesthetic issues are more frequently encountered in international disputes involving non-state actors, in the image politics of anti-whaling activists and climate action groups, for example. In these guises, aesthetics partakes in the political battleground itself, rather than being a subject that the law adjudicates.

In conclusion, we should not expect any methods for adjudicating disputes over aesthetic impacts to generate a definitive consensus of opinion, yet socially legitimate decisions may ensue where authorities enable public debate and assessment of the merit of aesthetic preferences. As argued in the opening chapter of this book, aesthetics should and can be taken seriously, despite individual or cultural variability in our aesthetic preferences. It can happen if participants have sufficient aesthetic literacy and capacity to make reasoned arguments to defend their positions. Environmental aesthetics cannot be reduced to a purely private domain, as though natural beauty is simply a matter of individuals' idiosyncratic taste; rather, it can inform defensible, collectively determined judgements that the law can respond to. That some people may remain dissatisfied is not an adequate objection, as differences of opinion permeate other realms of environmental governance as they do for innumerable other fields of law and policy. Indeed, as I have already argued, dissent can be a positive force, as found in the culture jamming artists challenging corporate hubris.

VI. ENDING

In facing the Anthopocence, environmental governance has prioritised economic tools and scientific evidence for solutions. We must also value the aesthetic realm, including the arts, in our emotional and ethical engagement with nature. Naïve appeals to natural beauty, however, won't get us very far. Aesthetic appreciation must ultimately align with the conservation of essential ecological processes and the web of life. An aesthetically pleasing but environmentally degraded landscape is hardly viable over the long term; or as Thayer puts it, 'landscapes that create an illusion of a better world while depriving us of the actual means of achieving it are not sustainable'.[182] The appearance, sound or other sensory qualities of landscapes and seascapes must dovetail with their material health and sustainability. But that does not mean that there is only *one* way to aesthetically experience or engage with nature, as though a holy grail can be sought out. Rather, what is appropriate will vary with time, geography and culture.

In calling for environmental law to take aesthetics seriously, I recognise that we confront momentous governance challenges. Natural beauty defies easy legal codification, and beauty itself can precipitate harmful environmental

---

[182] R Thayer, 'Gray Heart, Green World' in S Swaffield (ed), *Theory in Landscape Architecture: A Reader* (University of Pennsylvania Press, 2002) 189, 189–90.

exploitation, especially when harnessed by unscrupulous commercial and political interests. Moreover, time and space disrupt or distort our sensory perceptions of nature, resulting in an absent aesthetics beyond our discernment. Aesthetic values must also seemingly compete with non-aesthetic knowledge, often coming off second-best. These present major concerns, but not – I believe – insurmountable objections.

Furthermore, I strenuously reject that we should view aesthetic values as a 'luxury' or lower-order priority for environmental governance, as though opportunities for experiencing natural beauty are trivial dalliances relative to meeting basic human needs or tackling climate change. Rather, aesthetics interact with key agendas of modern environmental law. For instance, the appalling food waste owing to supermarkets' rejection of aesthetically imperfect fruits and vegetables levies a huge burden on the hungriest and nature itself. Likewise, aesthetic activism, including culture jamming, can helpfully stir public awareness of the plight of the politically marginalised and advance social justice. A critical aesthetics can also forge aesthetic appreciation of the value of places overlooked by the dominant narratives of beauty, such as landscapes treasured by Indigenous peoples. Fundamental rights for people's well-being and basic needs, as found in South Africa's national constitution, are capable of encompassing aesthetic values, suggest seasoned scholars.[183]

Although authorities will struggle to prescribe aesthetic values into any timeless or universal legal formulae, their governance still matters vitally for shaping their expression and value in the public realm. A successful social aesthetics draws people together to help overcome the void between individuals' aesthetic perceptions. Coming together to experience a place, to participate in making art or just hiking through the forest, may not necessarily lead to common aesthetic values but they can at least foster a common aesthetic *experience*, and forge a constructive dialogue about aesthetic values to inform environmental laws. If we reduce nature to just objects of passive observation, detached from context, we are more likely to disagree in our aesthetic judgements. Governance must also engage our senses with nature more intimately, while accepting our vulnerability to nature's engagement in our lives. Accepting our place within nature, not apart from it, demands this reciprocal relationship. The aesthetics of engagement and vulnerability have concrete implications for legal governance, from expanding rights for the public to roam in nature to managing our exposure to environmental adversity. The law equally matters for curbing manipulative corporate marketing that masks environmentally dubious practices.

The arts also contribute to curating a critical aesthetics, both in representing beautiful or degraded nature and as a participatory, aesthetic practice. In Romantic art, nature was sometimes depicted as the physical embodiment of

---

[183] A du Plessis, 'The Promise of "Well-being" in Section 24 of the Constitution of South Africa' (2018) 34(2) *South African Journal of Human Rights* 191, 200.

God, available only through transcendental experiences. Since the 1960s, Western artists have worked to deconstruct the worn-out paradigm of nature as 'other', as a variety of art genres from non-Western cultures have done for eons. Initially, this involved Earthwork artists recycling land for new uses – principally sculptures and gestures in arid landscapes. In the 1970s artists went further in their attempts to recycle land – seeking to rehabilitate and restore, and forging alliances with environmental NGOs and scientists. Since the 1980s, the relationship between capitalism, technology and social injustices in human-nature relationships has received closer scrutiny, offering a more penetrating challenge to the colonising dynamics of capitalism. Today, the subject of climate change dominates much of this critical art practice. Of course, art cannot save the world's environment or ourselves, but it can help humanity to see itself embedded in a broader community with nature, and it can challenge the consumer culture and the accompanying institutions and ideologies.

The *Art of Environmental Law* thus behoves us to recognise how aesthetic experiences associated with nature have implications for what we notice and value. Governing with aesthetics addresses our sensory interactions with the natural world and reshapes their influence on our environmental behaviours and impacts. A critical aesthetics offers a way of understanding the realm of environmental aesthetic experiences that is more social, creative and intimate, to enable us to better confront the ecological crises of our times. Environmental lawyers must take aesthetics seriously.

Index